Media and Its Role in Protecting the Rights of Children in Africa

Olusola Oyero
Covenant University, Nigeria

A volume in the Advances in Media, Entertainment, and the Arts (AMEA) Book Series

IGI Global
DISSEMINATOR OF KNOWLEDGE

Published in the United States of America by
IGI Global
Information Science Reference (an imprint of IGI Global)
701 E. Chocolate Avenue
Hershey PA, USA 17033
Tel: 717-533-8845
Fax: 717-533-8661
E-mail: cust@igi-global.com
Web site: http://www.igi-global.com

Library of Congress Cataloging-in-Publication Data

Library of Congress Cataloging-in-Publication Data

Names: Oyero, Olusola, 1973- editor, author.
Title: Media and its role in protecting the rights of children in Africa / Olusola Oyero, editor.
Description: Hershey : CyberTech Publishing, 2019. | Summary: "This book examines media roles, challenges, theories, and strategies to ensuring the realization of the rights of the children in Africa"-- Provided by publisher.
Identifiers: LCCN 2019021157 | ISBN 9781799803294 (hardcover) | ISBN 9781799803300 (softcover) | 9781799803317 (ebook)
Subjects: LCSH: Mass media and children--Africa, Sub-Saharan. | Children's rights--Africa, Sub-Saharan.
Classification: LCC HQ784.M32 A3575 2019 | DDC 302.230830967--dc23
LC record available at https://lccn.loc.gov/2019021157

This book is published in the IGI Global book series Advances in Media, Entertainment, and the Arts (AMEA) (ISSN: 2475-6814; eISSN: 2475-6830)

British Cataloguing in Publication Data
A Cataloguing in Publication record for this book is available from the British Library.

For electronic access to this publication, please contact: eresources@igi-global.com.

Advances in Media, Entertainment, and the Arts (AMEA) Book Series

ISSN:2475-6814
EISSN:2475-6830

Editor-in-Chief: Giuseppe Amoruso, Politecnico di Milano, Italy

MISSION

Throughout time, technical and artistic cultures have integrated creative expression and innovation into industrial and craft processes. Art, entertainment and the media have provided means for societal self-expression and for economic and technical growth through creative processes.

The **Advances in Media, Entertainment, and the Arts (AMEA)** book series aims to explore current academic research in the field of artistic and design methodologies, applied arts, music, film, television, and news industries, as well as popular culture. Encompassing titles which focus on the latest research surrounding different design areas, services and strategies for communication and social innovation, cultural heritage, digital and print media, journalism, data visualization, gaming, design representation, television and film, as well as both the fine applied and performing arts, the AMEA book series is ideally suited for researchers, students, cultural theorists, and media professionals.

COVERAGE

- Products, Strategies and Services
- Arts & Design
- Sports & Entertainment
- Color Studies
- Gaming
- Digital Heritage
- Blogging & Journalism
- Design of Interiors
- New Media Art
- Environmental Design

IGI Global is currently accepting manuscripts for publication within this series. To submit a proposal for a volume in this series, please contact our Acquisition Editors at Acquisitions@igi-global.com or visit: http://www.igi-global.com/publish/.

The Advances in Media, Entertainment, and the Arts (AMEA) Book Series (ISSN 2475-6814) is published by IGI Global, 701 E. Chocolate Avenue, Hershey, PA 17033-1240, USA, www.igi-global.com. This series is composed of titles available for purchase individually; each title is edited to be contextually exclusive from any other title within the series. For pricing and ordering information please visit http://www.igi-global.com/book-series/advances-media-entertainment-arts/102257. Postmaster: Send all address changes to above address.

Titles in this Series

For a list of additional titles in this series, please visit:
https://www.igi-global.com/book-series/advances-media-entertainment-arts/102257

Gender and Diversity Representation in Mass Media
Gülşah Sarı (Bolu Abant Izzet Baysal University, Turkey)
Information Science Reference • copyright 2020 • 338pp • H/C (ISBN: 9781799801283) • US $195.00 (our price)

Handbook of Research on Deception, Fake News, and Misinformation Online
Innocent E. Chiluwa (Covenant University, Nigeria) and Sergei A. Samoilenko (George Mason University, USA)
Information Science Reference • copyright 2019 • 651pp • H/C (ISBN: 9781522585350) • US $295.00 (our price)

Popular Representations of America in Non-American Media
Floribert Patrick C. Endong (University of Calabar, Nigeria)
Information Science Reference • copyright 2019 • 361pp • H/C (ISBN: 9781522593126) • US $195.00 (our price)

Handbook of Research on Consumption, Media, and Popular Culture in the Global Age
Ozlen Ozgen (Atilim University, Turkey)
Information Science Reference • copyright 2019 • 454pp • H/C (ISBN: 9781522584919) • US $295.00 (our price)

Understanding Rivalry and Its Influence on Sports Fans
Cody T. Havard (The University of Memphis, USA)
Information Science Reference • copyright 2019 • 307pp • H/C (ISBN: 9781522581253) • US $175.00 (our price)

Handbook of Research on Transmedia Storytelling and Narrative Strategies
Recep Yılmaz (Ondokuz Mayıs University, Turkey) M. Nur Erdem (Ondokuz Mayıs University, Turkey) and Filiz Resuloğlu (Kocaeli University, Turkey)

For an entire list of titles in this series, please visit:
https://www.igi-global.com/book-series/advances-media-entertainment-arts/102257

IGI Global
DISSEMINATOR OF KNOWLEDGE

701 East Chocolate Avenue, Hershey, PA 17033, USA
Tel: 717-533-8845 x100 • Fax: 717-533-8661
E-Mail: cust@igi-global.com • www.igi-global.com

Editorial Advisory Board

Table of Contents

Detailed Table of Contents

The journey to realising the rights of the child could be traced back to almost a century ago with the Geneva Declaration of the Rights of the Child in 1924. But the most significant and most impactful event for children took place 30 years ago with the declaration of the United Nations: the Convention on the Rights of the Child (UNCRC) in 1989. It is this convention that has recognised and specified the important role that the media can play in supporting the rights of the child. This chapter thus tries to place media role in child rights promotion and protection with an historical context for the purpose of knowledge flow on the subject. It further discusses the theoretical basis for media intervention in child rights issues while at the same time it attempts to assess how the media has performed in the task assigned to it in the UNCRC. It offers some suggestions on better media performance to galvanise the effort at realising child rights for sustainable development.

Education is the 'right' of every child and should not be a privilege. As signatories to the United Nations Convention on the Rights of a Child (CRC), every country in Africa has a fundamental responsibility in the global commitment towards the

Studies have revealed that children constitute more than one-third of the world's population and half of the world's population is under the age of 25. In the age of globalization, media institutions and services are controlled by the market forces. Critically speaking, media institutions have not lived up to their expectations towards child rights advocacy and development. This chapter discusses the plight of children in Africa. It argues for the child rights advocacy as well as discusses the challenges and constraints that hinder the media from performing their role adequately. It concludes that the mass media plays an important role in promoting and sustaining the child rights advocacy. The chapter recommends that all media houses must strive to live up to the expectations of the people no matter the constraints and challenges that might stand in their way.

Children rights feature prominently in global news discourse as children continue to suffer abuse in an increasingly insensitive world. The theme of the 2018 Day of the African Child "Leave No Child Behind in Development" underscored the urgency of mainstreaming children rights in development programs. Arising from the media discourse generated around this event, this chapter employs a thematic frame analytic approach to interrogate how six mainstream East African newspapers framed issues around the theme. Selected stories were content-analyzed for themes and related frames underpinning the place of children in development discourse within the region. Findings depict a media discourse recognizing children as the future of Africa yet still 'passive' players in development occasioned by socio-economic and cultural barriers.

Chapter 7

This chapter describes Kenyan media narratives and portrayals of children and their rights. The chapter examines how Kenyan media frame child rights stories. Through qualitative content analysis of child stories in selected Kenyan media platforms, the authors interrogated what these narratives tell us about how children and their rights are viewed and the implications of the media frames used. Findings showed that child rights stories are yet to receive the comprehensive coverage needed. The findings further indicated that Kenyan media framed the child in stereotypical and patriarchal ways with the voice of the child most times left out. In addition, many of the stories analysed were found to lack depth, context, and link to child rights. Some of the challenges that hamper effective media coverage include inadequate training on child rights reporting, lack of media desks tackling children stories, and insufficient knowledge on child rights.

Chapter 8

This study discusses photojournalism ethics in portraying photographs of children in Tanzanian media. The study is guided by gatekeeping and semiotic theories. The authors used both quantitative and qualitative approaches to examine photojournalism ethical practices with regard to how children's photos are presented in Tanzanian newspapers and readers' perceptions regarding how children's photos are portrayed in Tanzanian media. Content analysis was to examine Habari Leo, the Guardian. and Uwazi newspapers published photographs from 1st May, 2017 to 31st May, 2018. The results showed that 591 out of 12,316 photos published by all the three newspapers were photographs of children. The results revealed that some media outlets published children's photos contrary to the ethics of photojournalism, the United Nations Convention on the Rights of the Child, and the African Charter on the Rights and Welfare of the Child. In order to improve photojournalism ethical practices, the authors suggested the use an approach base in classical philosophy by photojournalists.

The chapter explored public and stakeholder perceptions of media coverage of child labour in Nigeria. It has been observed that most studies are deficient in information on the interplay between media coverage of children issues and public perception of such coverage. This study therefore adopted the convergent mixed method design to elicit responses from audiences. Respondents were drawn from Babcock University on the assumption that individuals are literate enough to understand newspaper reports. Civil society organizations across Nigeria that deal specifically with children issues and some State Ministries of Women Affairs were sampled. The survey showed that people have knowledge of child labour issues from newspapers which in turn affect their attitude; however, their reactions to the reports are moderately favourable to the cause of abused children. It was recommended that newspapers give more coverage to child labour issues so that the public will have more knowledge and in turn make informed decisions.

This chapter examines the relationship amongst displacement, education, and sustainable national development. It pays attention to the effects of displacement on the rights of children to education in Nigeria. Data for the study were obtained via in-depth interviews from key informants and focus group discussions (FGDs) amongst internally displaced women in a government-managed and faith-based IDP camps in the Adamawa State as well as informal settlements in the Federal Capital Territory (FCT), Abuja on the quality of education offered in the camps. Findings from the study show that wide gaps exist between the education received by displaced children and the expectations of the Convention on the Rights of the Child. The study argues that the educational exclusivity of displaced children would have adverse effects on the sustainable development of the Nigerian state as it would decrease awareness of values about their civic duties needed for sustainable development. It thus recommends for increased media advocacy in pushing for better implementation of inclusive education in Nigeria.

A few abusive occurrences in the Third World escape the lenses of the media, portending danger to our collective existence. One such social ill that defied the radar of news coverage is the growing transient consummation and abortion of conjugal relationship implicating male gender and instantiating abuses affecting the children from such relationships. Regrettably, the 'hit and run parenthood' posture attendant of this practice often populate the crime cells cross-culturally and raises the probability of social dislocation laden with colossal cost to societies. Consequently, this chapter attempts to descriptively investigate the depth of this sexual pervasion and the predicaments of children raised under such milieu. A passionate appeal is thus made to galvanize dissuasive participation in such practices and to generate more media attention in order to alleviate the excruciating socio-economic condition and discourage crime among the affected children.

The study is premised on social responsibility and social epidemiological theories and examined the exposure of back-wrapped babies to health risk during street trading. Data were collected using structured face-to-face interviews and snowballing techniques among 228 Street trading women (with children aged $\leq$ 11 months), in one local government area of Ogun State, Nigeria. Data analyses involved univariate and multivariate methods. The results show that 58.3% of women interviewed wrapped their babies at their back while trading on the streets, ≥80% were not aware of any campaign against baby back-wrapping, 35% viewed baby back-wrapping as medicinal for the baby, and as traditional practice (59.2%). The multivariate analysis revealed that children wrapped while trading on the street are at higher risk of exposure to illness than those not back wrapped (OR=1.778, p=0.042). The authors suggested media campaign against back-wrapping baby while trading on the street to reduce exposure to diseases, mortalities and possibly achievement of sustainable development goal (SDG-3).

This essay examines media and child rights protection in Nigeria, using Kuje IDPs Camp in Abuja, FCT as a case study. It argues that the media has important and indispensable roles to play in enabling the promotion of the United Nations Convention on the Rights of the Child and Nigeria's Child Rights Act, 2003. The study adopted the qualitative method through interviews and focus group discussions conducted at the Kuje IDPs Camp. Findings suggest that the Nigerian government is not committed to implementing the prescription of the United Nations Convention on the Rights of the Child and the Child Rights Act, thus further jeopardizing the already fractured rights of the of children in IDPs camps in Nigeria. Similarly, the media is not paying attention to the plight of the displaced children. The prescriptions advanced in this study as well as the conclusions reached are relevant for policy makers at the national, regional, and international levels responsible for the rights of the children, especially the Nigerian child.

Demands on the actors include ability to interpret the writer's scripts, memorise the lines, and be at rehearsals anywhere, anytime, and anyhow; obvious dilemma is associated with the involvement of child actors. A child has the right to survival and development, education, leisure, amongst others, which are to be undertaken under the guidance, supervision, and care of parents. If a child actor has a dutiful parent or guardian, effectiveness may be attained in creating a balance between acting and other areas of needs; without a conscientious parent, where the child actor is overwhelmed by the acting environment, his education may suffer even as he can commit himself to the lifestyle of the make-believe world of acting. Drawing from two child actresses in Nigeria, this chapter exemplifies the dilemma of child actors and the challenge it poses to such child rights. It offers suggestions on how the effect of the dilemma could be resolved.

Preface

Since the adoption of the United Nations Convention on the Right of the Children (UNCRC) in 1989, global attention has focussed more on the issues that affect children. This attention, triggered by the UNCRC, has underscored the role that the media has to play in the effort at serving children and their rights. This attention to children is quite significant against the backdrop of global quest for sustainable development, taking cognisance that children are the future generation and the fact that making the world sustainable is only possible through them, and in fact meant for them.

While so much is being done by international organisations and non-governmental organisations to realise the objectives of UNCRC, not much has been done in academics circles to address children rights, especially as it connects with the media. This book therefore is an addition to direct more attention to the role of the media in the pursuit of the rights of the child, especially in Africa whose children and young people are mostly the victims of the challenges confronting the continent.

The book contains 14 chapters, which are divided into three sections. Section 1 with five chapters is titled "Media in Child Rights Issues." Chapter 1 lays the foundation for the book, giving historical background of child rights and the media. It examines media performance in the service of child rights and sets out future pathways for media intervention. Chapter 2 discusses the imperatives of education to the development of the African child and the role of new media technologies in this process. Chapter 3 focusses on media cultural content and childhood education in Nigeria. It stresses the need for indigenous, culturally fit media content in the education of children. Chapter 4 discusses some dysfunctional aspects of media contents, especially entertainment that are injurious to children. It recommends that media contents should focus on the protection and promotion of the rights of the child. The last chapter in this section (Chapter 5) identifies the challenges and constraints hindering the media in performing their roles. It urges the media to do more of advocacy journalism.

Section 2 is titled "Media and Child Rights: Narratives, Portrayal, and the Audience." This section with four chapters begins with chapter 6 interrogating how, the media frames issues of children and development. The findings show a media discourse recognising children as the future of Africa, yet still ''passive'' players in development occasioned by socio-economic and cultural barriers. Chapter 7 analyses child rights issues in Kenyan media. Findings show that many of the stories lack substance, detail and context, and a link to child right. It suggests a more comprehensive approach to reporting about children. In chapter 8, photojournalism ethics in portraying photograph of children in selected Tanzanian press came under interrogation. The results show some violations of ethical codes. It recommends journalists should comply with the ethical codes. Chapter 9 concludes this section by investigating public and stakeholders' perception of newspaper coverage of child labour, with recommendation for the media to push out substance that will enhance people's knowledge of the issue.

The third section, "Child Rights, Abuse, and the Media," has five chapters focussing on issues that affect the right of the child. Chapter10 addresses how children education has been affected by their displacement due to armed conflict; thus, calling for increased media advocacy in pushing for better implementation of inclusive education in Nigeria. Chapter11, is an essay on transient marriages and their effects on the rights of children. The chapter believes that the media has a role to play in changing the situation. In Chapter 12, we see a study of how child swaddling affects child's health and the need for media campaign against the practice. Chapter 13 focuses on the rights of children in the internationally displayed people camps (IDPs) and what is expected of the media. It is found out that children in these camps are grossly neglected by the media. It calls for a change in the trend. The last but not the least chapter (Chapter 14) deals with child actors and how roles performance in acting can affect their rights, especially to education. The chapter prescribes some measures to guarantee the rights of child actors without jeopardising their acting potentials.

It is believed that this book is a timely contribution to the ongoing conversation on the role of the media in promotion and preservation of the right of the child and to sustainable development of Africa. It will be of immense learning materials to students and researchers in child rights issues and development communication. It will also be a good reference material for policy makers, development agencies and as many who take interests in media, child rights issues and sustainable development.

Acknowledgment

This book is a contribution to expand the frontiers of knowledge on child right and the media, an area that not too many persons have taken interest in. Many thanks to all the contributors to this book who did not just show interest but also pulled through the review process to the completion of their chapters.

I also want to appreciate the effort of all the reviewers who devoted time to review the articles offering very candid opinions and suggestions on how to improve the quality of the chapters.

My appreciation also goes to the publisher, the IGI Global, for agreeing to publish the manuscript and giving adequate time for more quality job to be done even after deadlines had been missed.

I want to express my sincere appreciation to the management of Covenant University for providing conducive environment for serious scholarship. I also appreciate my colleague in the Department of Mass Communication, Covenant University, for the great support I received as the Head of Department, their cooperation in executing various administrative duties made enough room for me to see this book through.

I thank my family and especially my wife Oluwatoyin Oyero for moral, social and prayer support to get this book done. Finally, I appreciate the most high God for health, strength and wisdom to complete this project

Section 1

Media in Child Rights Issues

Chapter 1
Media and the Rights of the Child in Africa: The Context and the Future Pathways

Olusola Samuel Oyero
https://orcid.org/0000-0001-7795-5516
Covenant University, Nigeria

ABSTRACT

The journey to realising the rights of the child could be traced back to almost a century ago with the Geneva Declaration of the Rights of the Child in 1924. But the most significant and most impactful event for children took place 30 years ago with the declaration of the United Nations: the Convention on the Rights of the Child (UNCRC) in 1989. It is this convention that has recognised and specified the important role that the media can play in supporting the rights of the child. This chapter thus tries to place media role in child rights promotion and protection with an historical context for the purpose of knowledge flow on the subject. It further discusses the theoretical basis for media intervention in child rights issues while at the same time it attempts to assess how the media has performed in the task assigned to it in the UNCRC. It offers some suggestions on better media performance to galvanise the effort at realising child rights for sustainable development.

INTRODUCTION

The centrality of children in society as being the future of any nation places them at the heart of decisions making and planning for that future. It is in this regard that the United Nations deemed it fit to institute an agency, the United Nations Children's

DOI: 10.4018/978-1-7998-0329-4.ch001

Fund (UNICEF), to work for the interests of children, the world over. It is thus not surprising that the first global attention to the issues of children was initiated by the United Nations- the Convention on the rights of the Child (UNCRC) in 1989. An important aspect of that Convention was the recognition of the media as an indispensable stakeholder in the preservation and promotion of the rights of the child. In the past thirty years, the Convention has propelled a lot of activities in form of advocacy, conferences, workshops, agreements, research, etc., as regards media inputs in the service of child rights. It is therefore imperative to introspect on what has been the progress made by the media in the task of serving children and to set future pathways for more progressive and impactful service in favour of children. This chapter thus traces the historical development of the rights of the child, the involvement of media as a partner for fulfilling child rights and prescribes modalities for more successful efforts that will favour the rights of the child.

HISTORICAL ANTECEDENTS TO CHILD RIGHTS

In order to comprehend and appreciate the efforts that have gone into child rights preservation and promotiom, it is important to place it in a historical context. Appreciation of the overall connection between instruments concerning human rights and international organisations that regulate the special position of children over time are thus presented. According to Mahkonen (n. d.), the situation, in terms of years, is as follows:

1. = Geneva Declaration of the Rights of the Child (1924 GDR)
2. = Universal Declaration of Human Rights (1948 UDHR)
3. = Declaration of the Rights of the Child (1959 DRC)
4. = Convention on the Rights of the Child (1989 CRC)

Geneva Declaration of the Rights of the Child 1924

The League of Nations (1919 - 1946) was an international organisation founded by the countries that were victorious in the First World War. Its most basic purpose was to guarantee lasting peace, and the organisation's objective was to resolve disputes by peaceful means, by the use of specific sanctions, reducing armaments and disarmament (Mahkonen, n.d.).

One of the primary targets of the League of Nations was to secure the rights of women and the special rights of children who had been orphaned by the hostilities of World War I. After several phases, a declaration of explicit children's rights was published in Geneva, Switzerland on the 26th of September 1924. Utmost recognition in this declaration was given to children who did not enjoy the protection of a traditional family. The introduction to the 1924 declaration stated: *"By the present Declaration of the Rights of the Child men and women of all nations, recognizing that mankind owes to the child the best it has to give."* The declaration contained five articles which were given the title of principles. These principles are as follows:

Principle 1

The child must be given the means requisite for its normal development, both materially and spiritually.

Principle 2

The child that is hungry must be fed; the child that is sick must be nursed; the child that is backward must be helped; the delinquent child must be reclaimed; and the orphan and the waif must be sheltered and succoured.

Principle 3

The child must be the first to receive relief in times of distress.

Principle 4

The child must be put in a position to earn a livelihood, and must be protected against every form of exploitation.

Principle 5

The child must be brought up in the consciousness that its talents must be devoted to the service of fellow men.

At the time of this declaration, these principles were not only modern, they were wide in scope. From today's perspective, however, a specific reservation in terms of coverage is appropriate. Mahkonen (n.d.) notes that 'Geneva Declaration of the Rights of the Child (GDRC) places children in a lower category than adults. This can be seen in *Principle 5.* It is also not an accident that while adults are referred to as "he" or "she", children are referred to as "it" '(p.14). It is however appropriate to point out that the GDRC was the first international instrument related to children's' rights. This is its value and significance.

Universal Declaration of Human Rights (1948 UDHR)

It was on December 10, 1948 that the *Universal Declaration of Human Rights* (1948 UDHR) was adopted and proclaimed by the United Nations General Assembly resolution 217 A/III. The preamble to the 1948 UDHR was wide and comprehensive. A quotation in the preamble says:

Whereas the peoples of the United Nations have in the Charter reaffirmed their faith in fundamental human rights, in the dignity and worth of the human person and in the equal rights of men and women, have determined to promote social progress and better standards of life in larger freedom.

The preamble thus placed emphasis on not only the importance of human rights, but also on the rights of adults ("the equal rights of men and women"), not the human rights of children and the significance of their special rights. It was only after the rights of all human beings had been established by this declaration that attention began to be paid to the rights of children.

Declaration of the Rights of the Child 1959

The Declaration of the Rights of the Child (DRC) was proclaimed by Resolution 1386/XIV of the United Nations General Assembly on the 20th November, 1959. As in the 1924 declaration, principles were used instead of articles. The difference was that the number of principles had doubled and that they had been extended, compared to the earlier declaration, by including a wider interpretation of the principle of children's best interests. Another significant difference was that the importance of children's rights (Article 1 in the DRC) was highlighted.

The summary of the ten principles of the Declaration goes thus:

- Principle 1-Equality without any kind of discrimination
- Principle 2-The best interests of the child
- Principle 3-Right to name and nationality
- Principle 4- Benefits of social security
- Principle 5- Disabled children and special care
- Principle 6- Full development of personality, love and understanding.
- Principle 7- Free and compulsory education Principle 8- The child as the first to receive protection.
- Principle 9- Protection against neglect, cruelty, and exploitation.
- Principle 10- Upbringing in a spirit of understanding, tolerance, and peace.

The DRC regulated children's rights in a more extensive way than the 1924 declaration. The 1924 declaration did not include issues such as name and nationality, the benefits of social security, the position of children with special needs and the right to receive education. The DRC was a significant extension of the special rights of children. Also new was the fact that the principle of children's best interests permeated the 1959 declaration. This was touched on in Principle 2 and Principle 7. In the 1924 declaration, children were placed in a position different from that of adults, in the 1959 declaration; this was no longer the case. One aspect of the 1959 declaration is however worth mentioning, the fact that boys have primacy - girls and boys were not treated equally.

Convention on the Rights of the Child 1989

The Convention on the Rights of the Child was born out of shortcomings observed in the 1959 declaration. It became evident that the 1959 declaration was not sufficiently-powerful instrument in connection with children's rights. This conclusion can be drawn from the opinions voiced in the middle of the 1970s as plans were being drawn up for the International Year of the Child. It can therefore be presumed that the 1959 declaration did not match the requirements viewed as essential in connection with children's needs, their position, and their rights. A probable biggest shortcoming was the fact that the DRC was a mere declaration of intent. It could not be ratified and included in national legislative systems. The DRC therefore lacked legally-binding status and obligations. This set the move for the codification that was framed in the 1970s and eventually adopted by the General Assembly.

The Convention on the Rights of the Child was adopted and opened for signature, ratification and accession by the General Assembly resolution 44/25 of 20 November 1989. It entered into force on 2 September, 1990, in accordance with article 49. It has since then been ratified by all countries except the United States of America. The Convention incorporates three forms of rights- provision, protection and participation (Ansell, 2005). It acknowledges that every child has certain basic rights, including the rights to life, his or her own name and identity, to be raised by his or her parents within a family or cultural grouping and have a relationship with both parents, even if they are separated.

The Convention obliges states to allow parents to exercise their parental responsibilities. The Convention also acknowledges that children have the right to express their opinions and to have those opinions heard and acted upon when appropriate; to be protected from abuse or exploitation, to have their privacy protected and that their lives should not be subject to excessive interference. The Convention also obliges signatory states to provide separate legal representation for a child in any judicial dispute concerning his/her care and requires that the child's viewpoint be heard in such cases. The Convention forbids capital punishment for children.

The Convention is child-centric and places the child's needs and rights first ahead of the parents or others. It requires that states act in the best interests of the child. This approach is different from the common law approach found in many countries that had previously treated children and wives as possessions or chattels, ownership of which was often argued over in family disputes. In many jurisdictions, properly implementing the convention requires an overhaul of child custody and guardianship laws, or at the very least, a creative approach within the existing laws.

The Convention also has two optional protocols, adopted by the UN General Assembly in May 2000, which apply only to those states that have signed and ratified them. One is on the involvement of children in armed conflict and the other is on the sale of children, child prostitution and child pornography (United Nations, 2000).

THE MEDIA AND THE UN CONVENTION ON THE RIGHTS OF THE CHILD

Very significant in the UN Convention on the Rights of the Child is the task given to the media in the protection and preservation of children's rights. While Article 12.1 stresses capability of children to form and express their views, Articles 13 and 17 specifically identify the role that the media have to play in the exercise of this right. Article 13.1 states: "The child shall have the right to freedom of expression; this right shall include freedom to seek, receive and impart information and ideas of all kinds, regardless of frontiers, either orally, in writing or in print, in the form of art, or through any other media of the child's choice". This article thus guarantees freedom of expression to the child just as the adults do.

Article 17 further elaborates on the role that the media is expected to play. It links this role to the all-round well-being of the child. Thus, the promotion of child's social, spiritual and moral well-being, as well as physical and mental health is paramount in the performance of media roles of information, education and entertainment, including their protection from injurious materials. The article states:

States Parties recognize the important function performed by the mass media and shall ensure that the child has access to information and material from a diversity of national and international sources, especially those aimed at the promotion of his or her social, spiritual and moral well-being and physical and mental health.

To this end, States Parties shall:

(a) Encourage the mass media to disseminate information and material of social and cultural benefit to the child and in accordance with the spirit of article 29;

(b) Encourage international co-operation in the production, exchange and dissemination of such information and material from a diversity of cultural, national and international sources;

(c) Encourage the production and dissemination of children's books;

(d) Encourage the mass media to have particular regard to the linguistic needs of the child who belongs to a minority group or who is indigenous;

(e) Encourage the development of appropriate guidelines for the protection of the child from information and material injurious to his or her well-being, bearing in mind the provisions of articles 13 and 18 (Article 17, UNCRC 1989).

With these provisions in the UNCRC, the media has become a partner in ensuring that the rights of children are both protected and promoted. The extent to which the media has fared in the performance of this duty is a different ball game.

OTHER EVENTS ON CHILDREN'S RIGHTS AND THE MEDIA

There have been several treaties, resolutions and charters to commit the media to better service as regards children's rights. The objectives of a number of meetings held have been to improve the profile of children's programming and other child media contents throughout the world, to prompt initiatives to advance the diversity and quality of children's broadcasting, and to promote research, co-operation, exchange and training for those concerned with children's broadcasting and other media. (Carlsson 2006). Furthermore, there are meetings with children, youth and media on the agenda arranged by UN agencies or on a regional supranational plane by, for example, the European Union. The objectives of these meetings have been partly to support states in their cultural policies, and partly to give media professionals ideas on how to promote and protect the rights of the child.

Some of these events include: The first World Summit on Television and Children, 1995; Violence on the Screen and the Rights of the Child, 1995; The Southern African Developing Countries' Summit on Children and Broadcasting, 1996; The Asian Summit on Child Rights and the Media, 1996; The UN Committee on the Rights of the Child, 1996; The first All African Summit, 1997; The Second World Summit on Television for Children, 1998; Journalism 2000: Child Rights and the

Media, 1998-2001; The Oslo Challenge, 1999, West African Regional Summit on Media for Children, 2000; EU Expert Seminar: Children and Young People in the New Media Landscape, 2001; The 3rd World Summit on Media for Children, 2001; MAGIC - An Oslo Challenge Follow-Up, 2001; Asian Seminar on Children and the Internet, 2001; 2nd Asian-Pacific Television Forum, 2002; The 4th World Summit on Media for Children and Adolescents, 2004 ; The Radio Manifesto, 2004; to mention but a few.

Worthy of emphasis are The Asian Summit on Child Rights and the Media, 1996; The first All African Summit, 1997 and The Oslo Challenge, 1999.The Asian Summit on Child Rights and the Media was held in July 1996 in Manila, the Philippines. The major organising members included the Asian Media Information and Communication Centre (AMIC), the Philippine Children's Television Foundation, the Asia-Pacific Broadcasting Union, the Council for the Welfare of Children (CWC), Philippines, and UNICEF. Issues examined at the Summit were: child rights and the media; influence of media; access to media; promoting cultural diversity; children's media; media and values; issues of portrayal; and media education. Delegates at the Summit - including ministers and senior officials of Asian governments, journalists, media executives, educators and child rights advocates - adopted the Asian Declaration on Child Rights and the Media.

The first All African Summit was arranged in Accra, Ghana, in October 1997. The most important thing that occurred at this Summit was the adoption of the Africa Charter on Children's Broadcasting. The Charter is an amendment of The SADC Children's Broadcasting Charter on 1996 and is in keeping with the international Children's Television Charter in 1995, but expands on issues relevant to the African continent, and includes radio as well. In particular, greater emphasis is placed on the educational and developmental needs of Africa's children and protection from all forms of commercial exploitation. The African Charter on Children's Broadcasting was ratified at the general assembly of URTNA (Union of National Radio and Television Organisations of Africa) in 2000 in Algiers, where all African broadcasters were asked to make necessary amendments. The final Charter was then further adopted by the Commonwealth Broadcasting Association (CBA) in 2000 in Cape Town, South Africa.

The Oslo challenge is a follow up to identify examples of good practice in fulfilling Articles 12, 13 and 17 of the Convention on the Rights of the Child (UN CRC), to forge co-operative links among the many sectors involved in the issue of children and media, and to produce a checklist for the UN Committee on the Rights of the Child to facilitate consideration of submission by State Parties in relation to these articles. In connection with an international working group of media professionals, young people, UN and voluntary sector workers, researchers and creative thinkers from different continents, The Oslo Challenge was launched on the 20th of November

1999 - the 10th anniversary of the UN CRC. The Challenge is a call to action with the aim to ensure that the overwhelming power of the media for good in the lives of children is identified, encouraged and supported, while the potential harmful effects are recognised and reduced.

It is a call to action. It goes out to everyone engaged in exploring, developing, monitoring and participating in the complex relationship between children and the media (The Mediawise Trust, 2003). This includes governments, organizations and individuals working for children, media professionals at all levels and in all media, the private sector, including media owners, children and young people, parents, teachers and researchers. One will observe that the challenge poses to different sectors indentified is in relation to the media.

The Challenge to governments is:

- to recognize children as an investment rather than a cost, and as potential rather than a burden, and to strive to integrate this reality into policy, including that related to the media; to meet national obligations set out under the Convention on the Rights of the Child and to report regularly to the Committee on the Rights of the Child on policies and actions aimed at fulfilling Articles 12, 13 and 17;
- to ensure that resources are provided so that children and young people have access to information;
- to explore ways in which, without compromising professional independence, support can be given to media initiatives aimed at providing greater access to children, serving their needs and promoting their rights; to recognize that an independent media is fundamental to the pursuit of democracy and freedom and that censorship and control are inimical to the best interests of both children and adults, and thus to create an effective and secure environment in which the media can work professionally and independently.

The Challenge to organizations and individuals working for children is:

- to respect the need for independence of the media as a component of democratic society; to work together with media professionals to promote and protect children's rights and to respond to children's needs;
- to provide effective media liaison services to ensure that media have access to reliable sources of information on children's issues;
- to facilitate accurate coverage of child-related issues by developing media liaison policies that discourage misrepresentation in the interests of publicity and fundraising.

The Challenge to media professionals at all levels and in all media is:

- to raise awareness in the media professions about the rights of children and how they can be protected and promoted by good professional practices or harmed through inappropriate policies or actions;
- to work ethically and professionally according to sound media practices and to develop and promote media codes of ethics in order to avoid sensationalism, stereotyping (including by gender) or undervaluing of children and their rights;
- to resist commercial pressures that lead to children's issues and the rights of children to freedom of expression, fair coverage and protection from exploitation, including as consumers, being given low priority;
- to work to enhance the relationship between children and the media so that both grow and improve in understanding of the positive and negative power and potential of the relationship.

The Challenge to children and young people is:

- to know and understand their rights as laid down in the Convention on the Rights of the Child, and to find and develop ways to contribute to the fulfilment of these rights, including the rights of access to information and to diverse points of view, and to find ways to promote their own active participation in the media and in media development.
- to learn as much as they can about the media so that they can make informed choices as media consumers and gain maximum benefit from the diversity the media offer;
- to grasp opportunities to participate in production of media output and to provide feedback to media producers, both positive and negative;
- to share their opinions about the media with those who can help to support a positive relationship between children and the media: parents, teachers and other adults and young people.

The *Challenge to the private sector, including media owners is:*

- to take into account the rights of children to access, participation, media education and protection from harmful content in the development of new media products and technologies;
- to make the best interests of the child a primary consideration in the pursuit of commercial and financial success, so that today's children become adults in a global society in which all people are protected, respected and free.

The Challenge to parents, teachers and researchers is:

- to acknowledge and support the rights of children to have access to media, participate in it and use it as a tool for their advancement;
- to provide a protective and supportive environment in which children can make choices as media consumers that promote their development to their full potential;
- to be as informed as possible about trends and directions in the media and, where possible, to contribute actively to forming such trends and directions through participation in focus groups, feedback mechanisms and by using procedures laid down for comment and complaints on media content.

THEORETICAL BASIS FOR MEDIA ROLE IN PROMOTION OF CHILD RIGHTS

The call to the media to play active role in the protection and promotion of the rights of the child is well grounded in several theoretical postulations on the role of the media in the society. From the normative perspectives, the social responsibility media and development media theories are applicable to what is expected of the media as regards children rights.

The social responsibility media theory stresses the obligation of the media to serve the public and be responsible in the performance of its duties while its freedom is not hampered in any way (McQuail, 1987, 2005). This theory state that the media can be used by anyone who has an idea to express but they are forbidden to invade private rights of disrupts social structures. It emphasizes the freedom of the press and places responsibility on the media practitioners to abide by certain social standards. It opposes media regulation but believes that the press is automatically controlled by community opinion, consumer protest and professional ethics. Central in the theory's tenets is the duty to protect the rights of the individual by acting as watchdog over the government. It thus follows that part of these rights to protect are the rights of children.

Development media theory advocates media support for government policies and programmes in order to enhance the development of the state (Folarin 2005). This suggests that child rights as government programme should attract the attention of the media and as such, give child rights the necessary support in awareness creation, educating people to instil appropriate and adequate knowledge of child rights, and expose activities that are inimical to the best interests of the child.

Another theoretical basis is the agenda setting. The media prioritises issues and determines those that are regarded as important in society through frequent and selective presentation of such issues. Our perception of the world is dependent not only on our personal interests, but also on the map that is drawn for us by the media practitioners (McCombs & Shaw, 1972 Baran & Davis, 2003). Hence, the media is thus well-positioned to make child rights issues important through careful presentation in various media types.

Closely related to agenda-setting is framing theory which states that the media focuses attention on certain events and then places them within a field of meaning ((Davie, n.d; Ardèvol-Abreu, 2015). In essence, framing theory suggests that how something is presented to the audience (called "the frame") influences the choices people make about how to process that information. Frames are abstractions that work to organize or structure message meaning. The most common use of frames is in terms of the frame the media place on the information they convey. They are thought to influence the perception of the news by the audience, in this way it could be construed as a form of second level agenda-setting – they not only tell the audience what to think about (agenda-setting theory), but also how to think about that issue (second level agenda setting, framing theory). The application of this theory to child rights entails the way the news media constructs the information given out to the audience about children. This will largely determine the audience perception about the rights of children.

THE STATE OF THE AFRICAN CHILD

The African child is the most neglected species in the continent as they suffer in their millions from malnutrition, discrimination, abuses and deprivation of good things including education Corry, 2017; Listverse, 2009). Manyasa (2017) while writing on the International Day of the African Child notes that the problems confronting children today include "denial of educational opportunities, subjection to violence, female genital mutilation, early marriages, child labour, exposure to child prostitution and drug pushing and abuse, and in worst cases, conscription into militias and criminal gangs". Oyero (2018) outlines several areas where children have been deprived such as education, health, nutrition, freedom of expression; as well as hardship they suffer as a result of poverty, armed-conflict, government neglect, child labour and sexual abuse. Millions of children remain in critical situation and their rights are trampled upon with reckless abandon.

With these challenges facing children in Africa, there is no gainsaying that something drastic needs to be done to rescue children from a blink future. It is not enough to pay a lip service to children's welfare while they continue to languish in all manner of suffering. If truly Africa believes that children are the future generation, all stakeholders must come together to show necessary commitment to better the lot of the African child.

MEDIA PERFORMANCE ON CHILD RIGHTS

The media have been playing some active roles as regards child's rights since the awareness of UNCRC is being created. News on different aspects of child rights occupy both the print and electronic media. However, one cannot really give kudos to the media for having done too good. McNamra (n.d) has reported that children and young people were under-represented in the British newspaper coverage. In fact, he noted that they were portrayed as needy, expensive, and a burden or as problematic for adults, Goddard and Sunders (2000) observed in their textual analysis of Australian and UK newspapers that children are objectified in the reportage and that some words used to describe the abuse of children may undermine the seriousness of the offensives. Another study by Alder and Pulk (2001) reviewed that journalist willing to advocate for children face the challenge of counter balancing negative images or 'demonisation' of children and particularly, of adolescents in print, television and film. Negative images of children and young people in the media may place obstacles in the paths of attempts to prevent their abuse and neglect.

McManus and Dorfman's (2002) study on how U.S newspapers portray child care shows that child care is all but invisible on the pages of the sampled newspapers. However, in Woodruff's (2001) study on child's nutrition policies, though there was not much news on nutrition policies what existed was substantive and well placed.

Again, Nwankwo and Okwemba (2002) examined how the media covers children's issues with a view to knowing whether it helps to expand or constrain the space and understanding of children's rights. They found out that children's rights issues receive lukewarm reception in the media as compared to other news. Children's issues are not in most cases as sensational as compared to other political issues, making them to be shunned by the media. Hence, the media tend to report children's issues only when they are sensational. One of the reasons why the media fail to educate their readers on CRC and other legislations could be that the writers are not themselves sensitised.

Oyero's (2009) study on children stories in the Nigerian and Ghanaian newspapers shows that the papers carried stories of child health, education, sexual abuse, armed conflict, child labor, freedom of expression, security, etc. However, the conclusion in the study is that children are not given the adequate representation in the news coverage. The newspapers adopted a variety of print media genres in the reportage of child rights including the use of pictures which help the readers to visualize the issue being reported on, and at times, pictures alone tell the whole story for readers to understand. However, there is low engagement of the public on the subjects of child rights, as reflected in the low coverage of opinion. Besides, children's stories were not given proper placement as they were buried within the newspaper pages, an indication of weak newsworthiness of child rights stories.

Omotosho, Oyero and Salawu's (2015) study on Nigerian television stations to assess their programming performance as regards children, shows a neglect of children on the sample TV stations, in the sense that the programs for children were very few. However, there was a balance in the focus of the program between entertainment and learning. Furthermore, none of the station has the policy on children's programming.

On the whole, the media performance as regards child right can be described as simply fair. This is because reportage of children's stories has always been reactive. Besides, most reports that advocate for children's rights appear mostly on children's day. Hence, there is still a whole lot the media can do in respect to the right of the child.

THE FUTURE PATHWAYS

The task assigned to media in the UNCRC demands greater commitment and more active role. If the media would accomplish the task of child right promotion, it must be well positioned and empowered to do so and there must be a strategic involvement of the media to accomplish the task. In positioning the media for better service for children is the need for training. There is need for journalists to be well educated on expectation from them as contained in the UNCRC and other documents such as the Oslo challenge,. There is the need for reorientation of journalists and media producers on the developmental approaches reportage as against nationalist and political angles which they are used to.

Again, emphasis should be placed on advocacy journalism which favors children's rights. Advocacy journalists are ready to stand by their position and pursue a cause until the desirable change is achieved. This is akin to the journalism of attachment, which deliberately takes a good cause and pursues it. "The aim of media advocacy and advocacy journalism is to increase the capacity of groups within society through in-depth and contextualized reporting, and in doing so to bring about social change" (Advocacy Institute cited in Salameh, 2005, p. 25)

Programming on television should also give a fair consideration to the right of the child. Adequate programmes that cater for the best interest of the child should be aired. A situation were children's programs are predominantly entertainment does not help me cause of children. Moreover, television programmes should also take care of the linguistic needs of children as contained in Art 17b of UN Convention on the Rights of the Child and Art 4 of the African Charter on Children Broadcasting, noting that "children should hear, see and express themselves, their culture and their language (ACCB, Art4). Recognising that Nigeria has three indigenous languages (Yoruba, Hausa and Igbo) as official languages apart from English calls to question the commitment of the stations to the performance of their duty' (Omotosho, Oyero & Salawu, 2015).

To make for consistency in the reportage of children issues, media organisations should set up children desk for this purpose. Special columns should be maintained while the broadcast also run special editions on weekly basis. There should also be persons designated as children reporters and writers whose duties are to write about children and educate the public about their rights, expose hills done against them and advocate their rights. Another very good gesture will be a collaboration among African media organisations. Oyero's (2018) notes that partnership would help to popularise the rights of the child as information are shared to different part of the continent. He further notes:

Such partnership could also galvanize the process of helping children when successful experiences in that direction in one part of the continent are shared with others. The aspect of media production for children will also benefit a lot from partnership among African media. There could be joint production of children's programs, thus reducing the burden of financial and human resources for such projects. It will also be easier to secure necessary funds from donors as a network to pursue children's media contents. Partnership could also facilitate sharing or exchanges of media content among various media organizations in different parts of the continent, thus fulfilling one of the UNCRC guidelines of encouraging "international co-operation in the production, exchange and dissemination of such information and material from a diversity of cultural, national and international sources" (Art 17b, UNCRC)

Moreover, there should be a balance in the programming to care for both social and mental wellbeing of children. Moreover, the aspect of cultural values should not be neglected. This suggests that TV programmess for child should not be only imported foreign programmess, locally produced programmes that focus on indigenous culture and moral values should be invested in and aired.

CONCLUSION

The paper has tried to trace the historical background of child's rights and the connection with the media. It also briefly assessed how the media has performed in accomplishing the fast set out in the UNCRC and other documents., While the media has fairly tried to focus on child rights issues, it activities have been largely reactive. There remains so much to be done for the media to receive kudos in what they do for children. Journalists must be trained to have the right perspective about children and media organisations should form alliances to deliver the best for the interest of the child. Media organisations too should understand paying attention to children is part of their social responsibility. The fact that children do not have economic power or do not have much commercial values should not discourage them from giving their best to children.

REFERENCES

Advocacy Institute. (2001). *What is 'advocacy'?* Retrieved on October 2, 2008 from http://www.advocacy.org/definition.htm

Alder, C., & Polk, K. (2001). *Child victims of homicide*. Cambridge.

Ansell, N. (2005). *Children, youth and development*. London: Routledge.

Ardèvol-Abreu, A. (2015). Framing theory in communication research in Spain. Origins, development and current situation. *Revista Latina de Comunicación Social, 70*, 423-450.

Baran, S. J., & Davis, D. K. (2003). *Mass Communication Theory: Foundations, Ferment, and Feature*. Belmont: Thomson-Wardsworth.

Carlsson, U. (Ed.). (2006). Regulation, awareness, empowerment: Young people and harmful media content in the digital age. The UNESCO International Clearing House on Children, Youth and Media, 239-251.

Cohen, B. C. (1963). *The press and foreign policy*. Princeton, NJ: Princeton University Press.

Corry, S. (2017). *Celebrating the day of the African child*. Retrieved from https://www.trustedclothes.com/blog/2017/06/19/celebrating-the-day-of-the-african-child/

Davie, G. (n.d.). *Framing Theory. Mass Communication Theory. Mass Communication Theory: From Theory to Practical Application*. Retrieved from https://masscommtheory.com/theory-overviews/framing-theory/

Folarin, B. (2005). *Theories of Mass Communication: An Introductory Text*. Stirling: Horden.

Goddard, C., & Saunders, B. J. (2000). The gender neglect and textual abuse of children in the print media. *Child Abuse, 9*(1), 37–48. doi:10.1002/(SICI)1099-0852(200001/02)9:1<37::AID-CAR586>3.0.CO;2-2

Listverse. (2009, July 6). *Top 10 terrible issues facing children worldwide*. Retrieved from http://listverse.com/2009/07/06/ top-10-terrible-issues-facing-children-worldwide/

Mahkonen, S. (n.d.). *Children's rights and the media*. Malaysia: AIBD. Retrieved on August 6, 2008 from http://download.aibd.org.my/books/Childrens_Rights_and_the_Media.pdf

Manyasa, E. (2017, June 16). *Challenges the African child faces in our time*. Retrieved from https://www.standardmedia.co.ke/article/2001243683/challenges-the-african-child-faces-in-our-time

McCombs, M., & Shaw, D. (1972). The agenda-setting function of mass media. *Public Opinion Quarterly, 36*(2), 176–185. doi:10.1086/267990

McManus, J., & Dorfman, L. (2002). *How U. S. newspapers portray child care. Issue 11*. Berkeley, CA: Berkeley Media Studies Group.

McNamara. (n. d.). *Silent victims and pretty props: The representation of young people in Irish national*. Retrieved from newspapers.www.nordicom.gu.se/cl/publ/electronic/PaulMcIreland1.pdf

McQuail, D. (1989). *Mass communication theory: An introduction*. London: SAGE publications.

McQuail, D. (2005). *McQuail's mass communication theory: An introduction*. London: SAGE publications.

Nwankwo, E. H., & Okwemba, A. (2002). *How the Kenyan media covers the children's rights issues: A content analysis*. A paper presented to International Federation of Journalists (IFJ), Nairobi, Kenya. Retrieved on October 22, 2008 from www.ifj.org/assets/docs/089/021/36f1759-cbfee15.pdf

Oyero, O., & Salawu, A. (2018). Building media capacity for children sustainability in Africa: Educational and partnership imperatives. *SAGE Open, 8*(1), 1–10. doi:10.1177/2158244018763930

Oyero, O. S. (2009). *A comparative study of child rights coverage in selected Nigerian and Ghanaian newspapers (1999-2003)* (Unpublished doctoral thesis). Covenant University, Ota, Nigeria.

The MediaWise Trust. (2003). *The Oslo challenge*. Retrieved May 8, 2007 from http://www.mediawise.org.uk/display_page.php?id=130

United Nations. (2000). *Assembly adopts two protocols on rights of child: Children in armed conflict; Sale of children, Child prostitution, Child pornography*. Accessed October 9, 2019 from https://www.un.org/press/en/2000/20000525.ga9711.doc.html

Woodruff, K. (1997). *Children's health in the news. Issue 4*. Berkeley, CA: Berkeley Media Studies Group.

Woodruff, K., & Dorfman, L. (2001). *Newspaper coverage of child nutrition policies*. Berkeley Media Studies Group.

KEY TERMS AND DEFINITIONS

Child Protection: To shield a minor from any form of danger, including harassment, violence and neglect, especially as guaranteed by Article 19 of the UN Convention on the Rights of the Child.

Child Rights Act: Adapted by Nigeria in 2003 through an Act of Parliament, it serves as a legal documentation that ensures the protection of children in Nigeria.

Childhood: The phase of life that covers infancy and adolescence, and when one still requires care and protection by others.

Convention on the Rights of a Child (CRC): A United Nation's human rights treaty that seeks to uphold and protect the rights of a child (defined as any person under the age of 18). The treaty came into force on the 2nd of September 1990. Currently, 196 countries, compromising all members of the UN are parties, with the exception of the United States of America.

Media: A broad term used to describe various channels of communication, including the traditional and digital communication platforms.

Sustainable Development: It is development that meets the needs and aspirations of the present without compromising the ability of future generations to meet their own needs. Thus, sustainable development is the organizing principle for sustaining finite resources necessary to provide for the needs of future generations of life on the planet.

Sustainable Development Goals (SDGs): The Sustainable Development Goals (SDGs), otherwise known as the Global Goals, are a universal call to action to end poverty, protect the planet and ensure that all people enjoy peace and prosperity.

UNICEF: United Nations Children's Fund.

Chapter 2
New Media Technologies and Childhood Education for Development Purposes in Africa

Silk Ogbu
Pan Atlantic University, Lagos, Nigeria

ABSTRACT

Education is the 'right' of every child and should not be a privilege. As signatories to the United Nations Convention on the Rights of a Child (CRC), every country in Africa has a fundamental responsibility in the global commitment towards the provision of childhood education in their respective states. However, the number of children in the continent that are 'out of school' has risen to the world's highest today. This chapter examines some of the problems encumbering childhood education in Africa, especially in terms of curriculum development, funding, and capacity building and interrogates the effectiveness of current mitigation strategies. It argues that childhood education holds the key to unlocking the potentials of the vast natural and human resources of the continent that are required to catalyze poverty reduction and socio-economic development in the years ahead.

INTRODUCTION

Africa is arguably the least developed continent in the world today. As creativity and innovation continue to spur radical changes in almost every sphere of human endeavor, the fear of a widening gap between Africa and the rest of the world is

DOI: 10.4018/978-1-7998-0329-4.ch002

increasing by the day. Many scholars believe that the key to bridging that gap or accelerating the pace of development of the continent lies in the education of its young and future generations. Education is irrefutably the most potent weapon against poverty and ignorance known to man, and Africa is probably the most endowed continent in terms of natural resources but remains the least developed because of its inability to convert natural resources to tradable goods and services. As the forces of globalization and virtualization continue to contract the world space, academics and professionals are searching for ways to reposition Africa for greater competitiveness in a rapidly changing world. In spite of divergent views about the end, there is increasing coalescence on the need to focus on the effective education of the African child as the fastest track to socio-economic transformation of the continent.

Without a doubt, advances in media and communication technologies offer new possibilities for childhood education that many African countries are yet to tap into because of several reasons. The first is the political will to craft a policy on education that will break the colonial heritage- a system of education that was based on ethnocentric assumptions and designed to compel Africans to conform to western ideals. A new policy on childhood education, anchored upon the emerging trends in pedagogy and leveraging on new media technologies, is required to propel Africa towards aggressive growth.

Apart from the lack of a policy direction in curriculum development, another constraint to childhood education in Africa today is the paucity of funding on the part of governments and the private sector for early education across the continent. In other parts of the world, childhood education is better funded and supported by stakeholders, especially as the increasing use of media technologies continues to introduce new cost implications into the delivery process. Important cost dimensions include the provision of suitable infrastructure, the procurement of necessary facilities and the expansion of access to digitized protocols of instructional delivery.

Besides, inadequate funding of childhood education, perhaps the most important hindrance to the application of tools to childhood education in Africa is the dearth of competent teachers that are sufficiently trained to use new media technologies in the classroom. At the moment, early education teachers in Africa are among the least qualified and remunerated in the world. There is, therefore, little or no incentive for well-trained teachers to accept such jobs in many countries across the continent. In Nigeria, for example, it was shocking to discover recently that over 25,000 primary school teachers in Kano State were unable to pass an aptitude test designed for their students (Daily Post, 2018). Without competent teachers, it will be impossible to explore the media landscape as a pathway for improving or benchmarking Africa's childhood education against the rest of the world.

This chapter explores the issues surrounding the adoption of media technology in childhood education in Africa, particularly in terms of how they address the rights of the child. In pursuance of that goal, however, the chapter focuses mainly on the three areas of concern highlighted above: curriculum development; improved funding and accelerated training of teachers. The arguments put forward in this chapter are anchored upon the postulations of the *Technological Determinism* and *Cognitive Development* Theories. Essentially, the chapter adopts a conceptual approach, drawing evidence to support analytical perspectives from secondary sources of data.

CONCEPTUAL FRAMEWORK

New Media Technologies and Childhood Education in Africa

New Media Technologies encompasses all forms of digitally-enabled means of transmitting or exhibiting information (Manovich, 2002). In a broad sense, media technology covers various forms of communicative devices such as radio, television, DVDs, video games, laptops, mobile phones, tablets, interactive boards, portable players, etc. Although some of these devices are no longer new by relative standards, the use of the word 'new' to describe them refers mainly to their interactive nature and connectivity which are fundamentally driven by Web 2.0. In general, new media technologies may differ in terms of their cultural, technological, social, and pedagogical attributes, but they share five characteristics in common: communication, collaboration, community, creativity, and convergence (Friedman & Friedman, 2008).

Unarguably, media technologies are fundamentally changing the way children learn and make sense of the world around them. Across western countries, empirical evidence indicates that that the exposure of children to new media technologies enhance the development of positive learning personalities and accelerate their acquisition of language, communication, and motor skills (Nikolopoulou, 2014; Roberts-Holmes, 2013; Pohio, 2009). In Africa, the adoption of technology for childhood education is still relatively new and evolving, but the impact has been quite significant. In Kenya, a study revealed that the implementation gap in the use of media technologies for early education is driven by the shortage of knowledgeable teachers in the use of ICT and a widespread negative perception of the teachers about the contributions of media tools to their effectiveness in the classroom (Momanyi, Norby & Strand, 2006). In some other African countries, militating factors range from the lack of policy initiatives, institutional frameworks and funding to weak regulatory and political support (Amolloh, Lilian, & Shaji, 2017; Omodara & Adu, 2014).

Nevertheless, new media technologies offer great opportunities for the transformation of pedagogy, which providers of early education in Africa can leverage. As the rate of internet penetration continues to increase across the continent, the percentage of children using digitally-enabled devices is rising astronomically. Televisions are becoming better 'baby sitters' than humans with the capacity to tell more captivating stories. Children aged six and seven are increasingly surfing the web to find materials for their school assignments. A growing body of evidence suggests that interactive media are now helping children to develop cognitive skills in specific contexts, including the following:

- attend and concentrate
- associate words and symbols with objects
- perceive and discriminate
- identify similarity and difference
- classify objects
- see order or relationships
- develop concepts – space, size, shape
- explore and be curious
- manipulate
- use creative imagination (Edgar & Edgar, 2008)

In his interesting book, *Don't bother me, Mom, I'm learning!* Prensky (2006) shows how computer games help in teaching children complex lessons about:

- cause and effect relationships
- complex system behaviors
- long term winning versus short term gains
- counter-intuitive results
- creating order from seeming chaos
- using obstacles as motivation
- second order consequences
- the value of persistence

As the conversation on the protection and implementation of the rights of the 'African Child' intensifies, the major question that is hanging in the air is how new media technologies can be adopted and extended for early education so that children born in the continent can grow up sufficiently empowered to compete with their peers in other parts of the world. There is a need to develop a framework, at the continental level, that will accelerate the integration of emerging technologies that are suitable for childhood education with 'content' that is 'indigenous' and capable of transmitting core African values. Otherwise, Africa may not only lose its cultural heritage in the years ahead but will also face the risk of another wave of colonialism

— the enslavement of the mind of its future generation. Media convergence offers amazing possibilities for the combination of various teaching methods—old and new — in a single device. Africans must be strategic about ICT development to reduce the current dependence on the west for both hardware and software applications. Early education anchored on new media technologies is a practical way to narrow that gap and safeguard the future of the African Child.

THEORETICAL FRAMEWORK

Technological Determinism Theory

The theory of Technological Determinism is assumed to have originated from the early works of a sociologist, Thorstein Veblen (1857–1929). The major idea espoused by the theory is that technology controls human behavior and thus determines social change. Technological innovation is perceived as an 'unstoppable force', driving progress in society and in every sphere of human activity ((Green, 2002). For instance, the transition from orality to literacy is conceived by Technological Determinists as a historical transformation catalyzed by the innovation of the printing press and not a random manifestation of progress in society. Therefore, technology is seen as central to the cognitive development of man and the changes he is able to make to his environment. However, critics of the Technological Determinism (TD) contend that the idea of determinism is reductionist in the sense that it negates the relevance and contributions of other factors to change in society. They argue variously that technology itself is socially determined, that technology and social structures co-evolve in a non-deterministic, emergent process, or that the effects of any given technology depend mainly on how it is implemented which is in turn socially determined (Adler, 2006). The debate over TD, it seems, has developed into three variant perspectives: The 'Hard Determinists' claim that technology is the major or only determinant of social change; the 'Soft Determinists' are of the view that technology is just one out of the other vital forces; while the 'Anti-TD' contend that technology is a 'neutral' contributor to social change and that its effects are mostly or completely dependent on the social context in which it is applied.

Media determinism (MD) is an offshoot of Technological Determinism philosophy which suggests that the media is the dominant force in the determination of how society evolves and adapts over time. Proponents of MD argue that advances in media technologies directly impact the development of both society and the human person. In his popular declaration that the 'medium is the message', Canadian born Sociologists, Marshal McLuhan, draws attention to how much ground-breaking transformations in society, across different historical epochs, have depended on innovations in mass communication technologies. For example, he describes the invention of printing as 'the typographic extension of man, which brought in nationalism, industrialism and mass markets, and universal literacy and education' (McLuhan, 1962; McLuhan, 1964). Since then, the advent of the internet and the growth of the electronic media has created a new information and knowledge age, which is radically changing the world and taking the notion of media determinism to a whole new level, especially in terms of how people learn or interact with each other. In alignment with this view, McQuail (2010), posits that media technological determinism is anchored upon four major postulations:

- Communication technology is fundamental to society
- Each technology has a bias to particular communication forms, contents and uses
- The sequence of invention and application of communication technology influences the direction and pace of social change
- Communication revolutions lead to social revolutions

Indeed, the overwhelming influence currently being exerted by the media on society appears to reinforce the arguments of the Media Technological Determinists that contemporary society and culture have become 'mediatized' and can no longer be separated from the 'media logic' (Hjarvard, 2008; Allwell & Ogbu, 2018). The relevance of the above propositions to this discourse is that it draws attention to the influence of the new and evolving dimensions of 'digital literacy' to the cognitive development of the child and how media technologies are particularly changing the methods of childhood education in Africa (Hauer, 2017; Servaes & Lie, 2008).

Cognitive Development Theory

The Cognitive Development theory originated from the groundbreaking work of Jean Piaget, a Frenchman who was employed by the Binet Institute in the 1920s to develop French versions of the English Intelligence Tests for children. Based on his study of the reasons that participants gave for failing the tests, Piaget (1936) concluded that children have different cognitive abilities conditioned by both their interaction with the environment they live in and their biological maturation processes. Before this study, it was commonly assumed that children were less competent thinkers than adults, but by beaming the light on the formation of knowledge blocks (schemas) in the minds of children and the biological steps in their cognitive development process, Piaget (1936) revealed that children actually think in amazingly diverse ways compared to adults.

Essentially the basic components of Piaget's Cognitive Development Theory (CDT) are made up of 3 categories (McLeod, 2018):

1. Schemas (building blocks of knowledge).
2. Adaptation processes that enable the transition from one stage to another (equilibrium, assimilation, and accommodation).
3. Stages of Cognitive Development:
    a. Sensorimotor stage (birth to age 2)
    b. Pre-operational stage (from age 2 to age 7)
    c. Concrete operational stage (from age 7 to age 11)
    d. Formal operational stage (age 11+ - adolescence and adulthood).

The stages of cognitive development indicate the steps through which children learn new things and make sense of the world around them as they grow from infancy to adulthood. While they may not necessarily think as adults do, Piaget (1945) insists that they learn through play and imitations. Although Piaget's CDT has been criticized, especially for its assumption that the learning competence of children can be measured through their biological maturation stages, its revelation concerning their ability to develop cognitive flexibility when exposed to schemas was extremely influential in the development of education policy and teaching practice for children in Europe in the 1960s. In the United Kingdom, the 1967 Plowden Report, which was the basis for the reform of the primary education, was strongly motivated by the recommendations of Piaget's (1957) work. As McLeod (2018) notes, the report's recurrent thrusts, which include individual learning, flexibility in the curriculum, the centrality of play in children's learning, the use of the environment, learning by discovery and the importance of a dynamic method of evaluation of children's advancement are the bases upon which a new curriculum was developed for primary education in the UK at that time.

The importance of CDT as a frame for this chapter is that it underlines the necessity of developing a curriculum for childhood education in Africa that is not only informed by indigenous research but deliberately designed to respond to the peculiar ways children in the continent learn, as they progress from one stage of their cognitive development process to the other. A better understanding of how African children learn is instructive because it opens the door to the interrogation of the current teaching methods used for childhood education and how they can be continually improved overtime to achieve the desired objectives.

MEDIA ROLE IN CHILDHOOD EDUCATION IN AFRICA: ISSUES, CONTROVERSIES AND PROBLEMS

In the past two decades, the amount of time spent by children on media-related activities worldwide has increased sporadically. Despite the pace of internet penetration and issues around affordance, the exposure of children to media content has been increasing exponentially across Africa as a result of the rise in media proliferation and convergence. Even in the villages, children are now able to watch television and movies, play games, listen to music and radio programs, create and share their own photos and videos by using smart mobile phones belonging to their parents or relatives, whether or not they own any device. Several studies indicate that apart from sleeping, children between the ages of 2 and 17 spend the greatest amount of their time these days on media screens (Arnett, 2007; Jackson, Brown, & Pardun, 2008; Ray & Jat, 2010). Obviously, the huge and increasing exposure of children to media contents present serious concerns as well as interesting opportunities for childhood education in Africa. However, the majority of the studies found in extant literature appear to be more interested in the negative effects of media on children, especially in terms of detrimental health and psychosocial consequences (Oyama & Ogbu, 2017; Bioulac, Arfi, & Bouvard, 2008; Hayne, Herbert, & Simcock, 2003), rather than its benefits, which include the enhancement of learning and cognitive development of young children (Hastings, et al., 2009).

From the revelations of the Cognitive development Theory, it is clear that the learning abilities of young children significantly increase as they mature and interact more with their environment. If children devote most of the time they are active interacting with media devices, the natural question to ask would then be: what are they learning through that process? What type of content are they consuming on media screens and to what extent can that be regulated to ensure that negative consequences are mitigated while expanding the positive outcomes? This is where the development of appropriate curriculum to harness media technology in the teaching of young children comes in. In many parts of Africa, including Nigeria, Egypt, Tanzania, Zimbabwe, and Mali, teaching methods are far behind the media revolution and no longer seem to excite children. There is a need for a deliberate, evidence-based and policy-driven reform of the curriculum for childhood education in Africa that will incorporate new media technologies and the positive values inherent in the cultures of the continent. At the moment, a majority of the content that young children in Africa are exposed to via televisions, video games, DVDs, computers, mobile phones, tablets, etc., are based on foreign cultures that are strange and only imaginable to them. Given that children learn by imitation and playing, it is no surprise that some Africans from childhood start to learn about foreign values and all through their journey to adulthood struggle with an inferiority complex and the aspiration of resembling the Europeans and the various characters they idolize in the media.

To develop the potential of the African Child and position him/her for the greatness that tomorrow holds, educators and policymakers must address the problem of obsolete curricular. Several studies have shown that children from the ages of 2-16 can learn faster the skills of spelling, mathematics and problem solving when such lessons are programmed on media devices than when they are taught physically in the classrooms (Kirkorian, Wartella, & Anderson, 2008; Hastings, et al., 2009). Yet, in many countries in Africa, articulating a modern and appropriate curriculum for childhood education is neither prioritized nor seen as an instrument for deliberate intervention in the overall plan to grow the manpower potentials of the continent and thus reduce the scourge of poverty pervading the land. Studies indicate that in several countries, including Lesotho, Rwanda, Zambia, Tanzania, Kenya, Nigeria, Ethiopia, Egypt, Cameroon, Ghana, Uganda and Zimbabwe, there are critical deficiencies in the design, implementation and regulation of early childhood education curricula (Mwamwenda, 2014 ; Mushoriwa & Muzembe, 2011; Mtahabwa, 2009; Morrison, 2001). In most of the countries, education at the preschool level (1-4) is still largely relegated to NGOs and private providers with little or no government participation or direction. As a result, a majority of the children in rural areas who do not have access to NGO sponsorships, and whose parents cannot afford to pay the high tuition for private education, start off being disadvantaged and ill-equipped to compete with their peers in other parts of the world.

Another significant dimension of media adoption in childhood education is the increasing cost of providing good quality education for children. In many African countries, including Nigeria, Namibia, Kenya, Ghana, Botswana, Tanzania, Ethiopia, South Africa, etc., free education is available to children at the primary school level, however, the facilities and quality of teaching provided for the public schools is far below the standard found in both the private schools and in similar public schools around the world. Although so much rhetoric about the imperativeness of increasing annual budgetary allocation to education in Africa to about 20% has been spewed at the relevant conventions of the United Nations and African Union, the political will to implement is lacking. Childhood education in Africa is still grossly under-funded. Many government-owned nurseries, primary and secondary schools have no teaching facilities and equipment, and no basic infrastructures, including suitable accommodation, electricity, internet, books, furniture, etc. Indeed, the introduction of media-based teaching methods, with often additional cost implications, remains a challenge that many governments in Africa have simply been unable to deal with. The consequence, however, is that a gap in the provision of good quality education for children has developed over the years, and private proprietors have been cashing in on that at the expense of struggling parents. On one hand, the effort to keep up with the cost of private education is significantly reducing the disposable income of the emerging African middle class and their chances of escaping poverty, and on the other hand the gulf between the children of the privileged few, who can afford good quality education and those of the masses who are relegated to ill-equipped public schools, is dangerously widening (in terms of life chances) with serious implications for social and economic stratification in the future (Alakwe & Ogbu, 2017; Alakwe & Ogbu, 2018). This is an infringement of the privileges of the African Child as enshrined in the United Nation's Convention on the Rights of the Child (CRC), which all the countries in Africa and all over the world have pledged to protect. Specifically, the rights to free and good quality education for every child are clearly spelled out under articles 17 & 28 of the CRC:

Article 17 (Access to information; mass media): *Children have the right to get information that is important to their health and well-being. Governments should encourage mass media – radio, television, newspapers, and Internet content sources – to provide information that children can understand and to not promote materials that could harm children. Mass media should particularly be encouraged to supply information in languages that minority and indigenous children can understand. Children should also have access to children's books.*

Article 28: (Right to education): *All children have the right to a primary education, which should be free. Wealthy countries should help poorer countries achieve this right. Discipline in schools should respect children's dignity. For children to benefit from education, schools must be run in an orderly way – without the use of violence. Any form of school discipline should take into account the child's human dignity. Therefore, governments must ensure that school administrators review their discipline policies and eliminate any discipline practices involving physical or mental violence, abuse or neglect. The Convention places a high value on education. Young people should be encouraged to reach the highest level of education of which they are capable (UNICEF, 1996).*

Similarly, Articles 13, 29, 30 and 31 of the CRC all affirm the obligations of governments to protect the rights of children to good quality education in one way or another. Therefore, the failure to fund technology-based childhood education in Africa does not only deprive children of their rights under international law, but it also places them at a disadvantaged position compared to others from other continents in the current race for knowledge acquisition and talent development. Specifically, Article 17 recognizes the emerging role of media technologies in the advancement of childhood education and supports the view of Technological Determinism theorists that modern education must be driven by the forces of technology. However, Article

28 concedes that while free education is a right of every child, poor countries may not be able to afford the cost without the help and support of their more affluent neighbors. Indeed, the funding of childhood education is a challenge for many countries in Africa (Adamu-Issah, Elden, Forson, & Schrofer, 2007), necessitating their dependence on grants from various development partners, such as USAID, DFID, GIZ, etc. In all fairness, the intervention of these transnational agencies has been instrumental to the expansion of access to childhood education in many poor African countries. However, in a lot of countries too, the resort to foreign aid for the funding of childhood education has led to the total negligence of that responsibility by the governments, the loss of regulatory and oversight rights of governments over implementation strategies, the negligence of indigenous values and mores in the training of the young children, and several other problems that are beyond the focus of this chapter.

Beyond the challenge of funding the provision of modern style childhood educational facilities and infrastructure, which is no doubt, an onerous task for poor African governments and their development partners, there is also the problem of sustainability and affordance on the part of citizens, the majority of whom still live below the poverty line. Media devices that children need for learning, such as mobile phones, tablets, DVDs, Televisions, Computers, Video Games, etc., are not exactly cheap. Certainly, many families, especially in rural areas cannot afford these devices and may not be able to provide the necessary support and guidance that children may need for multimodal learning. Besides, most media technologies depend on electricity supply and internet access which are usually not available to the poor and rural dwellers. Unfortunately, the funding strategies for childhood education by governments and NGOs in Africa are cached in silos and, therefore, have been unable to respond to these multifarious challenges in any comprehensive manner.

Perhaps, the greatest challenge facing childhood education in Africa today is the shortage of competent and trained teachers with the capacity to deliver the quality of learning outcomes that can stimulate the innovative and creative energy of the 21st Century African child. The internet revolution is impelling the growth of a digital generation that is now able to acquire digital literacy almost from birth through early exposure to various types of media, communication and electronic devices. This digital generation lives in an era of global civilization that is far ahead of the world that many of their teachers, especially in Africa, grew up in and are still stuck in. As Bento, Lencastre, & Pereira (2016) observes:

We live in a society that has developed in almost all areas, yet it is slow to update in education. Generally, students live in the twenty-first century, with teachers who run after them with pedagogies from the twentieth century in classrooms that remain frozen in time and comparable, in all too many cases, to classrooms from the nineteenth century

The inability of teachers to use new media technologies affects their perception of the relevance of multimedia tools for teaching, and their inclination to deploy them in instructional delivery. In a broad sense, the knowledge gap fosters resistance of teachers to reforms in pedagogical methods, especially at the levels of pre-school and primary education in Africa. Even in circumstances where the teachers are cooperative and willing to introduce new methods of teaching in their classrooms, they are mostly unable to offer guidance and learning support to the children because they are still struggling to understand these new technologies themselves. The 'disconnect' between the teachers and students in this context undermines the potentials of childhood education in Africa and distorts the learning experience of children. In other parts of the world, mobile devices, tablets, and computers are increasingly being used for teaching games and role play (Kjartansdóttir, 2016; Colvert, 2016), reading and comprehension skills (Bento, Lencastre, & Pereira, 2016), social skills (Brito & Dias, 2016), cultural sensitivity (Amante, 2016), word and language learning skills (Sarı, Başal, Takacs, & Bus, 2016), etc. Unfortunately, the use of multimodal instructions for childhood education is still very limited or mainly restricted to a few private schools reserved for the privileged few. In many countries in Africa, there are no policy initiatives or comprehensive programs for the training of teachers in the use of media technologies for childhood education. This means that Africa may remain far behind other continents in terms of advancement in human capital development until this knowledge gap is closed. Even if they wanted to, teachers, just like everyone else, cannot give what they don't have.

Another important dimension of the problem is that teachers at the pre-school and primary school levels in Africa are among the most poorly remunerated workers in the world, in contrast to the practice in other climes. Therefore, it is difficult to attract and retain the younger, more competent and better-trained teachers who understand new media technologies and how to apply them to the teaching of young children. Given the present structure of remuneration at that level of teaching practice, only the old and retired, who are mostly digital immigrants are willing to accept the job offers. From these indications, the future of childhood education in Africa appears bleak and may not likely get brighter until these fundamental issues are addressed.

CONCLUSION

This chapter has identified the lack of an appropriate curriculum for childhood education in Africa as a major challenge hindering the development of learning capabilities in children. There is a need for a broad policy intervention at the level of the African Union that will compel African governments, who are all signatories to the CRC, to prioritize the creation of a 21st-century curriculum for childhood education in their respective states. Article 28 of the CRC treaty clearly affirms the right of every child in Africa to education.

However, the type and quality of education that is provided to the child is equally of great importance to the achievement of that objective. As can be deduced from the submissions of the Cognitive Development Theory, children have different cognitive abilities that can be developed only when the appropriate mix of teaching methods are deployed. A curriculum for childhood education will enable governments and development partners to interrogate implementation strategies, cost implications, and delivery objectives so that all providers (public and private) can be on the same page and be properly guided. In countries like South Africa, Namibia, and Botswanan, where models such as the 'Montessori' are used as the basis for curriculum development, periodic revision of learning outcomes is recommended to ensure that instructional methods leverage emerging new media technologies and are in sync with global best practices. This is in tandem with the view of Technological Determinist theorists who insist that it is dangerous to ignore the dynamic influence of technology on every sphere of human development, especially education.

The funding of childhood education is a complex matter that requires a creative solution. In situations where governments and citizens are poor, as is the case in many African countries, there is really no easy way around this problem. The dependence on foreign assistance or aid has not been a perfect solution. As much as it serves as a useful stop-gap in mitigating the problem, it is not sustainable and cannot be considered as a 'safe' approach to educating Africans given the various cultural, social and psychological implications associated with it. Therefore, what is required is more or less the political will to invest more in childhood education and to explore creative avenues for funding that will respond to the short, mid and long term needs in the sector. This chapter recommends that further research is conducted in this regard to examine available options and innovative funding strategies that will work for the continent.

Regardless of the curricula and funding mechanisms articulated to enhance childhood education in Africa, competent teachers will be required for implementation, at least until robots are deployed to the classrooms. To address the knowledge gap and the widening gulf between expectation and performance, there is a need for an urgent and aggressive training and re-training of the teachers currently involved in the conception, design and implementation of instructional methods at that sensitive level of pedagogical practice, especially in the adoption and adaptation of media technologies in the classroom. Adequate training will reduce the level of incompetence and resistance that currently exits to the introduction of new teaching methods and also increase the confidence of the teachers in experimenting with the new media technologies. Going forward, it will be useful to develop a coherent strategy for the training of future teachers in childhood education that will capture the dynamic nature of the social, health, cultural and psychological risks associated with the application of new media technologies to pedagogy. Also, it is recommended that the remuneration of teachers in childhood education should be reviewed in many countries in Africa to attract competent individuals and enhance their retention. If this is not done, even the effort and funds invested in training them will be wasted because they may migrate to other parts of the world where teachers are better paid and appreciated.

Generally, it appears that the performance of pupils in pre-school, primary and secondary schools in many African countries has been declining for several years now. This has become a matter of grave concern to parents, educators and policymakers. This chapter admits that the problems responsible for this downward trend are multipronged and has made its recommendations to support the search for enduring solutions. The key position of this study is that media influence on childhood education is humongous, irreversible and still evolving. New media technologies are converging in portable devices like mobile phones, tablets, wristwatches, etc., making it impossible for humanity to escape mediatization. It is now increasingly difficult to live or even imagine our lives without media gadgets. We spend most of our active hours glued to screens, using them for work, entertainment, communication, and learning. Children born into the digital age become attached to media devices form birth and grow up spending almost their non-sleeping hours fiddling with them. It is, therefore, not possible to conceive a future for childhood education that will not be determined by how well media technologies are leveraged.

Africa is a continent that must hurry to level up with other parts of the world on so many different fronts. The key to unlocking its vast potentials, including natural and human resources, so that they can be channeled towards accelerated development and poverty reduction is education. This chapter lends a voice to the call for a transformation of the pedagogical approach to childhood education in Africa and the integration of media technology in future instructional design strategies. However, it is important that adequate caution is exercised in determining the speed and extent of the application of media solutions to the teaching of young children. Despite obvious and assumed benefits, several studies have discovered a correlation between prolonged use of media and the manifestation of various health and psychosocial ailments in children, including obesity (Wang & Lobstein, 2006), depression and decreased attention span (Heim, Brandtzaeg, Karre, Endestad, & Torgersen, 2007), violence and aggression (Olson, et al., 2009), poor self-esteem and social incompetence (Shen & Williams, 2011), and poor academic performance (Hofferth, 2010; Jolin & Weller, 2011; Jackson, Brown, & Pardun, 2008). In view of these risk factors, educators and policymakers are advised to strike the right balance, in such a way that the implementation strategies of deploying new media technologies to childhood education in Africa are designed to mitigate the negative consequences of media use while the positive outcomes are harnessed. It is also imperative that these efforts are guided by the commitment to uphold and enforce the fundamental rights of the African child, as espoused in the 54 articles of the CRC.

REFERENCES

Adamu-Issah, M., Elden, L., Forson, M., & Schrofer, T. (2007). *Achieving universal primary education in Ghana by 2015: A reality or a dream?* New York: UNICEF.

Adler, P. S. (2006). Technological Determinism. In S. Clegg & J. R. Bailey (Eds.), *The International Encyclopedia of Organization Studies*. Thousand Oaks, CA: Sage Publishing.

Alakwe, K., & Ogbu, S. (2018). Communication and the Shaping of Human Personality; Deconstructing the Nature/Nurture Debate in Light of the Menace of Street Children in Nigeria. *Advanced Journal of Social Science*, 23-33.

Alakwe, K., & Ogbu, S. U. (2017). *Media and Society: Deconstructing the Role of the Media in Fostering Social Cohesion in Contemporary Nigerian Society*. Research on Humanities and Social Sciences.

Allwell, O. N., & Ogbu, S. U. (2018). Mediatization of Life: Exploring the influence of the mobile and other media in Nigeria. *Observatorio (OBS*)*, 72-84.

Amante, L. (2016). Childhood, digital culture and parental mediation. In The Digital Literacy and Multimodal Practices of Young Children: Engaging with Emergent Research (pp. 205-212). Braga: Centro de Investigação em Educação (CIEd).

Amolloh, O. P., Lilian, G. K., & Shaji, M. G. (2017). *Adopting Digital Technology in Teaching and Learning Environment in Early Childhood Education Classes in Nairobi County*. Asian Education Studies.

Arnett, J. J. (2007). *Encyclopedia ofchildren, adolescents, and the media*. Thousand Oaks, CA: Sage Publications. doi:10.4135/9781412952606

Bento, M., Lencastre, J. A., & Pereira, Í. (2016). The use of mobile devices in the development of reading comprehension skills. In The Digital Literacy and Multimodal Practices of Young Children: Engaging with Emergent Research (pp. 24-35). Braga: Centro de Investigação em Educação (CIEd).

Bioulac, S., Arfi, L., & Bouvard, M. P. (2008). Attention deficitlhyperactivity disorder and video games: A comparative study of hyperactive and control children. *European Psychiatry*, *23*(2), 134–141. doi:10.1016/j.eurpsy.2007.11.002 PMID:18206354

Brito, R., & Dias, P. (2016). 'The tablet is my BFF': Practices and perceptions of Portuguese children under 8 years old and their families. In The Digital Literacy and Multimodal Practices of Young Children: Engaging with Emergent Research (pp. 35-43). Braga: Centro de Investigação em Educação (CIEd).

Colvert, A. (2016). Teachers supporting transmedia play with classes of young children in the UK: Exploring new literacies through Alternate Reality Game design. In The Digital Literacy and Multimodal Practices of Young Children: Engaging with Emergent Research (pp. 51-60). Braga: Centro de Investigação em Educação (CIEd).

Daily Post. (2018, July 28). Retrieved from http://dailypost.ng/2018/01/01/sacked-22000-teachers-kaduna-el-rufai-finally-speaks/

Edgar, P., & Edgar, D. (2008). *Television, Digital Media and Children's Learning*. Discussion Paper. Victorian Curriculum and Assessment Authority.

Friedman, L., & Friedman, H. (2008). The New Media Technologies: Overview and Research Framework. *Electronic Journal*, 1-30.

Green, L. (2002). *Technoculture: From Alphabet to Cybersex*. Sydney: Allen & Unwin.

Hastings, E. C., Karas, T. L., Winsler, A., Way, E., Madigan, A., & Tyler, S. (2009). Young children's video/computer game use: Relations with school performance and behavior. *Issues in Mental Health Nursing*, *30*(10), 638–649. doi:10.1080/01612840903050414 PMID:19742374

Hauer, T. (2017). Technological determinism and new media. *International Journal of English, Literature and Social Science*.

Hayne, H., Herbert, J., & Simcock, G. (2003). Imitation from Television by 24- and 30-Month-Olds. *Developmental Science*, *6*(3), 254–261. doi:10.1111/1467-7687.00281

Heim, J., Brandtzaeg, P. B., Karre, B. H., Endestad, T., & Torgersen, L. (2007). Children's usage of media technologies and psychosocial factors. *New Media & Society*, *9*(3), 425–454. doi:10.1177/1461444807076971

Hjarvard, S. (2008). The mediatization of society: A study of media as agents of social and cultural change. *Nordicom Review*, 105–134.

Hofferth, S. L. (2010). Home media and children's achievement and behavior. *Child Development, 81*(5), 1598–1619. doi:10.1111/j.1467-8624.2010.01494.x PMID:20840243

Jackson, C., Brown, J. D., & Pardun, C. J. (2008). A TV in the bedroom: implications for viewing habits and risk behaviors during early adolescence. *Journal of Broadcasting and Public Media*, 349-367.

Jolin, E. M., & Weller, R. A. (2011). Television viewing and its impact on childhood behaviors. *Current Psychiatry Reports, 13*(2), 122–128. doi:10.100711920-011-0175-5 PMID:21267680

Kirkorian, H. L., Wartella, E. A., & Anderson, D. R. (2008). Media and Young Children's Learning. In Children and Electronic Media (pp. 39-63). Princeton, NJ: Princeton-Brookings.

Kjartansdóttir, S. H. (2016). Creative and playful learning with Biophilia in preschool, after-school classes and primary schools in Iceland. In The Digital Literacy and Multimodal Practices of Young Children: Engaging with Emergent Research (pp. 90-103). Braga: Centro de Investigação em Educação (CIEd).

Manovich, L. (2002). New Media from Borges to HTML. In *The New Media Reader* (pp. 1–29). Cambridge, MA: The MIT Press.

McLeod, S. A. (2018, June 6). *Jean Piaget's theory of cognitive development.* Retrieved from www.simplypsychology.org: https://www.simplypsychology.org/piaget.htm

McLuhan, M. (1962). *The Gutenberg Galaxy: The making of typographic man.* London: Routledge.

McLuhan, M. (1964). *Understanding Media: The Extensions of Man.* MIT Press.

McQuail, D. (2010). *McQuail's mass communication theory.* London: Sage Publications.

Momanyi, L., Norby, R., & Strand, S. (2006). The need for integration of technology in K-12 school settings in Kenya, Africa. Association for the Advancement of Computing in Education Journal, 154-177.

Morrison, J. W. (2001). Early Care and Education in Ghana. *Childhood Education*, 77–85.

Mtahabwa, L. (2009). Early Child Development and Care in Tanzania: Challenges for the Future. *Early Child Development and Care, 179*(1), 55–67. doi:10.1080/03004430600923436

Mushoriwa, T., & Muzembe, H. (2011). Attitudes of Primary school teachers towards Early Childhood Development in Zimbabwean primary schools. *International Journal of Educational Studies*, 117-128.

Mwamwenda, T. S. (2014). Early Childhood Education in Africa. *Mediterranean Journal of Social Sciences*. doi:10.5901/mjss.2014.v5n20p1403

Nikolopoulou, K. (2014). ICT Integration in Preschool Classes: Examples of Practices in Greece. *Creative Education*, 402-410.

Olson, C. K., Kutner, Ł. A., Baer, L., Beresin, E. V., Warner, D. E., & Nicholi, A. M. II. (2009). Mrated video games and aggressive or problenl behavior among young adolescents. *Applied Developmental Science*, *13*(4), 188–198. doi:10.1080/10888690903288748

Omodara, O. D., & Adu, E. (2014). Relevance of Educational Media and Multimedia Technology for Effective Service Delivery in Teaching and Learning Processes. *Journal of Research & Method in Education*, 48-51.

Oyama, O.-A., & Ogbu, S. U. (2017). Television and Content Censorship: The Impact of Violent Content on the Developmental Stages in the Personality of the Nigerian Child. *Advanced Journal of Social Science*, 30-39.

Piaget, J. (1936). *Origins of intelligence in the child*. London: Routledge & Kegan Paul.

Piaget, J. (1945). *Play, dreams and imitation in childhood*. London: Heinemann.

Piaget, J. (1957). *Construction of reality in the child*. London: Routledge & Kegan Paul.

Pohio, L. (2009). *The implementation and integration of information and communication technologies in early childhood education: Teachers' perspectives* (Unpublished thesis). UNITEC Institute of Technology, Waitakere.

Prensky, M. (2006). *Don't bother me mom, I'm learning*. St. Paul, MN: Paragon House.

Ray, M., & Jat, K. R. (2010). Effect of electronic media on children. *Indian Pediatrics*, *47*(7), 561–568. doi:10.100713312-010-0128-9 PMID:20683108

Roberts-Holmes, G. (2013). Playful and creative ICT pedagogical framing: A nursery school case study. *Early Child Development and Care*, 1–14.

Sarı, B., Başal, H. A., Takacs, Z. K., & Bus, A. G. (2016). Using Electronic Storybooks to Foster Word-learning in Turkish Children. In The Digital Literacy and Multimodal Practices of Young Children: Engaging with Emergent Research (pp. 116-173). Braga: Centro de Investigação em Educação (CIEd).

Servaes, J., & Lie, R. (2008). Media Globalization through Localization. In J. Servaes (Ed.), *Communication for Development and Social Change* (pp. 58–68). Thousand Oaks, CA: Sage Publications. doi:10.4135/9788132108474.n4

Shen, C., & Williams, D. (2011). Unpacking time online-connecting internet and massively multiplayer online game use with psychosocial well-being. *Communication Research, 38*(1), 123–149. doi:10.1177/0093650210377196

UNICEF. (1996, March 9). *FACT SHEET: A summary of the rights under the Convention on the Rights of the Child.* Retrieved from UNICEF for Every Child: www.unicef.org/crc

Wang, Y., & Lobstein, T. (2006). Worldwide trends in childhood overweight and obesity. *International Journal of Pediatric Obesity; IJPO, 1*(1), 11–25. doi:10.1080/17477160600586747 PMID:17902211

ADDITIONAL READING

Cuc, M. C. (2014). The influence of media on formal and informal education. *Procedia: Social and Behavioral Sciences, 143*, 68–72. doi:10.1016/j.sbspro.2014.07.359

Gamage, S. N., & Tanwar, T. (2017). *Strategies for training or supporting teachers to integrate technology into the classroom. Ottawa: International Development Research Centre*. Ottawa, Canada, and the Department for International Development.

Munni, R., & Kana, R. J. (2010). Effect of Electronic Media on Children. *Indian Pediatrics*, 561–568. PMID:20683108

Okafor, G. O., & Malizu, C. F. (2013). The Nigerian Mass Media and Childhood Socialization. *Journal of the Humanities and Social Sciences*, 6–10.

Paciga, K., & Donohue, C. (2017). *Technology and Interactive Media for Young Children: A Whole Child Approach Connecting the Vision of Fred Rogers with Research and Practice*. Latrobe, PA: Fred Rogers Center for Early Learning and Children's Media at Saint Vincent College.

Preeti. (2014). Education and Role of Media in Education System. *International Journal of Scientific Engineering and Research*, 18-29.

Rogulj, E. (2014). Influence of the New Media on Children's Play. *Croatian Journal of Education*, 267-277.

Treapăt, L.-M. (2017). The Influence of Mass-Media upon Students' Education: A Two-Edged Sword. *European Journal of Business and Social Sciences*, 1-18.

Valkenburg, P. M., & Piotrowski, J. T. (2017). *Plugged in: How Media Attract and Affect Youth.* New Haven: Yale University Press. doi:10.12987/yale/9780300218879.001.0001

KEY TERMS AND DEFINITIONS

Childhood Education: All kinds of educational programs and strategies designed for the training of children from birth up to 8 years of age.

Convention on the Rights of a Child (CRC): A United Nation's human rights treaty that seeks to uphold and protect the rights of a child (defined as any person under the age of 18). The treaty came into force on the 2nd of September 1990. Currently, 196 countries, compromising all members of the UN are parties, with the exception of the United States of America.

Curriculum: A deliberately designed document detailing the academic content of a particular course or educational program.

Digital Generation: A generation of people born in the digital era that has grown up with access to digital information and the abilities to navigate the new communication technologies.

Digital Immigrants: Individuals who were born before the spread of digital technology and were not exposed to them in their early ages. Generally, people who were born prior to 1985 are considered to be digital immigrants.

Media: A broad term used to describe various channels of communication, including the traditional and digital communication platforms.

Media Convergence: The merging of distinct media technologies including old and new media into digitized formats that can be accessed using portable devices such as smartphones, computers, tablets, smart televisions, etc.

New Media Technologies: A generic term used to describe all forms of computer-based or web-related communication technology characterized by creative participation and interactive user interface such as mobile phones, blogs, wikis, video games, social networking sites, virtual worlds, etc.

Non-Governmental Organization (NGO): A non-profit organization that is independent of any government but works towards the achievement of a humanitarian cause, including social, economic, political and educational progress in society.

Chapter 3
Media and Cultural Contents for Early Childhood Education in Nigeria

Olusola Samuel Oyero
https://orcid.org/0000-0001-7795-5516
Covenant University, Nigeria

Oluwafolafunmi Afolabi
https://orcid.org/0000-0003-1593-8635
Covenant University, Nigeria

Lanre Amodu
Covenant University, Nigeria

Oladokun Omojola
https://orcid.org/0000-0001-8362-4588
Covenant University, Nigeria

ABSTRACT

The media have become major players in the socialization of children in modern African societies. Television, in particular, and its related products are at the center stage of early childhood education. Due to the attractive nature of television, children get fascinated as early as 3 months old. Thus, television begins to influence children's learning processes from the cradle. However, there emerges a conflict between media reception and social realities around children, creating a learning dissonance in them. This chapter explores the learning dissonance in children and the impact this has on early childhood education in Nigeria, in particular. It also attempts suggestions on how the situation could be redressed to the advantage of children in their early education.

DOI: 10.4018/978-1-7998-0329-4.ch003

INTRODUCTION

Early childhood education (ECE) is the basis for children's development. It is accepted by the Nigeria National Policy on Education of 2012 as the bedrock of a child's educational life. While the period of ECE varies from one nation to another, in Nigeria, it is the education a child receives between ages 3 and 5 which prepares him/her for the severities of primary education and education beyond primary education. According to Musa, Abubakar & Danladi (2017), ECE is any planned association that intended to improve and encourage the mental, expressive, sensitive, physical and lingual ability of children from the time of their birth up to the age of 8. Hence, it has different kinds of nomenclature such as pre-primary school, nursery school, the crèche, the kindergarten, and others.

The Nigerian educational system did not plan for children's early education as obtainable with primary education which commences at age 6 and other higher levels of education. As a result, early childhood education was carried out informally at home. It was not until a few decades ago that societal dynamics compelled the establishment of early childhood schools. Improvement in the education of women and economic pressure necessitate women to seek employment, thus having less time to spend with children. These are among several reasons for early childhood education. Some even do not see this as serious schooling and as such give it some funny names such as '*Jeleosinmi*' that is 'let there be peace at home'. Consequently, the introduction of early childhood school was seen as a means of avoiding children's many troubles at home. Even when the government introduced the idea of education before primary school in its policy, it was deficient in funding for its proper functionality. It is the private schools that came to make this as an opportunity to establish their business.

The proliferation of private schools that have pre-primary schools as part of their system offers opportunities for children's early education. Government schools still do not make actual provision for early childhood education, though it was included in their policy. Hence, the actual main providers of early childhood education in Nigeria are the private institutions (National Bureau of Statistics, 2015). Unimpressively, pre-primary schools are not properly regulated. Each school's administration is dependent on the experience, style, expertise, and resources of the owner. This does not make for the proper improvement of early childhood education in Nigeria. Therefore, the qualities of early education a child receives is a function of those afore-mentioned factors and more importantly, the financial capacity of the parents and guardians. Generally, schools whose fees are very high have better qualities in terms of the learning environment, quality of teachers and care-givers, learning materials used, and so on.

A common feature of these schools across board is their tendency to appear exogenous in their approach. These pre-primary schools, in their attempt to appear sophisticated and foreign, adopted media contents which they expose to children. These media products are imported video pedagogical materials and games which are completely culturally unfit for the children. Imagine Nigerian children watching white children sing rhymes. The pattern of word pronunciation alone is even different from the ones coming from their teachers. The children in the video play with materials that are not even available for them to see. The illustrations in the video are completely foreign and the children cannot relate with them. Again, there is a language contradiction. A set of children growing up in a language environment is already used to meanings of certain things and has developed affinity with those things. With the system of education where foreign materials are used for learning, the child gets confused because a different name is being given to what they are used to before. This leads to learning dissonance as children would not properly relate to what they are being taught against the cultural environment in which they grow up. This chapter thus situates the subject within the body of relevant literature and theory, pinpoints the significance of early childhood education, discusses the learning dissonance resulting from foreign pedagogical materials and proffers solution to solve the problem.

LITERATURE AND THEORETICAL BASIS

Dissonance in students' learning patterns can be traced to the individual difference study by Meyer (1991) who noted that features of knowledge forms that are hypothetically dissimilar with one another remained essentially verifiably linked. Vermunt and Verloop's (2000), corroborated this and identified five occurrences of discord: absence of variations inside education mechanisms; non-existence of incorporation amid education mechanisms; mismatch of education schemes, origins and bearings; losing knowledge flair rudiments; and a nonexistence of different practical-focused education. Thus, dissonance in student learning reflects as the lack of connections amid education notions, directions and plans that hypothetically should be there, or as the occurrence of interactions amid these education mechanisms that hypothetically should not be there. The theory thus explains the precarious situation in which children found themselves at early stage where the methodologies of education counter their cultural composition and environment, resulting in learning disconnection and creating dissonance which affects their overall mental development with impact on their future learning endeavors.

PURPOSE OF EARLY CHILDHOOD EDUCATION IN NIGERIA

The significance of pre-primary education cannot be overstated. This is because it empowers children to increase their self-assurance from the time when they are given a chance to communicate with their mates and grownups too. Pre-primary education gives room for individual endeavors and aids in stopping the inclination of children that are extremely violent during cluster actions. Children's collaborations with their mates and grownups do broaden their perspective of comprehension as they advance in their biosphere. Pre-primary education is of great essence to the family and humanity. Besides helping to transpose the child from the house to school, it also creates a fresh basis for socialization beyond the home. According to Obiweluozor, (2015), pre-primary school helps to improve children's intellectual area through educational rhymes and tunes; while playing on the glides and swings fosters bodily improvement and forms their physiques. Organized play with construction blocks and puzzles, baby dolls, and teddy bears encourages expressive and sensitive improvement of children.

At the pre-primary school phase, children acquire the knowledge to segment and collaborate with other children as a substitute for increasing their self-centered propensities. Contact with pre-primary education does a lot to educate every child on how to comprehend and achieve their feelings. The establishment of pre-primary education supports career-driven fathers and mothers, who have no relative, babysitter or housemaid, to secure their children while they are at the office. The children will also be introduced to reading and writing while the children who have been open to early childhood or pre-primary curriculums are more probable than other children to continue in primary school and attain decent grades.

As earlier noted, private schools in Nigeria prompted the start of early childhood education in their curriculum in the 1980s while public schools were obligated to implement the same curriculum. In recent times, some of the state governments in Nigeria have started to accept and implement early childhood education in their curriculum. This has influenced the National Educational Research and Development Council (NERDC) to formalize an early childhood education curriculum for both public and private schools to attain the specific targets of the National Policy on Education (2004), in Nigeria (Okewole, Veronica, & Osinowo, 2015).

One of the key purposes and policies of ECE is to safeguard all Nigerian native and cultural values, especially its languages and to guarantee the development of children in their natural environments. Therefore, it was noted that children should receive all instructions in their mother tongue from the beginning of ECE to Primary 3 class, with English language included as part of the subjects taught in the curriculum Salami, (2016). Some other key purposes of ECE was to secure the children in a formal and educative setting while their parents are at work, to offer prospects for the children to socialize and improve their intellect, to give children opportunities to maximise their full potential based on the nature of inspiration the children have received in the household, to form the right character and to give opportunity to children with intellectual and physical problems with hearing and sight, to be quickly noticed and attended to. This level of education cannot be overlooked (Akinbote, Osuji, & Salawu, 2014). In addition to the afore-mentioned, ECE aims at ensuring a smooth transition from home to school; preparing the child for the primary level of education and providing adequate care and supervision for the children while their parents are at work (on the farms, in the markets, offices, etc.). Besides, ECE intends to indoctrinate communal and ethical standards and ideals in children; instil in the child the essence of questions and imagination via the study of nature, the setting, art, music and structurally playing with toys, building blocks and puzzles, baby dolls, teddy bears and others, from the birth of a child to the age of 6; impart the essentials of numbers, letters, colours, shapes, and forms through play; widen their scope of understanding and enable them to gain mastery of the world around, them. Further, ECE seeks to develop a sense of cooperation, resilience, self-control, self-confidence and team spirit. For early childhood education, the instructions and tutelage given to children during their formative years are not only to enable the children to enjoy the childhood stages of their lives but also to shape their personalities towards socially acceptable ones that will be beneficial for all.

IMPACT OF EARLY CHILDHOOD EDUCATION IN NIGERIA

Although there was a push by the federal government of Nigeria to create and implement ECE curriculum in all public and private schools in Nigeria, much progress has not been made, as the curriculum seems to be unproductive (National Bureau of Statistics, 2015). It can be noted that ECE has not had any measurable impact in Nigeria, as at the time of this writing. To measure the impact of ECE in Nigeria, two past studies will be examined.

A study by Okewole, Iluezi-Ogbedu, & Osinowo (2015), examined the curriculum of the National Educational Research and Development Council (NERDC) as implemented by the schools in Osun State. The study adopted the survey design and observational method with questionnaire, and observational checklists as data-gathering instruments. The study evaluated the teaching recruits, learning facilities and infrastructure on ground, and the observed curriculum in line with the expected curriculum and the challenges being faced during and after the execution of the curriculum. Findings showed that there were many untrained ECE teachers, as well as resources and facilities that enabled and eased ECE (p. 48). Findings also indicated that only one school actually implemented the curriculum (p. 52). In another investigative study by Amadioha (2018) in Port Harcourt, Rivers State, 200 parents, whose children were pupils undergoing the ECE curriculum, were randomly sampled. The challenges discovered were high tuition, congested classes, and low drive and incentives for the teachers, many of whom were inadequately skilled to handle the ECE curriculum (p. 130). All these outcomes are proof that ECE has had no much impact in Nigeria since its creation.

McCoy, Peet, Ezzati, Danaei, Black, Sudfeld, et al. (2016, p. 1), in their study on the intellectual and/or socio-emotional capabilities in Low/Middle Income Countries (LMICs), showed that 80.8 million children, aged 3 and 4 years (95%, 48.1 million, 113.6 million) in LMICs experienced low cognitive and/or socio-emotional development in 2010, with the largest number of affected children in sub-Saharan Africa, including Nigeria (29.4.1 million; 43.8% of children ages 3 and 4 years). The number of children who are deteriorating and unable to attain their potentials is very high globally (p. 2).

The ECE is crafted to help kids familiarize themselves with their immediate environment. Akinbote, Osuji and Salawu (2014), and Nakpodia (2011) note that learning is easier this way as they are positioned to acquire the knowledge with which they can contribute to their community. As a social and cultural requirement, the curriculum document specifies that all instructions in pre-primary schools should be given the child in the local language of the community where he or she resides. English will still be relevant and it will be taught as a compulsory subject. The document also strongly recommends that textbooks and other instructional materials should be produced in the local language for use in the schools.

Unimpressively, however, this ECE recommendation has largely been ignored by the implementers of the curriculum. Instructions are still being given in English while a child is asked to select a local language to learn, as a way of fulfilling the global academic righteousness which prescribes that some components of learning should be localized. It is important to note that the motive for localizing learning at the pre-primary stage is to safeguard and promote Nigerian customs and traditions as well as foster intra- and inter-ethnic cohabitation among Nigerians, using children as arrowheads of the efforts. The ultimate objective is to create a platform for harmony in a nation where tribal differences are highly pronounced. By this non-performance, implementers have relegated the mother tongue to oblivion and exalted a foreign language, thereby creating an obstacle between the child and his environment.

It is worrisome to note that parents are also part of this problem! Many parents and guardians have been seen boasting about their children's proficiency in English and are hardly enthusiastic about wards' affinity with the local language. This is highly surprising going by the studies which have shown substantially that children develop better mentally, socially and emotionally when interacted with in their native language (Salami, 2016). What is more, this problem is not limited to the pre-primary system. Primary and secondary schools also skew their activities toward foreign taste. The implication of all of this is that ECE has been largely unimpactful.

For ECE impact to be felt by the individual pupils, their community and the nation in general, the government should take the responsibility of compelling the teachers and administrators to implement it to the minutest details. Parents should be enlightened on the advantages of learning in the mother tongue. Other stakeholders in the education sector should be carried along in this implementation as opposition from any group can create problems (Salami, 2016)

CHALLENGES CONFRONTING EARLY CHILDHOOD EDUCATION IN NIGERIA

The challenges of ECE in Nigeria include the fact that many of these pre-primary schools are located mostly in urban areas, as opposed to rural areas. Many are substandard and not equipped enough to implement ECE, even in the urban areas. Quality is not and has never been a priority to the government, the community or any of the private individuals who own those pre-primary schools. The evaluation from the government via the federal Ministry of Education and the ministries of education of different states in Nigeria are not prioritized enough while actions to tame control the over-commercialization of the pre-primary schools are not visible. High costs of tuition far above that of government schools, vis a vis the quality of the service provided, have not been dealt with in accordance with the ECE recommendations. These challenges have made Nakpodia (2016) conclude that the policy is a failed one.

One major problem confronting ECE is the prevalence of non-implementation in Nigeria. Salami 's (2016) findings of a study on Nigerian early childhood education policies and practices for sustainability show that a substantial part of the policy failed the execution process in most regions in the country and it wouldn't make any difference whether the school was privately or publicly owned. The findings also show that there was no regular assessment of the implementation while people who do not have the requisite knowledge are being asked to monitor or supervise it. Lack of knowledge, in this case, means that things are not being done scientifically. Salami adds that a proper assessment carried out by those who qualify for the job can turn the policy around as a beneficial instrument for improving the quality of education (p.81). Specifically,

The body that sets the minimum standards on the criteria, goals, intentions, and approaches as outlined in the ECE curriculum is called the National Minimum Standard for Early Child Care Centres in Nigeria (NMSECCC). The body also decides the level of stakeholders' involvement, supervision, resources - human and material - and the level of protection they can enjoy. For the policy to achieve its set goals, the need exists for regular checks by this body. Akinrotimi and Olowe (2016) note that owing to lack of checks, less qualified persons, most of them old women, have been paraded as teachers because of the assumption that they can play a 'motherly role'. This is the same set of people who have been found bereft of qualification in teaching or educational management. Moreover, there is no professional development training for teachers and caregivers. Lack of professional qualification and training, according to the authors, is a cause of the implementation failure of the ECE curriculum (p. 34-35).

Moreover, the teacher-pupil ratio in pre-primary education is a big problem. Several studies have shown that in Nigeria, the ratio of staff to children is often high. If a single staff is given a few number of children, he or she can concentrate better on the needs of each child and can better navigate the curriculum in favor of the children but the reverse has always been the case in most situations. The UN Special Envoy for Global Education has expressed disappointment regarding this development, noting that classes in early childhood development (ECD) centers in Nigeria are congested, with an average of 130 children per class in the North (The Good Planet Foundation, 2013). Moreover, wages are very low (Sooter, 2013).

Funding, which takes care of tuition, resource materials, feeding, immunization, monitoring, investigations, and training and re-training of staff and regular research, is a huge concern. Government's funding is insufficient (Akinrotimi & Olowe, 2016; Musa, Abubakar & Danladi, 2017). The problem of language policy implantation also exists, as it has disconnected Nigerian children from their culture. Investigations show that approximately 93.2% of instructions and education in Nigeria's pre-primary schools have been achieved in the English language. The 6.8% use of the mother tongue exhibits a strong apathy to native dialects and linguistic attributes of a societal setting. Sooter (2013) explains that the consequences of all these are that the children are presented with "inferior" and "unbalanced or lopsided" education that cannot guarantee the future (p178). An ECE curriculum acceptance will require a collaborative effort between government, parents/guardians, the schools and all other stakeholders (p. 176).

TEACHING AND LEARNING AS COMMUNICATION

The role of communication cannot be overemphasised. It is how we keep in touch with other persons. It is a two-way process that involves feedback. It is the transfer of ideas, messages, thoughts, data and information from (a) sender(s) to (a) receiver(s) through a channel or medium. The process involves listening, processing the information, comprehending or interpreting the information and giving feedback to the information received (Center for Literacy Studies, 2017). Effective communication is when your communication has an anticipated outcome. This means that the communication was a successful and effective interaction. Communication must have a purpose or a reason, a tactic-which is a preferred way to communicate and an acknowledgement of the reception of the message or a feedback (Center for Literacy Studies, 2017). Effective communication, in academia, is based on how clearly one can express his/her views and ideas. It must be confident, clear, concise and it must successfully reveal one's content and smartness to the class. Communication between students and teachers can go in two ways - either effective or problematic (Muste 2016). The instructor is a unique influence of conversation and transfer of information.

The accomplishment of the educational or impartation knowledge depends on the teacher. The teaching-learning procedure is dependent on the teachers' ability to transfer knowledge successfully to students. This is where communication plays an indispensable part. The process of transferring knowledge from teachers to students is verbal communication. This environment of verbal communication can facilitate the exchange of ideas, opinions, and facts, feelings from teacher to student and from the students to their teachers. The role of communication in education is very vital to the education process (Deepti, 2016).

It is required that when communicating with a child, you have to describe what will be done, give simple directives, and show a typical example of the process, using comprehensible language and visual aids. You are also to ask if the child comprehends and describe each step (Center for Literacy Studies, 2017). The classroom is usually complex. Future needs must be identified in order to simplify the classroom-communication-education process (Muste 2016).

According to (Muste 2016), 2016, p. 430), the techniques of learning-teaching communication includes:

1. Use of rich vocabulary; at list a minimal use of specialised language;
2. Use of language (in the general context of communication); use of information technology;
3. Information search skills;
4. Argumentation skills of personal opinions;
5. Non-verbal skills;
6. Networking skills in group.

According to Muste (2016), the qualities of a good teacher include the 'ability to establish positive interrelations with students (to demonstrate "care" for them); exercise authority and provide structure and clarity of rules without doing so in a rigid, threatening way, or following the use of punishment; and make learning fun by using creative teaching strategies'.

The process of teaching and learning in education includes, watching teachers-who are great influencers and typical examples of proficient communication and principled behaviour, watching videotapes-which can be a prevailing influential tool; role playing which is imitating someone's role in a social context and group work-which is to improve comprehension, social skills and learners' sense of membership (Muste 2016).

MEDIA AND EARLY CHILDHOOD EDUCATION IN NIGERIA

As stated by Greene, Wilder, Levine and Nemeth (n.d), in teaching children through the media, there are 3 Cs to be considered. They are the contents, the contexts and the child. Researchers have shown that children who view educational programmes on television, show a higher level of cerebral competence, heightened communal skills and better readiness for pre-school. For instance, Sesame Square, a type of the United States' Sesame Street, is a widespread program for children, and was aired for over forty years. It was one of the most popular children television programmes in Nigeria as it was in the United States. Sesame Street was not only an entertainment, but an edutainment-which is a combination of education and entertainment. The programme had a lot of retentive and recitable songs, with interesting and educative storylines which includes letters, numbers and all-round social skills. Sesame Square like Sesame Street delivered children with a valued addition for preschool education (Unite for Sight, n.d.). This is a typical example of helping children to become media literate. Media literacy is defined as aiding children to enhance the techniques of life that they need, to become critical intellectuals in the audio-visual setting, which is a semblance of reality (Greene, Wilder, Levine and Nemeth, n.d).

Children use television for viewing. They spend time watching television than any other waking activity. It was reported that pre-schoolers spend approximately 25-35 hours a week on television viewing in the United States. Over 2000 violent contents may be viewed within this period and about 500 will be preserved in their memories (Clements, & Nastasi, 2012). They also use television for attention and comprehension. Studies have shown that television viewing, especially by babies and pre-schoolers is not passive (p. 252). Another vital use of television is advertising. Over 22,000 advertisements are viewed by pre-schoolers in the space of just one year. Exposure to television, however, does not mean that the average pre-schooler would easy understand the message displayed in the advertisements. Children may also show certainty in premium offers displayed in these advertisements, without comprehending the reason for the commercials. Children's use of computers have been widely reported to have raised concerns about the disturbance of socio-emotional development. Sometimes, television only delivers entertainment to children (Omotosho, Oyero & Salawu, 2015) Omojola, et al. (2018). It was, however, recommended that it should be used in appropriate contexts, preferably with the supervision of an adult-either a caring teacher or a parent/guardian.

ADOPTION OF ENDOGENOUS CULTURAL CONTENT IN NIGERIAN EARLY CHILDHOOD EDUCATION

The ECE in Nigeria has adopted the use of media products in the system, especially the private schools. Many now have television, video products, and games with which they instruct children. The problem that arises with this development is that these materials and foreign-produced media contents are completely alien to the children being taught. There is, therefore, a situation where children are learning what they cannot relate with in their cultural environment. Besides, as earlier mentioned, they are equally taught in a language that is not generally spoken by everyone in the environment. While English language is the officially language in Nigeria, its use is common in formal setting mostly; and in fact, people still use their indigenous language for conversation even in-formal settings. This is apart from the fact that the type of English that is spoken is generally described 'Nigerian English' going by the heavy influence of the indigenous languages in both phonological and syntactic compositions. The implication of this is the dissonance that occurs in the learning process as children try hard to comprehend the media contents they are being exposed to.

The Wilbur Schramm's communication model underscores the importance of field of experience in effective communication (Lee, n. d.). Where there is an overlap between the source of the message and the receiver's fields of experience, effective communication takes place and in this context effective learning occurs. This necessitates the need for cultural contents in early childhood pedagogical materials to ensure effective learning (Omojola, Odiboh & Amodu, 2018). When children are taught with materials they can properly relate with, it enhances their understanding and increases their cognitive ability. That was the case of Sesame Square, a type of the United States' Sesame Street, which was popular in Nigeria in early 1980s. It was contextualised to fit into the Nigerian cultural environment, by incorporating contents, not just from Nigeria but also from other African nations, hence the kind of success it had.

Some messages in songs sometimes used in early childhood schools that adopted only foreign ideas have also been criticized for misleading children. For example, for the song:

Rain, rain
Go away
Come again another day
Little Johnny wants to play

The notion here is that rain may never go away and the child may be affected by entering the rain. Whereas an indigenous song captures what should be the appropriate message to children:

There are also many other short songs, poems and rhymes that teach children about hard work, honesty, cleanliness, sacrifice, respect for the older persons, avoiding covetousness, good character and so on. They do not just aid children's intellectual capacity but also teach ethics and etiquettes in the society. Consider the following:

Table 1.

Yoruba	Interpretation
Ojo nro *Sere ninu ile* *Ma wo nu ojo* *Ki aso re ma baa tutu* *Ki otutu ma baa mu o*	*It's raining* *Play within the house* *Don't ever enter the rain* *So that your clothes don't get wet* *So that you don't catch cold*

Table 2.

Yoruba Language	Interpretation
Imo toto, *Lole segun arun gbogbo,* *Imo toto ile,* *Imo toto ara,* *Imo toto ounje,* *At'ayika eni,* *Imo toto lole segun arun gbogbo.*	*Cleanliness is the key to good health,* *Cleanliness of the house,* *Cleanliness of the body,* *Cleanliness of food,* *And cleanliness of your environment,* *Cleanliness is the key to good health.*
Ise Logun ise *Mura si se re, ore mi* *Ise la fi ndeni giga* *Bi a ko ba reni fehin ti* *Bi ole la ri* *Bi a ko ba reni gbekele,* *A te ra mo se ni.* *Iya re le lowo lowo lowo* *Baba re le lesin lekan* *Ti o ba gbojule won* *O te tan ni mo so fun o*	*Work is the antidote for poverty* *Work hard and work smart, my friend* *Hard and smart work brings success* *When there is no one to rely on* *It's like we are lazy* *When there is no one to trust* *We focus more on our work* *Your mother might be rich* *Your father might own a thousand and one horses* *If you rely on them* *In truth, you might be on sinking ground*

Back to the issue of indigenous language as a means of instruction. There are studies as well that have confirmed the positive impact of the use of indigenous language on E.C.E. (Afolayan, 1984, Fafunwa, Macauley & Sokoya, 1989, Chumbow, 1990, and Akinnaso, 1993). Top on the list is the UNESCO-sponsored project carried out by Fafunwa, Macauley & Sokoya (1989). It was discovered that the best language for good concept formation at a very tender age is the indigenous language. The research was carried out at the Institute of Education of the University of Ife (now Obafemi Awolowo University, Ile-Ife) in Osun State, Nigeria. Popularly known as The 'Ife Six-Year Primary Project', it was designed to use indigenous language-Yoruba language as a medium of instruction in primary schools. The research was based on the premise that the child will benefit culturally, socially, linguistically and cognitively, and that the child's command of English will be improved if he is taught English as an entirely separate subject by a specialist teacher through the six years. The data collection and analysis were done between 1971 and 1983 and it revealed that the experimental group of schools performed better than the controlled group in all school subjects at the end of primary school education. The two assumptions were found to be correct. The result attracted much publicity in Nigeria in the media and it was suggested that the language of the immediate environment that is Yoruba (home language) should be adopted as the medium of instruction throughout the six-year period of primary education.

CONCLUSION AND RECOMMENDATIONS

It is important that for wholesome development of children from their childhood, the E.C.E. should take into consideration, the cultural environment of the children so as to avoid the problem of learning dissonance in the instructional processes. The content of pedagogical materials, and the context must be culturally fit. The use of indigenous language is very important in this direction (Oyero, 2003). This does not mean that they (children) must be taught only indigenous and culturally relevant content alone. Children still need ideas, orientation and contents that are exogenous, as well as in order to expand their learning horizons, expose them to things they might encounter in the future, since we operate in a globalised world and prepare them for that future. But these must be have a good balance and in fact, the formulations should be the cultural content upon which other learning materials could be built.

It follows then that agencies of the government in African countries in charge of early childhood education should develop policies and guidelines that will specify the kind of early childhood education to be delivered. There is also the need to develop pedagogical materials that will make possible the delivery of culturally suited E.C.E. These materials should be on various formats such as texts, graphics, videos, using various methods.

There is also the need to enhance the capacity of care providers and instructors at early Childhood schools through training in other to properly deliver the kind of education discussed here. In addition to this is the need to ensure compliance through various means, so that the purpose of the recommended system will be accomplished. Then, the media too should cater for the interest of children as they have the social responsibility to work for the overall development of children by catering for their social, mental, cultural and linguistic needs as specified in the UN Convention on the Rights of the Child and other related treaties (Abioye, Oyesomi, Ajiboye, Omidiora, & Oyero 2017). When the afore-mentioned are properly implemented, early childhood education will be at its best to prepare children to master their future.

REFERENCES

Abioye, T., Oyesomi, K., Ajiboye, E., Omidiora, S. & Oyero, O. (2017). *Impacts of the media on African socio-economic development*. Academic Press. doi:10.4018/978-1-5225-1859-4

Afolayan, A. (1984). The Six-Year Primary Project in Nigeria. In A. Bamgbose (Ed.), Mother Tongue Education. The West African Experience, (pp. 113-134). London: Hodder and Stoughton.

Akinbote, O., Osuji, U., & Salawu, I. (2014). *Origin and development of early childhood (Course Module)*. Lagos: National Open University of Nigeria.

Akinnaso, F. (1993). Policy and Experiment in Mother Tongue Literacy in Nigeria. *International Review of Education / Internationale Zeitschrift Für Erziehungswissenschaft / Revue Internationale De L'Education, 39*(4), 255-285. Retrieved from http://www.jstor.org/stable/3445126

Akinrotimi, A. A., & Olowe, P. K. (2016). Challenges in implementation of early childhood education in nigeria : The way forward. *Journal of Education and Practice, 7*(7), 33–38.

Al Odhayani, A., & Ratnapalan, S. (2011). Teaching communication skills. *Canadian Family Physician Medecin de Famille Canadien, 57*(10), 1216–1218. Retrieved from http://www.ncbi.nlm.nih.gov/pubmed/21626902%0Ahttp://www.pubmedcentral.nih.gov/articlerender.fcgi?artid=PMC3076489 PMID:21998240

Amadioha, S. (2018). Challenges of early childhood education in Nigeria: implication for assessment of early childhood curriculum implementation in Port Harcourt, Rivers State. *Australian Journal of Arts and Scientific Research, 22*, 125–129.

Bakken, L., Brown, N., & Downing, B. (2017). Early childhood education: The long term benefits. *Journal of Research in Childhood Education*, *31*(2), 255–269. doi:10.1080/02568543.2016.1273285

Center for Literacy Studies. (2017). Communication process. In *Learning guide Communication process theory* (2nd ed.; pp. 79–86). Christchurch, New Zealand: Careerforce. Retrieved from www.cls.utk.edu/pdf/ls/Week1_Lesson7.pdf

Chumbow, B. S. (1990). The place of the mother tongue in the national policy on education. In E. N. Emenanjo (Ed.), *Multilingualism, minority languages and language policy in Nigeria* (pp. 61–72). Agbor, Nigeria: Central Books Limited and Linguistic Association of Nigeria.

Clements, D. H., & Nastasi, B. K. (2012). *Electronic media and early childhood education*. doi:10.1080/00094056.2014.952218

Fafunwa, A. B., Macauley, J. I., & Sokoya, J. A. F. (1989). *Education in Mother Tongue: The Ife Primary Education Research Project (1970-1978)*. Ibadan: University Press.

Greene, E., Wilder, A., Levine, M., & Nemeth, K. N. (n.d.). *Technology and digital media in the early years : big ideas, best practices and future directions*. Academic Press.

Ibhaze, F. O. (2016). *Issues and challenges of implementation of early childhood education in Nigeria*. Academic Press.

Lee, D. (n.d.). *Developing Effective Communications*. Retrieved from https://extension2.missouri.edu/cm109

McCoy, D. C., Peet, E. D., Ezzati, M., Danaei, G., Black, M. M., Sudfeld, C. R., ... Fink, G. (2016). Early childhood developmental status in low-and middle-income countries: National, regional, and global prevalence estimates using predictive modeling. *PLoS Medicine*, *13*(6), e1002034. doi:10.1371/journal.pmed.1002034 PMID:27270467

Meyer, J. H. F. (1991). Study orchestration: The manifestation, interpretation and consequences of contextualised approaches to studying. *Higher Education*, *22*(3), 297–316. doi:10.1007/BF00132293

Meyer, J. H. F. (2000). The modelling of 'dissonant' study orchestration in higher education. *European Journal of Psychology of Education*, *15*(1), 5–18. doi:10.1007/BF03173163

Musa, M. M., Abubakar, I. B., & Danladi, N. Y. (2017). Early childhood education : Development, challenges and prospects in Nigeria. *International Journal of Education and Evaluation*, *3*(10), 47–58.

Muste, D. (2016). The Role of Communication Skills in Teaching Process. *The European Proceedings of Social and Behavioural Sciences.*, *430-434*, 430–434. doi:10.15405/epsbs.2016.12.52

Nakpodia, E. D. (2011). Early childhood education : Its policy formulation and implementation in Nigerian educational system. *African Journal of Political Science and International Relations*, *5*(3), 159–163.

National Bureau of Statistics. (2015). *Nigerian Formal Education Sector: Summary Report 2010-2012*. Author.

Obiweluozor, N. (2015). Early Childhood Education in Nigeria, Policy Implementation: Critique and a Way Forward. *African Journal of Teacher Education*, *4*(1), 1–9. doi:10.21083/ajote.v4i1.2930

Okewole, J. O., Iluezi-Ogbedu, V. A., & Osinowo, O. A. (2015). An evaluation of the implementation of early childhood education curriculum in Osun State. *Journal of Education and Practice*, *6*(4), 48–54. Retrieved from http://www.iiste.org/Journals/index.php/JEP/article/viewFile/19793/20357

Okewole, J. O., Veronica, I.-O. A., & Osinowo, O. A. (2015). An evaluation of the implementation of early childhood education curriculum in osun state. *Journal of Education and Practice*, *6*(4), 48–55.

Omojola, O., Odiboh, O., & Amodu, L. (2018). Opinions as Colors: A Visual Analysis Technique for Modest Focus Group Transcripts. *Qualitative Report*, *23*(8), 2019–2035. Retrieved from https://nsuworks.nova.edu/tqr/vol23/iss8/16

Omojola, O., Amodu, L., Okorie, N., Imhonopi, D., Yartey, D., & Adesina, E. (2018). Assessing the One-Lecture-One-Test Learning Model in Undergraduate Journalism Program Using Cohort Design. *The Journal of Social Sciences Research*, *4*(12), 591–597.

Omotosho, Y., Oyero, O., & Salawu, A. (2015). Children's Programmes on Nigerian Television Stations: a Case of Media Negle. *E-Bangi: Journal of Social Sciences and Humanities, 10*(1), 135–153. Retrieved from http://www.ukm.my/e-bangi/papers//2015/135-153 Olusola CHILDREN'S programme on TV.pdf

Oyero, O., & Salawu, A. (2018). Building Media Capacity for Children Sustainability in Africa: Educational and Partnership Imperatives. *SAGE Open, 8*(1), 1–10. doi:10.1177/2158244018763930

Oyero, O. S. (2003). Indigenous Language Radio for Development Purposes. In E. O. Soola (Ed.), *Communicating for Development Purposes* (pp. 185–195). Ibadan: Krafts Books.

Salami, I. A. (2016). Nigerian early childhood education policies and practices for sustainability. *European Journal of Research and Reflection in Educational Sciences, 4*(5), 71–85.

Sooter, T. (2013). Early Childhood education in Nigeria: Issues and Problems. *Journal of Education and Social Research., 3*(5), 173–179.

Sylva, K. (1994). School influences on children's development. *Child Psychology & Psychiatry & Allied Disciplines, 35*(1), 135–170. doi:10.1111/j.1469-7610.1994.tb01135.x PMID:8163626

The Good Planet Foundation. (2013). *Accelerating progress to 2015. Nigeria.* A report series to the UN Special Envoy for Global Education. Working Paper. Retrieved from http://educationenvoy.org/wp-content/uploads/2013/07/Nigeria-Unse-Final.pdf

Unite for Sight. (n.d.). *The role of social media in early childhood education: the sesame workshop*. doi:10.1598/RT.58.1.9

Vermunt, J. D., & Verloop, N. (2000). Dissonance in students' regulation of learning processes. *European Journal of Psychology of Education, 15*(1), 75–89. doi:10.1007/BF03173168

KEY TERMS AND DEFINITIONS

Childhood Education: All kinds of educational programs and strategies designed for the training of children from birth up to 8 years of age.

Convention on the Rights of a Child (CRC): A United Nation's human rights treaty that seeks to uphold and protect the rights of a child (defined as any person under the age of 18). The treaty came into force on the 2nd of September 1990. Currently, 196 countries, compromising all members of the UN are parties, with the exception of the United States of America.

Media: A broad term used to describe various channels of communication, including the traditional and digital communication platforms.

New Media Technologies: A generic term used to describe all forms of computer-based or web-related communication technology characterized by creative participation and interactive user interface such as mobile phones, blogs, wikis, video games, social networking sites, virtual worlds, etc.

Nigerian Children: A minor of Nigerian descent who is required to remain under the tutelage of their parents or guardian till they attain maturity.

Socialisation: The adoption of the norms of a people.

Values: A set of important principles and ethos by which an individual or a group of people are bound.

Chapter 4
Child Protection and Development in Nigeria:
Towards a More Functional Media Intervention

Stellamaris Ngozi Okpara
https://orcid.org/0000-0001-6374-5681
Pan-Atlantic University, Lagos, Nigeria

ABSTRACT

It is unarguably true that one of the social institutions from which children need protection is the media. This is because some media content violates and poses a harmful influence on their development. The media has been accused of being weak in protecting the rights of Nigerian children from the standpoint of the content it disseminates. This chapter focuses on the power of the media to advocate for the child's rights and shape the childhood process through its content. The study discovered that media outlets are not predisposed to reporting issues regarding child rights but rather place more attention on entertainment programmes that attract big sponsors. The study recommends that media content should focus on promoting child rights issues in Nigeria.

INTRODUCTION

The impact of the media on children varies from age to age. It enables children to gain the ability to grasp abstract ideas and metacognitive thoughts (Huston & Ripke, 2006). In addition, since the social context in which children develop cognitive

DOI: 10.4018/978-1-7998-0329-4.ch004

abilities is collaborative process which involves adults and peers, the cognitive shift from middle childhood to adolescence is marked by increased hypothetical reasoning and an ability to determine whether fictional media content is realistic or probable in real life (Flavell, Miller & Miller, 2002). Therefore, the media's role in ensuring the protection and positive development of children cannot be overemphasised. The media has a strategic contribution as an agent of socialisation and offers the platform for identity development of children. Therefore, from the manner in which the media frames its contents, it is obvious that its influence shapes a lot of the experiences of children, their perspectives and perceptions of themselves and the world around them.

In view of the social role of the media in the development of the child, the media has been accused of not ensuring the protection of children's rights from the standpoint of the content it disseminates to the public. There are indications that the media may advertently or inadvertently produce and show contents that may be harmful for children's development. Furthermore, the media is castigated for its inability to perform its surveillance function in detecting harmful practices customs, attitudes and issues which negatively affect children (Sambe, 2005). As the Fourth Estate of the Realm, the watchdog of the society and the voice of the voiceless, it behoves the media to produce contents that are in the best interest of the child. The media has to ensure the protection of children, using ethical media frames, in the contents they produce and as well in how children and their interests are projected as subject or object matters. They are supposed to champion the cause of responsible governance, dignity and freedom of the human persons and make truthful, objective, accurate, ethical and fair presentations at all times (McQuail, 2007). This is because the media has a strategic contribution as an agent of socialisation and offers the platform for the identity development of children.

This chapter will place special emphasis on the power of the media in advocating children's rights and in shaping the childhood process through its contents, which are readily accessible by these children.

BACKGROUND

Childhood is a significant period in human life, characterised by physical as well as poignant immaturity and susceptibility, unlike adulthood, resulting in a lack of autonomy and social dependence. The chronological age used in marking the boundary between childhood and adulthood is mostly set at 18 years, although social markers such as migration, labour, and physical markers such as height, facial hair, or the start of menstruation may be more important than age in signifying adult status in some locations (Evans, 2012). It must be stated that there are disparaging views on the concept of a child. Mosby's Medical Dictionary (2009) avers that a child is a person between the time of birth and adolescence. Further, Article 2 of Children and Young Persons Act (CYPA), enacted in Eastern, Western and Northern regions of Nigeria defined a child as a person within the age bracket 0 and 14 years of age (Oyero, 2010).

Jacomy and Stevens (2004:9) opine that the categorisation of a child cannot be restricted to persons under the age of fourteen but to include any "young person who has attained the age of fourteen years and under the age of seventeen years." In accordance with this assertion, the UN Convention on the Rights of the Child (UNCRC, 1989) defined a child as every human being below the age of eighteen years. In the Nigerian context, Okunola (2002) conceived a child as any being who has not attained the age of political right, which is 18 years as specified in the Nigerian 1999 constitution. Similarly, the Nigerian Child Rights Act (2003) operationalised a child within the framework of its enforcement as anyone who has not attained the age of eighteen. For the purpose of clarity, the child, as conceptualised operationally in this chapter, is a human person below the age of fourteen. The period of childhood is the foundation for all other stages of human development.

Adulthood cannot be attained without childhood; hence childhood can be regarded as the most significant stage in human development. However, not all children make it to adulthood. Physiologically, children's make-up can be said to be the same all over the world. Also, their interests, needs, growth and development patterns are similar. Thus, majority of the differences often observed in children can be mainly attributed to hereditary and environmental factors. However, academic discourses have presented childhood as a universally biologically and psychologically determined phase of human development; it is a period of inexperience, vulnerability and growth during which children are in need of adult protection and care. They are expected to receive formal education in schools and are separated from the adult domains of work, sex and politics considered to pose dangers to children (Wyness, 2006).

The variations of childhood experiences across countries are determined by cultural, political, personal and economic factors. Child-raising skills are determined by cultural attitudes and social behaviours that are necessary to succeed in a particular socio-cultural and economic setting. Children raised in many poor urban areas of the world may work on the streets in order to fend for their younger ones as early as age five (Manderson and Liamputting, 2002). In industrialised societies, children may have to depend on their parents for economic and personal support for more than the first twenty years of their lives (Manderson and Liamputting, 2002). Furthermore, children from the same family or society experience differences in their work, study and social responsibilities that are affected by factors such as gender, birth order, caste and disability. Girls and boys may be encouraged to develop different aptitudes and skills, which are influenced by the roles they are expected to play as adults. UNICEF (2011) duly reports that Nigerian children are highly

Figure 1.

vulnerable not only to income poverty but also to a wide variety of other economic and social deprivations. This appreciation of the various experiences of childhood across different cultures, chronological periods and socioeconomic settings has thus resulted in a new paradigm of childhood studies globally.

The primary agent of socialisation for the young, regardless of nationality, is the family (Abideen and Salaria, 2009). The family is the child's first contact with socialisation. The family's setup is such that can affect children in diverse ways including violently. A useful concept for understanding family differences is that of intergenerational contracts which see family relationships as a set of implicit understandings concerning roles and responsibilities of members (Evans, 2012). Parents or guardians have a duty to facilitate their children's wellbeing and growth as well as provide an environment where they are protected and cared for. Children without proper parental care and supervision are easily abused, particularly sexually (Olusegun and Idowu, 2016). Parents who send their daughters on errands at night, give them goods to sell, leave them for several hours or days in the care of housemaids, or allow them freedom of choice in lifestyle and clothing are putting them at a higher risk of being abused.

Sometimes, children are compelled to hawk by their parents, guardians or caregivers and are punished for their inability to finish the amount of goods or article of trade allocated to them to sell for the day. In Nigeria, thousands of children are engaged as house helps or placed under the care of relatives who use them in various forms of forced labour on farms, factories and private homes or establishments. Violation of a child's rights interferes with his or her ability to develop significantly (Terr, 2010). Violated children demonstrate a consistent pattern of socially unpleasant behaviour and are usually oddballs in the society. The child may display multiple psychosomatic and behavioural problems as well as experience a difficult time developing and maintaining healthy relationships.

This neurotic behaviour in turn increases the risk of long-term decreased productivity, economic reliance and generally lowers a child's level of satisfaction with life as an adult. Abusing children at the hands of parents or guardians is a long-standing challenge across cultures, from ancient times to the present in many societies, including Nigeria. Under the English Common Law, children are regarded as property duly owned by their parents especially their fathers who have greater opportunity over their conduct and behaviour regulation. Such legal view was ultimately integrated into the early laws in the United States and has also been applied to operations in Nigeria (Al-Shail, Hassan, Aldowaish & Kattan, 2012). Unfortunately, laws cannot stop such abuse from recurring. Despite the creation of laws to protect children from abuse, lack of proper care from parents and other family members is likely to cause abuse to occur and persist. Culture is a crucial determinant of child violation in Nigeria. The difference between what is tenable as child abuse in more developed countries of the world and a developing country like Nigeria is based on cultural perceptions and elements.

Children are characteristically curious and always dig things out for themselves. They often achieve this through the exploration of their environment and by asking questions from people with whom they have everyday contact. Some of them are encouraged to interact with their environment by providing them with toys or other objects. This signifies that children are very conscious of their traditional environment. Conversely, in today's global world, child development is no longer restricted to traditional environments but also well played out in online environments. The continuous breakup of families and subsequent disregard for traditional values due to parents' search of formal employment has affected childrearing negatively. This has resulted in children's heavy reliance on media such as books, magazine, social media, television and radio to get the much-needed information for their growth and development in different aspects including sexuality and modelling.

Media is a secondary agent of socialisation which is arguably becoming dominant in Nigeria. Studies have shown that the media is powerful and can have great effects on people, although media effects are difficult to ascertain due to certain physical and psychological factors (Akinbote, Osuji & Salawu, 2006; Nnam & Njemanze, 2016). However, there are scholars who strongly support the perception that regardless of other factors, children are influenced and vulnerable to the media content they consume (Bushman & Cantor, 2003; Zakeri, Zainab & Yakubu (2016). Media has become the very fabric of children's lives such that youngsters may not be aware of the many dangers the negative and offensive contents they get from media usage poses to them. This is more as society is increasingly dependent on the media for almost all mundane issues. This presupposes that whatever the media gives out as information is likely to be received as the truth, including lifestyle and values. Media therefore plays a role in shaping opinions, altering attitudes and behaviours of children because the media have become like the family - indispensable to society.

The media arguably plays many positive roles in the socialisation of children. The values, beliefs, customs, language and morals of any particular society can be transmitted to children through the media. This is because transmission of cultural heritage is one of the major functions of the media as can be attested to all over the world. This function of the media can manifest in any type of media channel: electronic, print and new media. For any society to produce children and youths that can become responsible adults, the type of characters, beliefs and values necessary for the actualisation of their vision must be transmitted through the media. More so, ever-growing new media platforms such as Facebook, Twitter, Instagram and other social network sites have enormous influence on their social and psychological development. New media thus affords a child access to his peers without parental intrusion or monitoring (Livingstone, 2009).

Nigerian children are not as exposed to the same hobbies as their counterparts in developed countries. Most Nigerian children only have access to recreational centres in a few cities such as Ibadan, Lagos, Port Harcourt, Kano, Abuja and some others. This, in turn, caused many children and youths to rely on watching television as a favourite pastime. Many of them watch television, home videos, music videos and such other contents for long hours immediately after closing from schools in the afternoon until late in the night. In the process, they are exposed to so many hours of television commercials and programmes, which eventually have consequential effects on their behaviour (Kadiri and Muhammed, 2011).

Nigeria's Child Rights Act expresses ways the child can be protected by the state through legislation at the different levels of the Nigerian government. However, there is a big gap in the provision of the Act regarding the protection of the child from media institutions. In as much as the Nigerian Constitution maps out laws that defend children, which are clearly explained by the Child Rights Act, it is important to also document how media deals with issues that affect children in Nigeria.

HISTORY OF CHILD PROTECTION IN NIGERIA

The concern for child protection in Nigeria was non-existent for a long time. Child abuse as a social problem has only gained recognition and acknowledgement in recent time in the country (Imo, 2015). The welfare of the Nigerian child was not a major concern during the colonial era. It was not until 1943 that efforts at legislation was first geared towards child protection in Nigeria when the Children and Young Persons' Act (CYPA) was circulated for use in any part of Nigeria (Okunola, 2010). Children's rights in Nigeria began to gain focus globally in 1979 when the United Nations chose the year as the International Year of the Child and drew up a list of children's rights. Notable among are the rights to love and understanding, adequate food and health, free education, play, identity and special attention for those with special needs regardless of colour, sex, creed, and national or social origins. The passing of the United Nations Convention on the Rights of the Child on November 20th 1989 by the United Nations General Assembly helped to concretise global efforts and focus attention on ensuring child development and protection against various forms of abuse or mistreatment (United Nations Convention on the Rights of the Child, 1989). The instrument is in three (3) parts with fifty-four (54) articles, with a preamble that states the aims and objectives, which the convention seeks to accomplish for the child.

In a bid to ignite global interest on the rights of the African child, Awosola and Omoera (2008:125) stated that the Organization of Africa Unity (OAU) proclaimed the 1990s as the 'Decade of the African Child' and set June 16 of every year as the 'Day of the African Child.' Every child must be protected against all forms of exploitation, indecent or degrading treatment, including child labour, abuse and torture, sexual exploitation, sale, abduction and drug abuse. Every nation that is a signatory to the convention is expected to make concerted efforts to protect children against all forms of abuse, through the enforcement of relevant instruments. Section 34 of the 1999 Constitution of the Federal Republic of Nigeria provides for the right of every individual to the dignity of his/her person. This section further prohibits "all forms of torture, inhuman or degrading treatment, and slavery, forced or compulsory labour." In other words, it ensures the child's right to dignity of their person. The very concept of children's rights is a western way of constructing child-adult relationships and contrasts with regional agreements such as the OAU Convention on the Rights and Welfare of the Child, which also refer to the child's responsibilities and duties towards family and society.

The rights of children are central to sustainable development. Since the future generation will naturally comprise of these children, the task of empowering them to maximise the potentials for their own development becomes significant. All children, regardless of legal status, nationality or statelessness, have the right to be protected from harm, to obtain such essential services as health care and education, be with their families, and have their best interests guide decisions that affect them. As cited in Oyero (2011), "the United Nations Children's Fund (UNICEF) notes that the central to the Convention the Rights of the Child (CRC) in its entirety is the development as well as survival of children. This guarantees them the right to education and leisure and to special protection from abuse, neglect and all forms of exploitation which interfere with their development." The CRC has been criticised for conceptualising children as independent rights-bearing individuals, rather than recognising that many societies adopt a social understanding of personhood, where children are primarily seen as members of an extended family, clan, or village (Ansell, 2005).

THE CHILD RIGHTS ACT (CRA) IN NIGERIA

A number of child rights articles emphasise the need for the protection of children. These include protection from sexual exploitation, trafficking and pornography. Underlying the principle of protection is the notion of the evolving capacity of children. Lansdown (2005) argues that the need for children to be agents of their rights must be balanced with the imperative of their protection in accordance with their age and maturity. Most human rights experts agree on the principle, hence the notion of designing interventions that are age-appropriate and content specific (Beers, Invernizzi, and Milne, 2006). Fatokun (2007) recorded that the rights of children have been extensively acknowledged and protected by legislations and constitutions in Nigeria. In a bid to ensure the eradication of violation of Nigerian children, the Federal Government of Nigeria passed a comprehensive Child Rights Act in 2003.

The Child Rights Act 2003 (CRA) was created to serve as a legal documentation for the protection of children's right and responsibilities in Nigeria. The Act also incorporates the rights of the "Convention on the Rights of the Child" (CRC) and the "African Charter on Human and Peoples' Rights" into the national law to provide the responsibilities of government agencies associated with the law and to integrate children-focused legislation into one comprehensive law. Although the Act was specially constructed to protect Nigerian children from any form of exploitation and abuse, till date some state governments have not implemented it. This is probably due to some limitations in financial and human resourcing, thus obstructing the effectiveness of the bill. The structure of the Act was informed by the mandate to provide a legislation, which incorporates all the rights and responsibilities of children, and which consolidates all laws relating to children in a single legislation. Section 264 (1) of the Act, provides for the establishment of a committee to be known as the State Child Right Implementation Committee (referred to as 'State Committee' in the Act). The State Committee has the duty to initiate actions that will ensure the observance and popularisation of the rights and welfare of the child as provided for in the CRA, CRC, and the AU Charter on the Rights and Welfare of the Child and the Declaration of the World's Summit for Children.

The Child Rights Act of 2003 provides that children must be protected from child marriage, child betrothal, tattoos and skin marks, exposure and use of narcotic drugs, abduction, removal or transfer of the child from lawful custody, child labour and unlawful sexual intercourse. It also acts as legislation against human trafficking since it forbids children from being separated from their parents against their will, except where it is in the best interests of the child. It is however disheartening to note that despite the various provisions put in place to protect the rights of children, they are continuously subjected to various forms of abuse, degrading treatment, cruelty and violence. When children are exploited or abused, they do not enjoy their childhood, which leads to several consequences in future. On the other hand, when children are protected from abuse, they grow up in a healthy and confident manner, achieve their potentials and contribute to the development of the nation (UNICEF, 2005).

Several legal provisions which seek to protect children have been enacted internationally and within Nigeria. However, these laws have not served as an effective tool in curbing the menace of child abuse, as originally intended. The purpose of enacting laws is to prevent a certain problem and decrease the frequency of its occurrence. When these laws are not effective, the purpose is defeated. Irrespective of the long-time existence of child abuse in Nigeria, scholars have noted that it has not gotten the appropriate attention by the Nigerian government. This seemingly cold attitude of the Nigerian Government can be said to have accounted for the less than required attention the Child Rights Act has received from educators, administrators, social workers, counselling psychologists, sociologists, criminologists and even politicians (Momoh, Aigbomian & Longe, 2008). Crimes such as breeding of street youth and children are direct consequences of child abuse and neglect due to the government's inability to enforce its local and international conventions (Awosola and Omoera, 2008). The obvious scenario of passing the Child Rights Act—with only lip service paid to its actualisation—depicts hypocrisy and indifference as far as the issues of child abuse is concerned.

It must be noted that the legislation on issues concerning children in Nigeria is in the residuary legislative list and as such depends on the state. Each state in Nigeria is expected to adapt the Child Rights Act. Some states including Abia, Anambra, Bayelsa, Ebonyi, Edo, Ekiti, Imo, Jigawa, Kwara, Lagos, Nassarawa, Ogun, Ondo, Rivers and Taraba have adopted the Child Rights Act (Isua, 2009). However, the Child Rights Act has not been domesticated in some states in Nigeria. In the states where the CRA has been adopted, there is very little commitment by the government to fully implement its provisions; lack of implementation has led to a continuance of menacing child abuse. A major reason for the lack of commitment is the cost implication of implementing the provisions of the CRA.

Poor enforcement and lack of sufficient documentation on the Rights' violation depict that the best interest of the child is mostly not rooted in government institutions and society. These deficits are notable in the nation's social protection systems and programmes (UNICEF, 2011). In the process of adapting the rights at state level, the definition of "child" based on age began to vary. Scholars are of the opinion that the perception of age as a definition of a child in Nigeria is dependent on the person defining and has been found to vary according to diverse cultural backgrounds. Hence, the lack of a generally agreed definition that is applicable throughout the nation is a major impediment with regards to the just application of the provisions of the law.

To facilitate the CRA effectively, States have to provide facilities including schools, as well as other equipment. Judges, magistrates, law enforcement agents, officers working for government-approved institutions and media agents would also have to be trained in child abuse protection processes; an abundance of resources will be required to achieve this goal. Literature has evidenced the importance of the roles played by the media to ensure the proper enacting of the Child Rights Act in Nigeria (Fayoyin, 2011). National development institutions also emphasise the critical importance of the media in enhancing a supportive public attitude to Child Rights Act implementation in Nigeria. Among other responsibilities, the media has to protect the integrity of the child. However, the media does not pay enough attention to the cognitive, physical and social development of Nigerian children in the Child Rights Act. A need for balance between checkmating media contents and roles in child protection should be given utmost priority on the national agenda for children in Nigeria

INFLUENCE OF MEDIA CONTENT ON CHILD DEVELOPMENT

The last few decades have witnessed a dramatic change in children's media landscape. The new digital media culture is on the rise due to the explosive growth of the Internet and digital media platforms. Today's media is more complex, stirring and

Figure 2.

fast-paced than prior times. Media comprises of the conduits of communications used to reach diverse audiences concurrently, including radio, television, cinema, interactive multimedia, diverse communication platforms through the Internet, email, mobile phones, among others (Zakeri *et al.,* 2016). Other forms of media include print, which comprises of newspapers, magazines, billboards, exhibition display, posters and leaflets. Cantor and Omdahl (1999), as cited in Zakeri *et al.* (2016), opine that people use mass media for purposes such as information gathering, knowledge acquisition and personal identification in order to gain insight into oneself and change the attitudes and conduct of the targeted consumers.

Researchers are of the opinion that changes in media may influence children's development. It has been established that the relationship between media and child development is not unidirectional but rather bidirectional. Thus, media does not only affect child development; child development may also influence media use (Vossen, Piotrowski, and Valkenburg, 2014). The factors that determine the type of media used by children include gender, age, race or ethnicity, social class, religion and place of residence, among others. Children differ in their access to different forms of media including books and magazines, radio, television, computers, Internet, music players and mobile phones. In some war and disaster-torn areas, children may have no access to any form of media at all. The process of technological and cultural globalisation is accelerating and access to various media is becoming more common, even in remote places.

However, access alone is not enough to make a positive difference for children. It is not only the ability to watch television or play computer games that may benefit them, but also the quality of television and computer content to which they are exposed. It is not the access to mobile phones or the Internet that would provide children with opportunities for growth and development, but the uses they are able to make of these media and the nature of the connections they foster. It is not a matter of just developing a puppet show for children, but ensuring that the message is developmentally and culturally appropriate as well as a catalyst for positive change. Despite the optimism on the power of the media, the scepticism surrounding its content also has its place. A proper understanding of the influential power of the media is needed in appreciating its role in the development and propagation of the Child Rights Act in Nigeria.

Findings about the influence of media in children's lives suggest that they can have both positive and negative effects depending on a number of factors including the content of the media, context of enjoyment, individual use and characteristics of the children using them. It was found out that children's exposure to media violence is positively related to successive belligerent behaviours, provocative attitudes and generally affects them negatively (Bushman and Cantor, 2003). This thus signifies that vicious tendencies and abnormal behaviour of children have a direct correlation with violent media content. Research conducted around the world suggest that good quality media products produced for children (television and radio programmes, books, Internet sites, mobile phone information services, public education street sign campaigns, puppet shows, dramas, etc) can be effective in promoting a host of development goals (Kolucki and Lemish, 2011).

Research with older media platforms, such as television, has established the significance of children accessing and watching only age-appropriate quality content (Blackwell, Lauricella, Carway & Wartella, 2014). Literature review on preschool television has also verified the consequence of age-appropriate content for younger children (Wright *et al.*, 2001), however research on older children and teenagers focuses on the negative influences of inappropriate content. Anderson (2003) and Lemish (2007) established the consequences of young people watching violent television content and playing violent video games. It was also established by Zakeri et al. (2016) that continual exposure to television violence has significantly influenced children to engage in physical altercation with their peers, teachers or parents when compared to those who are less exposed. Abideen and Salaria (2009) also found that daily and continuous exposure of children to many forms of the media has an incredible impact on their thinking, values, attitudes, actions and decision-making skills.

Furthermore, concerns about children interacting with strangers online as well as the negative influence of Internet on their socialisation have also been established (Subrahmanyam and Lin, 2007). Research has also shown that younger adolescents who interact with strangers online tend to display more risk-taking behaviours and poor maturity in these interactions, which further raises concerns about the influences social networking sites have on children (Valkenburg, Schouten, and Peter, 2007). Longe, et al (2007) discovered quite a disturbing drift on the exposure of Nigerian children from ages 7-12 years to Internet pornography, an age band known to be least hesitant to taking steps to reduce its effect on them because of their impressionistic minds. A study by Longe and Longe (2005) estimates that close to 10 million Nigerians visit pornographic sites a week: 40% focusing on sex sites and 60% distributed among searches such as academic, entertainment, migration, and sports.

With a statistically high percentage of children (7-18 years) constituting over 32% of Internet users, it is argued that this age group may be excessively exposed to Internet pornography. There are reports in many parts of the world that young people are *sexting*, which signifies sending sex-related images instead of, or in addition to, texting. Mburu (2004) reported a significant increase in violent behaviour among secondary school students and these to some extent was influenced by exposure to the media who most times do not consider the repercussion of these contents on these children who are predisposed to act and try out behaviours observed. This demonstrates that access to and use of Nigerian media by children may in fact be contrary to some elements of the Child Rights Act agenda, especially the concept of the emerging capacity of these children.

THE NIGERIAN MEDIA AND CHILD PROTECTION

Lasica (2003) notes that media in recent times is characterised by the utilisation of various communication formats such as images, videos, text and audio files, mostly driven by information and communication technology using the Internet. As documented by Chaffee and Metzer (2001), notable features of the media include decentralisation and democratisation of information resources, enhanced dialogues, erosion of traditional gate-keeping and agenda-setting functions. Some other peculiarities include interactivity, speed, user-generated content, multi-directionality of information, among others (Waters, 2011). As communication is key to the development of any nation, the media can play active roles in that process because of their capability in efficient information dissemination.

The expected role of the media in the propagation and protection of children's rights is clearly stated in Article 17 of the Convention on the Rights of the Child (UNICEF, 2002). The media has the power to play a fundamental role in supervising to ensure the authentic implementation of the rights of the child. The media is able to penetrate every sector of the society and successfully influence people's perspectives especially in the environment in which they find themselves (Oyero, 2011). Maley (2000) found that media representations are the primary sources of information on social problems. Media agents play a major role in defining contents regarded as deviant from normal. Goddard and Saunders (2001) draw attention to the essential role of the media in increasing the society's awareness of and response to child abuse and neglect. The fact that the media is known as the Fourth Estate of the Realm, the watchdog of the society, and the voice of the voiceless makes it imperative for the media to protect the Nigerian child and their interests. Media attention, in form of news and features used to report child abuse cases, research, and intervention strategies, can positively influence public opinion and solicit professional and political responses to the conditions in which children find themselves. Oyero (2011) duly recorded that it seems that children are generally underreported in the print media. It was gathered that this attitude can be explained from the perspective of journalists considering young people as unimportant in societal decision-making, undeveloped, ill-informed and uninterested in current affairs.

More so, it was revealed that because children do not purchase newspaper, journalists are probably not predisposed to reporting issues affecting them. Also, journalists' ethical codes in Nigeria and some other African countries do not permit journalists to interview or photograph individuals under the age 18 on matters regarding their personal welfare especially in the absence or non-consent of their parents or guardians. These constraints thus discourage journalists from prioritising children's stories due to associated editorial delays. It therefore can be said that the special status of children works against them in terms of media coverage but if children rights are to be realised, newspapers among other media forms need to give ample attention to them. Nigerian newspapers should assume the responsibility of ensuring the actualisation of children's rights through appropriate coverage.

The presently centralised and commercialised media in Nigeria cannot effectively deliver the demand of the rights of the child. There is thence, a crucial need to refurbish current media structures if the media would be properly suited to perform its roles in child protection in Nigeria. Despite the liberalisation of the Nigerian media system since the deregulation of broadcasting in the 1992, key factors such as democratisation and localisation have not been guaranteed. These factors are however important in ensuring media responsiveness to the Child Rights Act in Nigeria (Oyero, 2010). It is also surprising to discover that local radio and television stations are commercial-oriented, selective and foreign in their contents. The major purpose guideline to their programmes is that of competition in order to succeed in the media sector. However, children—especially those below the age of eight—do not have the ability to comprehend the television's commercial cognitive development. They tend to have a predisposition to believe whatever advertisement they see on television or hear on radio and even feel cheated when they are not provided with such advertised products. This behaviour is primarily due to the predominant egocentricism associated with their stage of development (Abideen and Salaria, 2009).

During a recent evaluation, children's programmes were found to be more entertainment- inclined as opposed to information and edutainment agenda. Children's parties are becoming the leading features of most Nigerian television programmes. Companies whose motive is to enlarge the market of their children-targeted products, rather than popularising the rights of the child, mostly sponsor such programmes. For the media to be better placed, the media structure must move beyond mere liberalisation to localisation and democratisation. It is necessary to note that the key participants concerned with children's rights are women, children

Figure 3.

and teachers at the community levels. These people need to know about the rights of a child, what the Child Rights Act entails, and the different roles they can play in fulfilling the rights. This would be better accomplished if the local media are successfully engaged in communicating these roles to them. The media can also bring forth children's issues by allowing children who have been working (in the worst form) as domestic servants, on the streets, in factories and mines/quarries, as well as those rehabilitated to participate in relevant media programmes (Parajuli, 2004).

Field experiences demonstrate that the media is being used to contribute to the child protection agenda in Nigeria (Fayoyin, 2011). Many development agencies and Non-Governmental Organisations in Nigeria are running social media and hotline projects that provide care and support for children and women who are victims or survivors of abuse, neglect, and exploitation. Considerably, the media has appeared sometimes to have more influence on child protection policy and practice than professionals working on the field. This phenomenon has been described as "legislation by tabloid." It is however undeniable that the media's portrayal of child abuse and child protection may have significant negative consequences for children and their families, but for children matters to gain attention from policymakers and political stakeholders, media coverage is highly essential. Nevertheless, the average Nigerian does not seem to be aware of the provisions of the Child Rights Act. It is even more worrisome in the light of the fact that most forms of youth violence, unrest and riots are linked with child abuse and neglect. Hence, the media has momentous roles to assume in ensuring that the rights of children are brought to the plane of dialogue.

FUTURE RESEARCH DIRECTIONS

Validating children's rights to be protected from harm may seem irreconcilable with the encouragement of their inclusion and involvement in the media. This is mostly so due to the absence of any international regulatory framework for the global media industry (UNICEF, 2009). It is thus worthy of note that through the media, children and young people are exposed to materials that negate the spirit and the letter of the Child Rights Act. Although the ramification of this challenge in Nigeria is yet to be fully understood, it is certain that there is a need for more child protection measures in the current digital age. Negotiating a fine balance between incorporating children into media agenda and minding the risk factors that accompany such involvement is most times difficult.

With the increasing influence of the media in every facet of society, the lack of sufficient measures to forestall a complete breakdown particularly towards safeguarding minors, and the other factors so far identified in this chapter, the adverse impacts of the media on the youngsters of present would become full-blown in a matter of time. With these likely impacts of current media consumption on the present day's youngsters manifesting fully, it is essential that more light is beamed on the results of the current media influence—whether uncurbed or minimally curbed—on the current generation of children and teenagers and more importantly urgent measures to prevent the emergence of delinquent generations.

SOLUTIONS AND RECOMMENDATIONS

Based on the study, it is evident that children can get influenced positively and negatively from their use of media and media contents. It is however suggested that:

- Children's media use should be better guided and monitored by their guardians, parents, family members, and other well-wishers.
- Parents and guardians should critically analyse media contents and help children differentiate between fictions from reality.
- Media contents should be framed to sensitise children about the CRA.
- Media contents should be framed to educate children about their rights and how the CRA can help, should those rights be violated.
- Individual states in Nigeria should empower media agents through trainings and capacity building to further the purpose of implementing the CRA.
- Media personnel should be trained on how to develop age-appropriate contents for children and also place some form of restrictions on X-rated sites that would disallow children from accessing them.
- Regulatory agencies should also implement censorial standards for media contents that would be made accessible by the Nigerian children.
- Government should focus and invest more in the use of media for child protection purposes.

CONCLUSION

Child rights issues are multifaceted and span numerous needs and services. Majority of children issues, especially in terms of rights violation, are well established within societal norms and culture requiring structural and systemic changes. Having established that the intervention of the media can ensure proper engagement of all stakeholders in the task of child protection in Nigeria; it also manifests some dysfunctional effects in terms of exposing children and young people to information that may be potentially harmful to their holistic development. Appropriate media contents have been found to be useful in improving children's participation in development activities including matters about their protection. There are, however, significant consequences when children are exposed to media contents that are not age appropriate.

It is widely argued that the proliferation of computer technology and the Internet has made the job of child predators easier, as children have become targets of Internet-based crimes. Risk-taking and violent behaviours in children have been linked to their unrestricted interaction with strangers online. The media has no way of restricting access of children to obscene and X-rated sites on media platforms. There is also almost no guide for the use of media by children, thus exposing them to the unlimited consequences attached to its advantages. This is an aspect in which the Child Rights Act has failed to protect the Nigerian child from its media contents. There is also a noticeable shortage of documentation on how the media can further ensure the enactment of the CRA at State levels and how media contents should be framed in order to promote what the CRA stands for.

REFERENCES

Abideen, Z., & Salaria, M. (2009, December 4). *Effects of television advertising on children: with special reference to Paskitani Urban Children*. Available at https:// mpra.ub.uni muenchen.de/22321

Akinbote, O., Osuji, U., & Salawu, I. (2006). *Origin and development of early childhood and education*. Lagos: National Open University of Nigeria.

Al-Shail, E., Hassan, A., Aldowaish, A., & Kattan, H. (2012). *The cultural reinforcers of child abuse*. Retrieved from http://cdnintechopen.compdfs-wm/37763.pdf.

Anderson, C. A. (2003). An update on the effects of violent video games. *Journal of Adolescence*, *27*(3), 113–122. PMID:15013264

Ansell, N. (2005). *Children, youth and development*. London: Routledge Press.

Awosola, K., & Omoera, O. (2008). Child Rights and the Media: The Nigerian Experience. *Study Home Communication Science*, *2*(2), 125–131. doi:10.1080/09 737189.2008.11885263

Beers, H., Invernizzi, A., & Milne, B. (2006). *Beyond Article 12: Essential Readings in Children's Participation*. Black on White Publications.

Blackwell, C., Lauricella, A., Carway, A., & Wartella, E. (2014). Children and the internet: Developmental implications of websites preferences among 8 to 12 years children. *Journal of Broadcasting & Electronic Media*, *58*(1), 1–20. doi:10.1080/08838151.2013.875022

Bushman, B., & Cantor, J. (2003). Media ratings for violence and sex. Implications for policymakers and parents. *The American Psychologist*, *58*(20), 130–141. doi:10.1037/0003-066X.58.2.130 PMID:12747015

Cantor, J., & Omdahl, B. (1999). Children's acceptance of safety guidelines after exposure to televised drama depicting accidents. *Western Journal of Communication*, *63*(1), 1–15. doi:10.1080/10570319909374628

Chaffee, S. H., & Metzer, M. J. (2001). The End of Mass Communication. *Mass Communication & Society*, *4*(4), 365–379. doi:10.1207/S15327825MCS0404_3

Child Rights Act. (2003). *Understanding the Child Rights Act 2003 (UNICEF).* Ministry of Social Welfare Rehabilitation.

Constitution of the Federal Republic of Nigeria. (1999). *Cap 23 LFN 2004*. Lagos: Simon Printers.

Evans, R. (2012). *Understanding Young People's Rights to decide*. Retrieved from http://www.ippf.org

Fatokun, K. V. (2007). Child abuse and the educational attainment of secondary school students in science subjects. *Journal of Research in National Development*, *5*(2), 1596–8308.

Fayoyin, A. (2011). Promoting children's rights through the new media: The Nigerian Experience. *Journal of Communication*, *2*(2), 57–65. doi:10.1080/0976691X.2011.11884782

Flavell, J. H., Miller, P. H., & Miller, S. A. (2002). *Cognitive development*. Englewood Cliffs, NJ: Prentice Hall.

Goddard, C., & Saunders, B. (2001). Child abuse and the media. *Child Abuse Prevention, 14*(2).

Huston, A. C., & Ripke, M. N. (2006). *Middle childhood: Contexts of development*. New York: Cambridge University Press. doi:10.1017/CBO9780511499760

Imo, N. A. (2015). Working with emotionality and sexually abused children: The therapeutic value of effective communication. *International Journal of Research in Arts and Social Sciences*, *8*(1), 151–161.

Isua, N. (2009). An examination of the child rights protection and corporal punishment in Nigeria: The Legislative and institutional framework of environmental protection in the oil. Academic Press.

Jacomy, S., & Stevens, A. (2004). *Rights of the child in Nigeria: Report on the implementation of the convention on the rights of the child by Nigeria*. Geneva: OMCT and Cleen Foundation.

Kadiri, K. K., & Muhammed, A. Y. (2011). Mass media as correlation of children's behavioural problems in Kwara state, Nigeria. *Journal of Media and Communication, 3*(5), 198–202.

Kolucki, B., & Lemish, D. (2011). *Communicating with children*. UNICEF Factsheet. Retrieved from http://www.unicef.org.ng/cwc/

Lansdown, G. (2005). The evolving capacities of the child. Firenze.

Lasica, J. D. (2003). *We media: How audiences are shaping the future of news and information. The Media Centre*. New York: The American Press Institute.

Lemish, D. (2007). *Children and television: A global perspective*. Hoboken, NJ: Blackwell Publishing.

Livingstone, S. (2009). *Children and the internet*. Cambridge, UK: Polity Press.

Longe, O. B., Chiemeke, S. C., Onifade, O. F., Balogun, F. M., Longer, F. A., & Otti, V. U. (2007). Exposure of children and teenagers to internet pornography in South Western Nigeria: Concerns, trends and implications. *Journal of Information Technology Impact*, *7*(4), 195–212.

Longe, O.B., & Longe, F.A. (2005). The Nigerian web content: Combating pornography using content filters. *Journal of Information Technology Impact, 15*(2), 59-64.

Maley, B. (2000). *The elite gatekeepers-How the media capture public policy*. Policy. Winter.

Manderson, L., & Liamputting, P. (2002). *Youth and sexuality in contemporary Asia societies in coming age in South East Asia*. Richmond: Curzon Press.

Mburu, S. (2004). *Shocking rise in rape cases unveiled. In The Daily Nation Newspapers*. Nairobi: Nation Media Group.

McQuail, D. (2007). *Mass communication theory*. London: Sage Publication Limited.

Momoh, S. O., Aigbomian, D., & Longe, B. O. (2008). Students' perception of the prevalence, forms and causes of child abuse in Edo state, Nigeria. *Investigaciones-REOP, 19*(1), 5–11.

Mosby's Medical Dictionary. (2009). *Child* (8th ed.). Elsevier. Retrieved May 29, 20 II http://medical dictionary.thefreedictionmy.com/Childrens

Nnam, M., & Njemanze, V. (2016). Culture as a determinant of child abuse in Nigeria: A sociological standpoint. *International Journal of Arts. Management and Humanities, 1*(3), 1–22.

Okunola, M. I. (2002). *A handbook for Nigeria Social Workers.* Daybis Limited.

Olusegun, O., & Idowu, A. (2016). Child abuse in Nigeria: Dimension, reasons for its persistence and probable. *Child and Family Law Journal, 4*(1), 1–23.

Oyero, O. (2011). How children are reported in Nigerian Newspapers: Implications for the realization of the rights of the child. *International Journal of Social and Management Sciences, 4*(1), 37–56.

Oyero, O. (2010). Child rights and media democratization: An agenda for realization of the MDGs in Nigeria. *International Journal of Communication, 11*, 202-215.

Parajuli, B. (2004, March 23). Child rights and media role. *The People's Review: A Political and Business Weekly*. Retrieved from http: //www.peoplesreview.com.np /2004/10/14102004 /c10.html

Sambe, J. A. (2005). *Introduction to mass communication practice in Nigeria.* Ibadan: Spectrum Books Limited.

Subrahmanyam, K., & Lin, G. (2007). Adolescents on the Net: Internet use and well-being. *Adolescence, 42*, 659–677. PMID:18229503

Terr, L. (2010). Childhood trauma: An outline and overview. *The American Journal of Psychiatry, 148*(12), 10–20. PMID:1824611

UNICEF. (2002). *A World Fit for Children.* New York: UNICEF.

UNICEF. (2009). *Childhood under Threat.* Retrieved from http://www.unicef.org/sowc05/english/sowc05.pdf

UNICEF. (2011). *Social Protection Diagnostic and Forward Agenda for UNICEF.* Retrieved from http://bit.ly/social-protection-nigeria

United Nations Convention on the Rights of the Child (UNCRC). (1989). *Adopted by the General Assembly of the United Nations on 20th November*. Geneva: United Nations Publication.

Valkenburg, P. M., Schouten, D., & Peter, J. (2007). Preadolescents' and adolescents' online communication and their closeness to friends. *Developmental Psychology, 43*(2), 267–277. doi:10.1037/0012-1649.43.2.267 PMID:17352538

Vossen, H., Poitrowski, J., & Valkenburg, P. (2014). *Media Use and Effects in Childhood. In Handbook of Lifespan Communication Chapter*. Peter Lang Publishers.

Waters, J. K. (2011). *The everything guide to social media*. Adams Media.

Wright, J. C., Huston, A. C., Murphy, K. C., St. Peters, M. F., Piñon, M. F., Scantlin, R. M., & Kotler, J.P. (2001). The relations of early television viewing to school readiness and vocabulary of children from low-income families: The early window project. *Child Development, 72*, 1347–1366. doi: 0009-3920/2001/7205-0005

Wyness, M. (2006). *Childhood and society: An introduction to the sociology of childhood*. Hampshire: Palgrave, Macmillan.

Zakeri, A., Zainab, B., & Yakubu, I. (2016). Examining children learned violent behaviour through mass media content: A study of Obasanjo model school, Jos, Nigeria. *Global Journal o Arts. Humanities and Social Sciences, 4*(11), 12–21.

ADDITIONAL READING

Allan, S. (2005). *Journalism: critical issues*. Maidenhead, England: Open University Press.

Anderson, C. (2011). *The impact of pornography on children, youth, and culture*. Holyoke, MA: NEARI Press.

Convention on the Rights of the Child (1989). Adopted by the General Assembly of the United Nations on 20th November.

Eadie, W. (2009). 21st century communication: a reference handbook. Thousand Oaks, California: SAGE Reference. (e-book).

Itat, U. (1999). A critical analysis of the United Nations Convention on the Rights of the Child and the Constitution of the Federal Republic of Nigeria. A paper presented at a seminar organised by Law Reform Commission, Akwa Ibom State, Nigeria.

Rasaq, K. A., & Osakue, S. O. (2008). } Child Rights and the Media. *The Nigerian Experience.*, *2*(2), 125–131.

Steinberg, C. S. (1972). *The communicative arts: An introduction to mass media*. New York: Hasting House Publishers.

Walvoord, G., & Rodney, P. (2010). *My body is private by Linda*. Newton, KS: Paw Prints.

KEY TERMS AND DEFINITIONS

Adulthood: The phase of life when one has come of age and can decide between right and wrong, and when one is expected to be responsible for minors.

Child Abuse: Any action that violates the rights of a child in any form, which can take various forms, including physical, psychological and social.

Child Protection: To shield a minor from any form of danger, including harassment, violence and neglect, especially as guaranteed by Article 19 of the UN Convention on the Rights of the Child.

Child Rights Act: Adapted by Nigeria in 2003 through an Act of Parliament, it serves as a legal documentation that ensures the protection of children in Nigeria.

Childhood: The phase of life that covers infancy and adolescence, and when one still requires care and protection by others.

Nigerian Children: A minor of Nigerian descent who is required to remain under the tutelage of their parents or guardian till they attain maturity.

Socialisation: The adoption of the norms of a people.

UNICEF: United Nations Children's Fund.

Values: A set of important principles and ethos by which an individual or a group of people are bound.

Chapter 5
Constraints and Challenges of the Media in Child Rights Advocacy and Development in Nigeria

Abdulhameed Kayode Agboola
Federal University of Technology, Minna, Nigeria

ABSTRACT

Studies have revealed that children constitute more than one-third of the world's population and half of the world's population is under the age of 25. In the age of globalization, media institutions and services are controlled by the market forces. Critically speaking, media institutions have not lived up to their expectations towards child rights advocacy and development. This chapter discusses the plight of children in Africa. It argues for the child rights advocacy as well as discusses the challenges and constraints that hinder the media from performing their role adequately. It concludes that the mass media plays an important role in promoting and sustaining the child rights advocacy. The chapter recommends that all media houses must strive to live up to the expectations of the people no matter the constraints and challenges that might stand in their way.

DOI: 10.4018/978-1-7998-0329-4.ch005

INTRODUCTION

Media indeed is a powerful instrument in raising the awareness of people of their rights, most especially of the children (Guru, Nabi & Raslana, 2013). Broadcast Journalists have responsibility of uncovering stories (through dramas, documentaries and news) of abuses occurring in the society that involve children. In these cases of abuses in the society, infiltrating sensitive stories, such as, child abuse is a must. Stories such as these have an overwhelming impact on society's attitude towards children which greatly affect the way the adult behave. It thus becomes an issue of concern to media practitioners to raise awareness of these children's issues and to avoid further exploitation these children who are extremely damaged by the abuses they went through.

Oyero (2010) rightly states that, the media provides a unique avenue through which children related issues are brought to the fore of public discourse. In recognition of this fact, the Norwegian Government and the United Nations Children Education Fund (UNICEF) launched the Oslo Challenge to call to action to ensure that the overwhelming power of the media for good in the lives of children is identified, encouraged, and supported, while the potential harmful effects are recognised and reduced. In this regard, it is not inaccurate to say that Nigerian children are faced with various challenges during their journey through life. Nigeria ranks among the worst nations in many children-related world ranking indices ranging from child health, out-of-school children, to child labour, child development index, among others. Several children-related issues abound that require urgent attention of stakeholders within and outside the country in order for the country to redeem her image as one that caters for the needs and protects the innocence of her children. The media was thus challenged to promote good ethical conduct to avoid sensationalism, stereotyping, or undervaluing of children and their rights (Child Rights International Network [CRIN], 2009).

CONCEPTS OF A CHILD AND CHILD RIGHTS

There is no generally accepted definition of a child or who a child is. However, in order to surmount the difficulty in defining a child, Sadeeq (2016, p.45) highlightes that, it is surprising to note that under the common law, the definition of the word 'child' varies with the statutes, so that a child is a child in one statute but not a child in another. Indeed, there is a legislative hesitation as to whether a child is properly to be termed a child, a minor or an infant; nor is this the only terminology to be considered. There are also juveniles and young persons to be woven into the legal fabric.

Sadeeq (2016) states further that the common law position which stipulates that a person who has not reached the age of 14 is a child applies in Nigeria. However, the current laws in Nigeria that deal with the child are the Constitution, the Child Right Act of 2003 and Children and Young Person's Law. In the Children and Young Persons Law, child is defined as a person less than 14 years while a juvenile or young person is any person who has attained the age of 14 years but has not reached 18 years. Even though the Constitution of Nigeria does not contain any provision specifying who a child is, it has been submitted that by prescribing 18 years as the voting age in the Electoral Act, it suggests a child to be a person under the age of 18. Also the Child Right Act defines a child as any person under the age of 18 years.

Child rights therefore can be said to mean the rights enjoyed by children that is specifically linked to their status as minors and to their needs for special care and protection. Child rights can also be said to mean the claims that all children have to survival, development, protection and participation. It could also mean the totality of obligations owed to children by both adults and the states. These rights are contained in several local and international instruments and they include right to life, right to health, right to welfare, right to education and right to freedom from physical or mental harm among others (Sadeeq, 2016).

STATEMENT OF THE PROBLEM

North America, Australasia, and Western Europe have made progress as regards improving the lives of children, but the position of children in the countries of Asia, South America, Eastern Europe, and Africa remains tenuous. The concept of child protection is often a distant dream, and the very structures of society negate the attempts to alleviate the position children find themselves in.

Therefore, with the unending challenges facing the Nigerian child, the task is on the media to drive change towards improving the status of the Nigerian child by drawing public attention to positive issues that can enhance their quality of life. But surprisingly, the Nigerian media is not living up to its responsibility in championing the course of the Nigerian child. The media can help to improve the plight of Nigerian children through extensive coverage, sensitisation, and proper positioning of children-related issues. The nature of such issues is also important if the desired change must be achieved. Premised on this argument, this paper thus examines the plight of the Nigerian child and how the media can help in sensitising the public on issues through and coverage in Nigerian media outfits.

PLIGHT OF CHILDREN IN NIGERIA

Oyero and Salawu (2018) have noted that among the most destitute species on earth, the African child numbered in them in millions because they are born and bred in abject poverty, deprived of education, suffer from various ailments, malnourished and discriminated against, and even abandoned and vulnerable to so much abuses, such as, child labour, child soldiers in warfare, etc. The issue of education remains problematic. Even with significant improvement in access to primary education, completion rates have remained abysmal as a result of high level of attrition. A World Bank report in 2012 revealed that completion rate at primary level in Central African Republic and Chad in 2009 was not less than 40% (World Bank, 2012). Hence, it is a great challenge to access to secondary schools in Africa (African Child Policy Forum [ACPF], 2013). Coupled with a significant gender dimension, there is a huge deficit of secondary school education.

In addition, it was highlighted that substantial number of children in many countries are still left out of secondary school education with exception of a few countries, such as South Africa, which has achieved considerable high level of access to secondary school education amongst its girls (97%) and boys at (93%) (UNICEF, 2012). Access to education is poor at both primary and secondary levels. For example, net enrollment for primary education for boys/girls is as low as 39%/37% in Liberia, 43%/38% in Eritrea, 47%/34% South Sudan, and 53%/56% in Sudan (ACPF, 2016). "More than half of the 59 million out-of-school children live in sub-Saharan Africa" and these children have limited prospects for re-entering school (UNICEF, 2016, p. 44). There are also problems with quality of education in form of unqualified teachers, overcrowded class rooms, and unacceptably high teacher-pupil ratio.

The situation is worsen by low pay for teachers with its attendant consequences of low morale, absenteeism, and teachers seeking for extra means of income generation to make ends meet at the expense of teaching the pupils. Some even completely abandon the teaching professions in favor of more rewarding businesses. "Out of 53 African countries, 20 have pupil-teacher ratios at primary level that are far below the recommended ratio of 1:40. In some countries, teachers are compelled to cater for 80 pupils or more" (ACPF, 2013, p. 17). Millions of children are also caught up in emergencies as exemplified with the Central African Republic, Nigeria, and South Sudan, with their education completely decimated, jeopardised and set for serious decadence, while many children are drawn into fighting as soldiers or forced to support armed groups (Human Rights Watch, 2016).

Child's health also largely remains at low ebb. The percentage of children under the age of five dying during the neonatal period is increasing. In 2015, neonatal deaths accounted for 45% of total deaths, 5% more than in 2000. High numbers of children are still dying before the age of 5 years with worst cases in Angola (157), Chad (139), Somalia (137), Central Africa Republic (130), Sierra Leone (120), Nigeria (109), and Benin (100) (UNICEF, 2016). Besides, opportunity for treatment and utilisation of health services is low. For example; "only about a quarter (26 per cent) of all HIV-positive children in sub-Saharan Africa had access to antiretroviral treatment (ART) in 2009" (UNICEF, Joint United Nations Programme on HIV/AIDS [UNAIDS], World Health Organization [WHO], and United Nations Population Fund [UNFPA], 2010, p. 5), though this increased to 40% in Eastern and Southern Africa (UNICEF, 2013, p. 11). However, the number of children living with HIV is still very high with countries such as Nigeria, South Africa, Ethiopia, and Democratic Republic of Congo topping the list (UNICEF, 2016). Moreover, chronic malnutrition determined by stunting is a more challenging difficulty in Africa. About 38% of children in Africa could not grow properly due to malnourishment and this situation has not witnessed any significant improvement over the past 20 years. A lot of children in Africa also lack basic micronutrients such as iron, vitamin A, and zinc, which are essential for growth and development - an issue classified as "hidden hunger." Many children born are stunted with Madagascar having 49%, Niger 43%, Malawi 42%, Rwanda 38%, and Nigeria 33% (UNICEF, 2016).

Similarly, not much has been achieved of the children's right to freedom of expression and their right to be heard. Child rights to free expression and to be listened to is globally recognised and well-articulated in Article 12 of the UNCRC, Article 7 of the African Charter on the Rights and Welfare of the Child, and other documents.

Drawing from these provisions, Lansdown (2011) mentioned that children should be listened to, and their views given due weight in accordance with their age and maturity, but the current situation is far from the case. Although there have been establishment of children parliaments in many countries, these parliaments are too elitist and the members, taken from the better-off urban schools, are not informed of the challenges faced by their poorer counterparts (McIvor, 2002). In many other places, children are not consulted even on issues that affect them. For example, more than 46% in West and Central Africa and 35% in East and Southern Africa maintained that decision-makers in their locality never consulted them whereas others were oblivious of existence of any consultative structure within local authorities. As for Côte d'Ivoire, Ethiopia and Malawi ranked the highest in term of countries where the number of children who said they were not consulted at all was found (ACPF, 2009). It is important not to compromise children and their critical needs as they constitute our future generation (cited in Oyero & Salawu, 2018).

In addition, Adeniran, Suleiman, Ajaga and Kayode (2015) made reference to Maplecroft's (2013) reports in which Nigeria was ranked among 11 worst countries with extreme cases of child labour. They noted that children wander aimlessly around in dirty conditions, deprived of education and other basic human rights. Universal Basic Education Act of 2004 makes education free and compulsory for the first nine years of a child's educational career, yet about 11 million children of school age are reportedly out of school despite the enactment of the Act (Adedokun, 2013) and the situation has not changed till now. The rise in insurgency in the country has undoubtedly reduced child enrolment and attendance in schools as insurgents now target schools in perpetrating their heinous crimes thus prompting parents/guardians in susceptible areas to withdraw their wards from schools in the hope of keeping them alive. The abduction of over 200 girls in April 2014 from a school in Chibok, Borno State with most of them yet to be released 5 years after continues to hunt the country. Although some of them were said to have been released after series of negotiations and a huge undisclosed ransom paid to their abductors, the situation has affected girl-child education in the country. Yet to our chagrin, in February 2018, approximately four years after the 2014 Chibok abduction, in the nearby town of Dapchi another 110 school girls were abducted by Boko Haram. Also study has revealed that the increasing attacks on schools have negatively affected school attendance in three states with high rate of Boko Haram insurgency in Nigeria.

Awosola and Omoera (2008) related that, in Africa, the Organisation of African Unity, before it was renamed the African Union, in Addis Ababa in 1990 during its Heads of State Summit adopted a Charter on the Rights and Welfare of the African Child. The charter, which was derived from the United Nations Convention on the Rights of the Child, takes into consideration the sociocultural characteristics prevailing amongst the African child. It notes that the situation of most African children remains critical due to the unique factors of their socio-economic, cultural, traditional and developmental circumstances, natural disasters, armed conflicts, exploitation and hunger and on account of the child's physical and mental immaturity, he/she needs special safeguards and care.

To further the mobilisation of attention on the African Child, Nigeria and the Rights of the Child (1999) reports that the Organisation of Africa Unity (OAU) subsequently proclaimed in Abuja 1991, the 1990s as the "Decade of the African Child" and set June 16 of every year as the "Day of the African Child". The document also reports that every child must be protected against all forms of exploitation, indecent or degrading treatment including child labour, abuse and torture, sexual exploitation, sale, abduction and drug abuse. It goes without saying that every nation who is a signatory to the convention is expected to make concerted effort at protecting children against all forms of abuses, through the enforcement of relevant instruments.

Section 34 of the 1999 Constitution of the Federal Republic of Nigeria provides for the right of every individual to dignity of his/her person. This section further prohibits "all forms of torture, inhuman or degrading treatment, and slavery, forced or compulsory labour". In other words, it ensures the child's right to dignity of his/her person. Accordingly, children should not be subjected to any form of torture or inhuman or degrading treatment, forced or compulsory labour. These saddening experiences have strong emotional impact on the victim. Often times, abused and neglected children are overwhelmed and shattered. This usually results in emotional imbalance, which eventually manifest in delinquency and deviance.

In Nigeria, for instance, youth crime and breeding of street children are direct consequences of child abuse and neglect. However, situation abounds where the government ratifies international conventions but fails to enforce such conventions locally. This is intolerable. A situation where the Child Rights Bill is passed and mere lip-service is paid to its implementation amounts to hypocrisy and apathy as far as issues of child abuse and neglect is concerned. Ademokun (2002) observes that there are cases of children in Nigeria being bludgeoned into child labour and prostitution by people who claimed to be philanthropists. Given these circumstances, the average Nigerian does not seem to be aware of the provisions of the Child Rights Bill needless to say the instruments before it. It is even more worrisome in the light of the fact that most forms of youth violence, unrest, riots are linked with child abuse and neglect. The media are undoubtedly persuasive instruments in man's struggle for self-liberation and development (Ademokun, 2002). In line with this, Steinberg (1972) advances that the mass media select and bring to waiting multitudes a constant flow of detail related to those fruitful dialogues of differences and concordance upon which free societies thrive (cited in Awosola & Omoera, 2008).

CHILD REPRESENTATION IN THE MEDIA

Over the years, studies have been done depicting the representation of children in the media across the world. A number of them recorded findings indicating that children's story remained on the back burner in the media and that most stories are outsourced stories, reflecting a tendency by media to react to issues rather than adopting a proactive role (Media Institute of Southern Africa, 2013). One of such is a study by Child Rights Alliance for England (CRAE) on children's portrayal in the British media, which acknowledged negative portrayals of children in the media - as troublemakers and deviant, or as victims (cited in Child Rights International Network (CRIN), 2009).

According to Lynn Geldof, UNICEF Communication Advisor for Central and Eastern Europe and the Commonwealth of Independent States, who says:

Media professionals are well placed to keep children's rights – and their abuse – on the news agenda, by scrutinising policies and legislation, and challenging those who fail to meet their commitments to children (Mediawise, 2010).

Journalists are champions of human rights. They act as the eyes, ears and voices of the public, drawing attention to abuses of power and human rights, often at considerable personal risk. Through their work they can encourage governments and civil society organisations to effect changes that will improve the quality of people's lives. Journalists, photographers and programme-makers frequently expose the plight of children caught up in circumstances beyond their control, or abused or exploited by adults. However, it is equally important to consider the 'children's angle' in more conventional news coverage. A good way of testing the value of changes in the law or fiscal policy, for example, is to consider the extent to which children will benefit or suffer as a consequence. The way in which the media represents, or even ignores, children can influence decisions taken on their behalf, and how the rest of society regards them. The media often depicts children merely as silent 'victims' or charming 'innocents'. By providing children and young people with opportunities to speak for themselves - about their hopes and fears, their achievements, and the impact of adult behaviour on their lives - media professionals can remind the public that children deserve to be respected as individual human beings (Mediawise, 2010).

The Media and Children's Rights

Commissioned by UNICEF and based on the practical experience of working journalists, *The Media and Children's Rights* is an attempt to assist media professionals and others to consider how the United Nations Convention on the Rights of the Child might impact upon the way children are represented in and by the media. Its purpose is to generate responsible coverage of children and the impact of adult behaviour and decisions on their lives, as well as to encourage media professionals to consider how best to protect the rights of children and help children to play a role in the mass media.

However, *Mediawise*, in collaboration with UNICEF, has developed principles and guidelines to help journalists report on children's issues in a way that enables them to serve the public interest without compromising the rights of children. Below are lists of principles and guidelines for reporting children:

Principles and Guidelines for Media Reporting on Children

According to Mediawise (2010), media reporting on children and young people should never put them at risk. UNICEF has developed principles and guidelines to help journalists report on children's issues in a way that enables them to serve the public interest without compromising the rights of children. These are six over-arching principles; six guidelines for interviewing children; and seven principles for reporting on children's issues.

Five Principles for Reporting on Children

1. Respect the dignity and rights of every child in every circumstance.
2. In interviewing (and reporting on) children, pay special attention to each child's right to privacy and confidentiality, to have their opinions heard, to participate in decisions affecting them and to be protected from harm and retribution.
3. Protect the best interests of each child over any other consideration, including advocacy for children's issues and the promotion of child rights.
4. When trying to determine the best interests of a child, give due weight to the child's right to have their views taken into account in accordance with their age and maturity.
5. Consult those closest to the child's situation and best able to assess it about the political, social and cultural ramifications of any reportage.

Six Guidelines for Interviewing Children

1. Do no harm to any child; avoid questions, attitudes or comments that are judgemental, insensitive to cultural values, that place a child in danger or expose a child to humiliation, or that reactivate the pain of traumatic events.
2. Do not discriminate in choosing children to interview because of their sex, race, age, religion, status, educational background or physical abilities.
3. No staging: do not ask children to tell a story or take an action that is not part of their own history.
4. Ensure that the child or guardian knows they are talking to a reporter. Explain the purpose of the interview and its intended use.
5. Obtain permission from the child and his or her guardian for all interviews, videotaping and, when possible, for documentary photographs. When possible and appropriate, this permission should be in writing. Permission must be obtained in circumstances that ensure that the child and guardian are not coerced in any way and that they understand that they are part of a story that might be disseminated locally and globally. This is usually only ensured if the permission is obtained in the child's language and if the decision is made in consultation with an adult the child trusts.

6. Pay attention to where and how the child is interviewed. Limit the number of interviewers and photographers. Try to make certain that children are comfortable and able to tell their story without outside pressure, including from the interviewer. In film, video and radio interviews, consider what the choice of visual or audio background might imply about the child and her or his life and story. Ensure that the child would not be endangered or adversely affected by showing their home, community or general whereabouts.

Six Guidelines for Reporting on Children

1. Do not further stigmatize any child; avoid categorizations or descriptions that expose a child to negative reprisals - including additional physical or psychological harm, or to lifelong abuse, discrimination or rejection by their local communities.
2. Always provide an accurate context for the child's story or image.
3. Always change the name and obscure the visual identity of any child who is identified as: i) - a victim of sexual abuse or exploitation, ii) - a perpetrator of physical or sexual abuse, iii) - HIV positive, or living with AIDS, unless the child, a parent or a guardian gives fully informed consent, iv)- charged or convicted of a crime.
4. In certain circumstances of risk or potential risk of harm or retribution, change the name and obscure the visual identity of any child who is identified as: i) - a current or former child combatant, ii) - an asylum seeker, a refugee or an internally displaced person.
5. In certain cases, using a child's identity (their name and/or recognizable image) is in the child's best interests. However, when the child's identity is used, they must still be protected against harm and supported in the event of any stigmatization or reprisals. For example: i) - when a child initiates contact with a reporter, wanting to exercise their right to freedom of expression and their right to have their opinion heard, ii) - when a child is part of a sustained programme of activism or social mobilization and wants to be identified as such, iii) - when a child is engaged in a psychosocial programme and claiming their name and identity is part of their healthy development.
6. Confirm the accuracy of what the child has to say, either with other children or an adult, preferably with both. When in doubt about whether a child is at risk, report on the general situation for children rather than on an individual child, no matter how newsworthy the story.

THEORETICAL FRAMEWORK

Social Responsibility Theory

Scholars have highlighted that the idea that emerged from the Hutchins Commission report of 1947 formed what is known today as the Social Responsibility theory of the press. The hub of the Social Responsibility theory is that the media should be used for the public good. It emphasises the need for an independent press that scrutinises other social institutions and provides objective, accurate news reports. Though it canvasses for the freedom of the press, such freedom places obligation on the press; it should be responsible to society for carrying out certain essential functions of mass communication in contemporary society (McQuail, 1987).

Social Responsibility theory calls on the media to be responsible for fostering productive and creative "Great Communities" (Baran & Davis, 2003, p.109), and it suggests that media should do this by prioritizing cultural pluralism- by becoming the voice of all the people - not just elite groups or groups that had dominated national, regional or local culture in the past. It also points out that the media, in carrying out their obligations, must adhere to the highest ethical standards.

McQuail (1987, p.16) summarized the basic principles of Social Responsibility Theory as follows:

1. To serve the political system by making information, discussion and consideration of public affairs generally accessible.
2. To inform the public to enable it to take self-determined action.
3. To protect the rights of the individual by acting as a watchdog over the government.
4. To serve the economic system; for instance by bringing together buyers and sellers through the medium of advertising.
5. To provide "good" entertainment, whatever "good" may mean in the culture at any point in time.
6. To preserve its own financial autonomy in order not to become dependent on special interests and influences.

In a nutshell, social responsibility is ethics that guides any action, be it in media or other organisations that put an obligation towards environment, society, culture and economy. The media like any other sector should not harm, but should promote environment and socio-cultural aspects in relation to the economy of the place. Just exactly, the media is saddled with the responsibility of creating awareness about the rights of child in our society, it must cover all cases of abuse and advocate, likewise, giving voice to the voiceless Nigerian children, and letting their voices be heard.

CHILD RIGHTS ADVOCACY: EMERGING AREAS OF IMPORTANCE

In line with UNICEF Global Communication and Public Advocacy Strategy and local priorities, UNICEF has highlighted the situation of women and children in Nigeria, especially those affected by the emergency in the northeast, to both domestic and international audiences, influencing policy and resource mobilisation decisions. UNICEF led international coverage of the crisis in the northeast, becoming a voice for children affected by the conflict, so that their concerns on education, protection and hygiene are presented. UNICEF facilitated a visit of Malala Yousafzai, Nobel Peace Prize winner and education activist, which created a strong advocacy momentum for education in the northeast. Visits by UNICEF senior staff, and UNICEF's press releases on the use of children as human bombs, further sparked the interest of the international media to cover the crisis and generate visibility on the issues children are facing. UNICEF Nigeria organized more than 20 strategic media dialogue meetings, including field visits, for Nigerian journalists and editors to raise awareness and generate action on children's issues including malnutrition, early childhood development, HIV/AIDS, and water, sanitation and hygiene (WASH). Media representatives at the events committed to covering children's issues. Over 40 international and national media visits, 20 press releases, events, briefings and press conferences resulted in 3,400 tracked UNICEF media mentions, almost all positive or neutral. UNICEF specialists were interviewed by media more than 215 times (UNICEF, 2017, p.6). The following areas of importance are highlighted for advocacy:

1. *Climate Change and Children:* UNICEF has deployed over 2,200 water supply systems, only technology options with clean energy, such as solar powered schemes and hand pump boreholes in flood-prone areas with adaptive technology options for sanitation and water supply facilities in communities and public institutions as part of resilience building. Also, populations in at-risk communities (especially children and adolescents) were trained on disaster risk reduction and resilience building.
2. *Accelerate Integrated Early Childhood Development (ECD):* In a 2017 conference, UNICEF increased engagement in early childhood development, especially in early learning through pre-primary education. Increased awareness on the need to invest early in every Nigerian child was achieved through a high-level ECD national conference initiated and funded by UNICEF in collaboration with the World Bank and the Global Partnership for Education and led by the Government of Nigeria. The ECD programme aims to strengthen convergence under the child-friendly community approach focusing on the whole child

especially young children. This is being modelled in southern Borno and is scalable at the community level through integrated Qur'anic schools beyond formal education.

3. *Refugee and Migrant Children:* Nigerians represented the highest number of identified migrants (14,000) arriving irregularly in Europe, with more than 600 unaccompanied or separated children, according to data from the UNHCR and IOM. Most children are originally from two southern states, Edo (72 per cent) and Delta (12 per cent). UNICEF requires additional resources to collect and analyse child-specific data on child migration to provide more in-depth evidence-based information on the living conditions of children in countries of origin and to inform good practice programming.
4. *Urbanisation and Children:* Based on the analysis of the situation of urban children carried out in 2017, the salient challenges requiring urban programming for children are: (i) the triple threat of urban diseases, urban lifestyles, and nutrition; (ii) road traffic accidents, particularly while going to school or playing in unsafe play spaces, and; (iii) child labour, which in urban Nigeria mostly occurs as domestic servants in wealthy urban families, informal work, and child prostitution (UNICEF, 2017, p. 6-7).
5. *Crackdowns on Child Rights Activists:* According to the Child Right International Network [CRIN] (2018), Children's freedom of expression is curtailed if the activities of representatives and activists are also restricted. CRIN has previously reported on the worrying attempts to censor or repress on child rights activists in different regions in the world.
6. *Children and Freedom of Expression:* Children Advocacy Network (CRIN) (2018) hinted that, everyone has the right to freedom of opinion and expression; this right includes freedom to hold opinions without interference, and impart information and ideas through any media regardless of frontiers" (Universal Declaration of Human Rights, Art. 19). The child shall have the right to freedom of expression; this right shall include freedom to seek, receive and impart information and ideas of all kinds, regardless of frontiers, either orally, in writing or in print, in the form of art, or through any other media of the child's choice. (Convention on the Rights of the Child, Art. 13).

In light of all of the above, CRIN (2018) declared that, Child Right International Network [CRIN] is especially passionate about press freedom because change is not possible without the 'democratisation of information', and that if people don't have access to information about children's rights, including children, then those rights can't be upheld.

MEDIA CONSTRAINTS AND CHALLENGES

The vast and fragmented nature of Nigeria's media, the volatility in the media market and the sheer number of media houses and media activities (at national and state level) make it an extremely complex sector to navigate. Some of the key challenges include countering the pervasive lack of media interest in child issues, and devising appropriate 'partnership' approaches that ensure wide media reach and buy-in while at the same time catering to the need for 'exclusive' media content. And where existing or potential opportunities are concerned, the media named a few literature festivals, certain national child-focus days etc. that could provide a temporary opening to raise the level of child rights coverage in Nigeria.

In addition, it is a clear fact that the Nigerian media houses are facing a lot of pressures in the discharge of their duties from political leaders and other private interests. These constraints limit their abilities in the development of the society; however, they must not allow these challenges to get into the way of their job. Though the media organisations in Nigeria are either privately or publicly owned, the reason for their existence is not to serve as a propagandist machinery of their owners. Media houses sociologically and philosophically exist to serve as the custodian of the rights of the masses and they are supposed to champion the cause of the masses, from the remotest portion of the society to the highest level. They are the Fourth Estate of the realm and they must stand up to the task when the situation demands (Kadiri, Muhammed, Raji, & Sulaiman, 2015).

For the mass media to live up to the expectations of the masses, their rights must be guaranteed by the state. However, the mass media is restricted from having access to information that has the potential to develop the society. The military decrees from past military eras still witch-hunt the mass media practitioners in the discharge of their duties. The press in Nigeria is still being checkmated by various previous decrees of the past military administrations in the country. Despite the fact that Freedom of Information bill has been accented to by the Federal Government, yet intimidation, harassment and incarceration of journalists still abound.

There are hundreds of district, state and national child rights networks in Nigeria; yet only few is dedicated to focusing specifically on connecting child rights advocates to the media. National-level child rights networks are usually theme-based and comprise numerous independently functioning district and state-level networks, with leadership structures varying across networks. Many networks in Nigeria have informal partnerships with media professionals/media houses and sometimes include individual journalists as members. A select few also engage in formal partnerships with the media.

However, the reality of achieving this is not so simple due to some factors that inhibit the media. Some of the factors identified by Internews Europe (2014) as cited in Uzochukwu, Morah and Okafor (2015) are as follows:

1. Lack of children voices: A patronising attitude towards children and youths severely limit the space that children get in the mainstream media and all but excludes their voices from public debate on child rights.
2. Lack of coverage: there is absence of meaningful, realistic and socially relevant media coverage or information flow on issues pertaining to child's right and protection.
3. Lack of professionalism: reporting on children issues and child's right is not widely recognized as a specialised field and this means that many journalists are not motivated or even capable of producing in depth coverage of children issues. This neglect starts from journalism schools and extends to almost all newsroom.

THE WAY FORWARD

The communication media has tremendous capacity of reaching out to a vast majority of people cutting across all barriers to communication. It has a responsibility to provide a balanced coverage of human rights violations and sensitise the various stakeholders regarding their social obligations with respect to arresting the problem of human rights violations. Mass media is providing limited services by highlighting the violations of human rights, sensitising the insensitive, stimulating action beyond discussion and initiating cases in which the culprits were brought to book. Siddegowda and Srinivasa (2015) cited Justice Reddy, who highlights that the social responsibility of media is thus:

The freedom that the media enjoy is the freedom for and on behalf of the people. Media play the role of communicator and as such they have to inform and not to misinform, dis-inform or non-inform the people on issues of vital importance. They have to educate, motivate, persuade and entertain. They must have their fingers on the pulse of the people and they have the pious obligation not to jeopardize or harm the welfare of the people. As the fourth organ, the media have also the responsibility of building the nation. They can promote economic development, social justice and reforms; bring about religious and communal harmony. The media can aid and assist in implementing development programmes meant for alleviating poverty, and for promoting health, education and literacy programmes. (Reddy, 2002, p.21)

Therefore, media practitioners must ensure they report news of both the urban and rural inhabitants. They must make sure that the news reported are those that have the tendencies of having positive impact on the lives of the people in general and with a special attention to children and their rights. Newsworthiness of the stories reported must not be based on the value-orientation of the Western media. As Sub-Saharan Africans and Nigerians in particular, we have robust cultural heritage upon which these rights must be based and disseminated to our people. News presented must be based on the values that it can have on the lives of the people in the rural and urban setting of Nigeria and Africa at large. However, if the information disseminated must have effective impact on the lives of the people, then it must be disseminated in the languages they understand most. Media houses must endeavour to reach the rural and urban dwellers in languages they speak for their easy comprehension.

Apart from reporting information about rural and urban dwellers, media practitioners must ensure that the information they report are from both the private and public establishments. The media personnel must ensure that they reduce their over-dependence on only one source of information. Journalists must involve themselves in investigative journalism, which is the cornerstone of development in any society. Getting different angles to a story has the potential of spicing up the news story thereby making it interesting for the end users, yet serving the public interest and the right to know. All geared towards informing on the rights of children and advocating for them.

CONCLUSION

This paper has argued and discussed that the rights of children are not well protected as expected in Nigeria and Africa as a whole. Children are still subjected to various maltreatments and abuses, such as, child labour, street hawking, trafficking, and many more unaccounted for maltreatments. Children are denied adequate representation by the media in their reports, and they were neither given appropriate prominence in their coverage. Their voices were barely heard, only when they are deemed as crime suspects or perpetrators. This scenario is not a good one for the Nigerian and African child in general. If we believe that children are tomorrow's leaders, there is a need to invest in them by ensuring that their rights are met. The media, therefore, need to wake up to its responsibility of informing and creating awareness among society in the plight of children by giving them adequate and appropriate coverage so that government and public attention could be directed to them.

Furthermore, the role that media plays in the development of a society cannot be over-emphasized; therefore, every media house must strive to live up to the expectations of the people no matter the constraints and challenges that might stand in its ways. The media is the last bastion of hope for Nigerian children and the bonds of the society. As the Fourth Estate of the realm, they must be willing to perceive children rights and advocacy as newsworthy events that must be given a thorough coverage with due consideration to their societies, environments and development needs of their people.

Finally, even if individuals and organisations work to eliminate all forms of child exploitation, this paper concludes that such efforts will only have a lasting impact if the media is able to raise awareness and mobilise public opinions to this end, even with the support of the government. Journalists should therefore place child rights' issues on their priority list by giving children fair representations in both the print and electronic media in Nigeria.

REFERENCES

Adedokun, N. (2013). Has Nigeria really made any progress? *The Punch*. Retrieved February 24, 2014 from http://www.punchng.com/opinion/has-nigeria-reallymade-any-progress/

Ademokun, F. (2002, Nov. 14). Children and the Lawmakers. *The Guardian*.

Adeniran, R., Suleiman, H., Ajaga, M., & Kayode, J. (2015). Representation of Children in the Nigerian News Media. *The Nigerian Journal of Communication, 12*(1), 160–183. Retrieved from https://www.researchgate.net/.../316794864_Representation_of_children_in_Nigerian_N

Awosola, R. K., & Omoera, O. S. (2008). Child Rights and the Media: The Nigerian Experience. *Studies on Home and Community Science, 2*(2), 125-131. Retrieved from www.krepublishers.com/...Awosola.../HCS-02-2-125-08-047-Awosola-R-K-Tt.pdf

Baran, S. J., & Davis, D. K. (2003). *Mass communication theory: Foundations, ferment and future*. Belmont: Thomas-Wardworth.

Child Rights International Network (CRIN). (2009). *MEDIA: Representations of Children in News Media: Revisiting the Oslo Challenge*. Retrieved February 24, 2014 from http://crin.org/en/library/publications/mediarepresentations-children-news-media- revisiting-oslochallenge

Child Rights International Network (CRIN). (2018). *Civil Rights: Freedom Of Expression And Children's Rights*. Retrieved from https://archive.crin.org/en/library/publications/civil-rights-freedom-expression-and-childrens-rights

Guru, B. P. M. C., Nabi, A., & Raslana, R. (2013). Role of Television in Child Development. The International Institute for Science, Technology and Education (IISTE). *New Media and Mass Communication*, *18*, 38-44. Retrieved from https://www.iiste.org/Journals/index.php/NMMC/article/view/8412/8512

Itat, U. D. (1999). *A Critical Analysis of the United Nations Convention on the Rights of the Child and the Constitution of the Federal Republic of Nigeria.* A paper presented at a seminar organised by Law Reform Commission, Akwa Ibom State, Nigeria.

Kadiri, K. K., Muhammed, Y. A., Raji, A., & Sulaiman, A. L. (2015). Constraints And Challenges Of The Media In The Development Of Nigeria. *Journal of Sustainable Development in Africa*, *17*(1), 44–60.

McQuail, D. (1987). *Mass communication theory: An introduction*. London: SAGE publications.

Media Institute of Southern Africa. (2013). *Promoting ethical reporting on children's issues in the SADC region.* Retrieved February 24, 2013 from http://misa.org/component/k2/item/2354-promotingethical-reporting-on-childrens-issues-in-the-sadcregion?Itemid=101#topofthepage

Mediawise. (2010). *The Media and Children's Rights*. Retrieved from http://www.mediawise.org.uk/wp-content/uploads/2011/04/The-Media-and-Children-Rights-2005.pdf

Oyero, O. (2010). Children: as 'invisible' and voiceless as ever in the Nigerian news media. *Estudos em Communicacado, 7*(2), 25-41. Retrieved from www.ec.ubi.pt/ec/07/vol2/oyero.pdf

Oyero, O., & Salawu, A. (2018). Building media capacity for children sustainability in Africa: Educational and partnership imperatives. *SAGE Open*, *8*(1), 1–10. doi:10.1177/2158244018763930

Reddy, K. J. (2002). Socio-Political Turmoil and the Role of Media. *Journal of Communication Studies*, *1*(3), 12–17.

Sadeeq, A. A. (2016). *Appraisal Of The Legal Framework For Protecting Rights Of The Child And The Role Of Unicef In Promoting Rights Of The Child In Nigeria* (Unpublished dissertation). Ahmadu Bello University, Zaria. Retrieved from http://kubanni.abu.edu.ng/jspui/bitstream/pdf /http://kubanni.abu.edu.ng/jspui/bitstream/123456789/9087/1/APPRAISAL%20OF%20THE%20%20LEGAL%20FRAMEWORK%20FOR%20%20PROTECTING%20RIGHTS%20OF%20THE%20CHILD%20AND%20THE%20ROLE%20OF%20UNICEF%20IN%20PROMOTING%20%20RIGHTS%20OF%20THE%20CHILD%20IN%20NIGERIA.pdf

Siddegowda, Y. S., & Srinivasa, D. (2015). Intervention Of Media In Child Rights Protection. *International Research Journal Of Commerce, Arts And Science, 6*(12), 64-73. Retrieved From http://www.casirj.com

Steinberg, C. S. (1972). *The Communicative Arts: An Introduction to Mass Media*. New York: Hasting House Publishers.

UNICEF, Joint United Nations Programme on HIV/AIDS, World Health Organization, & United Nations Population Fund. (2010). *Children and AIDS: Fifth stocktaking report*. Retrieved from https://www.unicef.org/publications/files/Children_and_AIDS-Fifth_Stocktaking_Report2010_EN.pdf

UNICEF. (2012). *State of the World's Children 2012: Children in an urban world*. Retrieved from https://www.unicef.org/sowc2012/pdfs/SOWC-2012-Main-Report_EN_21Dec2011.pdf

UNICEF. (2013). *Towards an AIDS-free generation—Children and AIDS: Sixth Stocktaking Report, 2013*. Retrieved from https://data.unicef.org/wp content/uploads/2015/12/str6_full_report_29-11-2013_78.pdf

UNICEF. (2016). *State of the World's Children 2016: A fair chance for every child*. Retrieved from https://www.unicef.org/publications/files/UNICEF_SOWC_2016.pdf

UNICEF. (2017). *Annual Report 2017 Nigeria*. Retrieved from https://www.unicef.org/about/annualreport/files/Nigeria_2017_COAR.pdf

Uzochukwu, C. E., Morah, N. D., & Okafor, E. G. (2015). Coverage of Child Rights and Protection Issues: Analysis of Selected Broadcast Media in Nigeria. *The Nigerian Journal of Communication, 12*(1), 272–297. Retrieved from http://tnjc.org.ng/wp-content/uploads/October2015/Coverage-of-Child-Rights-and-Protection-Issues.pdf

Section 2

Media and Child Rights: Narratives, Portrayal, and Audience

Chapter 6
Mainstreaming Children in Development:
A Thematic Frame Analysis of Print Media Discourse in East Africa

Joseph Njuguna
Jomo Kenyatta University of Agriculture and Technology, Kenya

ABSTRACT

Children rights feature prominently in global news discourse as children continue to suffer abuse in an increasingly insensitive world. The theme of the 2018 Day of the African Child "Leave No Child Behind in Development" underscored the urgency of mainstreaming children rights in development programs. Arising from the media discourse generated around this event, this chapter employs a thematic frame analytic approach to interrogate how six mainstream East African newspapers framed issues around the theme. Selected stories were content-analyzed for themes and related frames underpinning the place of children in development discourse within the region. Findings depict a media discourse recognizing children as the future of Africa yet still 'passive' players in development occasioned by socio-economic and cultural barriers.

INTRODUCTION

Globally, violation of children rights is considered rampant, despite this social problem attracting huge interest during events that commemorate children, for example, International Day of the Child and Day of the African Child (Human

DOI: 10.4018/978-1-7998-0329-4.ch006

Rights Watch, 2018). In such campaigns, the media are regarded key allies in the fighting against the vice, with evidence demonstrating that media reporting of such an issue may shape people's understanding of it. This makes media critical to policy formulation (Weatherred, 2015; Lonne & Parton, 2014).

Evidence suggests that media have generally been reactive rather than proactive in covering children issues as 'news items'. In a study on media coverage of children issues in southern Africa, the Media Institute of Southern Africa (2013) found that children stories were scant and mostly outsourced. Furthermore, studies indicate that where children are covered by media (e.g. studies by Saint-Jacques et al., 2012; Weatherred, 2015; Serag, 2015), issues mostly highlighted violation and abuse of their rights.

Other studies show that children stories are gaining prominence since the 'ideology of childhood' is a narrative device that invokes emotions of vulnerability that may drive action to protect them. Using framing analysis, Weatherred (2015) conducted a systematic review of 17 quantitative studies on media coverage of children in the US. In line with other studies (e.g. by FrameWorks Institute, 2011; Gordon, McAlister & Scraton, 2015; Internews, 2014), findings showed that media treated children issues as single events (episodic framing) like sexual violence, child labour and teenage crime as opposed to providing a wider context on the children rights (thematic framing).

A guide on children reporting by the International Federation of Journalists, underscores journalists' critical role in shaping public opinion on children rights by reporting and educating the public on the wider ramifications of protecting children rights. By analyzing how media cover issues like children rights, evidence shows that journalists highlight or frame certain features of the issue, by 'constructing reality' through the language and symbolism they employ. This framing contributes to different audience interpretations of the issue by the media audiences, with scholars positioning stakeholders as critical in understanding the problem and possible solutions (Foster & Bochner, 2008).

FOCUS OF THE CHAPTER

The focus of this chapter is to conduct a thematic frame analysis of stories published in leading East African print media to identify the prominent themes and attendant frames that underpin the discourse of 'leaving no child behind' in development. The central question explored is: how do different media actors in the East African community position children rights in the context of national development? To explore this question in a wider context, the author assesses how issues affecting children mainstreaming in development and possible solutions are framed.

SPECIFIC OBJECTIVES OF THE CHAPTER

1. To analyse how the mainstream East African print media portrays children as players in development
2. To identify prominent themes and frames in the newspaper discourse on mainstreaming children in development
3. To analyse how the East African print media frames solutions towards mainstreaming of children rights in development

Altheide & Schneider (2013) argue that examining discourse in media enables a researcher to see how language shapes people's perceptions. In the current, study, the researcher posits that how media portrays the mainstreaming of children in development is indicative of the extent to which different EAC actors have succeeded or failed to live up to the provisions of the Conventions they have signed or policies developed.

BACKGROUND

The 2018 Day of the African child presents a watershed moment to reflect on the strides taken by countries in the East African region in mainstreaming children development within the Sustainable Development Goals. Although all East African Community countries have ratified and developed policies supporting children rights protection (East African Commission, 2016), the extent to which these countries have adhered to the spirit of children rights advocacy and protection is largely unexplored, especially within regional media discourse.

The African Union Agenda 2063 envisages a people-driven continent with women and children fully empowered under the African Charter of the Rights and Welfare of the Child. This Charter contextualizes the United Nations Convention for the Rights of Children (UNCRC) rights to the African continent by foregrounding African values that affect children. Under the Convention, governments commit to establish the right conditions for children's holistic growth and development. The Convention envisaged a 'holistic, child-centered approach' entrenched in Poverty Reduction Strategy Programs (PRSPs) (African Union Commission, 2015). Some African countries continue to operationalize the African Charter with reports indicating some success, for example, fewer children dying of preventable diseases and more children accessing education (UNICEF, 2016).

Under the motto *One people, One destiny,* the 5 countries that make up the East African Community (EAC), i.e. Kenya, Uganda, Tanzania, Rwanda and Burundi, recognizing that children form more than 50% of population in the region and face nearly similar challenges, developed the EAC Child Policy aligning to global priority interventions of the Sustainable Development Goals. The Policy also conforms to the aspirations of Article 120(c) of the Treaty Partner States and Article 39 of the Common Market Protocol to the EAC Treaty that aim at harmonizing social protection approaches to disadvantaged and marginalized groups such as children and the elderly persons.

Judging from the adoption of relevant child rights framework by many countries, Sloth-Nielsen & Mezmur (2014) argue that children's right to participate in development seems to have struck a positive code to the rights-based philosophy, the forerunner of welfarist protectionism, which viewed children as objects as opposed to subjects of human rights. The authors position such participation as tools of children empowerment to make own development-conscious choices. However, 'swift' ratification of UN Convention on the Rights of the Child has not matched action. It has been contended that with so many child rights violations, children's interests seem to be 'invisible' on many national debates. On the other hand, even with abundant rhetoric on children participation in development, the Overseas Development Institute (2009) considers children's discourse of vulnerability an excuse to disallow them from meaningful participation in development.

ROLE OF MEDIA IN CHILDREN EMPOWERMENT

As a powerful force in society, the media conveys social issues like children rights to the general public thereby influencing and persuading their opinion. Studies have found a relationship between media coverage of child rights issues and the volume of cases reported to child welfare organisations (Saint-Jacques, Turcotte & Ivers, 2012). To address the marginalisation of child rights in development discourse, Harper, Jones & McKay (2009) advocate for a cross-sectional and macro-level approach that gives a 'more sophisticated understanding of child wellbeing that looks beyond health, nutrition and education' (p.12). News media have played a key role in promoting adherence to human rights since the adoption of the Universal Declaration of Human Rights in 1948.

Through the United Nations General Assembly resolution 44/25 of November 20, 1989 on the Convention of the Rights of the Child, news media were noted as key players in not only protecting the rights of the child, but also ensuring that children have access to diverse information and material that promote their holistic wellbeing. In the context of human rights, Vlad (2017) argues that the press should go beyond pinpointing the relevance of the human rights to the audiences but also show the extent to which such rights have been abused by different stakeholders. Such revelations sometimes trigger debates which lead to change of laws and policies.

Internews (2014) adopts a theory of change belief that, in communicating the protection of child rights, media needs to be empowered to provide credible and realistic information which is widely shared in a society to gain understanding of appropriate standards for treating and protecting its children. As some researchers have argued, few issues generate as much high profile, emotionally charged news coverage and public outcry as the abuse of children. Such coverage, they argue, is key in generating public debate and sometimes jolts policy makers into taking appropriate action (Lonne & Parton, 2014).

STATEMENT OF THE PROBLEM

The 1999 Oslo Challenge considered the relationship between media and children as an "entry point into the wide and multifaceted world of children and their rights to education, freedom of expression, play, identity, health, dignity and self-respect, protection; and that in every aspect of child rights, in any element of the life of a child, the relationship between children and the media plays a role" (Onumah, 2004:65). Since news media are key in shaping the public discourse of an issue and most media audiences are active consumers of news, it is expected that what appears in the news and how it is portrayed can profoundly influence their attitudes, beliefs and behaviours (Sutherland, McCormack, Pirkis, Easteal & Holland, 2015). Researchers argue that news media coverage of children issues such as maltreatment not only affects policy, but also incites individual action especially when they realize the need to report cases of child abuse to relevant authorities (Jones, Finkelhor, and Halter (2006), and Whitehead, Chiodo, Leschied, and Dermot, 2004).

Given the efforts that East African countries have taken to put children issues on the national development agenda through the different policy frameworks, the news media in the region are uniquely positioned to investigate and report on the level of implementation of these policies across the region. According to UNICEF (2007), research is required to examine how well news media have fared in the championing the plight of children and their active involvement in protecting the interests of the African child. To fulfill their public interest responsibility, the East African media have variously promoted and advocated for the protection of the rights of children through their news reporting on different child-related issues. A glance at different news media outlets reveals that this section of the population forms a regular news item, albeit in 'victim' circumstances like child abuse, domestic violence and child labour. Unexplored is how the news media relate children rights and the children's role in development. Specifically, how the discourse of mainstreaming children in development by protecting or promoting their rights plays out in given news media is of concern. The theme of the 2018 Day of the African Child "Leave no child behind in development" aptly captures a discourse moment interrogating what different actors in the EAC member states conceive of the Day and how mainstreaming child in development issues is framed.

THEORETICAL FRAMEWORK

This study draws from the media framing theoretical framework which demonstrates how news media package and present issues in ways that influence how audiences interpret those issues, basing on how they are selected and made salient (Scheufele & Tewksbury, 2007). Since the media can influence the importance attached to an issue through their framing, FrameWorks Institute (2011) argues that analyzing children rights discourses in such a study presents important empirical measurement on how children issues are constructed and the implications of this on perceptions of children in different development contexts. Furthermore, although an issue may be interpreted differently, Jorgensen & Phillips (2002) consider the competing discourse packages as constituting a struggle between different different understandings of the issue. Nevertheless, Stubbs (1985) argues that analyzing such different discourses can show the direction of consensus or divergence on a social problem amongst the claims-makers.

This study employs the frame elements of Entman (1993) to contextualize the print media discourse of children mainstreaming in East Africa. The frame elements are: (i) problems and causes (framing the problem definition and forces creating or contributing to it) (ii) moral judgments (how the problem-causers are judged or conceptualized in the stories) and iii) solutions (how the remedies to the problem are portrayed). From the social constructionist perspective that views truth and reality as socially constructed (Amineh & Davatgari, 2015), this study analyses how the above frame elements played out in the discourse of mainstreaming children in development was framed in selected mainstream East African newspapers. The discussion of the use of the frame elements is done concurrently under each identified theme.

METHOD

This content analytic study conveniently sampled stories from 6 daily newspapers considered as dominant players in the East African mainstream media. The newspapers were: *The Daily Nation* and *The Standard* (Kenya), *The New Times* (Rwanda), *The New Vision* and *The Daily Monitor* (Uganda) and *The East African* (regional – circulated in all EAC countries). To standardize analysis, only English dailies were selected. All selected papers are national in character and enjoy wide readership and circulation in their respective countries. The web versions, through the respective newspaper websites (in the month of June 2018) and broad Google searches were used to gather the sample stories relating to the 2018 Day of the African Child. In some cases, like the *New Times* and *Daily Nation*, the researcher had access to the hard copy version of the newspapers.

Despite the digital revolution, researchers justify the use of newspapers for their news agenda setting influence drawing from their rich discourse in news genres such as editorials and opinion pieces (see Lonne & Parton, 2014). Furthermore, more expert sources are likely to feature in mainstream media than others (Vasterman & Ruigrok, 2013), as mainstream media carry deep, hard facts and rational news compared to tabloid media (Lonne & Parton, 2014). To identify the stories of interest, online searches that captured the breadth of coverage on children issues in development included terms such as '2018 Day of African Child', 'mainstreaming children in development', children rights and development' 'children policy', 'child abuse', etc. Relevant stories appearing in the whole month of June 2018 qualified for selection. This period was considered a critical 'discourse moment', during which articles on or referring to the Day of the African Child were likely to feature.

Before textual data preparation, the researcher read the selected stories twice to immerse himself in the content (as recommended by Elo & Kyngas, 2008 and Nikander,2008) and identify the themes and frames that discussed the issues surrounding the mainstreaming of children in development within East Africa. Since the child rights is a potential conflict of ideologies and practice in different countries, Scheufele & Tewksbury's (2007) frames associated with controversial situations (attributions of responsibility, conflict, economic consequences, morality and human interest) were used, where possible, to thread the discussion of the analysis:

RESULTS AND DISCUSSION

Sixteen stories were analysed. They were in the form of opinion pieces, hard news and feature stories. Table 1 shows the distribution of news stories in the selected East African newspapers.

The story distribution was as follows: *The New Times* (4 stories, i.e. 2 opinion pieces, 1 feature and 1 news piece), *The New Vision* (7 stories, i.e. 3 news pieces, 2 opinion stories and 2 feature stories), *The East African* (2 feature stories), *The Standard* (1 opinion story), *The Daily Nation* (1 feature story) and *The Daily Monitor* (1 opinion story).

The findings are discussed under themes and the related frames embedded in the themes to depict how children rights in development contexts are discussed or understood in the different stories. In the analysis, references to the stories in the

Table 1. Selected stories in the East African newspapers

Name of Newspaper	Story Title	Story Genre	Author	Date	Story Code
The East African	Child sex for a dollar on Kenya's palm-fringed beaches	Feature	Thomson Reuters Foundation	14/6/2018	EA1
	Progress on health is not good enough for Africa's children	Feature	Nathan Mulure And Magdalene Kuria	16/6/2018	EA2
The Daily Nation	Girl-child, boy-child or just a child?	Feature	Faith Mwende	26/6/2018	DN1
The Standard	Let's do more to eliminate hurdles facing Kenya's children	Opinion	Mark Oloo	16/6/2018	TS1
The New Vision	Children mark the Day of the African Child	News	Sarah Kisakye	16/6/2018	NV1
	First Lady graces the Day of the African Child celebrations	News	Sarah Kisakye	16/6/2018	NV2
	Children can aid development	Opinion	Justine Nakiwala	16/6/2018	NV3
	Children demand protection from Government	News	Ismael Kasooha	16/6/2018	NV4
	Support children with HIV to realize their potential	Opinion	Administrator	16/6/2018	NV5
	Children can equally contribute to development	Feature	Dorothy Nassolo	18/6/2018	NV6
	Millions of Ugandan children still struggling	Feature	Carol Kasujja	18/6/2018	NV7
The Daily Monitor	Protect African child from HIV	Feature	Annet Nakibuuka	17/6/2018	DM1
The New Times	Consolation Walk: Commemorating International Day of the African Child	Opinion	Moses Opobo	15/6/2018	NT1
	First Lady calls for joint efforts for children's rights welfare	News	Jean D'amour Mbonyinshuti	17/6/2018	NT2
	Day of African Child: nurturing seeds of transformation	Feature	Martine Umukunzi & Kassy Irebe	25/6/2018	NT3
	Partnering to ensuring that all Rwandan children achieve their potential	Opinion	Joseph Mudingu	26/6/2018	NT4

newspapers are indicated in codes (e.g. *EA1* is the first story of *The East African*; *EA2* is the second….; *NV3* is the third story on *The New Vision*, etc. in the chronological order in which they appeared in the respective newspapers). For all the story codes, see Table 1.

THEMES

Five key themes underpin the discourse of mainstreaming children in development issues. These themes are:

1. Commit to future of humanity
2. Socio-cultural impediments to children's participation
3. Disease as disabler of children's progress
4. Education the panacea for child empowerment
5. Collective action for children's rights adherence

Commit to Future of Humanity

Mainstreaming children in development is framed in the context of 'what stakeholders consider children to be'. In the stories analysed, children are variously framed as the key to the survival of humanity using descriptors such as ' the future', 'hope of society', 'pillar of society', 'bedrock and strength of society', 'guardians of society' 'seeds of transformation' and, 'strategic resource' for Africa.

From a human interest frame perspective, *The New Vision* constructs a world without children as 'non-existent', with children portrayed as foundation of a nation's development (NV1). This resonates well with an opinion from Rwanda's first lady, Jeannette Kagame, who frames children as 'the future and the strength of Rwanda […] with a great value'. By attributing responsibility for productivity on the children themselves, the first lady positions children's success on how they ensure 'all the efforts parents and teachers invest in taking care of you' will be productive (NT2).

By employing a human interest frame, *The East African* positions children as the 'future of mankind' and 'shoulders on which the future of states is placed' and attributes the responsibility of ensuring African children's survival on the eradication of diseases like malaria, diarrhea and pneumonia that ravage them. From a morality frame perspective, the story urges nations to be conscious of how such challenges are ruining the future of mankind and 'do what is right for our offspring […] by being genuine guardians to their dreams and ambitions' (EA1)

Children are also depicted as 'future experts'. Consider *The Daily Monitor* statement that foregrounds the economic consequences of children's survival beyond six years: '…it assures not only prosperity for the society but also make it gain extra scientists, teachers, poets, entrepreneurs…' for the economy (DM1). Given the prominent characterization of children by the different media stories, the theme of the 2018 Day of the African Child 'leaving no child behind in development' aptly captures a near-consensus of interpretation among the stories. The analysis showed an overwhelming media interpretation of the Day as an opportunity to renew efforts and obligation to ensure this 'great resource' is well mainstreamed in all development activities. By the nature of children 'holding the future' of society, commemorating the Day was considered an opportune moment to relook at efforts of realizing children rights under the Sustainable Development Goals" *(DN1)*, "remind adult stakeholders on their obligation to children as potential agents of change" (*NV2),* "continue to safeguard the sanctity of children's lives and rights…" (*NT2)* and, "focus on the severe vulnerabilities that continue to afflict Kenyan children [...] especially those with special needs" (*DN1*).

By positioning the championing of children rights as critical in development discourse, *The New Vision* depicts children as strategic partners whose issues need to be 'budgeted for' in the endeavour to include them in different development contexts. The source advocates for adequate resources 'to implement legal and policy obligations relating to children' (NV3). The importance of this Day is thus positioned in the context of what remains to be done by stakeholders to ensure children assume their rightful place in development discourse.

Scholarly debate finds concurrence with the foregoing debate of the need to empower children, as the keepers of tomorrow's society. For example, the Uganda National Children Authority (2018) positions investment in children as a win-win situation, where countries gain from children who live to their full potential and become productive citizens. Serag (2015) aligns with the UN Convention's vision of children as neither a commodity nor hapless objects of charity but human beings complete with independence and competence as members of the society. It is also argued that since 'the actions and inactions' of duty-bearers have a stronger impact on children than others, any short-sighted policy-making that relegates children to the periphery will be largely to blame for undermining the role of children (UNICEF, 2007).

Despite the greatest burden of children's development placed on the shoulders of stakeholders like parents, scholars seem to concur with the principle of the African Children's Charter that requires children to play their role by obliging them to

respect their parents, superiors and elders at all times and to assist them in case of need and […] contribute to the best of their abilities at all times and at all levels, to the promotion and achievement of African Unity (Sloth-Nielsen & Mezmur, 2014).

By emphasizing on the role of children in their own development, the discourse seems to shift to the idea of 'holistic' development which many stakeholders believe should go beyond providing the basic needs to developing the 'whole person' in line with African values (Save the Children, 2014; EAC Commission, 2016)

Socio-Cultural Impediment to Children's Participation

The role of children in safeguarding the future notwithstanding, media analysis depicts children as 'vulnerable' and victims of an unjust society, pandering to bad social and cultural values. Emphasizing children as 'Africa's most precious resource' and identifying this as strong reason to give them a voice to shape their destiny, *The Daily Monitor* portrays a regretful negative image of this powerful resource being relegated to the periphery of development thanks to poor policies and lack of political will to follow through children rights (DM1).

The children as 'vulnerable' frame finds concurrence in research which has portrayed childhood on dependency terms – that children depend on adults and therefore, are subject to their whims. Considering childhood as a developmental stage, Gordon, McAlister & Scraton (2015) paints an image of children as moving from the 'angelically pure' to the marginalized 'problematic' individual who engage in 'anti-social, irresponsible and rebellious behavior.

A source in *The New Vision* echoes this marginalization by depicting children's empowerment as largely not 'all-inclusive', with vulnerable groups like 'children living with HIV, street children, orphans, children in conflict situations, […] being peripheral players in their own development (NV7). The 'vulnerable child' frame also relates to the "mean world" media syndrome where children are defined by their vulnerability to risks emanating from all sides — starting from their parents to the larger environment, including the media (FrameWorks Institute, 2011). In the opinion of a *New Vision* source, children's vulnerability is better positioned in the level of inequality in treatment (e.g gender) and 'security' for survival (medical care, personal safety and relevant infrastructure). This 'security for survival' is exemplified with an economic consequences perspective which depicts '80% of Ugandan girls feeling unsafe in public places […] due to high incidences of rape, defilement and theft' as the powder keg that 'ruins their aspirations for sustainable and inclusive national development' (NV4)

The failure to install child protection mechanisms is positioned as the perfect manifestation of denial of children rights with grave economic impact – higher costs of capital development, wasted potential and reduced productivity. This position is echoed by a *New Times* source who attributes the responsibility of children's compromised future to a conflict between 'poverty alleviation' and 'pursuit of education' where child labour is prioritized to address immediate physiological needs at the expense of long term child empowerment through education (NT2).

The discourse of culture as a causal agent in children development is framed under the 'opportunity cost' of engaging in practices that deprive children their identity and chance to play their role in development. *The East African* views poverty as the ultimate price for early child marriages with the economic consequence of such marriages being evident in lost lifetime earnings. Furthermore, the consequences of early child marriage are framed using descriptive phrases such as 'impediment to prosperity', 'curse to future generations', bride's 'vulnerability to domestic violence' and 'health risks' to children. To exemplify the notion of early children marriages as 'multipliers of poverty', *The East African* news source depicts the marriage as not only 'stifling girls' education, health and employment but also seriously hampering the development of her children who grow into the cycle of poverty (EA1). Stopping early marriages is therefore positioned as the 'panacea' to a better standard of living for the girls, an idea which is supported by another source who states that "by ridding Africa of child marriage, we can help alleviate poverty and ensure that girls everywhere have access to a brighter future" (EA1).

In concurrence with sentiments in the media stories, the African Children's Charter posits that child marriage 'violates the cardinal principles of child rights and other rights protected under the Charter' (African Union Commission, 2015). Furthermore, the media discourse of the negative effects of child marriage finds agreement with researchers such as Anju (2011) and White (2008) who attribute the responsibility of addressing this vice to the family and the community, where norms regulating marriage are set and implemented. In particular, White (2008) considers early marriages as 'poverty multipliers' by demonstrating how the 'impoverished young adults' eventually 'bequeath' the poverty to their children creating a vicious cycle of hopelessness.

Denial of children rights is represented as a 'barrier to a fair start in life' where a *New Vision* story source employs a morality frame to suggest that though children have no say on where they are born or into what circumstances, their future depends on how the environment nurtured them during childhood (NV3). A source in *The New Vision* laments such undemocratic exclusion of children's voice in decision making as akin to unfairly denying them a platform to express themselves, thereby shutting their voices in development issues that concern them (NV1). This view draws parallel with a source in *The East African* who uses the 'denial of rights as tragedy' frame to denounce the act of some parents removing children from schools and forcibly circumcising and marrying them off, something that multiplies the hopelessness of such children (EA1). In another example depicting the frame, *The New Vision* demonstrates the 'tragedy' facing children survival by depicting Uganda as 'host to millions of children affected by conflicts [...] compounded by rising cases of child trafficking, defilement, kidnapping and murder'. The story source goes on to argue that the millions of girls in Uganda still facing serious inequalities and regular violations of their rights [...] are ultimately unable to effectively participate on the development agenda. Using an economic consequences frame, the source portrays children in conflict and emergency situations as facing compromised future work prospects and financial independence as adults (NV3). The tragedy caused by denial of children to realize their full potential is further reinforced by a source in *The New Times* who associates child labour with children's poor performance at school (NT2).

As a strategy of ensuring children participation, children need to directly participate in planning of the Days commemorating their rights and play different roles. This can be in the form of children giving speeches, submitting own petitions for consideration and having their voice on different media channels. This is in line with the principle of non-discrimination of the CRC which seeks to position children as equal participants in development, irrespective of their sex, disability, ethnicity or other grounds (African Child Policy Forum, 2015).

Unbalanced gender treatment is framed by some news stories in the context of the 'global women emancipation efforts' that seem to prioritize the girl-child at the expense of the boy-child who seems to feel threatened and 'relegated to the periphery of development'. One *Standard* newspaper source attributes responsibility for this to a 'conflict of ideology' in understanding the meaning of gender equality, with this seemingly lop-sided development of gender being blamed for the growing social deviance in the society (TS1). A news story in *The East African* uses the 2014 Kenya Demographic and Health Survey report to attribute the 'worrying statistics' of increased social deviance among boys and early deaths to perceived unfair societal discrimination (EA1). Although *The Standard* source positions this conflict as 'healthy' since both gender have different needs that should be recognized without undermining each gender, she employs a morality frame to advocate for a balanced narrative of 'non-discrimination' that treats children as just children, irrespective of gender (TS1).

News stories frame culture as a 'militant' against the fight for child mainstreaming in development activities, with duty-bearers seemingly 'standing by" as if to sanction the crimes committed against children. A story in *The East African* "Child sex for a dollar on Kenya's palm-fringed beaches" depicts child prostitution as having been 'socially accepted', 'sanitized' or 'normalized' thanks to a culture of silence involving many stakeholders:

Sometimes it's the parents telling them to go out and bring home food, sometimes the girls do it on their own - the problem is, it's highly normalized [...] everyone is benefiting in some way - the families get some money from the girls, the bars and nightclubs get customers because of the girls, the taxi drivers get something for taking the customers to the girls. This means people don't even see it as a crime.... (EA1).

A government minister is quoted in *The East African* denouncing cultures that denigrate girls (through female genital mutilation and early marriages), with the source positioning the minister as the 'much-needed power' to move words into action to tame the vice. From the perceived inaction by stakeholders, media stories depict the complacency on child prostitution as the new normal characterized by 'political opportunism' where sanctioning a crackdown on this vice is equated to 'loss of votes' among the beneficiaries of the vice (EA1). Furthermore, children have also been framed as a commodity for sale as stated by one media source: 'some parents do not want to work, hoping that they will marry us off for money' (NV1). This constructs the society as devoid of 'humanistic values' where a certain clique of people has no qualms about commoditizing the rest of the population for political ends, at the great expense of the dignity of children (EA1).

Arguments have been made against countries who deny children rights like reentry of pregnant girls to schools. For example, the Human Rights Watch (2018) castigated the Tanzanian president, John Magufuli, for stating that as long as he remained president of Tanzania, 'no pregnant students will be allowed to return to school'. The president was portrayed as not only discriminative but also 'insensitive' and running counter to the ideals of the African Charter on the Rights of the Child by tending to 'criminalize' pregnancy. Save the children (2014) contends that with persistent violations of children's rights across the world, this demonstrates the gap between the policy declarations often made by different actors and the realities of children. The author suggests that with other competing national priorities, children's concerns seem to be largely considered "soft". To stem this tide of passivity to children's issues, the African Child Policy Forum (2015) advocate for 'more actions and few words' in developing concrete measures that go beyond the mere ratification and signing of policies to action points towards realizing children's rights in development.

Disease as Disabler of Children's Progress

In the analyzed stories, the media largely portrays the burden of disease as negatively affecting children's participation in development. In Uganda, a *Daily Monitor* source paints an image of the loss of many children before their fifth birthday attributing this to 'state inertia' where the state players fail to take appropriate measures to 'save children from preventable and treatable diseases' thereby missing a golden opportunity to safeguard the country's future (DM1). In the opinion of another *Daily Monitor* source, a disease like HIV AIDS 'disturbs' children's peace in Uganda and that efforts should be prioritized to defeat this 'agitator' that has left 'more than 130,000 children in Uganda struggling [...] thus exposing them to stigma and discrimination. This 'securitization' of the HIV AIDS scourge among children is depicted in the context of having left most children with low esteem, stunted growth and 'insecure'. (DM1).

Despite representing children as 'gift to an ageing world', a *Daily Monitor* source laments the prevalence of preventable childhood diseases that militate against children's survival. The source locates the low contribution of children to Africa's development to poor healthcare – inadequate access to appropriate healthcare leading to lifelong limitations: 'the children who survive are not contributing as much as they could to Africa's development...for lack of proper access to medical care' (DM1).

To put the health situation into clearer perspective, a *New Vision* story attributes most children diseases to the 'living environment' and positions urbanization as key trigger for chronic children 'diseases like asthma due to the polluted environments in which they play' (NV3). By quoting from the Save the Children Fund's End of Childhood Index 2018 Report, the *New Vision* paints a picture of children's vulnerability where 'one in four families cannot afford to visit a health facility or buy medication for sick children' (NV3). To safeguard children's rightful roles in development, *The New Times* seems to suggest that developing human capital in children should be underpinned by 'proper nutrition' enabled through campaigns on a personal basis - 'individual households'. Employing an economic consequences frame, the story source identifies balanced diet as bearing direct impact on how poor communities can shape their socio-economic development (NT2).

Although the progress in the fight against HIV AIDS in children has been variously framed positively by different East African media, the war is considered far from won. Consider a *New Times* source who, quoting a 2010 UNAIDS report, constructs the efforts to HIV AIDS eradication as 'tremendous' and a drop of new HIV infections by 56% in Africa as 'promising'. However, the source argues that unless people are continuously empowered with the right information, the fight against HIV AIDS and other sexual reproductive issues affecting the youth will only be half-won (NT3). Aligning to this view, media analysis also shows that some news stories view 'openness' [among parents] in the fight against HIV AIDS among children as the antidote to arresting this scourge. Indeed, one *Daily Monitor* writer locates the stigma and discrimination against children living with HIV AIDS [...] to

a culture of silence where parents and caretakers are not willing to disclose their children's HIV status to the school administration to enable the children to get help (DM1).

Several media stories depict children with special needs as requiring special nurturing to position them as equal players with others, without stigma and discrimination (NV5, TS1, NT2, EA2). An example is when one *New Vision* story source employs a morality frame to depict HIV children as 'innocent' requiring to be guided to be responsible citizens. Thus discriminating such groups is viewed as travesty of justice on the innocent children (NV5).

In some stories, the fight against HIV/AIDS among children is positioned as a 'conflict' between traditional and modern beliefs of medical practice. This is exemplified by a *Daily Monitor* news source who regret how some parents administer 'crushed-up bitter pills that children often spit out' instead of the modern 'child-friendly malaria formulation that expert doctors worked hard to develop'. Using another example in the same story, such behavior is attributed to the 'old habits die hard' syndrome affecting some expectant mothers who still consult traditional birth attendants despite the risks being made clear:

we still have expectant mothers refusing to attend antenatal care in health facilities and instead go to traditional birth attendants, who lack experience in handling HIV preventive child births, antenatal and post natal care and as a result, pregnant women end up producing HIV/Aids positive babies (DM1)

The *Daily Monitor* source constructs the remedy for this behavior as 'mindset change' which should disabuse the perception of an African's poverty of the mind 'that makes us accept that children in Africa are 15 times less likely to survive beyond 6 years than children in Sweden' (DM1).The central focus on promoting special vulnerable children groups, is argued by the FrameWorks Institute (2011) as moving away from having an 'undifferentiated and homogenous' group whose individual developmental differences that may require specific attention are emasculated. This is even justified by the promise made by signatories to the Sustainable Development Goals (SDGs) that underlines a deliberate effort to 'reach out to most excluded in the society – those who are the furthest will be reached first" (Save the Children Foundation, 2018)

Education as Panacea to Children Empowerment

From a conflict frame perspective, poverty is positioned as a dilemma between the choice of 'pursuing an education and looking for basic survival needs' among most children. This view is exemplified in a story in *The Standard* titled: "Let's do more to eliminate hurdles facing Kenya's children", where the source seems to argue against the vanity of pursuing an education in an 'empty stomach' especially where children are ravaged by conflict and economic difficulties. With such odds stacked against children, the article presents an image of children in deeper vulnerability to vices such as prostitution and child labour (TS1).

Effects of poverty notwithstanding, education for child development is seen as the magic wand for putting children on positive development discourse. According to Rwanda's First Lady, Jeanette Kagame, the ideal early childhood development education is 'holistic' where learners become 'all-round' in the service of the society:

the ECD centres you have helped build, have become havens of holistic growth to thousands of Rwandan children, and have given them a chance to prepare for the world that they will one day, pioneer (NT2)

In support of the Early Childhood Development, one parent testifies that the proximity to an early childhood education centre presents 'added advantages' – it will not only improve the welfare of the child but also relieve the parent to engage in more development activities (NT2). The first lady seems to consider early childhood centers as 'avenues of investment for the children's future' by locating the development of 'open-minded and positive mind-sets' among children in such schools. She states that

[...] districts and other institutions need to include early childhood development programmes in their activity plans so as to invest in children's education (NT2).

From an economic consequences frame perspective, the *New Times* attributes more children opportunities and better productivity to the foundation given by early childhood education. This education is thus identified as a 'great social and economic equalizer' with the potential to break the cycle of poverty in a country (NT2). In the words of the Executive Director of Uganda National Children Authority (2018), Martin Kiiza, entrenching children in development is like creating a ready market for the future: "If you do not invest in young children today, you will have no business tomorrow".

A source in *The New Times* identifies the 'promotion of children's education and health' as the panacea to full realization of children's participation in development. In this story, a human interest frame is employed to depict children as 'able to drive the sustainable development of this continent' and therefore, requiring more access to quality education and healthcare to be more 'empowered and dignified' (NT3). The competitiveness of a child is viewed as a product of a 'nurtured and developed mind' attributing this to early childhood development efforts. From a moral angle, a *New Times* source portrays children educated with the right 'values and mind-set' as set for success and self-actualisation. This source seems to foreground and reinforce the role of early childhood education as 'key to jump-starting' children's progress (NT2). In support of the above arguments, empirical evidence points to the potential benefits of educating the girl child. According to a 2015 report by the Committee of Experts on the Rights and Welfare of the Child of African Union, improving girls' access to education has considerably reduced the chances of early marriages in most African countries (African Union Commission, 2015)

Children's development discourse is also framed in the context of 'building confidence to face the future'. In a feature story entitled "Day of African Child: nurturing seeds of transformation", a *New Times* source attributes dropping out of school to 'discouragement by poor performance' among some children. This story seems to depict students as lacking confidence to 'face another chance to fail' and offers a moral explanation for a project, *Twige Neza Dutsinde* (Let us study well and succeed) of Imbuto Foundation (an girl-promotion initiative of Rwanda's First Lady) which seeks to offer a 'second chance in life' to such children through remedial learning. The source considers 'children as leaders of tomorrow' only if they are equipped with the right tools, mindset and values that will help them reach their full potential (NT3). This seems to imply that children empowerment is hinged on a proper educational foundation with the right supporting environment. Consider how one *New Vision* story source conditions their continued schooling on safe learning environments:

we fear going to school and even returning home because of increased kidnaps in the country […] we demand that the Government protects us from these kidnaps if we are to get involved in the development of our country Uganda (NV4).

Collective Action for Children's Rights Adherence

In several articles, empowering children to realize their development potential is constructed as 'work-in-progress' by various sources. *The East African* represents the child development as a 'walk in the long journey' of empowering children involving many players, underlining the importance of the collective action among different stakeholders (EA2). Using the HIV AIDS among children as an example, *The Daily Monitor* positions the 'collective effort' of health professionals, faith groups, NGOs and companies as an effective way to create avenues for 'speaking up' and 'reporting cases of defilement, torture…and encouraging expectant mothers living with HIV AIDS to seek treatment so as to avoid passing on HIV to children in Africa' (DM1). Using the rational appeal of figures to show the severity of the disease problem, one *New Times* source securitizes disease by framing the process of addressing stunting among children as an 'all-out war' in which all must participate:

[…] fighting stunting among children requires everyone's efforts if the country's target to reduce stunting from the current 38 per cent to 19% by 2024 is to be achieved (NT4).

The fight against stunting is also framed in the context of the magnitude of resources required. Although appreciable progress has been made in arresting stunting, the news source depicts the problem as one whose solutions are still 'work-in-progress' and that it seems to requires concerted multi-agency effort (NT4). An economic consequences frame is invoked by a *New Times* story source who suggests that partners especially parents need to go beyond 'finding food and shelter for children' and explore ways of empowering children through candid discussions that 'direct their thoughts, using innovations like ICTS that develop their families' something that 'will help build the Rwanda and Africa we want' (NT1).

Using a human interest frame, an article in the *New Times* "First Lady calls for joint efforts for child's rights welfare" depicts the first lady as betting the country's future generation's survival on strong partnerships driven by the need to ensure that children rights are respected and vices such as child labour eliminated. This seems to imply that without concerted efforts of 'everyone' on the child rights problem, no meaningful child development will be realized. The import of children empowerment in this regard is best captured by the first lady's statement:

If a child is taken care of, it helps them in better growth and living peacefully with others as it also awakens their brains, hence preparing them to become future leaders depicting the urgency of safeguarding this group (NT2)

The news media positions partnerships in girl empowerment programs as setting a direct path towards poverty eradication, inclusive economic growth and sustainable development. According to *The New Vision*, this partnership can be located in 'unity of purpose' to break the intergenerational poverty cycle and focusing on economic independence. The story source seems to attribute the responsibility of concretizing such changes on parents who need to 'complement government efforts' by providing necessary basic materials to ensure the girls start and complete school. By roping in parents' direct participation, the source foregrounds the notion of shared responsibility where players in the child empowerment efforts 'co-own' the process and feel the obligation to contribute (NV3). In the opinion of Sloth-Nielsen & Mezmur (2014), parents, as the primary care-givers and nurturers, are positioned as the agents of direction to their children as they prepare to take up roles in society.

Some news stories suggest the need for 'innovative approaches' in addressing child development, portraying current techniques as inadequate to deliver expected results. For example, a source in *The New Vision* frames the efforts to end HIV/

AIDS by 2030 among children as requiring a rethink of strategies. Despite portraying appreciable efforts through training, provision of anti-retroviral treatment and economic capacity building, the source seems to condition an HIV/AIDS-free Uganda on the complementarity of efforts by different partners, by designing appropriate interventions that specifically address 'socio-cultural barriers' militating against the war against the disease among children (NV5). By framing the collective effort of government and society as 'very essential' in ensuring a holistic development for children, a *New Times* source seems to suggest that the efforts might falter if resources are not pooled together in a united resolve to address the plight of children. The source positions a 'strong public-private and civil society partnership' as a key driving force to achieving this goal (NT4). This echoes Rwanda's first lady's suggestion that if the ideals of the Day of the African Child and those of the World Day against Child Labour are merged, the drive towards children mainstreaming in development would be more 'holistic' when resources are pooled together (NT2).

In mainstreaming children in development matters, Vandenhole, Hammonds & Vlieghe (2008) argue for a sober debate, using the children rights as basis, on the perception of childhood and what it means to develop a standard of living that capture a child's holistic development. Such a discussion, the authors argue, would imply shifting focus on the implementation of children rights to interrogating the 'meaning of the children rights in the societal context. Furthermore, by foregrounding strong stakeholder partnerships in mainstreaming children in development, various stakeholders depict this as not only a funadamental human right but also an important ethical and moral imperative towards realizing the SDGs (Commonwealth Secretariat, 2017; International Labour Organisation, 2010; UNICEF, 2016).

CONCLUSION AND RECOMMENDATIONS

This chapter interrogated how East Africa's print media framed the 2018 Day of the African Child under the theme "Leave no child behind in development". Five key themes underpinned the media discourse on children in development: 'commit to children as future of humanity', 'socio-economic impediments to children's development', 'disease burden in children welfare', 'education as panacea to empowerment' and 'collective action for children'. From the analysis, the essence of children as key to development has been variously framed in the context of their promise and potential – as 'hope', 'future', 'strategic resource', 'guardians of the future' among other descriptors. Committing to the children's course in development is therefore positioned as the sure way of safeguarding the survival of the society. This aligns well with Commonwealth Secretariat's (2017) view that real mainstreaming ensures different social groups benefit equally from the fruits of development and in accordance with their full human potential. In the media discourse, various story sources likened the Day of the African Child to stakeholder memorialization of their obligation to uphold and follow through children rights as ratified and implemented by the different countries.

While efforts to mainstream children in development are acknowledged, there is near-consensus among story sources that more is required to fully emancipate children from being passive players in development. Particularly, *The East African*, *Daily Monitor* and *New Times* dedicate deep coverage on how African children are still subjected to mistreatment greatly delaying their development efforts (see EA1, DM1, NT3). While many East African countries have instituted relevant policies, media analysis paints an image of more words than action. The articles cite several issues that militate against the fight for children mainstreaming in development – socio-economic and cultural factors like gender discrimination (e.g TS1, DN1, EA1), political opportunism (e.g EA1), child labour and early marriages (e.g EA1, TS1) and disease burden (see EA2, NV5, DM1). While attributing children mainstreaming in the human interest frame perspective (value of developing children to the society), various story sources frame poverty, disease and lack of education as creating an 'insecure' future of children. The media also frame these socio-economic and cultural barriers to children development in economic perspectives such as 'opportunity costs' of early marriages and 'early pregnancies as 'poverty multipliers'. Children health is debated in the context of failure by the states and other actors to institute mechanisms of addresses otherwise preventable diseases. The media and other players in this discourse argue for concerted efforts in addressing the multiple effects of lack of access to proper medical care and education on the development of children rights. Education and appropriate healthcare are particularly foregrounded as the panacea to realizing the full potential of children (see TS1, NT4, EA2)

In tandem with Serag's (2015) argument that the media are able to demonstrate the successes and failures of a country's efforts though their coverage, this study uncovers a consensus of opinions on the framing of children mainstreaming in development in East African context. Children rights issues discussed in the media text tend to converge with various reports by bodies like Human Rights Watch (2018), African Union Commission (2015) and Save the Children (2014) in confirming the fight for children rights in development in East Africa as far from won.

By using frame analysis to explore how media portrayed 'children in development', findings are in line with previous studies (e.g. Gordon, McAlister & Scraton 2015; Vlad, 2017) that foreground children's rights as threatened and requiring collective action to protect. The themes identified depict a region that is struggling to fulfill its obligation to mainstream children in development. Future research could broaden the focus and target regions like the Scandinavian where research has consistently positioned children rights as being scrupulously observed and defended. How media in such countries represent 'children in development' would define how the various instruments protecting the rights of the child are understood.

REFERENCES

African Child Policy Forum. (2015). *Implementing child rights in Tanzania: What is working well, what is not? Background paper to the African report on child well being*. Addis Ababa, Ethiopia: ACPF.

African Union Commission. (2015) Concept note on the DAC 2015. Addis Ababa, Ethiopia: The African Committee of Experts on the Rights and Welfare of the Child (ACERWC).

Altheide, D. L., & Schneider, C. J. (2013). *Qualitative media analysis* (2nd ed.). Thousand Oaks, CA: SAGE Publications. doi:10.4135/9781452270043

Amineh, R. J., & Davatgari, H. A. (2015). Review of Constructivism and Social Constructivism. *Journal of Social Sciences. Literature and Languages*, *1*(1), 9–16.

Anju, M. (2011). Solutions to end child marriage: what the evidence shows. International Center for Research on Women, 11.

East African Commission. (2016). *EAC child policy*. Arusha, Tanzania: EAC secretariat.

Elo, S., & Kyngas, H. (2008). The qualitative content analysis process. *Journal of Advanced Nursing*, *62*(1), 107–115. doi:10.1111/j.1365-2648.2007.04569.x PMID:18352969

Entman, R. M. (1993). Framing: Toward Clarification of a Fractured Paradigm. *Journal of Communication*, *43*(4), 51–58. doi:10.1111/j.1460-2466.1993.tb01304.x

Foster, E., & Bochner, A. P. (2008) Social constructionist perspectives in communication research. Handbook of constructionist research, 85-106.

FrameWorks Institute (2011). *Framing Early Childhood Development in a Global context: An Analysis of Children's Issues in International News Media*. A FrameWorks Research Report.

Gordon, F., McAlister, S., & Scraton, P. (2015). *Behind the headlines: Media representation of children and young people in Northern Ireland. Summary of research Findings*. Belfast, UK: Queen's University.

Harper, C., Jones, N., & McKay, A. (2009, Sep.). *Including Children in Policy Responses to economic Crises: Lessons from the Past and Policies for a Sustainable Future*. ODI and UNICEF Synthesis Conference Paper.

International Labour Organisation. (2010). *Mainstreaming child labour issues in key development policies and programmes in Sri Lanka. Report of a Preliminary Review*. Colombo, Sri Lanka: ILO.

Internews. (2014) *Protecting the rights Of children: the role of the media Lessons from Brazil, India and Kenya.* Internews Europe.

Jones, L. M., Finkelhor, D., & Halter, S. (2006). Child maltreatment trends in the 1990s: Why does neglect differ from sexual and physical abuse? *Medline*, *11*(2), 107–120. PMID:16595845

Jørgensen, M., & Phillips, L. (2002). *Discourse analysis as theory and method.* London: Sage. doi:10.4135/9781849208871

Lonne, B., & Parton, N. (2014). Portrayals of child abuse scandals in the media in Australia and England: Impacts on practice, policy, and systems. *Child Abuse & Neglect*, *38*(5), 822–836. doi:10.1016/j.chiabu.2014.04.020 PMID:24942126

National Children Authority (Uganda). (2018). Day of the African Child. *Souvenir Magazine.*

Nikander, P. (2008). Working with Transcripts and Translated Data. *Qualitative Research in Psychology*, *5*(3), 225–231. doi:10.1080/14780880802314346

Olowu, D. (2002). Protecting children's rights in Africa: A critique of the African charter on the Rights andWelfare of the Child. *International Journal of Children's Rights*, *10*(2), 127–136. doi:10.1163/157181802401005403

Onumah, D. (2004). Media literacy and the Nigerian child. *The Guardian,* 65.

Overseas Development Institute. (2009). *Raising the game: mainstreaming children's rights.* Briefing paper, 56.

Saint-Jacques, M. C., Villeneuve, P., Turcotte, D., Drapeau, S., & Ivers, H. (2012). The role of media in reporting child abuse. *Journal of Social Service Research*, *38*(2), 292–304. doi:10.1080/01488376.2011.627232

Save the Children. (2014). Universal Periodic Review: Successful examples of child rights advocacy. *Child Rights Governance Global Initiative.* Save the Children.

Scheufele, D. A., & Tewksbury, D. H. (2007). Framing, agenda setting, and priming: The evolution of three media effects models. *Journal of Communication*, *57*(1), 9–20.

Secretariat, C. (2017). *Youth Mainstreaming in Development Planning: Transforming Young Lives*. Loughborough, UK: Commonwealth.

Serag, E. M. (2015). *The Coverage of Children's Issues in Egyptian Newspapers* (Unpublished MA Thesis). American University in Cairo, Egypt.

Sloth-Nielsen, J., & Mezmur, B. (2014). A dutiful child: The implications of Article number 31 of the African Children's Charter. *Journal of African Law*.

Stubbs, M. (1985). Discourse Analysis: The Sociolinguistic Analysis of Natural language. *Language*, *61*(2).

Sutherland, G., McCormack, A., Pirkis, J., Eastal, P., Holland, K., & Vaughan, C. (2015). *Landscapes: Media representations of violence against women and their children: State of knowledge paper. Landscapes, No. 15*. ANROWS.

United Nations Children Fund (UNICEF). (2016). *The State of the World's Children*. UNICEF.

United Nations Children's Fund (UNICEF). (2007). *Children's rights and journalism practice: a rights - based perspective*. Dublin Institute of Technology.

Vandenhole, W., Hammonds, R., & Vlieghe, K. (Eds.). (2008). Children's rights in a globalized world: From Principles to Practice (comprehensive report). International Interdisciplinary Course.

Vasterman, K., & Ruigrok, C. (2013). Pandemic Alarm in the Dutch Media: Media coverage of the 2009 Influenza A (H1N1) Pandemic and the Role of the Expert sources. *European Journal of Communication*, *28*(4), 436–453. doi:10.1177/0267323113486235

Vlad, D. (2017) Perspectives on media representation of children. *Social Sciences and Education Research Review*, *4*(1), 114-124.

Watch, H. R. (2018). *World Report 2018*. Washington, DC: HRW.

Weatherred, J. L. (2015). Child sexual abuse and the media: A literature review. *Journal of Child Sexual Abuse*, *24*(1), 16–34. doi:10.1080/10538712.2015.976302 PMID:25635896

White, P. (2008). *Representations of children in a monopoly print medium* (Unpublished Doctoral dissertation). University of Western Australia, Perth, Australia.

Whitehead, P. C., Chiodo, D. G., Leschied, A. W., & Dermot, H. (2004). Referrals and admissions to the children's aid society: A test of four hypotheses. *Child and Youth Care Forum*, *33*(6), 425–440. doi:10.100710566-004-5265-7

ADDITIONAL READING

The Institute for the African Child. (2018). *Childhood in Africa: An Interdisciplinary Journal*. Ohio University.

KEY TERMS AND DEFINITIONS

Children's Rights: The freedoms and entitlements of children in a society.

Content Analysis: A research method that aids in discovering certain attributes of a story text like themes.

Convention: An agreement between states on expected ways of behaving or treating an issue affecting the society.

Duty Bearer: Actors obliged to advocate, promote, defend, and realize a specific duty to the society.

Framing: The essence of a news story as relates to values or angles used in telling it.

Human Interest: Depicting a feeling or experience with which people can relate their own lives.

Mainstreaming: Integrating an issue on the agenda to become part and parcel of life of an entity.

News Source: The person or organization to whom a quote or paraphrase in a news story is attributed.

Theme: The central or main idea or essence in a text, like a story.

Chapter 7
Media and Child Rights in Africa:
Narrative Analysis of Child Rights in Kenyan Media

Ukaiko A. Bitrus-Ojiambo
St. Paul's University, Kenya

Muthoni E. King'ori
Daystar University, Kenya

ABSTRACT

This chapter describes Kenyan media narratives and portrayals of children and their rights. The chapter examines how Kenyan media frame child rights stories. Through qualitative content analysis of child stories in selected Kenyan media platforms, the authors interrogated what these narratives tell us about how children and their rights are viewed and the implications of the media frames used. Findings showed that child rights stories are yet to receive the comprehensive coverage needed. The findings further indicated that Kenyan media framed the child in stereotypical and patriarchal ways with the voice of the child most times left out. In addition, many of the stories analysed were found to lack depth, context, and link to child rights. Some of the challenges that hamper effective media coverage include inadequate training on child rights reporting, lack of media desks tackling children stories, and insufficient knowledge on child rights.

DOI: 10.4018/978-1-7998-0329-4.ch007

INTRODUCTION

Global social structures have undergone fundamental changes. African countries have also been affected, willingly and / or unwilling, by global trends and treaties at various junctures in history. The global snapshot by mid-1970s is that 39 countries or a quarter of the world's independent countries were democratic compared to two decades later when 66 percent had momentous societal transformations (Schwartzman, 1998, p. 159). The African media industry's evolution took another turn in the 1990s and continues till the present time. At that time, many African state-controlled media were partially privatized, allowing for pluralization, or diversity of entrants and voices in the mediascape (Barber, 2009, p. 15; Ugangu, 2012). Those with access to media were still among the few; media owners were Western conglomerates or the minor urban elites (Goretti, 2009). These changes, particularly, liberalization, commercialization, democratization, and globalization, brought about structural shifts in media access, use, and depictions.

Children's rights, being human rights, are concerned with the prescribed ways that children are perceived by members of society, how those members relate with them, and protect them. Frames demonstrate the powerful role of media in shaping how audiences expect to see or hear an issue to make sense of it (Baran & Davis, 2009; King'ori & Bitrus-Ojiambo, 2016). Media is a socio-cultural institution that provides a social function for society (Collins, 1985). The stories produced influence society through frames or paradigms that reach the audience who consume this content as 'truth' due to the credibility of institutional authority (Lull, 2000). Such standardized presentations shape one's views of a group, phenomenon or issue. The media provides a lens or mirror from which members of society can examine their cultural participation, worldview, and lives through narratives or stories.

As a democratic tool, media is assumed to live up to the ideals of giving citizens opportunities through information, representation, and participation (Jensen, 2002b; Foley, Hayes, & O'Neill (2012). It is argued, in this chapter, that although Kenyan media cover stories about children along a variety of topics, the quality of the reports are wanting (Internews Europe, 2014). Writing styles, time and space constraints, and lack of sense of duty limit media practice and hence forces a likely narrative structure in this mediascape. It is argued that media practitioners are driven by commercial interest, first and foremost, and that the media does not live up to its role and duty in providing a platform for children's issues and rights to be understood within a rights framework.

Assumptions about media and media practice are that they present free and fair, objective information and tell society the 'truth'. Media are a powerful democratic tool that can both articulate and / or mute perspectives, voices, and groups. In as much as they can be used for development, democracy, and nation building, the media can be used to sustain authoritarianism, to exploit and to exclude (Zaleza, 2009, p. 19).

Views about children are shaped by media through the stories that are told about them, the language that is used about them, and the images that are presented of them. Media narratives are not neutral, and are framed in certain ways, regardless of the intent. Media literacy needs to be addressed to not only include media use, but critical analysis of frames that are inherent in storytelling, political and ownership affiliations and positions of media owners, and distinct roles of media in society.

Chapter Objectives

The objectives of this chapter are:

1. To examine how Kenyan media covered child rights stories between January and March 2019.
2. To analyse the media frames used in the child rights stories covered by the Kenyan media between January and March 2019.
3. To explore the implications of the media frames used in the child rights stories analysed.

BACKGROUND

In the Kenyan context, a child is someone below the age of 18 (Children Act, 2001). The Kenyan Constitution 2010 explicitly addresses rights of children as: free and compulsory basic education; basic nutrition, shelter and health care; protection from abuse, neglect, harmful cultural practices and other forms of violence; and parental care and protection.

Other Kenyan laws that protect children are the Sexual Offences Act, 2006, Prohibition of Female Genital Mutilation Act, 2011 and the Children Act of 2001. In addition to these laws, the Code of Conduct for the Practice of Journalism in Kenya which is part of the Media Council Act of 2013 explains how journalists should cover children issues. Article 19 of the code of conduct cautions journalists against identifying children when covering sexual offences cases. Journalists are also cautioned against interviewing or photographing children without consent of parents or guardians.

In addition to various laws enacted to protect children, the Kenya Children National Assembly was launched in 2012. The children's parliament is "expected to engage children on matters affecting them" (Mutembei, 2012). The first president of the Children's parliament, Janet Mkandoe promised to tackle "critical issues affecting children such as child labor and the right to education and especially girl child education" (Mutembei, 2012). Although there has been this great move towards giving children a voice within the democratic space, this children's parliament is not linked to, and operates separately from the Parliament of Kenya (Save the Children.net, 2014).

KENYAN MEDIASCAPE

The Kenyan mediascape is diverse and robust, including traditional and new media technology and platforms. Traditional media existed before the colonial era, through oral literacy and live performances. Mass media structures, namely radio and TV, developed and moved live performances onto those platforms (Barber, 2009). In post-independence Kenya, the main media station was Kenya Broadcasting Corporation (KBC) which produced content that broadcast on radio and TV. Over five decades later, the picture is very different, with a liberalized, commercialized, and democratized mediascape (Ugangu, 2012; Zaleza, 2009).

Media liberalization means non state-owned media were licensed to practice in Kenya; alluding to a 'free and fair' media (Foley, Hayes, & O'Neill, 2012). Globalization has given humans a chance to see a diffusion of practices and an increase in globalized consciousness (Ritzer, 2004). In terms of relations, people now have shorter, faster, and direct means of communication accelerated by technology, changing the way the local-global relate (Goretti, 2009). This has been evident during several social movements of our times, such as, the Arab Spring, Black Lives Matter, and Pakistani child activist for girl's education, Malala Yousafzai, now a Nobel laureate.

During the period of study, three notable narratives were visible in both local and international mediascapes. First, in mid-January, the national focus, hence front-page agenda, was on the terror attacks at the Nairobi DusitD2 hotel at Riverside Drive. Few stories about children made it to the front pages. Second, in February was the Catholic church's visible and vocal denouncement of child sexual offenses, being vocalized during a Vatican conference. Third, was the recurrent coverage of high-profile American musician, R. Kelly, accused of abuse by many women who were in sexual relationships with him, as minors. These three stories provide a socio-political context from which the stories reviewed in this chapter are positioned.

Lastly, it may be pertinent to mention here that, the newspapers assessed have children's magazines, whose stories and sometimes authors are children, 'for children, by children.' The scope of this research was to assess the *metanarratives* framed and perpetuated by mainstream media (sources being adults) and the audience members being those who control society and make decisions on behalf of different social groups, including children, at the policy level.

Theoretical Framework

This study was based on two theories: narrative and media framing. Narrative theory, developed out of linguistics and semiotics and provides a taxonomic and descriptive, not interpretive frame (Herman, 2008). Media framing is the process of media content production, packaging, and presentation. Frames can include or edit out as much of what a storyteller wishes an audience to pay attention to (de Vreese, 2005; Carter, 2013; McQuail, 2005). Use of frames means that readers or audiences only receive an angle that the storyteller decides *should be* told. Frames present a particular view of a topic to the reader, society, and the world (Carter, 2013; King'ori & Bitrus-Ojiambo, 2016). It is like a mold that places boundaries around a narrative. Thus, media frames shape the manner in which society views children, their rights, and how they should be treated.

Connected to media narrative reporting style and framing theory is critical theory. This theory provides the angle of social power structures, based on critiquing taken-for-granted systems, and asking 'whose interests are being served by power' including oppressive structures (Collins, 1985). The influence of power structures can be either positive/negative latent or manifest. The issue with media mainstreaming is that it allows the voice of those in power to be the dominant one. Language is thus seen to be a powerful means of maintaining and reinforcing dominance in society because it carries the ideologies of those who are in control of material means to produce that content (Littlejohn & Foss, 2004; Collins, 1985; Lemert, 1999). This means of production is implicit, demonstrating the negative latent function of media content (Collins, 1985).

Though implicit, the commercial interests of media influence how journalists frame issues (Sharanappa, 2018). The media text itself takes many forms, including text, images, and audio bites. Furthermore, agenda setting and cultivation effects, as part of the gatekeeping production processes (Tuchman, 2002), describe the very act of bringing to the public, an agenda or issue that one has framed or selected. The media select the story, *how* to tell it, *when* to tell, and *for how long*. The media profession itself, through news writing methods, standardizes how occurrences are recounted. One method, via the inverted pyramid begins with key details and ends with less important content.

Legal narratives and reporting structure are important to this discussion. The frame of the legal narrative is based on retelling; based on who is listened to, and shaped by the context in which it is heard. This is similar to Giddens' reflexivity, or technical integration where humans (re)interpret / renegotiate their thoughts and actions discursively (Jensen, 2002, p. 2; Lull, 2000). Explicit narrative structures are found in cases of rape, which pre-eminently offer competing stories with dramatically different outcomes and interpretations (Brooks, 2008, p. 417). Due to the 'narrative glue' or the way the incidents and events are made to combine in a meaningful story, the outcome is called "consensual sex" or "rape,' and is based on the judge's view of standard behavior (or recasting of the story) (Brooks, 2008, p. 417).

Verbal and nonverbal frames can be used to reframe the story of children, their rights, and the gaps to reaching those rights (Brooks, 2008; Gee, 2011; Jandt, 2007; King'ori & Bitrus-Ojiambo, 2016). Shortfalls in language used, content and context presentation, and incomplete retelling dehumanizes children and does not advocate for their rights.

Scholarship on Media Stories About Children

Scholars around the globe have highlighted the role of media in creating awareness about children's rights. In Ghana it was found that although newspaper stories raised awareness about the plight of children in society, low coverage was seen to be problematic and akin to deliberately keeping children issues from public discourse (Asare-Donkoh, 2017). Similarly, in Singapore, media covered topics on children related to health, education, and protection. However, Singaporean media downplayed the "capabilities and competencies of the child" in their portrayals (Warrier & Ebbeck, 2014, p. 145). In South Africa, children were portrayed negatively, stereotypically, and sensationally, as victims (Foley, Hayes, & O'Neill, 2012). In the US and UK, it was found that 1990s media caused a moral panic through coverage of children's internet access (Facer, 2012). Media depicted parents as people with little knowledge of a space their children could easily access and operate (a dangerous place with predators and perverts).

Some studies on media coverage of children found gaps in practice. Wanguba (2011) analyzed two major newspapers in Kenya; findings revealed that the newspapers showed negligence in their coverage of child rights, particularly related to privacy. Two studies compared the *Daily Nation* and *The Standard* newspapers' coverage of children; both found that prominence was not given to children issues (Kahiu, 2015; Ortum, 2013). This was the case, despite it being October, the month when the international day of the girl child is celebrated (Ortum, 2013). In South Africa, media narratives about children were found to be under-represented (Foley, Hayes, & O'Neill, 2012).

Internews Europe studied the role of the media in protecting children's rights in Brazil, India and Kenya. Findings showed five major issues that hamper media from playing its role as a protector of child rights (Internews Europe, 2014), including: widespread attitude that undermined children and youth in the three countries, thereby denying the two groups a voice in the public discourse on children/youth matters; a general lack of media coverage about child rights; failure by media in the three countries to recognize child rights issues as a key area in media reporting; mistrust between media and child rights activists; and lack of guidelines on ethical reporting of child rights issues.

METHODOLOGY

The authors used qualitative content analysis (Priest, 2010) to examine child rights frames used by Kenyan media between January and March, 2019. The authors looked at child rights stories published by Kenya's two leading papers, the *Daily Nation* and *The Standard* newspapers. In addition, the authors analyzed child rights stories published on online platforms of Kenyan media. Purposive sampling was used to select four trending news stories on child rights. The authors examined how the four stories were covered by websites of different Kenyan media houses. The analysis of the stories on the websites was included so as to provide a broader perspective on the child rights frames used by Kenyan media. In addition, the authors conducted an in-depth interview with an editor from a local TV station to explore the strategies media houses use when reporting child rights stories.

Analysis of Child Rights Stories Covered on Kenyan Online Media Platforms

1. Hijab Story

One of the stories the researchers analyzed was a story discussing a ruling by the Supreme Court on whether schools can determine whether Muslim girls should wear hijab as part of their uniform. What was the genesis of the hijab issue? The matter arose in Isiolo in 2014 when county officials gave a directive asking that Muslim girls in one of the secondary schools there be allowed to wear religious attire (hijab and trousers) as part of the uniform (Methodist Church in Kenya vs Mohamed Fugicha & 3 others, 2016). The Methodist Church, a sponsor of the secondary school in question, filed a case in the high court challenging the directive arguing it was discriminatory and elevated Islam above other religions. A ruling by the high court in 2015 reversed the directive terming it "discriminatory, unlawful, unconstitutional and contrary to the rules and regulations of the school" (Methodist Church in Kenya vs Mohamed Fugicha & 3 others, 2016). Mohamed Fugicha, a father of three girls attending the school contested the high court ruling (Methodist Church in Kenya vs Mohamed Fugicha & 3 others, 2016). He won the appeal in 2016, a move that saw the Methodist Church move to the Supreme Court of Kenya.

In court, the Methodist Church had argued the school did not act in a discriminatory manner against the Muslim girls as parents and students had signed a dress-code policy (Methodist Church in Kenya vs Mohamed Fugicha & 3 others, 2016). The Supreme Court of Kenya set aside the Court of Appeal ruling on a technicality - the lower courts had ruled on matters that had not been properly filed, thereby denying the church an opportunity to be heard (Methodist Church in Kenya vs Mohamed Fugicha & 3 others, 2016). In the ruling, the Supreme Court noted the matter "is an important national issue, that will provide a jurisprudential moment" that needs to be determined "in the future" (Methodist Church in Kenya vs Mohamed Fugicha & 3 others, 2016).

- **How did news websites cover the story?** The headlines were varied: "Opinions differ in hijab ruling as lawmakers vow action" (*Daily Nation* website); "No hijabs in school: Supreme court overturns appeal decision" (K24 TV website); "Blow for Muslim students as Supreme Court overturns rulings on hijabs" (Citizen Digital). Supreme Court ruling on hijab will predispose students to al-Shabaab recruitment - Muslim leaders" (Tuko news). The sources quoted in the stories included Muslim clerics and lawyers and legislators; none quoted education experts. Only one story from *the Star* Newspaper (an opinion piece from a lawyer), explained that the court had ruled on a technical matter and not on the constitutionality of allowing hijabs in schools. Lastly, the stories analyzed gave one view, as the reporters relied on quotes and sound bites from Muslims and failed to get the other side of the story - that of the Methodist Church.
- **Framing:** The framing of the story appeared to be that the Supreme Court had banned the wearing of the hijab in schools, thereby infringing on the rights of Muslim students. The wording of the headlines was sensational with reporters veering away from the original issue which was school policy on dress code. Thus, the frame took a religious tone, with various media websites reporting on the repercussions that the ruling was likely to have on Muslim-Christian relations. Similar to the studies analyzed in the literature review, the hijab stories did not give a voice to the child. The child's voice was drowned in the religious war of words that was waged in the media reports. The reports did not examine the views of child rights advocates in the matter.

2. Rastafarian Story

Another article that was covered widely by Kenyan media was a story about a girl who reported for her first year in high school but was turned away because of her dreadlocked hair. The *Standard Digital* and the *Nairobi News* websites reported the story in a similar way. The *Standard Digital* reported that the girl wore her dreadlocks in a turban, a style attributed to followers of the Rastafarian faith, was sent away by the Deputy Principal who told her that only Muslim students were allowed to cover their heads (Ogila, 2019). According to the girl's father, when she sought admission to the school, the girl had indicated that she identified with the Rastafarian religion (Ogila, 2019).

- **How did they tell the story?** *Standard Digital* story revealed the identity of the student. The story quoted the girl telling of her excitement at joining high school, and her distress when she was ordered to either remove the turban and cut the dreadlocks or go home. The sources of the story by the *Nairobi News*, an online paper that is owned by one of the top Kenyan media houses, Nation Media Group, were the girl, the mother and the father. The father's argument was that his daughter should not be denied education because of her Rastafarian faith (Kimuyu, 2019).

Kenyans.co.ke, a blog reported a decision made by the Education Cabinet Secretary directing the school to allow the girl to continue with her studies. The cabinet secretary argued that there was a court ruling declaring that no child should be denied education on account of religion. The story also quoted a former presidential candidate who said it was wrong for schools to discriminate the girl on basis of her Rastafarian faith, yet students of other religions were allowed to study while donning their religious attire.

Citizen Digital and *the Star* covered the court ruling that ordered the school to allow the girl back for studies. *The Star* which has a tendency to report in a sensational style, had a headline that read: "Rasta girl back to class as dreadlock ban overturned. " Citizen Digital's headline was: "Court orders school to allow Rastafarian girl to resume studies." *The Star* story included details of the testimony of the girl's father, while the *Citizen Digital* simply reported on the orders granted by the court.

- **Framing**: The girl, her family, and even her faith are framed as underdogs. The girl and the Rastafarian community were portrayed as oppressed and as people denied equal rights when compared to followers of other religions. The fact that the girl's family came from Kibra, an area where a big segment of Kenya's poor live, helped to subtly frame the narrative of the oppression of the downtrodden. The Rastafarian story had various themes which included education, religion and constitutional rights. The framing of the story depicted the girl as a victim whose constitutional rights were violated by the education system.

3. Court Ruling Suggesting a Revision of Age of Sexual Consent

In March 2019, one of the big media stories on child rights was based on a court ruling suggesting that the age of sexual consent be revised downwards from 18 to 16. Some of the articles praised the ruling, while others opposed the court's argument. The ruling arose from an appeal lodged by a man who had been sentenced to 15 years by a magistrate's court for impregnating an alleged 17-year-old (Wambui vs Republic, 2019). He had been charged with defilement and convicted under the Sexual Offences Act, 2006 (Wambui vs Republic, 2019). However, in his second appeal at the Court of Appeal, the man argued that the prosecution did not prove that the girl was under 18 and that he was only arrested after he failed to raise money that the girl's parents had demanded from him as compensation for impregnating their daughter (Wambui vs Republic, 2019). In their ruling, three judges of the Court of Appeal said:

Our prisons are teeming with young men serving lengthy sentences for having had sexual intercourse with adolescent girls whose consent has been held to be immaterial because they were under 18 years. The wisdom and justice of this unfolding tragedy calls for serious interrogation. (Wambui vs Republic, 2019).

- **How did they tell the story?** A *Citizen Digital* story said teachers, parents, child rights advocates and other authority figures were apprehensive about the repercussions of lowering the sexual consent age. The article further stated that this "could expose girls to the difficulties associated with pregnancies, motherhood and early marriage" (Muigai, 2019). The *Standard Digital* had a story explaining why the court proposed a revision to the law. According to the *Standard Digital* story the court's concern was "lengthy jail terms imposed on young men convicted of defilement" (Muthoni, 2019). A story by Kenya's national broadcaster, *KBC Channel 1* that was posted on YouTube told of Kenyans anger at the proposal by the judges. The *KBC* story had a sound bite of a member of parliament who opposed the court's argument. Although the heading of the story was "Kenyans condemn the ruling that seeks to lower the age of sexual consent", the report had only one sound bite (of a politician) condemning the proposal. The *Daily Nation* told of divided opinion among Kenyans (Nation Team, 2019). The story quoted health experts, a politician, parents, church leaders and a child rights activist. The health experts said the main concern should be sex education, not lowering the age of sexual consent. Church leaders were quoted as strongly opposing the proposal saying it would expose girls to early marriages and sexual abuse. The activist opposed the proposal but the politician supported it arguing that Kenyans were afraid of discussing a sensitive issue.

Among the articles analyzed, only one story; that from *the Star* had quotes from minors, the people who would essentially be affected if the proposal is implemented. The story quoted teenage girls and a number of mothers who were married off at an early age. The teens who were from poor backgrounds were worried that greedy relatives would take advantage of the law to marry off young girls. One of the teens interviewed felt the court should have talked to children before making such a proposal. A gynaecologist argued that at 16, girls' bodies are still not fully developed to handle the risks of pregnancies.

- **Framing**: Sexual consent stories were framed from the girl-child point of view. The stories that were analyzed hardly mentioned the boy. The articles ignored the fact that boys also suffer sexual abuse. The girl was framed as a victim whose rights would be jeopardized if the age of sexual consent was lowered. The stories argued that girls were likely to get early pregnancies, be sexually abused by pedophiles, or be married off at an early age. Other stories framed the proposal as a moral issue, which if allowed, would go against African values.

4. American Missionaries Accused of Sexually Abusing Orphans

Another big story touching on child rights is a report about an American couple accused of defiling orphans in Bomet County, Rift Valley, Kenya. A 38-minute feature story posted by *NTV* on YouTube was titled *#Preying Missionaries.* The report told of sexual abuse that allegedly happened at a Children's Home established by an American man, Gregory Dow and his wife, Mary Rose. Dow is alleged to have sexually molested girls at the home and engaged in cruelty that led to the deaths of three children. When Kenyan authorities issued an arrest warrant in 2017, Dow fled to the United States. His wife was arrested but later jumped bail. International news reports claimed that Dow is a convicted sex offender who served time in an American jail before he came to Kenya.

- **How was the story told?** The *NTV* story relied on various sources: the girls (their faces were concealed), a number of people who had worked at the orphanage, some relatives of the children who had stayed at the home and government officials. According to the story, Mary Rose took the girls to a health clinic where they were forcefully put on birth control. The girls also narrated in length the sexual abuse they suffered at the hands of Dow.

- **Framing:** The story framed the children as vulnerable and poor, and the couple as arrogant and cruel. The couple is framed as two people who took advantage of the remoteness of the village, their privileged background as white missionaries from America and the lethargy of government officials. The interviews with the children give the minors a voice to talk about what they went through. One interview with a health official portrays the lethargy shown by people who should protect children.

Content Analysis of News Stories on Child Rights Covered by the Daily Nation and The Standard Newspapers

The two newspapers had stories that touched on children's lives, well-being, and protection. Stories on health and safety showed the stringent environments in which children live: murders and threat of suicide and death, bandit attacks, assault to their body, family killed over witchcraft (children also), displacement/homelessness/ dormitory raising, exposure to and use of drugs, trafficking, defilement (girls) and sodomy (boys); while stories on education showed hurdles in transitions from one level of school to another, funding barriers, lack of infrastructure in schools, new curriculum debate, marks in top school being cancelled, and use of tablets in schools. Ten positive stories were covered, in all the sampled papers.

1. Daily Nation

The reporting style within the DN was varied. Stories to do with education were written with a historical framework, with names of decision makers and their statements being quoted, and policies (statements that reflect upon or present them). Stories that mentioned minors (particularly sexual offenses) used either a summary lead or shotgun lead. Court-stories referred to individuals by the use of initials, "MO" to conceal the identity of the minor. Where the minor died, by suicide or by another, the reporter did not mention the name of the minor. However, some positive features, such at the Weekend Saturday Nation, February 23, 2019 "13-year-old girl steals the show in African Writing competition" mentions Salem Teshome, an author, by her names. Similarly, the story of the "Boy, 2, with rare ability to read" on DN Sunday February 24, front page, finds the boy is named, so are his parents, his age, and the name of estate where they live. Similarly, in the story of the family of 6 who got a home from the President; the names and ages of the family members, adults and children are listed. (Brooks, 2008; Crewe, 2010)

The other distinct frames used in the DN newspaper is the manner in which pictures are presented. Images were not consistently captioned; neither was there consistency found in credits to the photojournalist. In some cases, the photojournalist is named, in other cases, "File | Nation" is used, in other neither is used. The health-related pictographs, included statistics and facts, steps to guide the interpretation of the data, and included expert sources, for example, on Saturday, February 23, 2019, Special Report, "Rate of C-section births alarms experts" is accompanied by a pictograph which is attributed to joint sources: Lancet series, MOH, WHO, and KNBS, the compiler, and graphic designer.

2. The Standard

The reporting style in TS typically followed a hidden lead, or historical style (Fang, 1991). The headlines presented the general outcome of the story, for example, "Couple won't be paid Sh4.3m for unplanned baby," of TS, Saturday, February 23, 2019. In the same story, initials AAAA are used to refer to the mother, the father is not named. This differed for the story in the Sunday TS, February 24, 2019, "Burden of childlessness; from weird treatments to baby theft, couples tell it all" (front page, pp., 2, 4-5), where the story names the professionals and gives their titles. The other adults are also named. The title, presented the daunting outlook for childless couples.

Stories were accompanied by images. The images covered were predominantly accompanying stories on safety and health (broadly), education, and sexual offenses (1). However, there was found to be lack of consistency in the manner in with the images were presented. Sometimes they were captioned and credited (name of photojournalist of "File", sometimes these elements were lacking).

The language of the media narratives needs to be discussed briefly. In one story (The Standard, crazymonday, of Monday, January 21, 2019, p. 9), the offender is an adult male, described in the headline, as "Boy, 24, imprisoned for life over sex with minor, 7." In the second story, on the same page, a headline reads, "Life imprisonment for dad, 50, who defiled his daughter, 9, infected her with HIV." In the latter story, the confidential health status of the minor is presented in the headline. This narrative structure follows Brooks (2008) views of how the legal narrative structure works to retell thus bound, and in so doing, omits information. Upon closer investigation, one may find gaps in story.

Narrative Frames for Reporting on Financially Needy Students

Particular frames were used in telling the stories of the students with financial needs, although the stories themselves varied, reflecting each individual's reality (Crewe, 2010). The titles themselves present the narrative glue, "Needy, bright students stranded over school fees" in TS, Monday January 21, 2019, p. 3 Crazy Monday feature. The three stories of financially needy students are presented in this way: names of the students, school attended, ages, marks achieved, and a brief description of their home situation. The name and phone number of a guardian is given (one an older brother; the writer; and lastly, the minor's mother). The phone line "will receive monies" is indicated. It is important to note that the full names of the students and their marks are published in each story.

Narrative Frame for Sexual Offenses Reporting in Both Newspapers

Although both DN and TS covered stories on sexual offenses, no one particular frame was used. The authors found that a legal narrative frame existed within all the stories, and the headlines presented a recasting frame (Brooks, 2008), for each story, "defilement, sodomy, or sex with a minor." The narrative glue is presented in the details: the full names of the adult and age is given, while the minor is not named. However, the minor's age, gender, and school are stated. The location where the act occurred, including town and county (including sub- location where relevant). The date is also given (date, month, and year). Also provided is the adult's relationship to the minor. In some narratives, there is an introduction to judgment ("convinced beyond any reasonable doubt…"), circumstances (familiar person, no need to fabricate stories), date offense was committed. Other experts cited are a doctor (or report, contents therein, which are retold). Lastly, the judgment is given (standpoint). Where a direct quote from a judge is restated, direct quotation marks are used. Finally, the authors of this chapter coined the *presenting opportunity* or circumstances that lead to the adult and child being alone are described and the *unfolding of the act* or the situation that succeeds the act which seems to unfold as the story is told. For example, the adult may tell the minor, 'not to tell anyone' or the child may have reported the incident to another adult (a parent, the mother), who then reports to the police.

Although media cover stories about children using both rights frameworks and historical frames, in varying degrees, the rights themselves are not consistently and substantially articulated (Internews Europe report, 2014). Similarly, the children's voices themselves were not always promoted or sought out. Where the stories were based on a legal narrative, for example sexual offense cases or the dress code (hijab) story, legal and rights approaches were seen to be taken in the language used, citing the constitution and presenting the outcomes. However, many of the stories in print did not present a full picture of the context, be it historical nor legal in terms of the rights of the children.

Where media coverage focused on the rights of the child, it was to legally protect the identity of the child in the reporting of sexual offenses cases, although this rule was not consistently followed. Sometimes this so-called objective process was done to show children's needs at the expense of contextualizing narratives on children's rights, which are complex in themselves (Crewe, 2010).

The newspaper stories that touched on children's safety / health, protection, and sexual offenses demonstrated the real, dangerous livelihoods of children and their vulnerability. This is similar to the narratives found in South Africa where children's stories were negative, underrepresented, and stereotypical (Foley, Hayes, & O'Neill, 2012). The findings of the various stories reviewed for this chapter showed different things first, in the sexual offenses' stories, the magistrates and / or judges use a legal narrative (Brooks, 2008), and retell in their judgement how trust was broken between the minor and adult. Second, that children depend on adults to ensure safe environments and how family and society have let them down. The exception being one story, which was given little space where street children are being placed in a program where they are being issued national identity cards to gain access to health. Third, in the stories, the children end up being harmed (beaten, abandoned, or defiled) or killed (suicide, by bandits, by negligence in hospital or others). This harm is not caused to them by adults alone. For example, in two of the stories, children die by the hands of other children; in one, a school prefect beats a student, his junior, who ends up dying, and in the other, a child takes a car and rolls over another child in an accident that leads to death. Sometimes the minors die by their own hands, as is seen in the stories of both boys and girls who died by suicide.

When it comes to the educational stories, a political force seems to dominate the narratives with mentions of historic, political, and systemic indicators. The students themselves are not consulted (for example, in the Forum discussion at a local University, adults are seen in the panel, no indication of children being key stakeholders); as mentioned earlier, national children's congress is not integrated into the Parliamentary structure. Images linked to stories on education showed either the children in different contexts learning with the aid of android tablets (3), learning under trees (1), reading in a library (1), and writing on a board (1), or leaders in the sector (3). In contrast, one image shows the new Education CS and children who are about to sit their exams. A closer look at the image shows the CS at a desk, perhaps appearing approachable (foreground, center), while the children of both genders are standing perhaps out of respect (background, L) and an armed guard is standing (background, R) perhaps as a bodyguard or on duty during exams, for the school.

Interview With Television News Editor

Kenya Television Network (KTN), owned by the Standard Media Group, the parent company of *The Standard*, has the second largest viewership in the country (Okulo, 2019). The editor who was interviewed revealed that reporters are guided by the Media Council Act, 2013 and the code of conduct for journalists in their reporting. The station ensures that extensive reporting on children matters is conducted during special days to celebrate the child. However, the editor pointed out that the newsroom does not have a desk that focuses on children stories or a reporter(s) assigned to report solely on child rights. Lastly, the editor pointed out that media needs to reframe the girl-child versus boy-child narrative.

The news editor pointed out some of the challenges that hinder the media from covering child rights issues competently and that lead to under-reporting include: inadequate knowledge of child laws, lack of financial resources to enable journalists to travel to remote areas to cover children stories, and inadequate training to enable reporters cover the stories competently.

DISCUSSION

In the stories reviewed across the different platforms, the power dynamics within the stories are symptomatic of society and the nature of human relationships. Patriarchy and nurture are cultural ideologies that emerge from the stories. For example, the minor's identity is generally protected (unnamed) and is presented as the victim; while the adult offender is named, their profession told, including other adults (magistrate, parents, and others). The media stories of minors, their frames, and outcomes, without the voice and position of the child disempowers them. A new angle that the authors found, is that, where a minor is also an offender, it is clear that the political environment is currently debating the meaning of this when a minor is tried in an adult court and jailed with adults. The other narrative emerging in the public, political and mediascape is the age of consent; but whose rights are being protected here?

Although the stories show us that the courts protect the rights of the child, the unveiling narratives, called here, "presenting opportunity," shows a situation where a minor is alone with a stranger or someone who takes advantage of the child; even when they were left in the care of a grandmother or other caregiver. Although they are viewed as needing care, the caregivers themselves are not held to account. Similarly, the narrative frames point to other types of psycho-social support needed for the children to which the narratives are silent. This in itself perhaps is telling of the social perception of children and the development gaps that need to be reached in society.

The media play a more hegemonic role in society than is sometimes addressed openly. Not only do they provide information, they make choices as to *what* frame of that information to provide. Although it is not always the case that this relationship is slanted, the literature shows that dominant ideologies can be normalized. Why this is so is because society relies on the credibility of institutional authority (Lull, 2000, p. 89). As the authors have here demonstrated, the media, being that socio-cultural institutional authority, has to consider its responsibilities to society and be more deliberate in some reporting areas.

CONCLUSION

On the surface, the media platforms reviewed covered various stories on children. That the stories themselves presented the rights of the child is debatable. The researchers' findings showed that although professional writing styles are in use, many of the stories lack substance, details and context, and a link to children's rights. Furthermore, in terms of prominence, the chapter's findings concur with those of Kahiu (2015) that children's stories hardly make it to the front pages of newspapers. Where they were presented as 'more human' was when they won prizes or published, and less than one percent of the stories; this did not include the children's magazine, which is targeted at children. That there were found to be few positive stories presents a negative picture about children, in itself. Stories about children were typically stereotypical, as they were shown as victims or minors (Foley, Hayes, & O'Neill, 2012). Media stories reviewed carried the voice of the elite, or showed the children as disempowered, while not deliberately inviting their perspective, despite the introduction of a children's parliament.

The authors argue that not only children's rights, their well-being, and protection need be at the heart of the story; their voice and representation also needs to be explicit (Crewe, 2010; Brooks, 2008). A common idiom, "Children are the future of tomorrow" would serve media writers and practitioners well, in seeing children, their rights and voice, as being part of each nations' development agenda and not as an appendix. That the media can play roles as educators, investigators, and advocates is clear, due to media reach and relationship of trust with its adult citizenry. However, there is more that can be done to fulfill these roles for children, their rights, well-being, and participation.

SOLUTIONS AND RECOMMENDATIONS

Solutions

Implications for Practice

That the media is a platform for voices to be heard, has been muted by the very nature of media practice globally: not providing resources, journalists, and specialists that can help promote and champion the rights of children through media (Zaleza, 2009; Panos Eastern Africa, 2013; Foley, Hayes, & O'Neill, 2012). Media training must be reviewed. As argued earlier, professional writing styles, editorial policies, financial challenges, and space and time constraints means that the stories themselves are not presented in a holistic manner. It has been found that when journalists are trained to cover stories on children, the focus is on ethical practice and feature writing, and not comprehensively on how to cover children's rights (Foley, Hayes, & O'Neill, 2012). Due to these professional constraints, the authors argue that the media then would not be fulfilling an advocacy role for the children. It would be using the media seemingly as a tool of information and power (and commercialization), but not explicit promotion of justice and the rights of the child.

This points to the need for tighter controls in practice, with professional, editorial decisions. Although Kenya has media regulatory bodies and legalized codes about children, how editors and journalists consistently, deliberately, and explicitly retell stories, which policies are applied for stories on children, and which rights are being promoted or limited, when and how images are captioned and credited needs to be monitored and reviewed. That the newspaper stories were captured in about the same amount (most in health and safety, then education, and other areas) shows the agenda setting goals of media and the commercial force through sensationalizing or politicizing headlines and / or frames (as seen in other digital platforms).

Narratives of and about children need not be presented sterilely, in isolation, or without a consideration of the total being of who that child is, complexities of the situation, and in relation to the rest of society. News writing and reporting is a skill that needs to be honed and developed with the knowledge that media narratives present social constructions of reality for users. This is also true for narratives on children. Narratives of children's rights are embedded within legal and right-based frameworks. This means that the stories themselves should have the language and style of the rights' perspective. The legal and rights-based approaches provide frameworks to monitor and measure legal, policy, and practice of protection of children rights, which incorporates the work and research of development agencies, NGOs, and other social institutions (Kilkelly, 2006; Brooks, 2008).

Recommendations

The authors thus make the following recommendations:

1. Investment and commencement of child rights and news coverage departments and staff within media houses that focus on the coverage of children and their lives, as with business news and sports news;
2. Continued discussions and inputs from development partners, NGOs, and ministries, including child representatives, and the media, to engage in an understanding, reframing, and defining of child rights, protection, voice and participation, and narratives;
3. Introduction of courses and degrees that focus on specialized media production and training, such as sports journalism, children reporting, gender reporting, health reporting, and legal reporting—with particular focus on children;
4. Targeted media literacy and journalistic writing programs and workshops for media professionals, including editors and journalists;
5. Policy direction and practical frameworks are needed from Media Council and such bodies to advise and monitor media practice within the mediascape.

FUTURE RESEARCH DIRECTION

Future of media research is to assess the different media platforms and their impact and effect on different audiences. This would include the intertextuality of the platforms and comparisons of media narratives that are being presented due to the interaction of media use and sharing of content by users. Secondly, future research needs to engage members of society, children and adults, together to establish a normative media practice that society wants, not one that the industry wishes to push, based on its own agenda. This engagement must be informed by sound development communication and media practice knowledge. Third is a deeper, critical investigation into the role of African media as a socio-cultural institution and perhaps a comparative angle among countries in sub-Saharan Africa. Lastly, assessments of media platforms and the narrative frames on audiences need to be conducted and findings shared as part of an aim to promote media literacy and to hold media practitioners accountable to their audience members.

REFERENCES

Children Act (2001). Retrieved from www.kenyalaw.org

Asare-Donkoh, F. (2017). Children in the media: How much space do they get in Ghanaian newspapers? *Journal of Children and Media*, *11*(4), 417–435. doi:10.1080/17482798.2017.1348370

Baran, S. J., & Davis, D. K. (2009). *Mass communication theory: Foundations, ferment and future* (5th ed.). Boston, MA: Wadsworth.

Barber, K. (2009). Orality, the media and new popular cultures in Africa. In K. Njogu & J. Middleton (Eds.), *Media and Identity in Africa* (pp. 3–18). Edinburgh, UK: Edinburgh University Press/International African Institute. doi:10.3366/edinburgh/9780748635221.003.0001

Brooks, P. (2008). Narrative in and of the law. In J. Phelan & P. J. Rabinowitz (Eds.), *In a companion to narrative theory*. Malden, MA: Blackwell Publishing Ltd.

Carter, M. J. (2013). The hermeneutics of frames and framing: An examination of the media's construction of reality. *SAGE Open*, 1–12.

Cheit, R. E., Shavit, Y., & Reiss-Davis, Z. (2010). Magazine coverage of child sexual abuse (1992 -2004). *Journal of Child Sexual Abuse*, *19*(1), 99–117. doi:10.1080/10538710903485575 PMID:20390781

Christians, C. G., Glassier, T. L., McQuail, D., Nordenstreng, K., & White, R. A. (2009). *Normative Theories of the media: Journalism in democratic societies*. Urbana, IL: University of Illinois Press.

Collins, R. (1985). *Four sociological traditions: Revised and expanded edition of the three sociological traditions*. New York, NY: Oxford University Press.

Crewe, E. (2010). Protecting children in different contexts: Exploring the value of rights and research. *Journal of Children's Services*, *5*(1), 43–55. doi:10.5042/jcs.2010.0116

de Vreese, C. H. (2005). News framing: Theory and typology. *Information Design Journal and Document Design*, *13*(1), 51–62. doi:10.1075/idjdd.13.1.06vre

Facer, K. (2012). After the moral panic? Reframing the debate about child safety online. *Discourse (Abingdon)*, *33*(3), 397–413. doi:10.1080/01596306.2012.681899

Foley, M., Hayes, N., & O'Neill, B. (2012). Journalism Education and Children's Rights: New Approaches to Media Development in CEE/CIS Countries. *Irish Studies in International Affairs, 23*, 47-58. Retrieved from http://www.jstor.org/stable/23489213

Gee, J. P. (2011). *Introduction to discourse analysis* (3rd ed.). New York, NY: Routledge.

Goretti, L. K. (2009). Reflections on the media in Africa: strangers in a mirror? In K. Njogu & J. Middleton (Eds.), *Media and Identity in Africa* (pp. 49–61). Edinburgh, UK: Edinburgh University Press/International African Institute.

Herman, D. (2008). Histories of narrative theory (I): A genealogy of early developments. In J. Phelan & P. J. Rabinowitz (Eds.), *In a companion to narrative theory*. Malden, MA: Blackwell Publishing Ltd.

Interviews Europe, . (2014). *Protecting the rights of children: the role of the media lessons from Brazil*. India Internews Europe. Available at https://www.internews.org/sites/default/files/resources/InternewsEurope_ChildRightsMedia_Report_2014.pdf

Jandt, F. E. (2007). *Introduction to intercultural communication: Identities in global community* (5th ed.). Thousand Oaks, CA: SAGE Publications.

Kahiu, C. W. (2015). *An investigation into the extent of child labor issues content in the Kenyan media: A case study of the Daily Nation and the Standard newspapers (Unpublished master's thesis)*. University of Nairobi. Retrieved from https://journalism.uonbi.ac.ke/sites/default/files/chss/journalism/journalism/Caroline

Kilkelly, U. (2006). Operationalizing children's rights: lessons from research. *Journal of Children's Services, 1*(4), 35-46. doi:10.1108/17466660200600030

Kimuyu, H. (2019, January 14). Form girl kicked out of school for being Rastafarian. *Nairobi News*. Retrieved from https://nairobinews.nation.co.ke/new

King'ori, M. E., & Bitrus-Ojiambo, U. A. (2016). Newspaper framing of gender-based (domestic) violence of women-on-men from Nyeri County. *African Multidisciplinary Journal of Research, 1*(1), 4–25.

Lull, J. (2000). *Media, communication, culture: A global approach* (2nd ed.). New York, NY: Columbia University Press.

McQuail, D. (2005). McQuail's mass communication theory (5th ed.). New Delhi: Vistaar Publications.

Media Council Act (ACT). (2013). *Laws of Kenya. Media Council Act No. 46 of 2013*. National Council for Law Reporting with the Authority of the Attorney-General. Available at www.kenyalaw.org

Methodist Church in Kenya vs. Mohamed Fugicha & 3 others. (2016). *Petition 16 of 2016*. Nairobi: Supreme Court of Kenya. Retrieved from http://kenyalaw.org/caselaw/cases/view/170043/

Muigai, R. (2019, March 27). Debate as court proposes sex consent age to be lowered to 16 years. *Citizen Digital*. Retrieved from https://citizentv.co.ke/news

Mutembei, P. (2012, May 6). Children's parliament launched. *Standard Digital*. Retrieved from https://www.standardmedia.co.ke

Muthoni, K. (2019, March 26). Why court proposed lowering sex consent to 16 years. *Standard Digital*. Retrieved from https://www.standardmedia.co.ke

Nation Team. (2019, March 29). Lowering the age of sexual consent talk divides Kenyans. *Daily Nation*. Retrieved from https://mobile.nation.co.ke/news/

Ogila, J. (2019, January 14). Kibera girl seeks justice after being rejected by school over dreadlocks. *Standard Digital*. Retrieved from https://www.standardmedia.co.ke/article/2001309413/k

Ortum, L. L. (2011). *An investigation into the extent of children content in Kenyan media: A case study of the Nation and Standard newspaper (Unpublished master's thesis)*. University of Nairobi. Retrieved http://erepository.uonbi.ac.ke/bitstream/handle/11295/60127/Ortum

Panos Eastern Africa. (2013). *The role of media in child protection: Challenges and opportunities in Uganda*. Kampala: Panos Eastern Africa.

Parliament of Kenya. (2018). *Senate debates*. Retrieved from http://www.parliament.go.ke/sites/default/files/2018-11/Thursday%2C%2029th%20November%2C%20 2018.pdf

Priest, S. H. (2010). *Doing media research: An introduction* (2nd ed.). Sage Publications.

Ritzer, G. (2004). *The McDonaldization of society (Revised New Century Edition.)*. Thousand Oaks, CA: Pine Forge Press/Sage Publications.

Ruggiero, T. E. (2000). Uses and gratifications theory in the 21st century. *Mass Communication & Society*, *3*(1), 3–37. doi:10.1207/S15327825MCS0301_02

Save the Children. (2014). *A lesson from Kenyan children*. Retrieved from https://kenya.savethechildren.net/news/lesson-kenyan-children

Schwartzman, K. C. (1998). Globalization and Democracy. *Annual Review of Sociology*, *24*(1), 159–181. doi:10.1146/annurev.soc.24.1.159

Sharanappa, A. (2018). *Mass media and social problem*. Raleigh, NC: Laxmi Book Publication.

Staksrud, E., & Milosevic, T. (2017). Adolescents and children in global media landscape: From risks to rights. *Annals of the International Communication Association*, *41*(3-4), 235–241. doi:10.1080/23808985.2017.1387503

The humanities in media and communication research. (2002). In *Handbook of media and communication research: Qualitative and quantitative methodologies*. London, UK: Routledge.

The Kenyan Constitution. (2010). Retrieved www.kenyalaw.org

The state of convergence in media and communication research. (2002). InJensen, K. B. (Ed.), *Handbook of media and communication research: Qualitative and quantitative methodologies*. London, UK: Routledge.

Thompson, K., & Anita Sharma, A. (1998, September). Secularization, Moral Regulation and the Mass Media. *The British Journal of Sociology*, *49*(3), 434–455. doi:10.2307/591392

Tuchman, G. (2002). The production of news. In K. B. Jensen (Ed.), *Handbook of media and communication research: Qualitative and quantitative methodologies*. London, UK: Routledge.

Ugangu, W. (2012). *Normative media theory and the rethinking of the role of the Kenyan media in a changing social economic context* (PhD thesis). University of South Africa.

Wambui vs. Republic. (2019). *Criminal Appeal 102 of 2016*. Nairobi: Court of Appeal. Retrieved from http://kenyalaw.org/caselaw/cases/view/170043/

Wanguba, F. M. (2011). *Subservience of children's rights in media coverage in Kenya* (Unpublished master's thesis). University of Nairobi. Retrieved from http://erepository.uonbi.ac.ke/handle/11295/4471

Warrier, S., & Ebbeck, M. (2014). Children's rights: Television programmes aired in Singapore. *Early Child Development and Care*, *184*(1), 138–148. doi:10.1080/03004430.2013.773991

Zaleza, P. T. (2009). The media in social development in contemporary Africa. In K. Njogu & J. Middleton (Eds.), *Media and Identity in Africa* (pp. 19–35). Edinburgh, UK: Edinburgh University Press/International African Institute. doi:10.3366/edinburgh/9780748635221.003.0002

KEY TERMS AND DEFINITIONS

Content Analysis: Methodology used to assess the content of the media texts as per qualitative content analysis methods. Coding of units of analysis were done before the assessment and discussion.

Journalistic Principles: Guidelines for professional behavior in the field of journalism including what makes news, writing structures, how to tell stories and present images of minors.

Legal Narratives: Story frame that is used in the legal profession to present a case and thereby a judgement.

Media Framing: The structure of media narratives, either due to professional writing styles and / or (more so) due to the meanings that the stories themselves present due to the way the story is told and retold.

Mediascape: A blended concept from the terms media and landscape. It refers to the global and local environments, independently and in concert that have shaped media practice, outcomes, and organizations.

Narrative Analysis: A Qualitative method for analyzing the meanings derived from stories and images based on certain criteria.

Professionalism: The outcome of being able to operate by and adhere to guidelines of one's profession and organization, especially the journalistic principles.

Texts: Content and formats, cultural by-products, for this chapter, content of news in all platforms, includes media texts.

Chapter 8
Photojournalism Ethics:
Portraying Children's Photos in Tanzanian Media

Kaanaeli Bariki Kaale
St. Augustine University of Tanzania, Tanzania

Mashaka Boniface Mgeta
St. Augustine University of Tanzania, Tanzania

ABSTRACT

This study discusses photojournalism ethics in portraying photographs of children in Tanzanian media. The study is guided by gatekeeping and semiotic theories. The authors used both quantitative and qualitative approaches to examine photojournalism ethical practices with regard to how children's photos are presented in Tanzanian newspapers and readers' perceptions regarding how children's photos are portrayed in Tanzanian media. Content analysis was to examine Habari Leo, the Guardian. and Uwazi newspapers published photographs from 1st May, 2017 to 31st May, 2018. The results showed that 591 out of 12,316 photos published by all the three newspapers were photographs of children. The results revealed that some media outlets published children's photos contrary to the ethics of photojournalism, the United Nations Convention on the Rights of the Child, and the African Charter on the Rights and Welfare of the Child. In order to improve photojournalism ethical practices, the authors suggested the use an approach base in classical philosophy by photojournalists.

DOI: 10.4018/978-1-7998-0329-4.ch008

INTRODUCTION

The Media Council of Tanzania (MCT) has provided guidelines for photojournalism in a code of ethics that emphasises norm of minimizing harm, using factuality, ensuring accuracy and fair captioning in order to prevent misconduct in the implementation of photojournalism ethics and professional behavior, particularly with reference to portraying children's photos in newspapers and social media. In addition, the guidelines insist that photojournalists avoid manipulating pictures, stereotyping, invading privacy, and using pictures of human suffering or victims of violence (Media Council of Tanzania, 2016). Despite these guidelines, there are growing concerns about unethical practices in the media, especially in social media (Patterson, & Wilkins, 2008). However, only a few studies have been conducted to investigate the ethical practices of photojournalists with regard to photographs of children and their rights. These rights are declared by the safeguards and remedies offered in the ethics of photojournalism, national laws, and international conventions (UNICEF, 2017).

Aims of the Research

The broad aim of this study is to find out how photographs of children ages 0-17 were portrayed in the media and how these portrayals affects their audience. Through information gathered from readers along with human rights activists, editors, and photojournalists, the authors address the following research questions: First, to what extent are children's photos presented in Tanzanian newspapers? Second, what are the ethical practices employed in portraying children's' photos in Tanzanian newspapers? And, last, what are readers' perceptions regarding children's photos in Tanzania newspapers?

Background

Nowadays, photojournalists are using advanced technology to manipulate photographs of children that are published in newspapers and on social media. Photojournalism is a sub section of journalism, which use images to tell a story. (Geraci, 1984; Lester, 2018). The history of photojournalism is connected to the history of photography over the last 180 years traces the emergence of a practice that has revolutionized understanding of visual communication (Gernsheim, 1969).

Photojournalists have the potential to be champions of human rights. Their reporting, writing, photographing, and filming of videos can act as the eyes, ears, and voices of the public, encouraging governments, civil society organizations, and communities to bring about changes that will improve the lives of children and their families as stated in United Nations Convention on the Rights of the Child (United Nations, 1989; UNICEF 2017), and the African Charter on the Rights and Welfare of the Child (Organization of African Unity, 1990). However, the advances in modern technology that makes it possible to enhance photographs and create impressive works of art and beauty. Also, modern technology have potentially negative consequences, making it just as easy to create lies and distorted versions of reality, discrediting the age-old adage that "the camera never lies," (Bossen, 1985, p. 30).

Various studies have been carried out on the ethics of photojournalism. Nottingham's (1978) ethnographic investigation of subject feelings during a photographic event, laid the groundwork for Newton's qualitative (1984) and quantitative (1991). Hartley (1981) conducted a study about media practitioners' perceptions of photographing the victim of a wreck. A few previous studies have been published concerning the ethics of photojournalism in the area of portraying children's photographs. A study of photojournalism ethics conducted by Ow-Yeong (2014) focused on photographs of children. In an article titled "Our Failure of Empathy: Kevin Carter, Susan Sontag and the problems of photography", Ow-Yeong investigated role of photography in relation to empathy by examining the visual impact, psychological effects, and emotional influence of photographic media. He used the case of a Pulitzer Prize-winning image by the late South African Photojournalist Kevin Carter taken during the 1993 famine in Sudan. The photograph shows a starving Sudanese girl who collapsed on her journey to the nearest feeding center. Kneeling over, she almost touches the ground with her forehead. The most distressing element in the picture is that a vulture lurks behind her, sinisterly waiting her death.

Many media scholars used Carter's photograph to caution photojournalists to be careful when choosing whether to photograph or help their suffering subjects (Ow-Yeong, 2014). Despite the many criticisms of Carter, violations of photojournalism ethics are growing more than ever because in the digital world news editors have access to ever-large amounts of visual materials from a multiplicity of sources (Gynnild, Nilsson; Simonsen, & Weselius, 2017).

A study done by Bhati and Eikenberry (2015), entitled "Faces of the needy: the portrayal of destitute children in the fundraising campaigns of NGOs in India," revealed that the prize-winning Italian photographer was not ethical because children were not happy with the photos.

The study attempted to answer two questions. Firstly, what are children's perceptions of their photographs used in fundraising campaigns? Secondly, how do photographers or managers/directors associated with NGOs view the portrayal of children as destitute? The study used different data collection technics, including analysis of images, focus group discussion with children, and interviews with photographers and campaign managers from different NGOs in India. Results revealed that children prefer to be portrayed as happy and in a "good light", telling the whole story of their lives including the hardships they face. The study pointed out that NGOs face a challenge in representing beneficiaries in a positive light while also showing "needs" to donors.

The study revealed that the children who participated did not know that their mages would be used negatively as a fundraising and marketing tool, which raises ethical concerns (Bhati & Eikenberry, 2016, Vos, 2018). Supporting these results, Batson, Lishner, Cook & Sawyer (2005) argued that charitable organizations often use children, as the "faces of need" in their promotional materials because displaying the most innocent and vulnerable is an effective way to elicit empathy leading to funding from potential donors. A study done by the Empowering Children and Media Monitoring project in partnership with Save the Children and UNICEF on representation of children and children's rights in the South African news media resulted in clear conclusions regarding unethical practices in photojournalism (UNICEF, 2004). In addition, a study done by *Media Wise* analyzed the content of some of the most important British newspapers. The results showed that out of 32 items about children, only two were positive (Vlad, 2017).

METHODOLOGY

This study used a descriptive research design based on both qualitative and quantitative research approaches. The combination of quantitative and qualitative approaches provides a clear understanding of the subject of this study (Creswell, 2015) In addition, the study incorporate the ideas of Johnson and Onwuegbuzie (2004) that the use of both qualitative and quantitative research approaches enables a researcher to extract the strengths, and diminish the weaknesses, of both approaches within a single study.

The study guided by gatekeeping and semiotic theories. Gatekeeping theory used to explain the process of filtering information before disseminating it to audiences using a definition of the news values of images constructed mainly through what is represented in the image (Caple & Bednarek 2016). The theory is useful in to the study of photos of children due to its emphasis on (Bissell 2000a, p.11) the individualistic decisions of photo editors, sometimes based on personal biases such as race, gender, age, or political orientation (Bissel, 2000b; Peterson & Spratt,2005).

The researchers also used semiotics theory as a tool for interpreting and analyzing photojournalist ethical practices by focusing on manipulation, minimizing harm, captions, grief, stereotyping and rights to privacy. Semiotics is a theory of the production and interpretative meaning of signs, language, and logic (Pierce, 1931; Eco, 1976) Signs and symbols help photojournalists to communicate effectively through shared experience and meaning in while putting in consideration culture, age, gender, and life experience (Littlejohn, & Foss 2009; Grange, 2013; Frierson, 2018).

The researchers used simple random sampling to select 140 respondents from 1,400 newspapers readers. The selection based on the principle of saturation and diminishing returns. The selection also was because sample size should be large enough to sufficiently describe the phenomenon of interest and address the research question at hand. The researcher used self-administered questionnaire with open and close-ended to obtain information about their perceptions regarding children's photographic portrayal in Tanzanian newspapers.

The researchers used face-to-face interviews to obtain information from 25 key informants, including human rights activists (5), editors (10), and senior photojournalist (10). Content analysis was conducted for 768 copies of three newspapers published between May 1, 2017 and May 31, 2018. The study used a purposive sampling procedure to select key informant and newspapers. The newspapers selected were, *The Guardian* (360 copies), *Habari Leo* (360 copies), and *Uwazi* (48 copies).

The selection of these three newspapers was based on a pilot study, which included 10 daily mainstream newspapers and five tabloid papers. Prior the actual study, the researchers conducted content analysis to find out which newspapers published children's photographs and the results showed that *Habari Leo* and *the Guardian* published more photos than other mainstream newspapers while *Uwazi* published more photos to compare with other tabloid newspapers.

This study used categorical descriptive statistical analyses to classify and summarize qualitative data. The researchers used excel to code and summarize the quantitative data in statistical format. The study used semiotic analysis to identify photos and themes and then interpreted them to understand readers' experiences and opinions about the photographs of children in the Tanzanian media.

Ethical Considerations

The researchers obtained data from recognized institutions, including the Tanzania Media Council, various mainstream newspapers published in Tanzania, and UN reports. The researchers followed the professional guidelines of research, which included obtaining consent from all parties involved in the study, and asking for permission from Mwananchi Communication Limited to use its Library to conduct this research. The respondents were invited to participate in this study voluntarily, and personal confidentiality was maintained during all research activities.

FINDINGS

Photographs of Children Published in Tanzanian Newspapers

The first specific objective was to determine the extent photographs of children published in Tanzanian newspapers, specifically *Habari Leo*, *The Guardian*, and *Uwazi*. The research findings showed that all the three newspapers published a total of 12,316 between May 1, 2017and May 31, 2018. *Habari Leo* published 6,082 photos, repreenting 49%, *the Guardian* had 5,345 photos, which is equivalent to 44%, while *Uwazi* published 889 photos, which is equal to 7% of all photos. The study revealed that all the three newspapers had published 591 children's photos out of 12, 316 photos, which is equivalent to 5%. Particularly, 452 out of 6,082 photos published by *Habari Leo*, were the photographs of children, which is equal to 7%. *The Guardian* had 113 children's' photos out of 5,345, which is only 2% and *Uwazi* published 26 photos of children, which was equivalent to 3% of 889 photos published by *Uwazi*. The research findings showed that photographs of children portrayed in newspapers were not given priority to be printed on the front page or in the prime pages numbered three and five. According to the study, only 13 out of 591 photographs of children (2%) published by all newspapers appeared on front page, 21 photos (4%) were published on page 3, and 18 children's' photos (3%) were on page 5. The remaining photos were in pages that were farther from the front page, such as page 5 to 20 or in the features pages. Generally, the study revealed that most of the photos of children published on the front page involved the children interacting with prominent figures such ministers, member of parliaments or religious leaders. Also, photos of children taken during disasters, including disease outbreaks, floods, hunger, or social and political conflicts, appeared on the front or premium pages.

For example, on the *Habari Leo* newspaper published on January 19, 2018, the front page had a photo of children affected by floods in Chemba district of Dodoma region. *The Guardian* newspaper published on February 5, 2018, included a photo of a child with albinism being served food by the Prime Minister on the front page. On February 19, 2018, *The Guardian* came out on the front page with a photo of a 12-year-old girl meeting with the Prime Minister during his official visit to Bunda district in Mara region. It is important to note that *Habari Leo* published more children's photos because it had two pullouts for children per week. One was titled *Uwanda wa Watoto* (Children's Forum) and came out every Sunday. In this pullout, at least 10 children's photos are published in a single edition. The other pullout, published photographs of children in the education section. This pullout, which was published every Thursday, carried the voices and views of children on the education sector in the country. The findings showed that within the time of this study, 240 children's photos were published in these two pullouts.

For *The Guardian*, the majority of photographs of children originated from events, particularly donations to children and children's centres, awards, and other related events. Few of the photos presented the views of the children. In addition, event-oriented photos appeared in *Habari Leo*, but they were never seen in *Uwazi*.

PHOTOJOURNALISM ETHICS IN PORTRAYING CHILDREN'S PHOTOS IN TANZANIAN NEWSPAPERS

The second research objective was to examine the ethical practices of photojournalism in portraying photographs of children in Tanzanian newspapers. The researchers used six elements to form a code of conducts for examining the ethical practices of photojournalism in publishing children's photos in Tanzanian newspapers. These included manipulation, minimizing harm, captions, grief, stereotyping and rights to privacy.

The research findings showed that out of 591 children's photo, 136 (23%) had violated at least one of these photojournalism ethics. Among these, 91 photos, equivalent to 15%, were published by *Habari Leo*; 33(6%), were published by *The Guardian*, and 12 (2%) were published by *Uwazi.* The study revealed that 13 children's photos violated the photojournalism ethic of manipulation, 27 photos violated the ethic of minimizing harm, 18 photos had captions published against the dignity of a child, 31 photos interfered with the privacy of children, 25 photos stereotyped the child, and 22 photos had intervened with the rights of a child. The research also found that photos published on pages 3 and 5, respectively, tended to involve events including people donating or speaking to children. Some photographs portrayed children's engagement in different activities, such as scrambling for food and walking out of a refugee's center or otherwise accompanying major stories on issues that affect children, such as getting tap water from leaking pipes. The findings showed that the tabloid *Uwazi* had children's photos, which depicted their personal issues, such as sickness, and other photos were manipulated in order to link with notable social issues. For example, the study showed that from March 20-27, March 28-April 2 and April 3-9, 2018, *Uwazi* published manipulated photos of children. Some of these publications showed photographs of children who looked at the skulls and bones of some of people who died in *Rwanda's genocide in 1994*. The children's photos were cropped and pasted beside the skulls and bones photos, which were published to support the feature article on the massacre, hence distort the actual message from the original photos. These photographs portray negative images and violate photojournalism code of ethics. Also, the tabloid newspaper exposed photos of children in Kahama district. It was claimed that these children drank a cup of porridge with pieces of glass in it. Another photo had exposed a child victim of *sexual harassment* from a family of beggars in Dar es Salaam streets. The findings showed that photojournalists did not seek consent from the children, their parents, or their guardians before taking those photos and published them.

MEDIA PRACTITIONERS

Photojournalists were interviewed to understand their views and experiences in ethical practices in portraying photographs of children. This study engaged both chief photojournalists - normally heads the photo desks in the newsrooms - and Photojournalists, sometime referred to as photographers, who were assigned to take photos from different occasions. Despite the significance of photography in conveying media messages, including political messages, photojournalists claimed that most media in Tanzania have not recognized them as part of journalism. The General Secretary of the Press Photographers Association of Tanzania (PPAT), Mroki Mroki, said that although the Media Council of Tanzania has provided guidelines for photojournalism codes of ethics, practically photojournalists are not regarded as professional media practitioners. Mroki said that despite the challenges facing photojournalists in Tanzania, the PPAT is keen to use modern technology to maintain excellence, trust, and high quality of photoproducts for both newspapers and television.

Mroki said that most of photojournalists in Tanzanian media are smart photographers who attend journalism seminars to become professional photojournalists, but they are facing numerous challenges that contribute to their violations of photojournalism ethics. For instance, cheap labor and lack of media owners' interests in investing in photojournalism have become major obstacles for the promotion of ethics in photojournalism in Tanzania. Most media owners are neither willing to employ photojournalists, nor provide working facilities for them, especially professional cameras and laptop computers.

Mroki said that there are more than 200 photojournalists who work in Tanzania media, but about 80% are not permanently employed, and 70% of them are working without a legal employment contract. He said most photojournalists use their own cameras, equipment, and facilities. Since the majority of photojournalists are not employed, the employers do not feel the need to provide them with facilities, seminars, or trainings about the ethical issues of photojournalism.

Mroki said the major challenges are in the newsroom, where journalists and editors undermine the work of photojournalists deliberately or due to lack of awareness about the role and importance of photojournalists in the news production process. Mroki claimed that although photojournalists are working in difficult situations as they supposed to be in the front line to capture events, they are not involved in final photo selection. This tendency leads to bad habits of using photos without bylines. In some incidences, one photo can be used three times in different years without captions or extra explanations to indicate that it is from a library of photos taken some years ago. These make readers skeptical about the role of photojournalism, especially in portraying photographs of children.

Since some of photographers are paid based on the number of published photos, sometimes bylines are removed deliberately in order to avoid compensation or payment. The omission of bylines and captions in photos contributes to violations of photojournalism ethics, especially to minimize harm. Plagiarism has increased the number of photos, which are published in the newspapers and magazine without bylines. Lack of involvement of photojournalists in the news process enforces graphic designers and feature writers to find photographs to accompany the news or feature stories. Therefore, they end up searching for photos on the internet and using them without giving proper acknowledgement or attribution to the source of those photos. Some media sources misuse the opportunity provided by digital knowledge. Instead of producing memorable photos and using the internet to promote the creditability of their product, the internet has become a key source of plagiarism. Although newspapers are losing credibility because of plagiarism of photos, it seems that the media is not aware of or is no longer sensitive to the issue of credibility of the uses of photos.

Sharing his experience in the field of photojournalism, the veteran photojournalist, Richard Mwaikenda worked with four different major media houses, but he has never attended any in-house training or seminars about photojournalism ethics. Mwaikenda said, "Sometimes we are prevented from attending seminars for journalists. Often, when photojournalists attempt to enter the seminar room, journalist colleagues will shout 'No! You are a photographer and this is for journalists. You're not needed here!'"

He said that most Tanzanian photojournalists lack adequate training and tend to rely on experience mostly gained through apprenticeships. Lack of photojournalism training not only affects photojournalists but also the entire journalism profession because news photo production also involves writers, particularly feature writers, editors, and graphic designers. Most photojournalists who were interviewed come with similar answers, stating that they are not engaged in selecting photos for the final publication. Instead, they are asked by their Chief Photographers to submit the best photos after their return from the field.

Some of the chief photographers and editors evaluated photojournalists' ability to take the best photos from different angles as the main criteria for being a good photographer without considering the issue of ethics. The respondents revealed that even though photojournalists knew the ethical restrictions involved in using children's photos, they do not have the power to make decisions of photos to be published so they took many photos to prove the quality of their work. The decision for publishing photos was in the hands of chief photographers.

Another respondent said that when it comes to children's photos, most photojournalists know that it is strictly unethical to take a photo that exposes children negatively. However, they do it purposely for the use in newsrooms to prove that they are good at taking photos. Sometimes, stiff competition in the media market forced editors to publish photos, which exposes children negatively, contrary to the ethics of photojournalism.

Senior Editors

Additionally, this study included interviews with 10 editors about the photojournalism practice in portraying photographs of children. The findings showed that all editors clearly know about ethical issues in portraying photographs of children. All editors said photojournalists are not fully involved in selecting photographs that are published in the newspaper because of nature of journalistic culture, which allows gatekeepers to make final decisions. All editors declared that in some cases, newspapers violated ethical issues in photojournalism because of ethical dilemmas, stiff competition in the newspapers, political reasons and when they published international news in local media. They clarified that international news carry stereotypes and manipulated photos that contribute to violation of journalism ethical such as portraying photographs of children suffering from diseases and violence.

The study involved five graphic designers who shared their experience in preparing news production. They explained that after receiving photos from chief photographers, their duty was to fill the space as arranged on the pages' layouts. According to the respondents, chief photographers spent less time with them during the photo production and paid limited attention to few photos, particularly those published on the front and premium pages.

Graphic Designers

In addition, photographers had commented that graphic designers often badly crop children's photos in newspapers' production. Respondents noted that graphic designers sometimes under or over-cropped the original children's photos, thus distorting the original message. Graphic designers do not study journalism, but rather, they study graphics and online or newspaper designs. They know few rules about editing photos, such as not cropping heads and publishing photos without head. Thus, whenever the chief photojournalists or editors failed to give more details on what to consider in putting the photos on pages, they used their expertise in graphics to select, design, and place photos in the newspapers, according to their desires. One graphics designer from *Habari Leo* said that they used to crop photos to fit the places provided for the particular photos. They are free to design and manipulate the photos, but the final decision of processing the photo to print is made by production editor. "We are free to select and temper with photo as much as we can, but we're strictly not allowed to process any photo or any page of newspapers to the final printing without approval of the editor," said a graphic designer from *Habari Leo.*

Another respondent from *Uwazi* said that he has never understood the procedures for which children's photo were selected in editorial processes. A respondent from *The Guardian* articulated that selection of photos that are published on the front and premier pages are made at the editorial meeting, which is normally held in the afternoon or in the evening to make final decision of what is to be published.

Advocates of Rights of the Child

This study interviewed 10 advocates for the right of the child. They all had drawn from Civil Society Organizations (CSOs), including associations of journalists, particularly the Tanzania Photojournalists Association, Medico Press, and Association of Tanzania Health Journalists. Other organizations were Save your Generation Tanzania (SAGETA) and Youth Alive Club (YAC). All of the respondents agreed seeing children's photos in the newspapers but criticised the way some newspapers portrayed children's photos negatively. Respondents felt upset to see children's photos published in newspapers with negative images and exposing them as victims of certain disasters like flood, poverty, war, or social conflicts. The Director of SAGETA that the majority of mainstream newspapers performed well in portraying children's photos compared to the tabloids, which were largely based on personalities and business interests. Furthermore, advocates from three journalists' associations, Medico Press, Tanzania Photojournalists Association, and Association of Tanzania Health Journalists, shared a similar idea and revealed that the ethics of photojournalism, which is used as the base for developing Child Act and other codes of conduct related to the rights of the child, must be strongly imparted to photojournalists.

Some respondents pointed out that the publication of children's photos has a number of internal and external influence. One of the influences mentioned was business companies and CSOs that claimed to pay the photojournalists in order to facilitate the smooth publication of photos that they want. Most of the photos submitted to the editors by these companies or organizations involve negative portrayal to the children.

PUBLIC PERCEPTIONS ON PHOTOJOURNALISM ETHICAL PRACTICE IN PORTRAYING CHILDREN'S

This study used a self-administered questionnaire given to 140 respondents to examine respondents' perceptions about the public perception regarding photojournalism ethics in portraying children's photos in Tanzania media. The findings showed that 98% of respondents had high access to newspapers and social media and they see children photos.

When they were asked if they knew that Informed consent is necessary for journalists to take photographs of children, 89% of the respondents said they were not. They clarified this point by relating that they thought photojournalists had a mandate to take children's photos without permission from their parents or guardians because they see them taking photos in many occasions where others were not allowed to do so. However, 11% of the respondents said they were aware that informed consent is very important but believed it is difficult to prevent photojournalist from talking photos because they are very aggressive in their pursuit of photographs. Sixty seven percent of respondents believed that photo manipulation is high. In addition, 87% of respondents said that photos often lacked a clear caption that might minimizing harm, creating pain and grief for readers.

Most of photos in the feature pages, especially international news and features, show children suffering from diseases, violence, and disasters. The findings showed that 91% of respondents said that there are stereotypes in the photos published in the newspapers, and 94% respondents said there is a lack of rights to privacy of the children photos who are published in the newspapers.

DISCUSSION

The findings revealed that Tanzanian newspapers have made a good will effort to implement international conventions and African charters on children's rights. The special children pages in *Habari Leo* is evidence of how photojournalists are promoting children's rights, as stated in articles 12, 13 and Article 17 of *Convention on the Rights of the Child* (UNICEF, 2017; United Nation, 1989).

The findings indicate that although the Media Council of Tanzania has provided a photojournalism code of ethics, 80% of photojournalists are not recognized as professional photojournalists. Most of them are professional photographers, they enjoy taking photos, regardless the low interest of media owners in investing in Photojournalism. Lack of journalism education among photojournalists in Tanzanian media has created questions on whether photojournalism is the combination of photography and journalism (Geraci, 1984; Lester, 2018). For the experience of

Tanzania, the latter remained as academic terminology that was used at schools of journalism, due the fact that the unfriendly environment for photojournalists in the media discourages photojournalism graduates to join the field. Generally, a photojournalist in Tanzania is a photographer who practices journalism. In this regard, there is a need for Tanzanian leaders to encourage media owners to invest in photojournalism to improve the working conditions of photographers, including providing them with education and seminars about human rights, particularly children's rights.

Images from different places or events often do not reflect reality, but they appear to be a reflection of the stereotypes and prejudices of the author of the photograph. For example, the most international features that are shared in *Habari Leo* and *The Guardian* depict stereotype that African children are poor and dying from hunger, diseases, and war. These findings are consistent with previous studies by Berger (2007) that a photo is an interpretation of reality, not reality itself. Lester (1991; 2018) said media photography researchers have found that stereotypes and prejudices have a big impact on decision-making and the process of photographing. The children's photos from disasters, such as floods, hunger, social and political conflicts, or diseases, were given weight to appear on front or premium pages. Some children's photos were focused on children's engagement in different activities, such as scrambles for food and walkouts of refugees, accompany major stories on issues affecting them. There is a need for media to change their mindset and avoid publishing negative images for the sake of fulfilling the goals of politicians or NGOs. Some NGOs have tendency to depict press and exposed children negatively to draw public attention as a strategy to search for funds from internal and external donors.

The findings indicate that photojournalists still apply what has been labeled as "Parachute Journalism", practiced by foreign journalists in Africa. In "Parachute Journalism", stories break that capture the world's attention, including widespread famine in Ethiopia or Somalia, genocidal warfare in Rwanda, rioting in Soweto, South Africa, And news about poverty and diseases that are accompanied by manipulated photos (Hachten,1993). The net result is to give the impression that most Africans are desperately poor, hungry, and incapable of improving their lives. In contemporary journalism, violent crimes and sex crimes are areas where news reporting is highly selective. The media prefers emotional stories, sobbing victims, and stories that fit into their political agenda and confirm images of the criminal as a monster (Altheide, 2002; Kilimwiko, 2009). This kind of journalism guides people toward fatalism and fears of global changes. It also continues to develop a generally negative impression about Africa. This is not an accurate reflection of reality, therefore, this study calls for the media to change their mindset and use the International Day of the African Child, which is celebrated on June 16th every year, and the International Day of the

Girl Child, which is celebrated on October 11th every year, to promote the African rights, talents, and values of African children .

In order to obey the code of ethics, the media should first consider Article 3 of Convention on the Rights of the Child, which states that in all actions concerning children, whether undertaken by a public or a private welfare institution, courts, administrative authorities, or legislative bodies, the best interests of the child are a primary consideration. Additionally, Article 17(e) encourages the development of appropriate guidelines for the protection of the child from information and material injurious to his or her well-being, bearing in mind the provisions of articles 13 and 18 (UNICEF, 2017). After the media practitioners are informed about children's rights, it will be easier for them to follow ethical principles, which will protect children, individuals, or groups from unacceptable abuse in the media.

Due to the competition and challenging environment facing photojournalists, this paper suggests that Press Photographers Association of Tanzania (PPAT) to implement the recommendation made by International Federation of Journalists (IFJ) (Warren, 2006). Warren urged journalists to establish the strong and independent unions that are necessary for press freedom and in order to speak with a collective voice that is independent of both governments and employers. The International Federation of Journalists insists that journalists and their unions know best their own working conditions. They have the fullest knowledge and experience of local traditions and know best what will work well in their own national situations. Photojournalists should seek their right to employment instead of working without official contracts. Through Press Photographers Association of Tanzania, they should search for funds for training so that they can become familiar with important subjects, including ethics and international and crosscutting issues involving children's rights.

CONCLUSION

Photojournalists in Tanzanian newspapers play a significance role in promoting children rights. However, to some extent media outlets are violating photojournalism ethics and publishing unethical photos of children. It appears that many Tanzanian Media owners are not interested in investing in ethical and professional photojournalism. In order to encourage ethical photojournalism practices, Tanzanian media must recognize the role and importance of photojournalists in the print media. Ethical Photojournalism would better enable the communication of visual language in order to promote children's rights.

In this era of digital technology, it is necessary for Media Council of Tanzania to influence the media to promote quality photojournalism and to set standards for the use of photos in order to maintain media credibility. This can be done by encouraging media owners to invest in photojournalism by employing and recognizing photojournalists as well as to sponsor them to attend seminars on photojournalism ethics. In addition, nations must create, publish, and enforce up-to-date ethical codes for photojournalists. Photojournalists themselves should use these media codes of ethics as well as systematic moral analysis and guidelines to address the ethical dilemmas posed by their profession and their professional practices.

GUIDELINES FOR MAKING ETHICAL DECISIONS

This study recommended that there is a need to develop journalistic ethical guidelines more robustly. This development can be guided by classical philosophical writings, such as those provided by Aristotle, Mill, Kant, W. D. Ross and John Rawls.

The photojournalists should apply Golden Mean as suggested by Greek philosopher Aristotle (Cunningham, 1999; Berry, 2013; Perebinossoff, 2012; Hooker, 2018)). The golden mean would help photojournalists to judge between personal interest and public interest in order to avoid biasness. The Biblical Golden Rule is sometimes phrased "love your neighbor as yourself." These ideas are reflected in the Media Council of Tanzania's (2016) recommendation that since photojournalists are human beings, they should avoid doing what they would blame others for doing.

A utilitarian concern emphases on minimizing harmful as a result of a decision for the greatest good for number of people as stated by John Stuart Mill (1806–1873). Taking an example of Utilitarian theories, this study suggests that all studied newspapers promoted children's rights for the interest of public and individual children. Utilitarian theories also enable photojournalists to make better decisions with regard to the right of privacy. In additional, journalism's ethical, codes can draw on the branch of philosophy known as duty ethics to improve photojournalism ethical practices. This kind of thinking already is part of a professional photojournalist's training to act as an objective reporter and work for the public good. For example, Code of Ethics for Press Photographers & Video Producers (Media Council of Tanzania, 2016, p.38) wanted photojournalists to seek and present the truth and publish photos or visual images which present a clear, comprehensive and accurate representation of the event or the situation depicted and they should never fake reality.

The German philosopher, Immanuel Kant (1724–1804) established the concept of the unconditionality of categorical imperative; the evaluation of consequences and the concept of the greater good that can also be used to help photojournalists to work professionally while they are taking and publishing photographs of children's (Lester, 2018). According to his schematic, media personnel and owners should bear in mind that they are not to use photographs of children to profit themselves.

Key elements of many journalistic codes of ethics are Kantian in nature: they provide directives of the duties that journalists, as responsible professionals, must carry out. These include the duty to seek the truth and inform the public, the duty to be accountable for their work, and the duty to minimize harm as much as possible without compromising the first two directives (Perebinossoff, 2012; Pearsall, 2013; Hooker, 2018).

A British philosopher, William David Ross (1877-1971), played a crucial role in evaluating photojournalism's ethical practices (Plaisance, 2014; Ross, 1930). Ross proposed, as fundamental in both moral practice and ethical theory, the prima facie duties of fidelity, reparation, justice, gratitude, beneficence, self-improvement, and non-injury when making an ethical judgement. Ethical intuitionism states that fundamental ethical truths can be known directly. Rossian intuitionism theories are still valid and can be applied to media ethics. For example, the Media Council of Tanzania (2016, p.24) has insisted that when photojournalist take photo of a situation of grief he/she must respect personal grief by making any necessary approaches and inquiries with sensitivity and discretion and by handling situations of grief with special attention and consideration for those affected. When dealing with photographs of dead persons, photojournalists should consider the culture, myths, beliefs and rituals of the people involved. For example -Media Council of Tanzania (2016, p.24) insisted that when photojournalist take photo of a grief he/she must Respect personal grief by making any necessary approaches and inquiries with sensitivity and discretion and handle situations of grief with special attention and consideration, for the sensibility of those affected. When dealing with photographs of dead persons, photojournalists should consider the culture, myths, beliefs and rituals of the people involved.

The results of this study also suggests that media practitioners should apply Rawls's theory of justice when (Rawls, 1999) evaluating their ethical practices. Theory of Justice enable photojournalists to consider minority and voiceless rights as indicated in Articles17, 23, and 30 of *the Convention on the Rights of the Child.*

Apart from the ethical guidelines provided by philosophers, this study also, points to the usefulness of analytic guidelines that simplify the study of ethics and make it more easily applied to media practitioners. Firstly, this study recommends the two-step Systematic Moral Analysis (SMA) that finding alterative of preventing people from harm (Elliott, 2017; Lester, 2018, 1991). These steps are conceptualization and justification, which are designed to help media practitioners to understand who might be harmed and how that harm can be minimalized. As Lester (2018) put it in his book, "Visual Ethics: a Guide for Photographers, Journalists, and Filmmakers," conceptualization means that photojournalists should asked themselves who might be harmed and how might that harm be administered by their action. For justification, photojournalists should ask themselves, "does breaking a moral rule prevent a greater harm from occurring or does the harm you cause legitimately address a more significant harm that was already caused? If an action causes the least harm to others, can withstand public scrutiny, and would be ethically permissible for anyone in a similar situation, it can be considered ethical," (Lecter, 2018 Ch.1). There is a great need to equip photojournalists with knowledge, skills and ethics guideline to improve ethical practice in portraying photographs of children.

REFERENCES

Altheide, D. (2002). *Creating fear: News and the construction of crisis*. New York: Aldine de Gruyter.

Batson, D., Lishner, D., Cook, J., & Sawyer, S. (2005). Similarity and nurturance: Two possible sources of empathy for strangers. *Basic and Applied Social Psychology*, *27*(1), 15–25. doi:10.120715324834basp2701_2

Berry, D. (2013). *Ethics and Media Culture: Practices and Representations*. Oxford, UK: Focal Press. doi:10.4324/9780080573809

Bhati, A., & Eikenberry, A. (2016). Faces of the needy: The portrayal of destitute children in the fundraising campaigns of NGOs in India. *International Journal of Nonprofit and Voluntary Sector MarketingInt*, *21*(1), 31–42. doi:10.1002/nvsm.1542

Bissell, K. (2000b). Culture and Gender as Factors in Photojournalism Gatekeeping. *Visual Communication Quarterly*, *7*(2), 9–12. doi:10.1080/15551390009363429

Bissell, K. L. (2000a). A return to "Mr. Gates": Photography and objectivity. *Newspaper Research Journal*, *21*(3), 81–93. doi:10.1177/073953290002100307

Bossen, H. (1985). Zone V: Photojournalism, ethics, and the electronic *age. Studies in Visual Communication*, *11*(2), 22–32. doi:10.1111/j.2326-8492.1985.tb00031.x

Caple, H., & Bednarek, M. (2016). Rethinking News Values: What a Discursive Approach Can Tell Us about the Construction of News Discourse and News Photography. *Journalism*, *17*(4), 435–455. doi:10.1177/1464884914568078

Creswell, J. W. (2015). Research design: A qualitative, quantitative, and mixed method approaches. Thousand Oaks, CA: Saga.

Cunningham, S. B. (1999). Getting It Right: Aristotle's "Golden Mean" as Theory Deterioration University of Windsor. *Journal of Mass Media Ethics*, *14*(1), 5–15. doi:10.1207/S15327728JM140101

Eco, U. (1976). *A Theory of Semiotics*. Bloomington, IN: Indiana University Press. doi:10.1007/978-1-349-15849-2

Elliott, D. (2017). Systematic moral analysis. *Ethics Unwrapped*. Accessed June 28, 2017 from http://ethicsunwrapped.utexas.edu/video/systematic-moral-analysis

Frierson, M. (2018). *Film and Video Editing Theory Film*. Abingdon, UK: Focal Press. doi:10.4324/9781315475011

Geraci, P. C. (1984). *Photojournalism: New Images in Visual Communication*. Dubuque, IA: Kendall/Hunt Publishing Company.

Gernsheim, H. (1969). *The history of photography*. New York: McGraw-Hill.

Grange, A. (2013). *Basic Critical Theory for Photographers*. Abingdon, UK: Focal Press.

Gynnild, A., Nilsson, M., Simonsen, A. H., & Weselius, H. (2017). Introduction: Photojournalism and editorial processes: Global similarities, local differences. *Nordicom Review, 38*(Special Issue 2), 1-5.

Hachten, W. (1993). *The growth of media in the third world: African failures, Asian successes*. Ames, IA: Iowa State University Press.

Hartley, C. (1981). *The reactions of photojournalists and the public to hypothetical ethical dilemmas confronting press photographers* (Unpublished master's thesis). University of Texas, Austin, TX.

Hooker, J. (2018). *Taking ethics seriously: Why ethics is an essential tool for the modern workplace*. London: Productivity Press. doi:10.4324/9781315097961

Kilimwiko, L. (2009). *Media power and political in Tanzania: Critical analysis of media trends and practice*. Dar es Salaam: Friedrich Ebert Stiftung.

Lester, M. (2018). *Visual ethics*. Oxford, UK: Focal Press. doi:10.4324/9781315455136

Lester, P. (1991). *Photojournalism: An ethical approach*. Lawrence Erlbaum Associates, Incorporated.

Littlejohn, S. W., & Foss, K. A. (2009). *Encyclopedia of communication theory*. London: SAGE Publications Inc. doi:10.4135/9781412959384

Media Council of Tanzania. (2016). *Code of ethics for media professionals*. Dar es Salaam: Media Council of Tanzania.

Newton, J. H. (1991). *In front of the camera: Ethical issues of subject response in photography* (Unpublished doctoral dissertation). University of Texas, Austin, TX.

Nottingham, E. (1978). *From both sides of the lens: Street photojournalism and personal space* (Unpublished doctoral dissertation). Indiana University, Bloomington, IN.

Onwuegbuzie, A. J., & Leech, N. L. (2004). *Enhancing the interpretation of significant findings: The role of mixed methods research.* Paper presented at the annual meeting of the Eastern Educational Research Association, Clearwater, FL.

Organization of African Unity (OAU). (n.d.). *African Charter on the Rights and Welfare of the Child.* Addis Ababa: OAU.

Ow-Yeong, W. (2014). Our Failure of Empathy': Kevin Carter, Susan Sontag, and the Problems of Photography. *Think Pieces: A Journal of the Joint Faculty Institute of Graduate Studies, 1*(1), 9-17.

Patterson, P., & Wilkins, L. (2008). *Media ethics issues and cases.* New York: McGraw-Hill.

Pearsall, S. (2013). *A photojournalist's field guide: In the trenches with combat photographer.* San Francisco: Peachpit Press.

Perebinossoff, P. (2012). *Real-world media ethics.* Oxford, UK: Focal Press. doi:10.4324/9780080557106

Peterson, A., & Spratt, M. (2005). Choosing Graphic Visuals: How Picture Editors Incorporate Emotion and Personal Experience into Decision Making. *Visual Communication Quarterly, 12*(1-2), 4–19. doi:10.1080/15551393.2005.9687439

Plaisance, P. L. (2014). Privacy. In *Media ethics: Key principles for responsible practice* (2nd ed., pp. 175–199). Los Angeles, CA: SAGE Publications. doi:10.4135/9781544308517.n10

Rawls, J. (1999). *A theory of justice* (2nd ed.). Cambridge, MA: Harvard University Press.

Ross, W. D. (1930). *The right and the good.* Oxford, UK: Clarendon Press.

Sontag, S. (2003). *Regarding the pain of others.* New York, N.Y.: Picador. doi:10.3917/dio.201.0127

UNICEF. (2017). *Reporting on children: An ethical guideline for journalists.* United Nations.

United Nations. (1989). *Convention on the Rights of the Child (A/RES/44/25).* New York: General Assembly.

Vlad, D. (2017). Perspectives on media representation of children. *Social Sciences and Education Research Review.*, *1*(4), 114–124.

Vos, T. P. (2018). *Journalism*. Boston: Walter de Gruyter Inc. doi:10.1515/9781501500084

Warren, C. (2006). *The nexus between independent journalists' unions, press freedom and poverty eradication: A Strategic Policy Discussion Between Donors and UNESCO* (Unpublished master's thesis). International Federation of Journalists.

Wilkins, L., & Clifford, G. C. (2009). *The handbook of media ethics*. New York: Routledge.

Zguri, P. (2014). *Ethical issues in photojournalism* (Unpublished Doctoral Thesis). University of Tirana.

Chapter 9
Public and Stakeholders' Perceptions of Newspaper Coverage of Child Labour in Nigeria

Oguchi Onyeizu Ajaegbu
Babcock University, Nigeria

Mofoluke Akoja
Babcock University, Nigeria

Taiwo Abolaji Ogunwemimo
https://orcid.org/0000-0003-0128-9013
Babcock University, Nigeria

ABSTRACT

The chapter explored public and stakeholder perceptions of media coverage of child labour in Nigeria. It has been observed that most studies are deficient in information on the interplay between media coverage of children issues and public perception of such coverage. This study therefore adopted the convergent mixed method design to elicit responses from audiences. Respondents were drawn from Babcock University on the assumption that individuals are literate enough to understand newspaper reports. Civil society organizations across Nigeria that deal specifically with children issues and some State Ministries of Women Affairs were sampled. The survey showed that people have knowledge of child labour issues from newspapers which in turn affect their attitude; however, their reactions to the reports are moderately favourable to the cause of abused children. It was recommended that newspapers give more coverage to child labour issues so that the public will have more knowledge and in turn make informed decisions.

DOI: 10.4018/978-1-7998-0329-4.ch009

INTRODUCTION / BACKGROUND

The chapter explored public and stakeholders' perception of media coverage of child labour in Nigeria. Children occupy an important position in the continuity of human existence as such their survival and development must be protected. It has been observed that most media coverage on different children issues are deficient in information on the interplay between media coverage of children issues and public perception of such coverage (Nwodu & Ezeoke, 2013).

It is the assumption of this chapter that child labour still thrives despite different advocacy efforts because the public do not fully understand the implications of the problem and the media as information sources to majority of people are also falling short in keeping people adequately informed, thus the adverse effects on the Nigerian child. Weatherred (2015) citing previous studies explained that most Americans get information on child sexual abuse through the media. Pickering (2016) added that the mass media are the vehicle through which social issues especially those of child welfare are relayed to the general public and thus, this makes them powerful in the society. Awosola and Omoera (2008 p.126) assert that "the media are persuasive instruments in man's struggle for liberation and development". Severin and Tankard (1979) explain that through the agenda-setting function, the mass media are to select and emphasize certain issues so that the public can perceive such issues as important.

Internews Europe (2014 p.8) in its study highlighted some reasons for the inadequate reporting of child labour issues; one of such is the lack of media-Civil Society Organizations cooperation. It explains that there is a high level of mistrust between both parties and this leads to failure to understand each other's needs and expectations. It should be stressed that both parties need to work in tandem to restore the dignity of the Nigerian child; the CSOs are to keep the media aware of their efforts at alleviating the situation of children not just for publicity purposes. The media are also to work with the CSOs as they could be viable information sources in exposing some ills that children go through. The media, the CSOs as well as the ministries of women affairs and social development are to work as partners in progress and harness strengths to handle the concerns of children.

This is especially mandatory in view of the fact that Nigeria is a signatory to the United Nations Convention on the Rights of the Child and has also ratified some other laws for the protection of children. It should be noted that any nation that is a signatory to such laws is expected to ensure a high level of protection for the children against abuse and other forms of exploitation. It is possible that lack of media education or the portrayal of child labour issues as a mere offense rather than putting it into context as a broader issue of concern, may have increased its prevalence. This means that the extent to which the mass media covers or fails to cover issues of child labour will affect the public's understanding and attitude to the issues. Pickering (2016) explains that media representation of child welfare positively and negatively impacts child welfare and indirectly affects how the public and policy makers perceive the issue. Nwodu and Ezeoke (2013), in their study examined the coverage of children and women's rights by the Nigerian press, recommended that there should be a more elaborate research to find out the correlation between press coverage of the issues and the audience perception and attitude to the issues. Weatherred (2015) implies that news media influences public perception of child sexual abuse which in turn impacts public policy. This shows that framing media reports on child labour as a problem requiring urgent attention and solution can lead to an improved public attitude to the issue.

The study takes into cognisance the fact that the concerted efforts of all stakeholders involved is equally important. Therefore, it seeks to examine public and stakeholders' perception of media coverage of child labour in Nigeria. The specific objectives are to:

1. determine the level of awareness of the public on newspaper's coverage of child labour issues;
2. explore the extent to which the public gained knowledge on newspaper's reports on child labour;
3. investigate the attitude of the public to newspaper reports on child labour;
4. examine the reactions newspaper reports on child labour provoke among the public;
5. ascertain how the public perceive the effectiveness of the newspapers in reporting child labour issues; and
6. determine the perception of stakeholders on the effectiveness of newspapers coverage of child labour issues?

LITERATURE REVIEW

Child Labour: An Overview

Even though all human beings are entitled by nature and international human right laws to enjoy some inalienable rights, children are often deprived these rights most especially by the same set of people entrusted with their care. This problem has continued to hamper the development of children. The practice of child labour predates the Industrial Revolution of the 18th century in the Great Britain. Children below the age of ten were made to engage in dangerous work in mines and factories for long hours with little stipend. This problem has remained an issue of global concern decades after. Although, it began among the agricultural societies, its rise has been linked to industrial production and capitalism (Kudjonu, 2016). With the trend dwindling and completely eradicated in countries like the United Kingdom among other developed nations, it has remained prevalent in Sub-Saharan Africa especially in countries with low standards of living. According to the International Labour Organisation (ILO), in its World Report on Child Labour in 2013, about 265million children in the world amounting to 17 percent of the world-wide population of children are working (Ortiz-Ospina & Roser, 2019).

Many attempts have been made to define child labour and over the decades so many views have sufficed. The International Trade Union Confederation (ITUC) has defined it as:

work that deprives children of their childhood, their potential, dignity and harmful to their physical and mental development. It refers to work that is mentally, physically, socially or morally dangerous and harmful to children and/or interferes with their schooling by depriving them of the opportunity to attend school, obliging them to leave school prematurely or requiring them to attempt to combine school attendance with excessively long and heavy work.

Clarifying further on its position, ILO convention 138 added that child labour is when children under the age of fifteen (15) are made to do work that is physically or mentally harmful and interrupts their education and social development. Generally, child labour is defined as the employment of children in any work that deprives them of their childhood and dignity, and that is harmful to their physical and mental development (Ortiz-Ospina & Roser, 2019). From the foregoing, what constitutes child labour will depend on the child's age, the number of hours worked, the type of tasks performed, the circumstances under which the work is performed and the objectives aimed at. This is because children are now encouraged to take part in practical education that will help them with skills to persist in the economical world. Thus, a child may work for pleasure, leisure, hobby, to assist parents, to make money or even meet an aspiration (Kudjonu, 2016). In short, there are positive reasons why children may work and depriving them of such opportunities could also hamper their total development. On the other hand, any kind of work may be harmful to children especially if it hampers their education. Thus work that does not interfere with education (light work) is permitted from the age of twelve (12) years under the ILO convention 138 (Kudjonu, 2016).

While mining constitutes the worst form of child labour, other forms such as trafficking, slavery, prostitution, domestic servitude, trading, small or large scale agriculture among others can be equally incapacitating.

CHILD LABOUR IN NIGERIA

In Nigeria, about 15million children below the age of 14 are engaged in one form of work or the other usually for long hours in unhealthy and dangerous environments and often handling responsibilities above their age. Often times, these children are deprived of education or are forced to work part time for their education. It is estimated that about 6million Nigerian children do not attend school, over 80 million manage to stay in school and work partly while one million are forced to drop out of school for several reasons including poverty, need to support family income, broken family, greed, family size, culture and illiteracy (UNICEF, 2006; Agbo, 2017). The money earned by a child member of family has become a significant source of income due to some of these reasons. The National Bureau of Statistics in conjunction with the National Primary Health Care Development Agency (NPHCDA) and the United Nations Children Fund (UNICEF) in the 2017 Multiple Indicator Cluster Survey (MICS) says about 50% of Nigerian Children, aged between five and 17 years, are involved in child labour (Business Insider, 2018).

The International Labour Organization (ILO) reports that despite several legislations by the Nigerian government, 43% of Nigerian children aged between five to 10 years are involved in child labour (Adepegba, 2019).

According to UNICEF (2006), places where children work in Nigeria may be categorised into four major aspects including public places such as streets and markets; semi-public settings such as cottage industries and mechanic shops; private households (domestic servants); and agricultural plantations (farm and quarry). Although efforts are being made to combat this menace, the practice persists as a cycle of child right violations are noticeable in Nigeria. Some of the existing measures include the adoption of the International Labour Organization (ILO) conventions proscribing a minimum age for the employment of children at sea, in industry and underground in addition to the signing of a Memorandum of Understanding in August 2003 in cooperation with ILO to launch a country programme under the International Programme for the Elimination of Child Labour (IPEC). The implementation of the West Africa Cocoa Agriculture Project (WACAP) and the passing of the Child Rights Act Sections 28 and 29 into law is another giant step taken by the Nigerian government to combat this problem. The Child Rights Act prohibits exploitative Labour and enforces sections 58 -64 of the Labour Decree of 1974, now the Labour Act. In some states, like Anambra State, children have been banned from working during school hours. Despite the existence of these legislative stands, legal enforcement remains abysmal leading to serious social and economic implications (UNICEF, 2006).

The rise in insurgency in the country is another factor incapacitating children in Nigeria. Adeniran, Hassan, Ajaga and Kayode (2015) noted that there has been a reduction in child enrolment and attendance in schools as insurgents now target schools in perpetrating their heinous crimes thus prompting parents/guardians in susceptible areas to withdraw their wards from schools to keep them alive.

At the individual level, it has been noted that child labour impairs the physical and mental development of children leading to an increment in the number of lay about, mentally demented, and stunted persons in the society (Ugal & Undyaundeye, 2012). Equally, Awosola and Omoera (2008) described the consequences as saddening experiences which have strong emotional impact on the victim as often times, abused and neglected children are overwhelmed and shattered resulting into emotional imbalance which eventually manifest in delinquency and deviance.

CHILD RIGHTS ACT IN NIGERIA

The Nigeria Child Rights Act (CRA) is a domesticated version of the United Nations Convention on the Rights of the Child (UNCRC). The Child's Rights Act is a law passed by the Nigerian National Assembly in July 2003 which incorporates all the rights and responsibilities of children as well as providing protection and care for the Nigerian child. Although this law was passed at the Federal level, it is only effective if state assemblies also enact it. States are to adapt similar version of the law and make it relevant to their specific situations. The reason for having states adapt this law to their situation is because it is a recurring issue.

Amalu (2010) states that more than seven years after the CRA was passed into law, only 22 States in the country have passed the Act. (Obozuwa, 2010). However, besides passing the law at the state level, the most important thing is strict enforcement. Poverty is a major cause of child labour and this means that the states have a huge role to play to eradicate poverty. It is not enough to have good laws, it is most important to have laws that are adequately enforced and practicable. As stated by UNICEF Country Communication Officer quoted by Amalu (2010) the states that have assented to the law are reluctant to enforce it because they feel it would make children grow wild.

Obozuwa (2010) citing a National Daily on August 22, 2005, reports that the Supreme Council for Shari'ah in Nigeria (SCSN) said:

Any law that seeks to give equal rights to male and female children in inheritance seeks to give an illegitimate child the same rights as the legitimate one, and establish a court (family court) that ousts the jurisdiction of Shariah courts on all matters affecting children, is unacceptable to Muslims.

The group said the Child Rights Act is an instrument to outlaw Shariah courts.

In Lagos state, the CRA was passed in 2007 and renamed The Child Rights Law; in Rivers state, the CRA was signed into law in 2010 and it is called the Rivers State Child's Right Act 2009, Cross River state adopted the law in 2009, In Akwa Ibom state where the Act has also been passed into law, children are still branded witches and wizard and are physically abused and neglected in a bid to make them confess to such allegations (ThankGod-Amadi, 2012; Uwaleke & Eghagha, 2009).

Ogun is one of the states in Nigeria that has recognized the need for the eradication of child labour in Nigeria. The state demonstrated its commitment and resolve with the inauguration of the State Steering Committee on Child Labour (SSC) in May 2012. Enumerating its action plan for the elimination of child labour in Nigeria (2014-2017), it listed one of its strategies for combatting this menace as advocacy and awareness creation on the evils and effects of child labour in the 21 LGAs of Ogun State. The plan noted a low level of awareness campaign on the hazards of child labour through the media (OSAPECLN, 2014). Ever since the launch of this document highlighting the different strategies and actions to be taken by all stakeholders, the practice of child labour in Ogun State is still a major source of concern.

The result of a study conducted in Sagamu Local Government of Ogun State among primary and junior secondary school students revealed a 64.5% prevalence rate, underscoring the high prevalence rates reported in Nigeria. The findings of this study also confirmed previous reports showing that children in Nigeria both school and work. Further, the study revealed a higher representation of girls than boys among working children reflecting a gender bias in upbringing with the intent of preparing the female child for traditional roles of small-scale economic trades to support the family. It equally revealed that Muslim children were more involved in child labour than their Christian counterparts suggesting a religious undertone in the practice of child labour in this part of the state. (Fetuga, Njokoma & Olowu, 2005).

MEDIA AGENDA SETTING AND CHILD LABOUR PRACTICE IN NIGERIA

As the fourth estate of the realm, the media is recognised as an institution powerful enough to set present certain issues as top-burners in public discourse and as such emphasise its importance through agenda setting. Propounded by Maxwell McCombs and Donald L. Shaw in 1972/1973, the agenda setting theory *proposes that the facts which people know about public issues tend to be those which the mass media presents to them. Also, the significance which they ascribe to the same issues tend to be proportionate to the amount of attention given to the same issues in the media. (Anaeto, Onabajo & Osifeso, 2008 p.89)*

The theory predicts that if people are exposed to the same media, they will place importance on the issues raised; explaining why people with similar media exposure place importance on the same issues. In line with this viewpoint, Sanchar (2002 p.40) had rightly noted that the media plays an important role in creating awareness among the general public and in emphasizing pertinent issues for the development of the child noting further that the media can also be very effective for the overall development of children through the advocacy for children's rights. Ugal and Undyaundeye (2012) affirmed the role of the mass media by explaining that the print and electronic media is aghast with news on the engagement of children in labour or work. Confirming further, these researchers realised that the media's concern has been that the world's population especially in the developing countries of Asia and Africa is made up of children (between ages 5-15) and about 60% of these children are engaged in one form of labour or another.

In the Nigerian context however, Awosola and Omoera (2008) in their study investigated the extent to which television has created awareness of child rights in Oredo local government in Edo state. They highlighted some television programmes that were created to address the problems of child labour however; they also explained that the degree of awareness by these programmes is not properly established. In a bid to understand how television has raised awareness, the study adopted the exploratory survey design to analyse the responses of 200 residents of Oredo local government in Edo state. They found out that television has raised awareness of child rights though the finding does not reflect with the practices in the locality where people still maltreat children. This means that though the people are aware of what child rights constitute, they have not been able to practice upholding children's rights.

Highlighting the major causes of child labour and human trafficking from press reports, Olube (2015) examined the role of the media by content analysing four Nigerian newspapers (*Vanguard, Champion, Sunday Punch* and *The Guardian*) by purposively collecting reports on child labour and women trafficking using a coding sheet with results measured in frequency counts and percentages. Following a review of 16 reports coded from the month of September 2003 – June 2004, results showed that all the reports are favourable, majority of the victims of child labour and women trafficking are born to parents of lower class levels who are uneducated and unskilled; some parents see their children as a source of income because of poverty, and as a result of ignorance give out their children to foster parents, relatives, masters, mistresses and friends for incentives which they usually don't get; and government agencies, the media and non-governmental organizations (NGOs) are involved in the fight against child labour and women trafficking.

Muhammed and Kadiri (2011) explored the mass media as correlates of children behaviour problems in Kwara State Nigeria emphasizing the role of television in particular as a critical force in the socialization of children. Based on an hypothesis testing the relationship between mass media and children's behavioural problems, it was found that the two variables were related with an observed calculated value of chi-square of 12,240.000 exceeding the table value of 124.342 at 0.05 with 225 degrees of freedom with a Pearson product moment correlation coefficient of 0.1000. The study concluded that children's behavioural problems can be linked to the amount of media children are exposed to. Thus, it was recommended that formulation of public policy by government should focus on eliminating violence scenes in the mass media, particularly television while the mass media provide instead programmes that serve the educational and informational needs of children.

Using two Nigerian newspapers, Nkememena (2009) investigated the performance of newspapers on the coverage of child trafficking in Nigeria by content analysing such issues across a period of 12 months with a coding sheet as the instrument for data gathering. A sample size of 118 was drawn systematically from September 2007 to August 2008. Findings revealed that the two newspapers did not give adequate coverage to the issue of child trafficking as most of the stories were tucked into the inside pages. It was concluded relegating child trafficking by the media will make it an entrenched criminal practice in Nigeria.

In a study analysing press coverage of child labour issues in Nigeria, Ajaegbu, Alao and Oloyede, (2018) explains that the press is saddled with the responsibility of exposing societal anomalies like child labour. The purpose of the study was to assess the extent to which the media gave coverage to child labour issues; three newspapers- *The Guardian*, *The Punch* and *The Sun* were selected for a period of five years 2010-2014. It was discovered that media did not give prominence to reports on child labour; straight news reports accounted for the majority; child abuse was the most reported child labour type and the reports were given an episodic angle of reporting. It was recommended that the media should give a broader context to child labour issues since it is a societal problem and not reporting stories from the individual-level angle that will yield flawed solutions.

In same vein, Oyero (2011b) studied how children are reported in Nigerian newspapers in an attempt to understand the news environment in which child rights is portrayed and the consequences it has for the realisation of the rights of the child. The study established that "the current coverage of children's issues by the Nigerian newspapers may not deliver much benefits as regards the realisation of the rights of the child due to low coverage and inadequate prominence given to children, lack of good treatment of the issue with appropriate genres, as well as poor engagement of children themselves on issues that affect them" (Togunde & Olawole ed., 2011 p.28).

Adeniran, Hassan, Ajaga and Kayode (2015) content analysed all news stories, features and editorials published in two national daily newspapers (*The Punch* and *The Guardian*) and two news magazines (*Tell* and *The News*) published between April to June 2013, the authors examined the coverage of children-related issues in the Nigerian print news media. The result showed that children-related issues are generally under-reported in the Nigerian press but when the children are involved in crime related issues, the media give them "adequate" coverage. It was thus recommended that the print media adopts a more cautious approach in reporting children and children-related issues.

Furthermore into how the mass media set agenda for what the public thinks about, different scholars have explored how the framing of issues by the media could influence the attitude of the public towards the issue. Mastin, Choi, Barboza and Post (2007 p.779) explain that "the manner in which the media present a health issue defines the problem, and in turn, influences individuals' and societies' decisions in regard to adopting one solution among several alternatives." This could be attributed to the type of frame used to construct the issue. The study by Mastin et al (2007) further explains that the way the media typify an issue generate public outcries and policy responses.

The manner an issue is framed, by inclusion and exclusion of certain aspects, suggests the solutions for such issues. By framing child labour in a certain way, it could influence the public attitude towards the issue. Iyengar's (1991) thematic and episodic frames show that the frame the media decide to adopt will go a long way to affect the solutions or the public reactions to a particular problem. Episodic frame addresses a social problem from an individual-level angle thus requiring an individual solution; on the other hand, thematic frame describes the issue from a more collective-level angle putting the issue in societal context. The implication of this is that, child labour will be seen as an individual problem from the episodic angle or be seen as a society's problem from the thematic angle.

Different studies have put these frames to test and it was discovered that the media reports child labour and abuse issues from an episodic perspective (Ajaegbu, Alao & Oloyede, 2018; Internews Europe, 2014; Arthur, 2012; Mastin, Choi, Barboza & Post, 2007; Kunkel, Smith, Suding & Biely, 2002).

STAKEHOLDERS INVOLVEMENT IN CHILD LABOUR

Different stakeholders have been involved in the fight for the child rights and ending child labour issues. At the local and international levels, these stakeholders are playing prominent roles which have led to the reduction in certain instances and more awareness in other contexts. However, there are concerns that many a times, stakeholders' efforts are not properly coordinated and as such, communication and action gaps are created leading to a slow realization of the objective of ending child labour. In places where the practice of child labour has been completely eradicated like the United Kingdom, stakeholders played significant roles in making it happen.

According to UNICEF (2014 p.8), engaging stakeholders on children's rights can help in "broad sustainability strategies, support the process of implementing human rights, inform materiality exercises, or enable a company to delve deeper into specific material issues to determine appropriate actions and responses".

Stakeholders may include civil society and international organisations, parents/caregivers, government, labour organisations, professionals in contact with children, media, community leaders, company personnel, youth organisations and the children themselves. Studies have revealed that often times in Nigeria, these stakeholders do not work together in the achievement of the overall goal of eliminating child rights and child labour issues mainly because of their unwillingness to work together. Atuma (2018) reported the outcome of a stakeholders meeting which held in Osun State sometime in 2018 blamed parents and guardians for using children and wards as street hawkers, marketers and custodians of house chores thereby exposing them to suffering and child trafficking options.

International and local agencies involved in tackling the problem have also been blamed for not living up to expectations due to the fact that not many of those involved have not been convicted thereby serving as deterrent to others (Ahiuma-Young, 2012). On the part of the media, the role of mobilising public support and involvement to help in preventing and combatting this problem has been grossly deficient despite the fact that the media possesses the ability to reach and mould public opinion as a powerful agent for social change.

Recently, the Ministry of Labour in Nigeria conveyed its renewed commitment in the fight against child labour in Nigeria recognising the fact that it portends a great threat to national peace and national development. The Ministry has developed a national template on the elimination of child labour in Nigeria so as to help in tackling the incidences of child labour across the country and serve as valuation mechanism to facilitate the identification of gaps in the implementation of multi-sectoral strategies and processes (PR Nigeria, 2018)

METHOD

The study adopted a mixed method design, comprising quantitative and qualitative methods. The specific type of mixed method used is the convergent parallel design.

The purpose of this design according to Creswell (2012 p. 540) is "to simultaneously collect both quantitative and qualitative data, merge the data, and use the results to understand a research problem". According to Creswell (2012 p.540), "the direct comparison of the two datasets… provides a convergence of data sources".

For the quantitative method, the chosen population was Babcock University, Ogun State. This is because on one hand, Ogun state has a high incidence of trafficking in persons and is a major transit point (Iyanda & Nwogwugwu, 2016). On the other hand, the chapter examines newspapers reader's perceptions of coverage of child labour issues, a university community with literate audience is considered appropriate. There is a supply of newspapers to different offices in the institution and to the University library for different users. Thus, Babcock university is appropriate for this study as individuals have access and read newspaper reports. However, the results of this study would not be generalised to represent the perceptions of all Ogun residents.

The institution comprises faculty and staff, it has a nursery and primary school, a secondary school, undergraduate and postgraduate schools', it also has a Teaching hospital which also houses a state-of-the-art heart and vascular centre, some financial institutions that cater to the campus and members of the host community. With these, the University attracts a daily population of about 10,000 people (Director of Security Services, Babcock University, 2019) from its immediate and surrounding environments.

Based on a population of 10,000, a sample size of 253 was calculated and respondents were picked using the convenience sampling from individuals around the campus who are willing and enlightened enough on the issue of child labour. Saunders, Lewis and Thornhill (2009) formula was used to calculate the sample size for the study. Therefore, it was assumed that 20% of the participants from the population may be knowledgeable about the subject of enquiry; hence p% and q% are 80% and 20% respectively. Although a total of 253 was administered based on the sample size calculated, 250 copies were returned at the end of the survey. However, only 200 copies were correctly filled and considered valid for final analysis.

Furthermore, in-depth interviews were conducted among key officers of select civil society organizations (CSOs) and State Ministries of Women Affairs and Social Development dealing with child labour issues. Their opinions on the issues were sampled based on their roles as major social actors in the fight against child labour. There are different civil society organizations that cater to different areas of the society. The selected CSOs are located in different areas of the country and were purposively selected based on the fact that they deal with children protection issues. The CSOs sampled were Women Trafficking and Child Labour Eradication Foundation (WOTCLEF), African Network for the Prevention and Protection against Child Abuse and Neglect (ANPPCAN) Nigeria Chapter, Child Life – Line (CLL), Idia Renaissance and Save the Child Initiative. Telephone interviews were conducted with the representatives as some of these CSOs are based in distant places; they were purposively chosen because they deal with child rights issues. Different CSOs were communicated but only the stated ones were willing to speak on the issue. However, there were no responses from WOTCLEF.

State ministries of Women Affairs from Lagos, Ogun and Oyo states were also included in this study purposively. There were no special criteria for the choice of the states as they were chosen based on convenience and proximity. This was important to get responses from the angle of the government though at the state level. The state Ministries are: Ministry of Women Affairs and Poverty Alleviation (Lagos state), Ministry of Women Affairs (Oyo State) and Ministry of Women Affairs (Ogun State). It cut across the ministries in these states to get more robust responses. Specific departments were selected in these ministries because of their involvement with handling children issues, they are: Department of Social Welfare Services, and Department of Child Development.

The idea basically is to ascertain their perception of the newspaper reports in creating awareness and educating the citizenry on the problem of child labour. While this study seeks to get the perception of the public on the coverage of the media generally, it will be more focused on newspapers.

NGOs and CSOs are one of the major social actors in the fight against child labour because they get to the grassroots and are able to mobilize communities to work toward its elimination. Most NGOs or CSOs work to promote the welfare and rights of children through campaigns and they also play a major part in national campaigns against child labour. Based on the reports of the media on child labour and on their own findings, they rally the government to create a protective atmosphere for children by instituting better policies and coming up with good enforcement mechanisms to the existing laws. Using mixed methods in data collection is appropriate because it answers the question from a number of perspectives and variation in data leads to greater validity of the results of the study.

For the instruments, this study adopted the use of a questionnaire and a structured in-depth interview guide. The interview guide was used to elicit responses from respondents in the selected NGOs/CSOs and also the State Ministries of Women Affairs.

The questionnaire was subjected to Cronbach Alpha reliability test to establish internal consistency of constructs in the research instrument and it yielded the following coefficients: level of awareness=0.784; knowledge of child labour issues from the reports= 0.940; attitude to newspaper reports on child labour issues=0.904; reactions newspaper reports have provoked in the public=0.857 and effectiveness of newspapers in reporting child labour issues=0.937. On an average note, the reliability score yielded 0.967, this shows that the questionnaire is highly reliable.

RESULT

This section shows the result of data analysis, interpretation and discussion of findings in respect of the investigation of public and stakeholders perception of child labour issues.

Majority of respondents to this survey are within ages 31 to 40 years (n=104, 14.4%) and there were more male respondents (n=113, 56.5%) than female respondents (n=87, 43.5%). Furthermore, there were more respondents with Master's degree (106, 53%) than there were with PhD (n=57, 28.5%) and Higher National Diploma and Bachelor's degree (n=37, 18.5). In addition, most of the respondents are married (n=137, 68.5%) and also most of the respondents said they have children (n=132, 66%).

The implication of demography is that it is possible that when one has a child, it could affect their attitude towards child labour reports and also the level of education could determine the extent to which they know about child labour issues from newspaper reports.

Respondents were asked how often they see child labour reports in the newspapers. Most respondents said they see newspaper reports on child labour sometimes (n=95, 47.5%) while others said often (n=62, 31%) and rarely (n=25, 12.5%) respectively; the least group said very often (n=18, 9%). This means that the respondents do not see child labour reports in the newspapers regularly even though the issue is one of great concern and this implies that the newspapers are not doing enough in the coverage of child labour issues.

The analysis in table 2 shows the awareness level of respondents and how they ranked the child labour issues they see most in newspapers. Respondents ranked child abuse as the highest ($\bar{x}$=3.79) followed by child trafficking ($\bar{x}$=3.53), this shows that these two issues were ranked on a high level. Domestic work ($\bar{x}$=3.29), street begging ($\bar{x}$=3.20), street trading ($\bar{x}$=3.10), commercial sexual exploitation ($\bar{x}$=3.09) and child slavery ($\bar{x}$=2.84) were ranked in the moderate level while children in armed conflict

Table 1. Frequency of child labour stories

Variable	Frequency	Percent
Very Often	18	9.0
Often	62	31.0
Sometimes	95	47.5
Rarely	25	12.5
Total	**200**	**100.0**

Table 2. Awareness of child labour issues

Issues	Mean ($\bar{x}$)	SD
Child Abuse	3.79	1.24
Child Trafficking	3.53	1.33
Domestic Work	3.29	1.57
Street Begging	3.20	1.49
Street Trading	3.10	1.50
Commercial Sexual Exploitation	3.09	1.34
Child Slavery	2.84	1.47
Children In Armed Conflict	2.16	1.30
Average Mean	**3.12**	**1.41**

Lowest Level 1<-----2--------3---------4-------5 Highest Level; *** Decision Rule; if mean is ≤1.49= Lowest Level; 1.5 to 2.49= Low Level; 2.5 to 3.49=Moderate Level; 3.5 to 4.49 = High Level; 4.5 to 5= Highest Level

was ranked lowest ($\bar{x}$=2.16). This shows that respondents are more aware of child abuse in the sense that it had the most occurrences in the newspaper reports. On an average note, respondents are moderately aware of child labour issues ($\bar{x}$=3.12).

Stakeholders

One major part of this study looked at stakeholders, that is, those who should be partners with the media in the fight to end child labour. It is assumed that the government at all levels and civil society organizations are partners in progress with the media in addressing the welfare of children.

Figure 1. Stakeholders/voices in the reports

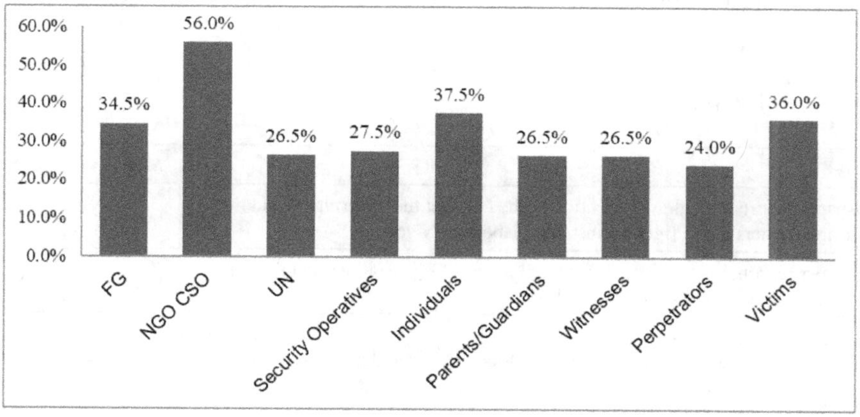

In addition, newspaper reports also reflect the voices of different persons, figure 1 shows that the respondents are of the opinion that civil society organizations or non-governmental organizations account for the most voices (56%) followed by individuals (37.5%). The voices of victims (36%) and perpetrators (24%) are also seen. The federal government (34.5) also features in the reports also and this is important because they are the policy makers where issues are concerned. Furthermore, the analysis in table 3 shows the opinion of respondents in relation to two major stakeholders.

This shows that the public believes that the government ($\bar{x}$=3.09) and civil society organizations ($\bar{x}$=3.42) are to moderate level partners with the media in the fight against child labour.

Table 4 shows the level of knowledge the public have acquired from newspaper reports. The table indicates that the public to a moderate level have gained knowledge from newspaper reports on child labour issues ($\bar{x}$=3.17). Respondents had moderate knowledge level across the parameters of knowledge on the issues: child abuse ($\bar{x}$=3.15); street begging ($\bar{x}$=3.13); street trading ($\bar{x}$=3.16); child trafficking ($\bar{x}$=3.38); domestic labour ($\bar{x}$=3.21); commercial sexual exploitation ($\bar{x}$=3.30); children in armed conflict ($\bar{x}$=3.27); and child slavery ($\bar{x}$=2.77). This implies that the public have not gained much knowledge of child labour issues from newspaper reports.

We also analysed newspapers reports on child labour issues; the respondents have a high level of disposition to newspaper reports on child abuse ($\bar{x}$=3.77); street begging/street trading ($\bar{x}$=3.57); child trafficking ($\bar{x}$=3.62); domestic labour ($\bar{x}$=3.64); commercial sexual exploitation ($\bar{x}$=3.54); and children in armed conflict ($\bar{x}$=3.55). However, they have a moderate attitude to reports on child slavery ($\bar{x}$=3.35). This means that the public have a favourable attitude to newspaper reports on child labour issues.

Table 5 shows that the public have a moderately favourable reaction to newspaper reports on child labour ($\bar{x}$=3.46). On an item basis, their reaction to child abuse ($\bar{x}$=3.47) was moderate, the reaction to street begging/street trading ($\bar{x}$=3.54);

Table 3. Major stakeholders

Items	Mean ($\bar{x}$)	SD
Newspaper reports have drawn attention to the fact that the government and the media are partners in the fight against child labour in Nigeria	3.09	1.22
Newspaper reports have projected that Civil Society Organizations and the media are partners in the fight against child labour	3.42	1.28

Lowest Level 1<-----2--------3---------4-------5 Highest Level; *** Decision Rule; if mean is ≤1.49= Lowest Level; 1.5 to 2.49= Low Level; 2.5 to 3.49=Moderate Level; 3.5 to 4.49 = High Level; 4.5 to 5= Highest Level

Table 4. Level of knowledge

Items	Mean ($\bar{x}$)	SD	AM
Child abuse			
Newspaper reports have helped me know the difference between child abuse and discipline	2.87	1.41	**3.15 (SD=1.28)**
Through newspaper reports, I know that child abuse involves sexual exploitation.	3.15	1.18	
Through newspaper reports, I understand that child abuse involves neglecting and denying children basic necessities	3.43	1.25	
Street begging			
From newspaper reports, I am aware that some parents send their children to the streets to beg to provide for the family	3.32	1.25	**3.13 (SD=1.25)**
From newspaper reports, I understand that some parents send their children to beg to pay their school bills	2.94	1.25	
Street trading			
Newspaper reports have made me understand that children involved in street hawking, could be involved in criminal activities to meet their daily target	3.13	1.21	**3.16 (SD=1.28)**
Newspaper reports have made me understand that children who engage in street trading may have daily target and in the process may beg to meet their daily target	3.19	1.34	
Child trafficking			
Newspaper reports have enlightened me that children are transported to different places for the purpose of exploitation	3.31	1.22	**3.38 (SD=1.31)**
I am sensitised through Newspaper reports that traffickers entice children and unsuspecting parents with the promise of education and better living conditions	3.44	1.40	
Domestic labour			
Newspaper reports have made me understand that there is a thin line between domestic service and training	3.01	1.21	**3.21 (SD=1.22)**
Newspaper reports have made me understand that domestic servants are more prone to exploitation	3.25	1.13	
Through Newspaper reports, I realized that engaging children as house helps is an abuse	3.38	1.32	
Commercial sexual exploitation			
Through newspaper reports, I understand that children are sold for sexual pleasure	3.39	1.23	**3.30 (SD=1.26)**
Newspaper reports have enlightened me on advocacy programmes against sexual exploitation of children	3.20	1.28	
Children in armed conflict			
Newspaper reports have me realize that children are involved in armed conflict	3.04	1.28	**3.27 (SD=1.26)**
I am aware through newspaper reports that children are recruited by extremist groups to take part in terrorist activities	3.50	1.24	
Child Slavery			
Through newspaper reports, I am aware that some parents give out their children to settle debts	2.93	1.28	**2.77 (SD=1.27)**
I am aware of the fact that newspapers report on labour laws protecting children even when they are used to settle debts	2.61	1.26	
Average Mean	**3.17**	**1.26**	

Lowest Level 1<-----2--------3---------4-------5 Highest Level; *** Decision Rule; if mean is ≤1.49= Lowest Level; 1.5 to 2.49= Low Level; 2.5 to 3.49=Moderate Level; 3.5 to 4.49 = High Level; 4.5 to 5= Highest Level

Table 5. Reactions newspaper reports have provoked

Items	Mean $(\bar{x})$	SD	AM
Child abuse			
Through newspaper reports, I am willing to draw a line between discipline and abuse	3.34	1.30	**3.47 (SD=1.25)**
Through newspaper reports, I intend to advocate stopping punishments that harm children	3.60	1.20	
Street begging / Street trading			
Through newspaper reports, I intend to rally a community of professionals to generate solutions to keep children off the streets especially during school hours	3.33	1.38	**3.54 (SD=1.31)**
I am encouraged to put pressure on policy makers to make laws to keep children off the streets	3.75	1.23	
Domestic labour			
Through newspaper reports, I am willing to report perpetrators of domestic abuse to the relevant authorities	3.48	1.30	**3.61 (SD=1.32)**
I am encouraged to advocate better ways of disciplining a child without abuse	3.73	1.33	
Commercial sexual exploitation / Child trafficking			
Through newspaper reports, I am willing to raise more awareness through different platforms on the sexual exploitation of children	3.54	1.32	**3.60 (SD=1.31)**
Through newspaper reports, I intend to speak against people with improper relations with children	3.66	1.30	
Children in armed conflict			
Through newspaper reports, I intend to engage my community in outreach programmes to rehabilitate children in armed conflict	3.16	1.41	**3.32 (SD=1.35)**
I intend to lend my voice to increase support for advocacy programmes for children in armed conflict	3.48	1.29	
Child Slavery			
I intend to sponsor a law or movement against child slavery	3.12	1.42	**3.24 (SD=1.37)**
I am willing to generate and disseminate professional ideas to help the plight of children	3.35	1.32	
Average Mean	**3.46**	**1.32**	

Lowest Level 1<-----2--------3---------4-------5 Highest Level; *** Decision Rule; if mean is ≤1.49= Lowest Level; 1.5 to 2.49= Low Level; 2.5 to 3.49=Moderate Level; 3.5 to 4.49 = High Level; 4.5 to 5= Highest Level

domestic labour ($\bar{x}$=3.61); commercial sexual exploitation/child trafficking ($\bar{x}$=3.60) were high. While their reaction to reports on children in armed conflict ($\bar{x}$=3.32); and child slavery ($\bar{x}$=3.24) were to a moderate level. This means that the reaction of the public to newspaper reports on child labour is moderately high.

Table 6. Effectiveness of newspaper in reporting child labour issues

Issues	Mean ($\bar{x}$)	SD
Newspaper reports on child labour have enlightened me on what child labour issues constitute	3.61	1.22
The level of reportage given to child labour in newspapers is laudable	3.39	1.17
Newspapers constantly sensitize the public on child labour issues	3.39	1.16
Newspapers reports have been able to place the problem of child labour in the minds of the public	3.36	1.13
Newspaper reports give pride of place to child labour issues	3.08	1.13
Newspaper reports give proper attention to child labour issues in Nigeria by setting it as an agenda for public discourse	3.17	1.19
Newspaper reports have been successful in mounting pressure on government to make child welfare policies	3.19	1.33
Average Mean	**3.31**	**1.19**

Lowest Level 1<-----2--------3---------4-------5 Highest Level; *** Decision Rule; if mean is ≤1.49= Lowest Level; 1.5 to 2.49= Low Level; 2.5 to 3.49=Moderate Level; 3.5 to 4.49 = High Level; 4.5 to 5= Highest Level

Table 6 shows the extent to which the public thinks newspapers have been effective in their reportage of child labour issues. On the average, the public rate newspapers effectiveness at a moderate level ($\bar{x}$=3.31). Newspaper reports on child labour have enlightened me on what child labour issues constitute ($\bar{x}$=3.61); the level of reportage given to child labour in newspapers is laudable ($\bar{x}$=3.39); newspapers constantly sensitize the public on child labour issues ($\bar{x}$=3.39); Newspapers reports have been able to place the problem of child labour in the minds of the public ($\bar{x}$=3.36); newspaper reports give pride of place to child labour issues ($\bar{x}$=3.08); newspaper reports give proper attention to child labour issues in Nigeria by setting it as an agenda for public discourse ($\bar{x}$=3.17); and Newspaper reports have been successful in mounting pressure on government to make child welfare policies ($\bar{x}$=3.19). This means the newspapers are fairly effective in their coverage of child labour issues.

Research Question 6: What is the perception of stakeholders on the effectiveness of press coverage of child labour issues?

To further validate the results gotten from the survey of newspaper readers, interviews were conducted on representatives of some selected Non-Governmental Organisations/Civil Society Organisations (NGOs/CSOs) and also on some representatives of Ministries of Women Affairs and Social Development in Lagos, Ogun and Oyo states.

The responses were used to contextualise the results of the survey to find out from the angle of major social actors if the media are performing the agenda-setting role in reporting child labour issues. Victims of some problems usually do not speak up and that is the same situation with children because of fear of being harmed. This section attempts to find out if the press are setting the right agenda on issues relating to child rights violations.

The analysis was to find out what these stakeholders think about media coverage of child labour issues, that is if the media are covering the issues of child labour adequately through their reports. The responses are summarised not on an individual basis but from the angle of the CSOs generally and the final statements in each of the themes will represent the voices of the representatives of the Ministries of Women Affairs and Social Development.

THEMES

Extent to Which the Press Cover Child Labour Issues

There were varying answers to this question. A respondent said the newspapers are not covering child labour issues adequately. However, they said that compared to what obtained in the 80s, newspaper coverage have improved greatly and people now know about child labour as compared to the 80s when people denied there was any form of abuse in the country. On how well the newspapers are doing, respondents said they are not doing enough and need to do more in terms of programmes, policies and laws.

The representatives of the ministries are in agreement that the media generally cover child labour issues. They are however of the opinion that is it not enough and there is more to be done.

Extent to Which People Have Been Sensitised on Child Labour Issues

The consensus was that the media reports have actually helped to sensitise people on the problem of child labour and raise awareness for the education of children. At least one area is that of child hawking as parents who used to send even their own children to hawk now send them to school.

The reports have not really being able to sensitize the public because the problem is still on, on the other hand another representative said that the media have tried to sensitise the public without which the public would not know anything about child labour or child trafficking.

If Reports Have Rallied the Government to Fight Child Labour

They answered in the affirmative that newspapers reports have rallied the government to come up with policies to protect the welfare of children especially at the Federal level. However, left to the newspapers alone, they just report and there is no follow up. A respondent said the government at the Federal level have done their own part with the passing of relevant laws like the Child Rights Act 2003, which is a domestication of the United Nations Convention on the Rights of the Child and African Union Charter on the Rights and Welfare of the Child; International Labour Organisation (ILO) Convention No. 136 and 138 which talks about age limit and extreme forms of child labour. Another respondent added that the government at the Federal level created a relevant agency NAPTIP which has the responsibility of sensitising the public, prosecuting offenders and lobbying government to pass relevant laws to address the issue of trafficking and general children issues.

However, as stated by a respondent, the problem is about the adoption of the Child Rights Act by States in Nigeria. Though some States have passed the Act, in terms of implementation, they are not doing much. For example, the issues of family court, some states have passed the Act but Family Court is not effective and in some other States, there are Family Courts but the Child Rights Act has not been passed into law. While there is agreement that the government have tried to come up with policies guiding children issues at the Federal level, the remaining States yet to pass the law at the State Assemblies are urged to do so and in sum all States should not just have laws guiding these children but should put strict enforcement mechanisms else the law becomes an ineffective instrument.

A respondent representing the Ministry in Ogun state said that media sensitisation have also gotten to the government and have led to the inauguration of a committee in the last two years concerning child labour (CHILD PROTECTION COMMITTEE), this committee go against child trafficking in any area of Ogun state.

Aspects of Child Labour the Media Focus on

Based on the responses, some child labour issues the media focus on are: domestic labour, street hawking, child battering, and child abuse.

Areas Media Have Done Well

One respondent was of the opinion that the media was instrumental in the passage of the Child Rights Act, they have done well in covering domestic labour, and also child battering being an aspect of child abuse. However respondents were in one accord on the fact that even with these reports, the problem is still prevalent and that there is so much to be done.

On the part of the Ministry representatives, they said the media have done well in reporting stories that have helped keep children off the streets. In addition a respondent said even the broadcast media have been instrumental by using radio and speaking different languages to ensure proper understanding of the issue.

Reasons Media Do Not Cover Child Labour Issues Adequately

Respondents spoke extensively on some reasons the media are not covering child labour issues and general children violation issues adequately. One respondent says funding is a major problem because child rights promotion is donor-driven. For instance, there was funding to promote the passage of the Child Rights Act in 2003 but now funds for promoting the rights of children is inadequate and this could cause a decline in media reportage of children issues. Also, there are lots of issues in the country needing media attention; Child Rights promotion is too little to gain prominence. There are other more important things like insurgency, politics, economic growth and even killer diseases. A disease like Ebola gained much prominence in the media because it was a rapid killing disease and with media attention, it was stemmed; child rights issues on the other hand are given little prominence because it does not kill rapidly and can be overlooked without taking recourse that it is a problem that has attendant effects on the human resource of the country.

The editorial policy of the media organisation also determines what goes into the papers and because most of these papers are privately owned and funded, they rather want to emphasise stories that will sell and even when there are occurrences on child rights violation, they are not given prominence. Also, cultural and religious factors have a role to play in our culture, children should assist their parents, and when policies or laws restrict that, people think it is against our culture. The problem of child fostering in Nigeria where a person who is well to do and lives in the city goes to the village to pick a child of a relative who is not doing very well to train such person and then abuse and exploitation sets in since such person is not his biological son or daughter. When laws come to address these issues it is seen as conflicting with our culture so people do not understand and that is why such stories do not make headlines.

Another challenge as highlighted by a respondent is that the level of investigative journalism by the media is low, he says "children are like silent features, they cannot complain directly about what is happening to them; even for us who work for children, we go out to interact with people look for these children because their cases will likely not reach us." The respondents further added that, the media personnel are not properly trained in handling child rights issues and as such they do not know their limits. A ministry respondent added that the media lack access to some of these information; others said, the media have more catchy or attractive information and do not consider children issues with so much importance.

AREAS OF IMPROVEMENT

Respondents suggested the following: there should be more investigative journalism by visiting places where these children are for instance at motor parks, restaurants, markets. The media can also look for researches done to promote child rights, link up and partner with child rights advocacy networks to know what they are doing to promote child rights to publicise it. The problem of child labour should be put in public glare and sphere of discussion as that will be one way to address it. Reporters can go through child protection laws like that of Lagos State and get educated on how to report children issues. There is need for professional training for the media personnel and also the child rights advocates. Currently, UNICEF trains media scholars on child rights reporting and is seeking to train more people and encourage its inclusion in the curriculum.

They also suggested that newspapers can devote weekend editions to the coverage of human interest stories like child labour; in doing this, they would have enough space to talk about the issues and also when people see this as the trend in weekend papers, they will be willing to read. In addition, the media though profit-oriented should not always put their interest above that of children. There is also need to strengthen the relationship between child rights advocates and the media as they should be partners in progress in addressing children issues. Representatives of the ministries suggested that the media should publish more reports to enlighten the public on the reduction of child labour and also to further advocate for children going to school through their reports.

DISCUSSION OF FINDINGS

This chapter examined the public and stakeholders' perception of child labour reports in the newspapers. It was discovered that child labour reports are not seen regularly in the newspapers. This led to a moderate level of awareness among the public as they can only be more aware of an issue that is prominently reported in the media. In addition, the most seen child labour issue in the newspaper report is child abuse followed by child trafficking, this is also reinforced by the response from the interviewees that child abuse is prevalent especially child battering. Ajaegbu, Alao and Oloyede (2018) in their study found out that child abuse was the most reported issue probably because there was a high occurrence of abuse cases within the period of study. Further finding show that the public have not gained much knowledge of child labour issues from newspaper reports and this could be attributed to poor coverage of child labour issues.

It was also discovered that there is a significant influence of public knowledge of child labour reports on attitude to the reports ($\beta = 0.493$, $R^2 = 0.547$, $p < 0.05$). This means that the respondents usually feel perturbed by the plight of children. The attitude in turn should cause a reaction on the issue.

Further finding showed that the reaction of the public to newspaper reports on child labour is moderately high ($\bar{x}=3.46$). It was also discovered that audience knowledge of child labour reports has a significant influence on their reactions to the messages ($\beta = 0.528$, $R^2 = 0.500$, $p < 0.05$). This means that when people are aware of child labour issues in media reports, it could affect their attitude and also cause them to seek ways to address the problem.

Another finding showed on the average that the public rate newspapers effectiveness at a moderate level ($\bar{x}=3.31$). This is corroborated by some studies that media are not doing enough to address the issue of child labour. Ajaegbu, Alao and Oloyede, (2018 p.630) concluded in their study that the newspapers did not give sufficient coverage to child labour issues. Nwodu and Ezeoke (2013) also reported that the frequency of mentions of child rights was low in the newspapers studied meaning that the press did not give sufficient attention to the issue (p.48). Oyero (2011a) also reported in his findings that the coverage given to child rights by the newspapers shows a gross under-reportage of children's issues… that children are invisible in the newspapers content (p.102).

Further finding showed that the level of education of the respondents has no influence on the knowledge of newspaper reports however the result was significant ($\beta = -4.360$, $R^2 = 0.039$, $p < 0.05$). The analysis showed that the level of education attainment had no significant influence on knowledge of child labour reports and this went contrary to the assumption of this study that the more educated people are, the more they will know about child labour issues. This could also be attributed to the fact that those with the terminal degree probably are too busy to read newspaper reports.

Results of the study further showed that NGOs/CSOs are the most voices in the reports they have seen. In related findings by Oyero (2011a), NGOs/CSOs and child rights advocates are predominant voices in Nigerian newspapers followed by government officials. However, in the findings by Nwodu and Ezeoke (2013), they reported that the major news and information sources in their study were International organizations/Agencies like UNICEF followed by Women Groups/Organisations and NGOs/ CBOs.

In addition, Nwankwo (2011) asserts that the media and human rights NGOs/CSOs are helpful to each other in the fight against human rights violations. Furthermore, that "the NGOs/CSOs serve as 'monitors' and 'sources of information' for human rights" (p.14). It was however noted by Internews Europe (2014) and by some of the responses from the interview that the CSOs and the media do not enjoy an interdependent relationship; they also assert that the "only time the child rights CSOs engage with media is when informing them to cover incidents of child rights violations or official functions" (p.65). Nwodu and Ezeoke (2013) explain that NGOs/CSOs are child rights advocates and major actors in the fight against child labour. This shows that these advocates have been in the forefront of setting the agenda for child rights in the country.

From the analysis of the interview responses, respondents were of the opinion that the media have done well in reporting child labour issues but others said they have not done well and need to do more for people to know about the problem. The media reports especially before the passage of the Child Rights Act in 2003 and based on the results of some research (Oyero, 2010; Oyero 2011a), were high but in the last ten years, there has been a decline and this a respondent said is due to inadequate funds and the fact that the media gives priority to some other issues they consider more important. These media reports were able to spur the government into the passage of the Act and also being signatory to some other laws like the ILO Convention No. 136 and 138 and some states have also passed some laws to protect children.

The respondents gave some reasons the media have not covered child labour issues adequately as follows: the editorial policy of the media organisations in the sense that these papers want to report what people would enjoy reading that are more thought-provoking and children issues are not considered so, funding was also identified as a major issues in the sense that media reports were heightened before the passage of the Child Rights Act in 2003 because of funding from International Organisations and there is decline in media reportage because of limited funds, also, there are lots of issues needing media attention and children issues are not considered hot topics for the media when there are more pressing issues, in addition, the cultural context of the issue is a hindrance, advocating for the rights of children is like giving them liberty to misbehave and that is something peculiar with the Western culture.

These laws are seen as conflicting with our culture and people do not agree with them. Respondents also said the level of investigative journalism is low, that the media need to seek these children out because they will not want to speak for fear of being harmed; on the relationship between the media and child rights advocates, this is supported by Internews Europe (2014) as they report that the media and CSOs do not understand each other's needs and expectations, and find it hard to work together constructively. Also, the media personnel are not properly trained to handle children issues; this is also reinforced by Internews Europe (2014), that most journalists are not aware of the International Federation of Journalists (IFJ) guidelines for media coverage of child rights, or the United Nations Convention on the Rights of the Child.

The areas of improvement as suggested by the interviewees are germane and they are summed up as follows: there should be more reports brought up for discussion and action, funding for the media organisations and also the child rights advocates to partner well with the media, investigative journalism because these children are scared of whoever they are working for, linking up and partnering with child rights advocate networks to know what they are doing to promote child rights. Internews Europe (2014) found out in their study that "the media- CSO relationship is characterised by mistrust and misunderstanding (p.65)"; they further stated that the media and CSOs 'have not developed professional, mutually supportive relationships' (p.65). This means that the media and CSOs need to see their relationship as a partnership for a given cause. Other areas are: the need for professional training for the media personnel and also the child rights advocates, the newspapers can also devote weekend editions to cover child labour and general children issues more extensively.

It was also discovered that one of the reasons the media do not cover child labour adequately is because of the editorial policy of the paper, as stated by the agenda setting theory, it is what the publisher, editor and reporters want people to know that they know about. Also if the media places emphasis on the issue of child labour, the citizenry will be more informed about it. This also underscores the tenet of the social responsibility theory in that the media should be used for the good of the society and also that the media should put public interest above their own. The press should be responsible to the society by performing the essential functions ranging from informational role and also interpretation of events (Oyesomi, Soola, Abioye & Oyero, 2014).

Further finding from the interview showed that the media did a lot in creation of awareness and sensitisation for the passage of the Child Rights Act in 2003 but in the years after, they have paid attention to other issues to the detriment of the Nigerian child. Though not all states have passed the CRA into law, the Act is seen as an end rather than a means to an end. Most state governments believe that once the law has been passed in their State Assembly they have fulfilled their part. This shows that the state governments are paying lip service to the Act.

As stated by Oyero (2010) in his study that spanned from 1999 to 2003, he discovered that reports on children issues were heightened in 2002 before the Child Rights Act was passed. In another similar study that spanned 2010 to 2014, Ajaegbu, Alao and Oloyede (2018) reported that State governments passed the Child Rights Act law at the state level meaning that the media reports and civil society campaigns encouraged the passage of this Act. This invariably shows a connection between media agenda setting, public agenda and policy agenda. In a particular state in the Eastern part of the country, there have been media sensitisations to impede parents and guardians from giving out their children for cheap labour in the name of better life for the family; this has paid off as most parents are wary about giving out their children. This reinforces the idea of the agenda setting theory in the sense that when the media gives salience to certain issues in terms of position and space, the public in turn discuss such issues and constant discussion of such issues can influence the policy agenda and cause decision makers to institute policies to address such issues. When the media constantly report child labour issues, there will be a push from the public which could in turn lead to the passage and enforcement of laws to address the issues.

CONCLUSION AND RECOMMENDATIONS

This chapter concludes that people are aware of child labour issues in newspaper reports with more focus on child abuse, meaning that the newspapers cover child abuse more than other issues. In addition, they do not regularly see reports on child labour issues probably because of inadequate reportage. The study also concludes that the more the media gives coverage to child labour issues, the more the public will know about it which will lead to a favourable attitude and therefore lead to reactions to help alleviate the plight of children in the country.

This study recommends that the newspapers give more coverage to child labour issues. The reports should also be written in clearer language to aid better understanding. In addition, different areas of child labour should be covered to give better representation of issues. Civil Society Organizations are also encouraged to have better working relationships with the media to further the cause of child protection in the country.

FUTURE RESEARCH DIRECTION

This study serves as a base for future studies. It is important that there is further research on what audiences in other prevalent regions of the country think about child labour reports. The study should be done on a larger scale so the results can be generalised to the country.

REFERENCES

Adeniran, R., Hassan, S., Ajaga, M., & Kayode, J. (2015). *Representation of children in Nigeria News Media on ResearchGate.net*. Retrieved from https://www.researchgate.net/publication/316794864_Representation_of_children_in_Nigerian_News_Media

Adepegba, A. (2019, May 3). 43% of Nigerian Children engaged in Child Labour-ILO. *The Punch*. Retrieved from https://punchng.com/43-of-nigerian-children-engaged-in-child-labour-ilo/

Agbo, C. M. (2017). The health and educational consequences of child labour in Nigeria. *Health Science Journal, 11*(1). Retrieved from http://www.hsj.gr/medicine/the-health-and-educational-consequences-of-child-labour-in-nigeria.php?aid=18408

Ahiuma-Young, V. (2012). Stakeholders re-strategize to combat human trafficking and child labour. *The Vanguard Newspaper*. Retrieved from https:// vanguardngr.com/Stakeholders-re-strategize-to-combat-human-trafficking-and-child-labour

Ajaegbu, O. O., Alao, S. E., & Oloyede, D. B. (2018). Press Coverage of Child Labour Issues in Nigeria (2010-2014). *International Review of Social Sciences, 6*(12), 618–632. www.irss.academyirmbr.com

Amalu, C. (2010, June 29). Nigerian child and the Child Rights Act. *The Vanguard*. Retrieved from http://www.vanguardngr.com/2010/06/nigerian-child-and-the-child-rights-act/

Arthur, J. B. (2012). *Framing child neglect: A content analysis of national and regional U.S. newspaper coverage* (Unpublished Master's Thesis). A Capstone Project Presented to the Faculty of the School of Communication.

Attoh, N. R. (2016, August 8). *The Child's Rights and Responsibility Law just passed in Enugu state*. Retrieved from https://www.educationalresourceproviders.com/child-abuse-and-the-childs-rights-and-responsibility-law-just-passed-into-law-in-enugu-state/

Atuma, U. (2018). Day stakeholders converged in Osun against human trafficking, child labour. *The Sun Newspaper*. Retrieved from https://sunnewsonline.com/Day-stakeholders-converged-in-Osun-against-human-trafficking-childlabour

Awosola, R. K., & Omoera, O. S. (2008). Child Rights and the Media: The Nigerian Experience. *Communication Science*, *2*(2), 1255-131. Retrieved from http://www.krepublishers.com/02-Journals/S-HCS/HCS-02-0-000-08-Web/HCS-02-2-087-08-Abst-Text/HCS-02-2-125-08-047-Awosola-R-K/HCS-02-2-125-08-047-Awosola-R-K-Tt.pdf

Business Insider. (2018, February 14). *Lifestyle 50% of Nigerian children engage in child labour – NBS- Pulse Nigeria.* Retrieved from https://www.pulse.ng/bi/lifestyle-50-of-nigerian-children-engage-in-child-labour-nbs/bnqqk33

Creswell, J. W. (2012). *Educational Research: Planning, Conducting, and Evaluating Quantitative and Qualitative Research* (4th ed.). Boston, MA: Pearson Education, Inc.

Director of Security Services, Babcock University. (2019). Speech delivered at the 2019 Annual Colloquium, Babcock University, Ilisan-Remo, Ogun State, Nigeria.

Europe, I. (2014). *Protecting the Rights of Children: The Role of the Media. Lessons from Brazil, India and Kenya.* Retrieved from https://internews.org/sites/default/files/resources/InternewsEurope_ChildRightsMedia_Report_2014.pdf

Iyanda, R. O., & Nwogwugwu, N. (2016). Globalization and Rising Human Trafficking in Nigeria. *Kuwait Chapter of Arabian Journal of Business and Management Review*, *5*(6), 17–31. doi:10.12816/0019031

Iyengar, S. (1991). *Is anyone responsible? How television frames political issues.* Chicago: University of Chicago Press. doi:10.7208/chicago/9780226388533.001.0001

Kadiri & Muhammed. (2011). Mass media as correlates of children's behavioural problems in Kwara State, Nigeria. *Journal of Media and Communication Studies*, *3*(5), 198–202. Retrieved from http://www.academicjournals.org/app/webroot/article/article1380115207_Kadiri%20and%20Muhammed.pdf

Kunkel, Suding, & Biely. (2002). *Coverage in context: How thoroughly the news media report five key children"'s issues.* Retrieved August 18, 2013, from http://www.mediawise.org.ukldisplay

Mastin, T., Choi, J., Barboza, G. E., & Post, L. (2007). Newspapers' Framing of Elder Abuse: It's Not a Family Affair. *Journalism & Mass Communication Quarterly*, *84*(4), 777–794. doi:10.1177/107769900708400408

McQuail, D. (2005). *McQuail's Mass Communication Theory* (5th ed.). Sage Publications Inc.

Nigeria, P. R. (2018). *Labour Ministry champions renewed fight against child labour in Nigeria.* Retrieved from www.prnigeria.com

Nkememena, A. C. (2009). *Press coverage of child trafficking in Nigeria: a content analysis of* Daily Sun *and* Vanguard *newspapers* (Master's thesis). University of Nigeria, Nsukka.

Nwankwo, V. C. (2011). *The Role of The Media in Promoting Human Rights: An analysis of the BBC documentary, 'chocolate: the bitter truth'*. An Unpublished MA Dissertation. Retrieved from http://munin.uit.no/bitstream/handle/10037/3500/thesis.pdf?sequence=1

Nwodu, L. C., & Ezeoke, C. B. (2013). An Evaluation of Press Coverage of Children's and Women's Rights in Nigeria. *Higher Education of Social Science*, *4*(2), 41–51.

Nwosu, I. E., & Nwodu, L. C. (2007). An Empirical analysis of the factors influencing child labour abuses and control in Nigeria. Towards the application of ACADA model. *The Nigerian Journal of Development Studies*, *6*(1), 23–45.

Obozuwa, D. E. (2010). *Nigeria @ 50 ... Protecting the future of this Nigerian child – The future leaders of this Nation: A look again at the Child Rights Act.* Retrieved from http://www.wali-uwais.com/?page_id=784

Olube, F. K. (2015). The influence of mass communication on social change: a study of press reports on child labour and women trafficking. *New Media and Mass Communication*, *36*, 31- 40. Retrieved from https://www.iiste.org/Journals/index.php/NMMC/article/viewFile/21765/21793

Ortiz-Ospina, E., & Roser, M. (2019). *Child Labor.* Retrieved from: 'https://ourworldindata.org/child-labor'

Oxford Advanced Learner's Dictionary. (2015). (9th ed.). Oxford University Press.

Oyero, O. (2010). Media Ownership and the Coverage of Child's Rights in the Nigerian Newspapers. *Nigerian Journal of Communication, 8*(1).

Oyero, O. (2011a). Presenting Children's Right Issues in Nigerian and Ghanaian Newspapers. Multidisciplinary Journal of the University of Fort Hare, 17.

Oyero, O. S. (2011). How children are reported in Nigerian newspapers: Implications for the right of the child. *International Journal of Social and Management Sciences*, *4*(1), 37-56.

Oyesomi, K. O., Soola, E., Abioye, T., & Oyero, O. (2014). Perception of women on the role of indigenous communication in politics: A study of Ado-Odo Ota, Ogun State, Nigeria. *Vision 2020: Sustainable Growth, Economic Development, and Global Competitiveness - Proceedings of the 23rd International Business Information Management Association Conference, IBIMA 2014, 1*, 2622-2644.

Pickering, T. (2016). *Print media and child welfare: A discourse analysis* (Master's Thesis). The University of Manitoba.

Saunders, M., Lewis, P., & Thornhill, A. (2009). *Research methods for business students* (5th ed.). Harlow: Pearson Education Harlow.

Severin, W. J., & Tankard, J. W. (1979). *Communication Theories: Origins, Methods and Uses*. Toronto, Canada: Copp Clark Ltd.

ThankGod-Amadi, S. (2012, May 27). *Domesticating Child Rights Law ...The Rivers Example*. Retrieved from http://www.thetidenewsonline.com/2012/05/27/domesticating-child-rights-law-%E2%80%A6the-rivers-example/

Ugal, D., & Undyaundeye, F. (2012). *Child labour in Nigeria: causes and consequences for national development*. Retrieved from https://www.researchgate.net/publication/228217064_Child_Labour_in_Nigeria_Causes_and_Consequences_for_National_Development

UNICEF. (2014). *Idea Box: Engaging stakeholders on children's rights (First ed.). A tool for companies*. Retrieved from www.unicef.org/cs

UNICEF fact sheet on child labour in Nigeria. (2006). Retrieved from https://www.unicef.org/wcaro/english/WCARO_Nigeria_Factsheets_ChildLabour.pd

Uwaleke, I., & Eghagha, B. (2009, June 9). *Child's Rights Act: The Cure For Trafficking*. Retrieved from http://www.nigerianbestforum.com/generaltopics/childs-rights-act-the-cure-for-trafficking/

Weatherred, J. L. (2015). Child sexual abuse and the media: A literature review. *Journal of Child Sexual Abuse*, *24*(1), 16–34. doi:10.1080/10538712.2015.976302 PMID:25635896

ADDITIONAL READING

Department of Labour Programme towards the Elimination of the worst forms of Child Labour (TECL) / ILO (2006). Commercial and Sexual Exploitation of Children and Child Trafficking: A South African National Situation Analysis. Community Agency for Social Enquiry.

Edet, G. E., & Etim, N. A. (2013). Child Labour in agriculture among poor rural households: Some issues and facts. *European Journal of Physical and Agricultural Sciences* Vol. 1 (1). UK: Progressive Academic Publishing. www.idpublications.org

Ekuri, E. A. (2013). Influence of African Independent Television as a watchdog against child abuse and labour with a particular focus to child trafficking (A study of Garki residents of Abuja Metropolis). An Unpublished BSc. Thesis Caritas University, Amorji-Nike, Enugu.

Esguerra, E. F. (2003). An Analysis of the causes and consequences of child labour in the Philippines. http://www.ilo.org/ipecinfo/product/download.do?type=document&id=3688

FOS/ILO/SIMPOC (2000/2001). Final Report on National Modular Child Labour Survey: Nigeria. A Project of the International Labour Organization (ILO) and Statistical Information and Monitoring Programme on Child Labour (SIMPOC) in conjunction with the Federal Office of Statistics (FOS).

Ibeme, N. P. (2014). Child Domestic worker in rural and urban areas of Nigeria: Implications for national development. *International Journal of Emerging Knowledge*, *1*(12), 219–231.

ILO. International Programme for the Elimination of Child Labour. (2004). Child Labour: A Textbook for University students. A Publication of the International Labour Office. Switzerland: Geneva.

Jabeen, T. (2014). Child protection Data: An analysis of newspapers coverage of child-protection issues in Pakistan. *South Asian Studies*, *29*(1), 123–135.

Jempson, M. (1997). Children in the picture: media ethics and the reporting of child labour. Background Paper for the International Conference on Child Labour, Oslo, 27-30 October 1997. International Federation of Journalists Media for Democracy Programme.

Merchant, R. (2010). Reframing child abuse: Changing media and public perceptions of the perpetrators of physical child abuse. Unpublished thesis. This research received no special grant from any funding agency in the public, commercial or not-for-profit-sectors.

Section 3

Child Rights, Abuse, and Media

Chapter 10
Displacement and Children's Rights:
Advancing Media Advocacy for Inclusive Education for Sustainable Development in Nigeria

Faith O. Olanrewaju
https://orcid.org/0000-0002-5242-0889
Political Science and International Relations, Covenant University, Nigeria

Lady A. Ajayi
https://orcid.org/0000-0002-5326-7732
Covenant University, Nigeria

Adekunle O. Olanrewaju
Covenant University, Nigeria

Oluwatimilehin Deinde-Adedeji
https://orcid.org/0000-0003-1531-3870
Covenant University, Nigeria

Ejiroghene R. Loromeke
Covenant University, Nigeria

ABSTRACT

This chapter examines the relationship amongst displacement, education, and sustainable national development. It pays attention to the effects of displacement on the rights of children to education in Nigeria. Data for the study were obtained via in-depth interviews from key informants and focus group discussions (FGDs)

DOI: 10.4018/978-1-7998-0329-4.ch010

amongst internally displaced women in a government-managed and faith-based IDP camps in the Adamawa State as well as informal settlements in the Federal Capital Territory (FCT), Abuja on the quality of education offered in the camps. Findings from the study show that wide gaps exist between the education received by displaced children and the expectations of the Convention on the Rights of the Child. The study argues that the educational exclusivity of displaced children would have adverse effects on the sustainable development of the Nigerian state as it would decrease awareness of values about their civic duties needed for sustainable development. It thus recommends for increased media advocacy in pushing for better implementation of inclusive education in Nigeria.

INTRODUCTION

The Universal Declaration of Human Rights (UDHR) declares that "all human beings are born free and equal in dignity and rights without discrimination" (UDHR, 1948). Thus, children's rights are human rights or reversely stated, human rights are also the rights of children too. However, the United Nations (UN) Convention on the Rights of the Child (CRC) adopted in 1990 remains the foremost legally binding treaty protecting the rights of children amongst which is the right to education. During emergencies, such as displacement and conflicts, these rights are often disregarded thereby leading to exposures to physical, psychological and sexual risks that violate their human rights. The situation is even more disturbing as displaced children represent at least half of the population in a conflict zone or during conflict.

The Nigerian displacement challenge has become a major global concern with grave consequences. Unfortunately, displacement does not have equal effects on men, women and children. Children and women, belonging to the most vulnerable groups, suffer the most (Skujyte, 2011). Asides the challenges such as malnutrition, fear, diseases, insecurity, sexual and gender-based violations, infant mortality, starvation, lack of portable water, poor shelter, trauma and insecurity that displaced persons face, education has been grossly affected by the Boko Haram insurgency induced displacement in Nigeria (Ajayi & Soyinka-Airewele, 2018). Very significantly, the vulnerability of displaced children is further exacerbated by their deprivation of inclusive education in spite of the legal obligation of the government to ensure freedoms of the citizens including children and the enjoyment of fundamental rights (Cotroneo, 2017).

A very salient reality remains that children in IDP camps go through traumatic experiences. However, the challenges that displaced children face are not made public and they are often left to the government which has proven to be insufficient in handling their situations. The media has tremendously contributed to the exposure of the daunting multifaceted challenges such as food insecurity, poor shelter, and health challenges confronting displaced children in Nigeria. Much efforts have not addressed the pronouncement of the disenfranchisement of the displaced children to inclusive education vis-à-vis their displaced counterparts. Hence, the need for the media as an interventionist tool or institution of publicity to expose to the public realm what displaced children are going through and to advocate for necessary / viable contributions or supports from individuals, NGOs, international community and other stakeholders and to also mobilise resources such as funds, personnel and training amongst other to change the fortune of the children. This chapter, therefore, addresses the social inequality as regards the education of displaced children viz a viz their non-displaced counterparts. It explores the current educational realities in IDP camps and examines the challenges displaced children experience with regards to the rights to education in Nigeria. It investigates trends in literature on the nexus between inclusive education and sustainable development and presents the possible effects of the educational exclusivity of displaced children on the sustainable development of the Nigerian state. Lastly, this chapter proposes the need for intensified media advocacy to ensure the inclusive and equitable quality education for displaced children in Nigeria knowing fully well that education is a germane aspect of sustainable development.

LITERATURE REVIEW AND THEORETICAL FRAMEWORK

Children's' Right to Education: A Global Overview

The Declaration of Geneva popularly known as the Declaration of the Rights of the Child adopted on September 26, 1924, by the League of Nations, recognized children as mere recipients of welfare (Sofoluwe, 2012). This perception continued with the UN Declaration of the Rights of the Child 1959, which stated that the child should be protected and provided with all the forms of care needed for them to develop in every ramification whether socially, morally, spiritually, mentally, and physically and it should be without discrimination. The 1959 Declaration formed the basis for the Convention of the Rights of the Child (CRC) which was adopted 30 years later (Moody, 2015). The CRC in Article 1 defines a child as "every human being below the age of eighteen years unless under the law applicable to the child, majority is attained earlier" (CRC, 1989). The underlining argument or postulation for the canvassing of the protection of the rights of the child in the CRC is that "children need special protection and priority care as a vulnerable group because they are in the developmental stages of their lives." The vulnerability of children is hinged on the fact that their capacities are still developing and depend largely on adults for protection, care, guidance and provision. Isokpan (2016, p. 16), providing a more explicit explanation on why children need special protection, argued that they are:

fragile, naïve, defenceless, often oblivious of danger and sometimes unaware and incapable of claiming their rights. Their physical, mental and psychological make-up predisposes them to greater hardship than adults. Children can neither negotiate special rights for themselves nor possess the necessary skill to acquire a stake in the resources of their communities.

The right to education as a human right has its foundations in the international human rights instruments such as the Universal Declaration of Human Right adopted on 10 December 1948; article 28 of the Convention of the Rights of Child (CRC) and articles 13 and 14 of the International Covenant on Economic, Social and Cultural Rights (ICESCR) amongst others (Sofoluwe, 2012). The right gained proper recognition at the global level after the birth of the UN system in 1948. According to the UDHR (1948):

Everyone has the right to education. Education shall be free, at least in the elementary stages. Elementary education shall be compulsory. Technical and professional education shall be made generally available and higher education shall be equally accessible to all on the basis of merit.

Though without specific reference to the rights of the child, the protection of human rights is stated in Chapter IV of the Constitution of the Federal Republic of Nigeria as amended in 1999. The Constitution of the Federal Republic of Nigeria does not guarantee the rights of the child to education but actually draws the government's attention to it in its second chapter as a vital objective and directive principle of state policy. However, in Section 18, it stresses the government's responsibility to direct its policies to ensure that there are adequate and equal opportunities for the education of all at all levels. Furthermore, it admonishes the government to ensure that illiteracy is eradicated. The government is also expected to provide compulsory, free and universal primary education and also free secondary, university and adult literacy education. This coincides with the provision of Section 15 of the Child Rights Act (CRA) 2003 that every child has the right to "free, compulsory and universal primary education" (Isokpan, 2016, p. 9). Sequel to the ratification of some international treaties on human rights by the Nigerian state, the Nigerian government adopted the National Policy on Education, which was a policy document and documentary guideline for the national educational objectives and goals. However, the policy lacked effective implementation (Folorunsho, Imam-Tamim., & Abdulraheem, 2014). The inefficiency of the policy reflects in the number of children that have access to education as well as the quality of education they receive.

Impact of the Boko Haram Insurgency on Education in Nigeria

Boko Haram is an Islamic, jihadist and radical movement formed by Yusuf Mohammed in northern Nigerian state of Maiduguri, Borno State. Agbiboa (2013, p. 71) asserts that the name, "Boko Haram," is derived from an amalgamation of a Hausa word, "Boko" which means book, and an Arabic word, "Haram" meaning something forbidden and ungodly. The nomenclature Boko Haram, therefore, means western education is forbidden, sacrilegious, ungodly or sinful. This is founded on harsh anti-western ideology. Mohammed Yusuf's quote stated below further reveals the harsh anti-democratic and anti-western ideology that founded the Boko Haram:

These European educated Muslims returned home only to confuse other Muslims, claiming that democracy is compatible with Islam, while jihad should only be for self-control... We are for jihad, and our jihad is to put an end to democracy, to western education and western civilization. The jihad is intended to make us [Muslims] return to the original state of Islam (Zenn, Barkindo, & Heras, 2013, p. 50).

It argues that the westernisation of Nigeria and the North specifically is un-Islamic and the root of the decadence and vices such as corruption, unemployment, poverty and instability in the Nigerian societies. It holds that the holiness of the Islamic faith has been contaminated by westernisation which makes it necessary for an Islamic Jihad in Nigeria that will necessitate the establishment of an idyllic Islamic society void of moral deprivation and political corruption (Pham, 2012). It is therefore not surprising that one of the major attacks by Boko Haram was on educational institutions. A UNESCO Education for All Global Monitoring Report (2011, pp. 124-125) states that:

Perhaps more than any time in history, school children, teachers and schools are on the front line of violence. Classrooms are destroyed not just because they are caught in the crossfire, but because they are targeted by combatants.

The violence against schools and education in northern Nigeria has been attributed to the systematic human rights abuses perpetrated by government's security forces against members of the sect, their children and wives as well as their raids of Quranic schools. The wrath of the insurgents was not spared from being meted out on both pupils and educational personnel such as teachers. Over a decade of

Boko Haram's onslaught has led to the disruption of education in northeast Nigeria making thousands of children miss out of education (Joshua & Olanrewaju, 2016). A report published by the Global Coalition to Protect Education from Attack (GCPEA), Education Under Attack disclosed that there have been 2,700 attacks on education between 2013 and 2017 and over 21,000 educators and students were harmed (Olaiya, 2018). Over 2,295 teachers were killed and 19,000 were forcefully displaced since 2009 (HRW, 2016). Male students were maimed and killed while female ones were abducted. For instance, in July 2013 a government boarding school in Mamusdo village, Yobe State, was invaded by insurgents. In the onslaught, 42 teachers and students were killed and the school was burnt down (Agba, Otuchikere, Odemwingie, Nda-Isaiah, & Esebonu, 2013). On February 25 2014, Boko Haram insurgents attacked the Federal Government College, Buni Yadi, Yobe state and over 59 male students were killed. Several buildings within the school compound were burnt down. Also, a suicide bomber, disguising as a member of the school community, invaded a school in November 2014 during a morning assembly and detonated a bomb that injured many and left about 47 pupils dead. Very significant abductions that have dominated the global media include the abduction of the 297 Chibok girls from the Government Day Secondary school Chibok, Borno state on the 1st of April 2014 and the 110 Dapchi girls abducted from the Government Girls Science Technical College, Dapchi, in Yobe State on (Olaiya, 2018). About 952,029 school-age children were estimated to have fled the violence and displaced as at early 2016 (NAN, 2016).

Asides the attacks on human elements such as teachers and pupils, educational infrastructures and facilities such as furniture and buildings were not left out. A report by the UNESCO Global Education Monitoring Report in 2019 on the effects of the Boko Haram insurgency on Nigeria's educational system states that, "out of 260 school sites, 28% had been damaged by bullets, shells or shrapnel, 20% had been deliberately set on fire, 32% had been looted and 29% had armed groups or military in close proximity" (UNESCO, 2019). The effect of the insurgency on education has been most felt in Borno state because it is the hottest zone of the insurgency. According to Olugbode (2017), over 57% of the schools in Borno were closed down due to the Boko Haram insurgency. As of 16 June 2018, the estimated number of IDPs in Adamawa, Borno, Bauchi, Gombe, Yobe and Taraba was 1,918,508 individuals comprising of 364,323 households. 27% of the IDP population are children under 5 years old. 46% of the IDP population are males, 54% are females. Thus, 25% of the estimated figure are children. 94% of the displacement is due to the Boko Haram insurgency. 61% of the IDP population reside in host communities while 39% are in camps/camp-like settings (IOM and NEMA Displacement Tracking Matrix, 2018). 600,000 of them lost access to education due to the insurgency and incessant attacks on the educational system.

The frequent and incessant attacks of the insurgent seriously disrupted school attendance and activities. It increased student drop-out rates and school closures. Student retention was made more difficult due to insecurity and fear of abduction (Abdulrasheed, Onuselogu, & Obioma, 2015). In addition to these, school attendance was also affected by the use of schools for military purposes by government security forces. While it placed the used schools at risk of being attacked by the insurgents, it also disregarded the Safe Schools Declaration endorsed by Nigeria in 2015. The declaration urges parties "not to use schools and universities for any purpose in support of the military effort" so that the rights of children to education are not hindered (Donnelly, Mausi, & Dele-Adedeji, 2016).

This study was anchored on the Interest theory which was propounded by Jeremy Bentham. He described it as an individual having a right to something of personal benefit while a person/body has the duty to provide it. Interest theory has been applied to different doctrines like moral and legal rights. Scholars like Kramer (2010) and Waldron (1985) have dwelt on the legal part of the theory which specifies that a person to whom a legal duty is owed holds the legal right correlative to that duty (Kramer, 2004). Closely related to interest theory is the will theory. However, unlike the will theory, interest theory allows for persons other than adults of sound mind to qualify as holders of legal rights. These categories of persons include: children, senile/lunatic persons, foetuses, animals, trees and dead persons (Waldron, 1985). Invariably, displaced children irrespective of the situation they found themselves have rights to basic education and parties involved should play active roles in other to achieve inclusive education in Nigeria.

METHODS

Study Design

This study is a part of an unpublished PhD thesis. Data for this study were extracted from the report of a larger study that used focus group discussions (FGDs) and in-depth interviews to investigate the extent to which IDP camps provide relevant solutions to the challenges of internally displaced women in Nigeria. The FGD allowed for a descriptive and in-depth narration of the ordeals of displaced women which gave insight into the quality of education that children displaced by Boko Haram receive. The choice of this method was necessary for the realization of the objectives of the research. The obtained information was analysed through framework analysis (Olanrewaju, Omotoso, & Alabi, 2018b; Amoo, Omideyi, Fadayomi, Ajayi, Oni, & Idowu, 2017).

Study Location

The study was conducted in three IDP camps, two in Adamawa state and one in the Federal Capital Territory (FCT), Abuja. Due to the security constraints in Borno, the hottest location of the insurgency, the researchers could not visit any IDP camps there. To cover this gap, two camps were visited in Adamawa state, the state with the second largest number of IDPs. The IDP sites were selected because of their rich ethnographic composition. Permissions were obtained from the management of each of the camps before interacting with the IDPs whose consents were sought before the commencement of the FGD sessions.

Recruitment of Participants

Participants of the FGDs were only women who were displaced by Boko Haram terrorism. Purposive sampling was used in the selection of the camps visited which were Abuja informal IDP settlements (AIS), the Federal Capital Territory, the Malkohi IDP camp (MIC) in Yola, Adamawa State (formal camp) and St Theresa's Catholic Church (STCC), a faith-based camp located in Jimeta, Adamawa State. Displaced women were selected and grouped into various FGD groups via stratified random sampling technique. The women live in the camps and have a good grasp of the education displaced children have access to. Furthermore, the sampling technique also allowed the population of the study to be distributed into homogenous sub-groups based on gender, socio-marital status and age. The various categories of FGD were elderly women (50 years of age and above), married women (between the ages of 20 and 49), single mothers (between 20 and 49 years) and single girls (between the ages of 7 and 19) (Olanrewaju, 2018). Lastly, for the focus group discussion, the simple random sampling technique was used to select women into each of the FGD key participants. Informants that participated in the in-depth interview sessions were also selected via purposive sampling technique.

Data Collection

A total of 12 FGs were held in all the camps. In each camp, there were four groups: - elderly women, widows, married women and single girls groups. This means that the groups were replicated in the selected camps. Each group had between 8 and 10 participants. All the groups except 2 had 10 participants each. Thus, there were a total of 116 participants in the FGD sessions. Each of the FGD lasted between 105 min and 150 min. The focus group discussion guide was adopted from Kruger (2002). Respondents were probed concerning their knowledge and assessment of the education of the displaced children in the camps.

Validity and Integrity of the Data

Most importantly, the diversity of participants' social characteristics such as their age and social-marital status made the findings more representative, as they assisted in both comparing and contrasting the views presented by the participants. The integrity of the data was further validated via the appraisal and reviews of the transcription by other researchers. This was to assist with the elimination of prejudice. Reports of the analysis were also subjected to the scrutiny of non-participating scholars.

Data Analysis

Notes were taken during all the FGDs and interview sessions. They were afterwards transcribed via the 'systematic-content-analysis' (Franzosi, 2007). Common themes were categorized using the 'scissors and paste' approach adopted by scholars such as Olanrewaju, Omotoso & Alabi (2018b) and Amoo et al (2017) in studies that adopted the FGDs and in-depth interviews for data collection. Using the consolidated criteria for reporting qualitative research (COREQ), the data was analysed and the report of findings was compiled (Tong, Sainsbury & Craig 2007) which conformed to qualitative research review guidelines (RATS). The FGD participants were referred to as "A1 to A10"; "B1 to B10"; "C1 to C10" and "D1 to D10" for the groups. "A1 to A10" was used to represent the single girl's groups; "B1 to B10" used to represent the elderly women groups; "C1 to C10" used to represent the various groups of widows and "D1 to D10" used to represent the married women groups (Olanrewaju, 2018). These FGD labels were replicated in referring to the four different FGDs across the different camps. That is, they were repeated across the camps but were distinguished by the names of the camps in the body of the work where the answers were thematically presented (Olanrewaju, 2018; Olanrewaju, Omotoso, & Alabi, 2018a).

Result

Marital status and age were the social characteristics used to describe the participants. Letter "S" was used to represent the single girls who were 30 in number representing 25.86% of total FGD participants. The elderly women's groups were represented with the letter 'E'. Elderly women were 30 making 25.86% of FGD participants. Letter "M" denoted the married women's groups across the camps. Similar with the elderly women's groups, married women were 30 that is 25.86% of the total FGD respondents while the widowed group which were represented with letter 'W' had a total of 26 IDP representations amounting to 22.41% of the total FGD participants (Olanrewaju, Omotoso, & Alabi, 2018a; Olanrewaju, Omotoso, & Alabi, 2018b).

This section actually presents the results of the data obtained from the IDPs during the FGDs and those obtained from the in-depth interviews on the educational realities in IDP camps. These included the assessments of the quality of education displaced children received and the challenges impeding effective education in IDP camps. The obtained data were used to complement or as the case maybe refute existing secondary data from journals and institutional outlets.

Quality of Education Available to Displaced Children

Table 1 is dedicated to discussing the responses derived from all the sessions of the FGDs amongst selected IDPs across the camps on the quality of education in the camps.

65.8 percent of all the respondents in Camp 3 (AIS) avowed that the quality of education available to displaced children was very poor (Coding Theme A). Single girls provided 26.3 percent responses, the widow's group had 15.8 percent responses while the married women had the least percentage response that is 10.5 percent. At the same time, 34.3 percent of the total respondents in Camp 3 also acclaimed that the quality of education available to displaced children was very fair. Equally, only 10 single girls respondents representing 26.3 percent revealed that the quality of education available to displaced children in Camp 2 was good (Theme C). Further interrogation of the respondents during the FGD sessions revealed some challenges. Respondents from the informal IDP settlements affirmed that displaced children had not had access to good education since they got displaced. This is due to insufficient facilities, absence of writing materials and a shortage of volunteer teachers. In the Abuja informal settlements, high tuition fees pose problems for the attendance of school located in the communities. IDPs also report discrimination against their children on admission into school to partake of free education at the primary level. The reasons include admission of children indigenous to the community before "foreign" displaced children if there are slots. This justifies the rating of education for children in Camp 3 which fell within the categories "poor" and "fair".

All the respondents in Camp 1 (100 percent) and 73.7 percent of the total respondents in Camp 2 acclaimed that the quality of education available to displaced children fell into the "Very Good" category. All the categories of respondents in Camp 1 had the same response rate of 25 percent each for the "very Good Category". While the married and elderly respondents represented by 52.6 percent of the total respondents in Camp 2 asserted that the quality of education available to displaced children was very good. This implies that all the categories of respondents in Camps 1 and 2 were satisfied with the quality of facilities available to them while a lot needs to be done in Camp 3 to facilitate a better standard of education in the camp.

Table 1. Quality of education available to displaced children

Coding Theme	Camp 1 (MIC)					Camp 2 (STCC)					Camp 3 (AIS)				
	S	**M**	**W**	**E**	**Total**	**S**	**M**	**W**	**E**	**Total**	**S**	**M**	**W**	**E**	**Total**
Poor	0	0	0	0	0	0	0	0	0	0	10	4	6	5	25
	(0%)	(0%)	0%	0%	0%	0%	0%	0%	0%	0%	26.3%	10.5%	15.8%	13.2%	65.8%
Fair	0	0	0	0	0	0	0	0	0	0	0	6	2	5	13
	0%	0%	0%	0%	0%	0%	0%	0%	0%	0%	0%	15.8%	5.3%	13.2%	34.3%
Good	0	0	0	0	0	10	0	0	0	10	0	0	0	0	0
	0%	0%	0%	0%	0%	26.3%	0%	0%	0%	26.3%	0%	0%	0%	0%	0%
Very Good	10	10	10	10	40	0	10	8	10	28	0	0	0	0	0
	25%	25%	25%	25%	100%	0%	26.3%	21.1%	26.3%	73.7%	0%	0%	0%	0%	0%
Total	**10**	**10**	**10**	**10**	**100%**	**10**	**10**	**8**	**10**	**100%**	**10**	**10**	**8**	**10**	**100%**

Note: S= Single Girls, M = Married Women, W =Widow, E = Elderly Women
Source: Fieldwork, 2017

Further Interrogation on the Quality of Education Displaced Children Access

Due to the discrepancies of the responses above to media projections on the education of displaced children, there was the need for further interrogation of the quality of education that displaced children had in the IDP camps. This was necessary as it exposed critical challenges or issues that should be nipped in the bud if future national security challenges and displacement issues must be addressed.

It was necessary to interrogate the provisions made for education in the camps despite the responses provided on rating the quality of education. This was because the responses provided for the quality of education in IDP camps did not tally with observed media publicities. Thus, the table shows that, 8(20 percent) of women from Camp 1 and 32 (84.3 percent) of the respondents from Camp 2 argued that there was improvement in the displaced children ability to read and write in English than they did before they were displaced. Only 1(2.6 percent) of the respondents from the informal camp, Camp 3 supported this claim. This implied that provision is made for better provision in Camp 2 than in Camps 1 and 3. Evidence to back up this claim was situated in the responses provided for in the coding theme "they go to school five (5) days a week" which showed that 20(50 percent) of respondent from Camp 1 stated that displaced children went to school every day of the week, while just 3(7.9 percent) gave the same reason in Camp 2. However, a more imperative reason was provided by a larger percentage of respondents from Camp 2 who argued that 32(84.3 percent) of the displaced children in their camp can read and write in English as against 7(18.4 percent) that gave the same reason in Camp 1. This could be based on the differences in the quality of education received in both camps.

A number of challenges were observed about education in Camp 3. In the Camp, 18 respondents constituting (47.4 percent) of the total respondents acknowledged that schooling was not every day. That is, there was no stable learning pattern for the education of displaced children there. 50 percent of the respondents in Camp 3 also affirmed that though the children could write, there was a need for improvement. Hence, the government and other stakeholders are required to develop strategies that will help to improve the educational standard of displaced children, especially in the informal camps. Just 1 respondent (2.6 percent) from Camp 2 and 19 (50 percent) from Camp 3 provided a response that could be categorised into the coding category "They can write but need to improve." The responses from the FGDs presented in the two tables above correspond with the findings of Sahara Reporters (2015) that children in the informal settlements located in host communities lack basic education beyond their peers in the government camps.

Table 2. Contains the responses given on the quality of education displaced children access

Coding Theme	Camp 1 (MIC)					Camp 2 (STCC)					Camp 3 (AIS)				
	S	**M**	**W**	**E**	**Total**	**S**	**M**	**W**	**E**	**Total**	**S**	**M**	**W**	**E**	**Total**
They can read &write in Eng. (A)	4	1	0	3	8	7	9	7	9	32	0	1	0	0	1
	10%	2.5%	0%	7.5%	20%	18.4%	23.7%	18.4%	23.7%	84.3%	0%	2.6%	0%	0%	2.6%
They go to school 5 days / week(B)	3	5	6	6	20	1	0	1	1	3	0	0	0	0	0%
	7.5%	12.5%	15%	15%	50%	2.6%	0%	2.6%	2.6%	7.9%	0%	0%	0%	0%	0%
A & B	3	4	4	1	12	2	0	0	0	2	0	0	0	0	0
	7.5%	10%	10%	2.5%	30%	5.3%	0%	0%	0%	5.3%	0%	0%	0%	0%	0%
Schooling is not everyday	0	0	0	0	0	0	0	0	0	0	10	0	8	0	18
	0%	0%	0%	0%	0%	0%	0%	0%	0%	0%	26.3%	0%	21.1%	0%	47.4%
They can write but need to improve	0	0	0	0	0	0	1	0	0	1	0	9	0	10	19
	0%	0%	0%	0%	0%	0%	2.6%	0%	0%	2.6%	0%	23.7%	0%	26.3%	50%
Total	**10**	**10**	**10**	**10**	**100%**	**10**	**10**	**8**	**10**	**100%**	**10**	**10**	**8**	**10**	**100%**

Note: S= Single Girls, M = Married Women, W =Widow, E = Elderly Women
Source: Fieldwork, 2017

Table 3. Challenges impeding the education of Displaced Children in IDP Camps

Category Code	Frequency of Category Code	% of Category Code	Coding Category
A	4./16	25%	Lack of adequate and qualified teachers
B	2./16	12.5%	Classes are not conducive for learning
C	1./16	6.3%	B & C
D	3./16	18.8%	Lack of adequate teaching materials
E	6./16	37.5%	There are adequate teaching and learning materials

Source: Fieldwork, 2017

Challenges Impeding the Education of Displaced Children in IDP Camps

Table 3 presents the responses of key informants on the challenges impeding the education of Displaced Children in IDP Camps.

Table 3 presents data on the emerging and common themes observed from in-depth interviews conducted with key informants such as camp officials and educational instructors in the IDP camps.

Thus, in addition to the evaluation of IDPs on the education of displaced children in IDP camps, responses in Table 3 showed that the key informants had more insight into the state of education in the IDP camps. They discussed matters bothering on the quality of teachers, the state of the classrooms as well as access to teaching and writing materials. 25 percent of the responses were of the opinion that IDP schools lacked qualified and adequate teachers. 12.5 percent argued that the classes were not conducive for learning at all. 6.3 percent agreed with the options in both categories A and B (Category C). This showed that displaced children lacked adequate and qualified teachers and the classrooms were not conducive for learning. 18.8 percent opined that there were limited supplies of teaching material, while 37.5 percent argued that there were inadequate teaching and learning materials for IDPs. They also stated that the textbooks donated by UNICEF were westernized, which has not been very helpful in helping IDPs learn. Below is an excerpt from a key informant on some of the challenges facing education in the IDP camps:

UNICEF did a wonderful job to provide these materials however we don't have adequate teachers. The students are usually more than the teachers. The only problem with the learning materials is that the textbooks are very westernized (Ibrahim, personal communication, MIC Camp Coordinator).

Generally, findings from these in-depth interviews (presented in Table 3) from the various camps and government agencies and coinciding with media reports show that that displaced children in the formal camp also do not learn under internationally approved standards. However, the condition is worse for those in Camp 3 as indicated in Tables 1 and 2. Half of the respondents provided negative information on the state of education provided for IDPs. The issues identified are westernized textbooks and limited number of qualified teachers. Existing classes are not conducive as they lack windows, adequate chairs, and sometimes even roofs and there is also lack of adequate learning and teaching materials. These responses were supported by scholars such as Sambo (2017) and Sanni (2017).

Another fundamental challenge is the poor funding of education. Egbas (2018) argues that the Nigerian budget and spending on education has been inadequate to quell the widening gap of illiteracy in the country. It is very disturbing that only 7% of the 2018's $24 billion budget was earmarked for education (African Development Bank, 2018). Below is an excerpt supporting this finding:

Government's neglect is the greatest challenge we face here. This has negatively impacted on funding and supplies to run the camp. Most of our supplies are from NGOs and various forms of charity organisations (Camp Coordinator, AIS, personal communication, 2016).

The submission noted above aligns with the findings of Lenshie & Yenda (2016) that limited funding has weakened the Nigerian government from handling problems faced by IDPs as it affects all the scopes of intervention including education.

Providing some disturbing figure on the availability of education to displaced children, Ajayi (2015) states that out of 78 IDP camps, 33 had no access to education while 45 camps that had access to education. For example, in a camp in Taraba State, displaced children never had access to education despite the fact that they had been in the camp for two years (Oyewobi, 2016). The lack of education is even worse for displaced children in the informal settlements. According to Sahara Reporters (2015), children in the informal settlements located in host communities lack basic education beyond their peers in the government camps. Some excerpts from the FGDs add some credence to the discrepancy between the access and quality of education IDPs in formal and informal camp receive:

Our children go to school Monday to Friday; before they could not write their names, but now they can do even more than writing their names (MIC, D7).

They can read and write however, they are not in the position I would have wanted them to be if not for the insurgency (STCC, B6).

Education does not really take place here. There are no permanent teachers. There are only volunteer teachers that come to teach the children when they are free. The classrooms are bad. Teaching ends when it starts raining because the classes are not well covered. This speaks volume about the quality of education displaced children get here. They even lack writing materials like books (AIS, D4)

These excerpts show that displaced children, especially in the government, managed camp and religiously controlled camps are getting some form of education even if they are not of the best quality. Scholars such as Aluko (2018) argue that the manifestations of challenges are because there is less emphasis on the educational needs of the displaced children in camps which violates Principle 23 of the Guiding Principles on Internal Displacement as well as affect the academic performance of pupils.

These challenges do not, however, discredit the fact that there are collaborations between the government, international organisations and NGOs. Due to the complexities of displacement and accompanying educational challenges, the Nigerian state receives supports from international organisations such as the United Nations (UN), United Nations International Children's Emergency Fund (UNICEF), US Agency for International Development, non-governmental organizations (NGOs) and concerned individuals to make education available to displaced children (Sanni, 2017). For instance, the limited role of government and other agencies in providing education was revealed from the encounters of IDPs in one of the camps in Sangere, Adamawa state. According to Ajayi (2015), the school in the camp is run by 58 displaced parents who receive assistance only from NGOs and kind-hearted individuals. The collaborations include the training of teachers, provision of textbooks, writing materials, school bags as well as the provision of tents to serve as temporary classrooms amongst other interventions.

Also, in Yobe, Borno and Adamawa, states with the highest attacks on education due to the intensity of the insurgency there, UNICEF provided school-in-a-box kits, 50, 000 school bags and other school supplies and tents to serve as momentary learning spaces for the education of IDP children. Also, US Agency for International Development in collaboration with the government and over 30 Nigerian organizations and international organisations such as International Rescue Committee launched a 3-year Nigeria Education Crisis Response program in October 2014 which focused on literacy and math in Adamawa, Bauchi, Borno, Gombe and Yobe states (Education Crisis Response Program, n.d.). Some excerpts are presented below on the collaborative roles of international organisations and NGOs:

The camp clinic is very fantastic and standard. Thanks to Nigerian Airforce, UNICEF and also the International Rescue Committee who partner with the government to sustain the camp clinic through their generous donations. Though we give first aid attention to the patients the drugs we prescribe are donated by IRC and UNICEF (Ibrahim, 2017 personal Communication with MIC, Camp Coordinator).

We access relief materials through the individuals, NGOs and INGOs. The federal governments relief appear at a very low level (Anonymous, personal communication with AIS Camp Coordinator).

The UN OCHA (2004) posits that principle 23 of the Guiding Principles on Internal Displacement established that concerned authorities should ensure that displaced children get compulsory and free education whether they are living in camps or not, and should get access to education as soon as the conditions permit it. It also states that nation-states have the primary role in the protection of the rights of IDPs and the provision of humanitarian assistance to IDPs within their territories. As stipulated in the GPID, the federal government is the major actor at the forefront of managing IDPs in Nigeria. Various interventions adopted have cut across the establishment of institutions and agencies, the formulation of policies, and collaboration with other local and international actors. With reference to the policy intervention, in January 2016, the Nigerian government approved a new Social Protection Plan that focused primarily on the improvement of the quality of education. In achieving this goal, the government hired about 500,000 university graduates to teach IDPs. Cash was also given as gifts to extremely poor parents that were willing to enrol their children in schools. The plan had a budget of US$ 302 million and was supported by the World Bank (HRW, 2016). One of the positive impacts of the education efforts is that previously out of school children are getting education. This is basically through campaigns and advocacy to enhance education. For instance, the Back to School campaign in Yobe and Borno led to the enrolment of 170 432 children that were hitherto out of school (Isokpan, 2016). Specifically, in the Muna Garage camp in Maiduguri, it was, estimated that 90 per cent of students were enrolled in school for the first time. Despite these achievements, there is a huge discrepancy between the rights stated in Article 28 of the Convention of the Right of the Child which states that "every child has the right to education" and what is obtainable in the Nigerian state.

Educational Exclusivity of Displaced Children and Sustainable Development in Nigeria

Sustainable development is the development that meets the needs of present generations and does not compromise the capability of future generations to meet their own needs also. Similarly, Ohunene and Ozoji (2014:596) define sustainable national development as the "process of improving the range of opportunities that will enable individual humans and communities to achieve their aspirations and full potential over a sustained period of time while maintaining the resilience of economic, social and environmental systems". The ability of future generations to meet their needs is often produced by a synergy of social development, economic development as well as environmental protection (Olagoke, 2017).

Inclusion in education has both wide and narrow definitions. The narrow definitions only accommodate a learner living with disabilities in a general education context. On the other hand, the wider definitions argue that educational environments must be suitable for all learners irrespective of their physical or bodily characteristics but must take cognizance of individual's needs. The wide sense of inclusion is used in this study. Inclusive education, according to UNESCO's (2009) Policy Guidelines on Inclusion is;

a process that involves the transformation of schools and other centres of learning to cater for all children – including boys and girls, students from ethnic and linguistic minorities, rural populations, those affected by HIV and AIDS, and those with disabilities and difficulties in learning and to provide learning opportunities for all youth and adults as well. Its aim is to eliminate exclusion that is a consequence of negative attitudes and a lack of response to diversity in race, economic status, social class, ethnicity, language, religion, gender, sexual orientation and ability. Education takes place in many contexts, both formal and non-formal, and within families and the wider community. Consequently, inclusive education is not a marginal issue but is central to the achievement of high-quality education for all learners and the development of more inclusive societies. Inclusive education is essential to achieve social equity and is a constituent element of lifelong learning.

It is expedient to mention that Nigeria's National Policy on Education recognizes these salient roles that education plays in the sustainability of a country. Specifically, the documents state that:

Education shall continue to be highly rated in the national development plans because education is the most important instrument for change: any fundamental change in the intellectual and social outlook of any society has to be preceded by an education revolution (Federal Government of Nigeria, 2004, p. 8).

While the statement above shows that the government has made significant policy steps towards its national development, Nigeria has persistently struggled with educating its citizens which have affected her national development (Onyemelukwe-Waziri, 2017; Duruji, Azuh, Oviasogie, & Ajayi, 2014). No wonder, the national development of Nigerian state has been ravaged by factors such as political dissatisfaction, religious and ethnic differences, illiteracy, unemployment, pervasive poverty and perceived societal neglect among the people, communal clashes and violent crimes which have arisen from the lack of inclusive education for all (Aboyi, 2014).

Persistent socioeconomic disadvantages such as poverty and illiteracy have negative effects on the life of many children (Ferguson, Bovaird, & Mueller, 2007). Poverty is one of the enemies of education which itself is a cure for poverty. Various forms of conflicts such as terrorism have remained one of the challenges that hinder the actualization of sustainable development. A substantial body of knowledge exists on the nexus between conflict and poverty. Research shows that slow economic growth and low per capita income severely escalates the chances that a country will experience conflicts (Ajayi, Fayomi, Abasilim., & Adepoju, 2015; Jolicoeur, 2011).

Therefore, these elements project a complex association that have enunciated a vicious circle in the Nigerian state. For instance, there is a general perception that most northerners hold an anti-Western education perception. The general belief about education in the Northern part of Nigeria is that the Quran and Islamic education are the only education necessary that children should be exposed to. As a result, most of the children lack basic skills. The Boko Haram terrorist group has largely hinged on the ideological notion that western education is evil and exhorts Islamic education and Sharia laws as the supreme guide of life and national governance. Thereby, using education amongst other socio-economic factors as tools for both reaching and radicalizing young people including children -which brought about the current displacement crisis in Nigeria. In light of this, Onuoha (2014) argues that,

While it is evident that illiterates do not manufacture the bombs that Boko Haram uses, arrest records suggest that the "real armies of suicide bombers and terrorists' foot soldiers are drawn from such "disadvantaged, stranded populations, suggesting how poverty, lack of education, and indoctrination contribute to terrorism.

Therefore, agreeing with President Obama that "ideologies are not defeated by guns, but by new ideas" (De Silva, n.d.), there is the internationalisation of the shift on leveraging education as a key to deradicalising young minds and preventing violent extremism ravaging some countries of the world including the Nigerian state today. No wonder education has been regarded as the 'fourth pillar' of humanitarian assistance to victims of conflict, feeding, accommodation and healthcare around the world. Quite unfortunately, despite the important role of education in development, many displaced children in Nigeria remain uneducated and worse, there is little action to improve access to education for displaced children. Such children, if not immediately provided with education, may pose a threat to the society. This is because illiteracy makes young people susceptible to embracing radical ideologies propagated by terrorist organizations. In other words, though the effects of the plight of displaced children on Nigeria's national development may be invisible now, it poses severe threats to the next generation because most educational opportunity risks force children to survive through a variety of illegal means because of the lack of education and a dysfunctional educational system breeds crime (Soyinka-Airewele & Yartey Ajayi, 2016).

Disturbingly, the use of children in poverty and illiteracy prone areas of Nigeria such as the northeast is not new. Corroborating this argument of poverty and unfavourable socio-economic conditions, some 35 kids between the age range of 9 and 15 years that were arrested in Borno State for burning schools in Maiduguri said they were given N5, 000 each to get the assignment done (Olanrewaju, 2018). This most significantly arose from their unawareness of knowledge, values and attitudes about their civic duties and responsibilities needed for sustainable development. Also, the failure of the Nigerian state to take action and educate displaced children across various parts of the country will result in worsening the child labour menace already prominent. In other words, the exclusion of displaced children from education if not remedied tend to be a pull factor towards a further radicalization of the region, exposure of the country to more conflicts, terrorism, and also plunge Nigeria into further displacement crisis which is all bane of sustained development affecting both present and future generations. This shows that the achievement of sustainable development does not exclusively domicile within the purview of adults. Children also have roles to play in its achievement just as they have been active players in the conflicts in Northern Nigeria. Arguing in support of the roles children can play in effective development, Feeny and Boyden (2003) argue that:

Children who are capable of lateral thinking and problem-solving can enhance their coping (in contexts of poverty) by identifying alternative options to their current circumstances and devising creative solutions (Feeny and Boyden, 2003, p. 13).

Thus, inclusive education has the capacity of preparing the younger generation for life and equipping them for the challenges that lie ahead. Furthermore, the inability of the government to educate displaced children is a pending disaster for the country. This is because education performs the function of empowering and educating people about their roles in the society. For instance, education ought to produce leaders of Nigeria who would manage the affairs of government and private sector industries. However, when such education is absent, it is impossible to have such leaders. Therefore, instead of training good leaders or at least good followers, exclusive education creates the opposite. Worse of is that illiteracy moulds a wrong attitude, mindset and a myopic perception of life in individuals.

In addition to the effects of past educational disparity in Nigeria, it can be concluded that the exclusion of displaced children is detrimental to Nigeria's sustainable because it expands the number of illiterates in the northern region of Nigeria. Educational exclusivity of the displaced children will only create more long-term economic inequalities for the country because the children would grow up without having the skills essential to be self-sufficient, and to contribute their civil and social duties as Nigerian citizens and her sustainable development. Therefore, the vicious cycle of poverty, illiteracy, national insecurity, underdevelopment and displacement is bound to continue making the realization of the SDGs in 2030 farfetched.

Media Advocacy for Advancing Inclusive and Equitable Quality Education for Displaced Children in Nigeria

Displacement resulting from the Boko Haram insurgency has been widely reported by both local and foreign media which has brought about humanitarian interventions for the various groups affected. Over time, one of the focus of the Nigerian media, has been on the promotion of inclusive education of children with special needs. This group refers to children with mental or physical disabilities as well as refugees. This has brought about philanthropic interventions tilted towards relief materials and health services. The focus of this section is not to highlight existing policies and models in inclusive education, but rather to identify the role of the Nigerian media in the enhancement of inclusive education for displaced children while paying special attention to northern Nigeria. Media Advocacy for advancing inclusive and equitable quality education for displaced children across Nigeria has not received much attention as sparse literature exists on this subject matter. Literature has dwelt mainly on the use of ICT, Gender, and Local Language as tools for inclusive education (Oyesomi, Soola, Abioye & Oyero, 2014; Eastwood & Imbiri, 2017; Goldsmith & Lotyam, 2017; Tauson, 2017). It is on this premise that this section sets out to highlight the role of the media in advocating inclusive education for displaced children in the northern region.

Increased Media Advocacy on Social Tolerance/Inclusion

Inclusive education proposals have been advanced stating the employment of community groups, family, non-governmental organizations as well as the media in the widespread awareness of the importance of inclusive education to tackle the challenge of ignorance at all levels. However, there is a need for a paradigm shift from the media just creating awareness about displaced children, to advocacy on the change of exclusionary patterns, practices, perceptions, behaviour and attitudes towards displaced children. Increased media advocacy in this light would help displaced children not to be socially segregated anywhere they find themselves. This would reduce the rate of social intolerance directed towards them which might have negative effect on their psychology thereby resulting in better performance in schools and achieving equitable and quality education irrespective of their background or social status. Media advocacy would better address the right to a creative and conducive learning environment (UNESCO, 2008).

Also, the media should advocate a total socio-cultural change targeted at increasing tolerance towards other excluded groups in the society. Identified groups include: people in rural areas or urban slums or marginalized areas, adolescent mothers, migrant mothers, adult learners, direct or indirect victims of HIV/AIDS, victims of war/insurgency or natural disasters, child soldiers, physical/mental disabilities or special needs, victims of rape/domestic violence and emotional abuse. These groups may have suffered stigmatization which has metamorphosed into the denial of their rights to basic human development and quality education.

Leveraging on the Potency of the New Media

The last two decades have witnessed a significant change in advocacy with the improvement of the internet and other related technologies as tools for social or political interactions, information participation and expression. Smartphones, tablets, desktop and laptop computers afford citizens the opportunity to actively engage millions of people via social media services like Twitter and Facebook (Hestres, 2017). This has revolutionized the methods by which advocacy is carried out. People regardless of their location can be involved in government legislation or policies that affect them. Media advocacy around the world has played a major role in harvesting public opinion and resources needed for a cause. All these and more have occurred as a result of leveraging on the potency of the new media. This course could be charted in Media Advocacy for advancing inclusive and equitable quality education for displaced children across Nigeria. A report by the Nigerian Communication Commission in 2017 puts the online presence of Nigerians at 91.6 million which represents 49.2% of the total population (Daily Sun, 2017). Building on this, social media can bring about awareness of the current situation of displaced children in northern Nigeria thereby connecting them to NGOs, volunteers and other notable stakeholders. This would help drive the achievement of inclusive and equitable education. Petitions can be signed through this means that later translates into legislation. Sponsored posts and the use of hashtags as was the case of the Bring Back Our Girls Campaign (#BBOG) which caught the attention of both State and Non-State actors. This can be employed to better address the challenge of displacement amongst children in Northern Nigeria (Hestres, 2017).

CONCLUSION AND RECOMMENDATION

This chapter interrogated the implications of internal displacement on the actualization of the rights of displaced children to quality education in Nigeria. It concludes that displacement exacerbates the illiteracy of children in northeast Nigeria which poses threats to the national and sustainable development on the Nigerian state amongst other long term predicaments disastrous for the future generations, as the lives of the educationally excluded children will be locked in the unending cycles of underachievement, poverty and poor human development that have hitherto characterized the northern part of Nigeria. While the media has made concerted efforts in exposing the educational plights of displaced children in various IDP camps in Nigeria, it still has roles to play especially in propagating the awareness of the public at the grassroots on the rights of children to education. The study, therefore, recommends that for the sustainable development of the Nigerian state, there is the need for government to invest both financial and human resources into providing better education at all levels thus ensuring that displaced children are receiving good education during their ordeal. In addition to the above, while the efforts of the government have been inadequate, the paper suggests that the role of the media in advocating for the promotion of the rights of these displaced children to quality and inclusive education cannot be overruled.

REFERENCES

Abdulrasheed, O., Onuselogu, A., & Obioma, U. G. (2015). Effect of insurgency on Universal Basic Education in Borno State of Nigeria. *American Journal of Educational Research*, *3*(4), 490–494.

Aboyi, A. E. (2014). Mass literacy and the attainment of sustainable democracy in African: The Nigeria Senario. *The 2014 WEI International Academic Conference Proceedings*.

African Develeopment Bank. (2018). African. *Economic Outlook, 2018*. Retrieved from https://www.afdb.org/fileadmin/uploads/afdb/Documents/Publications/African_Economic_Outlook_2018_-_EN.pdf

Agba, G., Otuchikere, C., & Odemwingie, E. (2013). *Nigeria: Boko Haram attack on Yobe school, "You'll burn in hell, Jonathan tells sect."* Retrieved from http://allafrica.com/stories/201307080649.html

Agbiboa, E. (2013). No retreat, no surrender: Understanding the religious terrorism of Boko Haram in Nigeria. *African Study Monographs*, *34*(2), 65–84.

Ajayi, A. (2015). *Boko Haram: Nigerian Human Rights Commission laments number of out-of-school children*. Retrieved from http://www.premiumtimesng.com/regional/nnorth-east/194074-boko-haram-nigeria-human rights-commission-laments-number-of-out-of-school-children. html

Ajayi, I. A. (2007). Achieving Universal Basic Education (UBE) in Nigeria: Strategies for improved funding and cost-Effectiveness. *Social Sciences*, *2*, 342–345.

Ajayi, L. A., Fayomi, O. O., Abasilim, U. D., & Adepoju, O. (2015). Girl-Child Education and Nigeria's National Development: A Study of selected Private and Public Secondary Schools in Ado-Odo Ota Local Government Area, Ogun State. *8th International Conference of Education, Research and Innovation (ICERI2015) held in Seville, Spain, 16th-18th November, 2015. Conference Proceedings*, 4819-4831.

Ajayi, L. A., & Soyinka-Airewele, P. (2018). Key Triggers of domestic violence in Ghana: A victim centered analysis. *African Population Studies*, *32*(1), 4097–4108.

Aluko, O. (2018). *Agency to train 60 education planners for IDP camps*. Retrieved from https://punchng.com/agency-to-train-60-education-planners-for-idp-camps/

Amoo, E. O., Omideyi, A., Fadayomi, T., Ajayi, M., Oni, G., & Idowu, A. (2017). Male reproductive health challenges: Appraisal of wives coping strategies. *Reproductive Health*, *14*(1), 90. doi:10.118612978-017-0341-2 PMID:28754166

Convention on the Rights of the Child. (1989). *Adopted and opened for signature, ratification and accession by General Assembly resolution 44/25 of 20 November 1989 entry into force 2 September 1990, in accordance with article 49*. Retrieved from https://www.ohchr.org/documents/professionalinterest/crc.pdf

Cotroneo, A. (2017). Specificities and challenges of responding to internal displacement in urban settings. *International Review of the Red Cross*, *99*(1), 283–318. doi:10.1017/S1816383118000164

Daily Sun. (2017). *Nigeria's internet users rise to 91.6*. Retrieved from https://www.ncc.gov.ng/thecommunicator/index.php?option=com_content&view=article&id=1572:nigeria-s-internet-users-rise-to-91-6m&catid=32&Itemid=179

De Silva, S. (n.d.). *Role of Education in the Prevention of Violent Extremism*. Retrieved from http://documents.worldbank.org/curated/en/448221510079762554/120997-WP-revised-PUBLIC-Role-of-Education-in-Prevention-of-Violence-Extremism-Final.pdf

Donnelly, E., Mausi, S., & Dele-Adedeji, I. (2016). *Boko Haram impacts on education in Northeast Nigeria*. London: Chatham House.

Duruji, M., Azuh, D., Oviasogie, F. O., & Ajayi, O. (2014). Education and Gendered Roles In Post-Adjustment Igbo Society. *International Conference on Education and New Learning Technologies EDULEARN14 Proceedings*, 5054-5061.

Eastwood, A., & Imbiri, H. (2017). Local language as a means to inclusive education in Indonesia: A remote area pilot project for kindergarten and primary children. In *Proceedings of 14th International conference of education and development* (p. 124). Oxford, UK: University of Oxford, United Kingdom.

Education Crisis Response Program. (n.d.). *Nigeria.* Retrieved from https://www.creativeassociatesinternational.com/past-projects/nigeria-education-crisis-response-program/)

Education for All Global Monitoring Report. (2011). *Armed conflict and education (part 2).* Retrieved from http://www.ungei.org/paris2011/docs/gmr2011-part2-intro.pdf

Egbas, J. (2018). *13.2 million Nigerian children now out of school, highest in the world, UNICEF says.* Retrieved from https://www.pulse.ng/news/local/132-million-nigerian-children-now-out-of-school-highest-in-the-world-unicef-says/ge754pc

Federal Government of Nigeria. (2004). *National policy on education* (4th ed.). Lagos: Nigeria NERCD.

Feeny, T., & Boyden, J. (2003). *Children and poverty: Shaping a response to poverty: A conceptual overview and implications for responding to children living in poverty, Children and Poverty Series Part III.* Christian Children's Fund.

Ferguson, H. B., Bovaird, S., & Mueller, M. P. (2007). The impact of poverty on educational outcomes for children. *Paediatrics & Child Health, 12*(8), 701–706. doi:10.1093/pch/12.8.701 PMID:19030450

Folorunsho, A.H., Imam-Tamim, M.K., & Abdulraheem, T.A. (2014). Children's right to education in Nigeria: Challenges and solutions. *Journal or Public Law and Constitutional Practice, 6,* 104-117.

Franzosi, R. (2007). *Introduction.* Retrieved from http://www.unive.it/media/allegato/Scuola-Dottorale/2011/allegato/Content_Analysis_-_Introduction.pdf

Goldsmith, C., & Lotyam, M. L. (2017). Using real-time, disaggregate, national education data to drive inclusive school enrolment and attendance in fragile and conflict-affected settings. In *Proceedings of 14th International conference of education and development.* (p. 26). Oxford, UK: University of Oxford.

Hestres, L.E. (2017, April). Tools beyond control: Social media and the work of advocacy organizations. *Social Media + Society,* 1-11.

HRW. (2016). *They set the classrooms on fire: Attacks on education in Northeast Nigeria.* Retrieved from https://www.hrw.org/report/2016/04/11/they-set-classrooms-fire/attacks-education-northeast-nigeria#

ION and NEMA Displacement Tracking Matrix. (2018). *Nigeria. Round 23 Report - June 2018.* Retrieved from https://reliefweb.int/sites/reliefweb.int/files/resources/Nigeria%20-%20Displacement%20Report%2023%20%28June%202018%29.pdf

Isokpan, A. J. (2016). *The Boko Haram insurgency and the child's right to education in Nigeria.* A Thesis submitted in partial fulfilment of the requirements for the degree of masters of Law (Llm (Ii)) In International and Human Rights Law.

Jolicoeur, D. (2011). *Understanding poverty and conflict.* Retrieved from https://www.mercycorps.org/research-resources/understanding-poverty-and-conflict

Joshua, S. & Olanrewaju, F. O. (2016). The impacts of terrorism on education: The North Eastern Nigeria's experience. *Journal of International Politics and development, 14*(1), 59-74.

Kramer, M. H. (2004). *Where law and morality meet.* Oxford, UK: Oxford University Press.

Kramer, M. H. (2010). Refining the interest theory of rights. *The American Journal of Jurisprudence, 55*(1), 31–39. doi:10.1093/ajj/55.1.31

Kruger, R. A. (2002). *Designing and conducting focus group Interviews - EIU.* Retrieved from http://www.eiu.edu/ihec/Krueger-FocusGroupInterviews.pdf

Lenshie, N. E., & Yenda, H. B. (2016). Boko haram insurgency, internally displaced persons and humanitarian response in Northeast Nigeria. *The International Journal of Humanities & Social Studies, 4*(8), 141–150.

Moody, Z. (2015). The United Nations Declaration on the Rights of the Child (1959): Genesis, transformation and dissemination of a treaty (re)constituting a transnational cause. *Prospects, 45*(1), 15–29. doi:10.100711125-015-9343-4

NAN. (2016). *910 students destroyed, 952, 029 pupils displaced by insurgency in North east.* Retrieved from https://guardian.ng/news/910-schools-destroyed-952029-pupils-displaced-by-insurgency-in-north-east/

Ohunene, O. C., & Ozoji, B. (2014). Science education and sustainable development in Nigeria. *American Journal of Educational Research*, *2*(8), 595–599. doi:10.12691/education-2-8-6

Olagoke, A. (2017). *Sustainable Development Goals In Nigeria: What Role(S) For Nigeria's Indigenous Languages?* Retrieved from https://www.idpublications.org/wp-content/uploads/2017/06/full-paper-sustainable-development-goals-in-nigeria.pdf

Olaiya, T. T. (2018). *Nigeria: Sparing a thought for harsh realities of refugees, IDPs.* Retrieved from https://allafrica.com/stories/201806210093.html

Olanrewaju, F. O. (2018). *Boko Haram insurgency and the crisis of internal displacement of women in Nigeria (2009-2017)* (Thesis). Covenant University, Ota, Nigeria.

Olanrewaju, F. O., Omotoso, F., & Alabi, J. O. (2018a). Datasets on the challenges of forced displacement and coping strategies among displaced women in selected Internally Displaced persons' (IDP) Camps in Nigeria. *Data in Brief*, *20*, 152–158. doi:10.1016/j.dib.2018.07.042 PMID:30112431

Olanrewaju, F. O., Omotoso, F., & Alabi, J. O. (2018b). Boko Haram insurgency and the crisis of internally displaced women in Nigeria: A situational analysis. *African Population Studies*, *32*(1), 3622–3633.

Olugbode, M. (2017). *Boko Haram: 57 percent of schools in Borno closed, says UNICEF.* Retrieved from https://www.thisdaylive.com/index.php/2017/09/30/boko-haram-57-percent-of-schools-in-borno-closed-says-unicef/

Onuoha, F. C. (2014). Why do youth join Boko Haram? Special Report. United States Institute of Peace. Special Report 348, June 2014.

Onyemelukwe-Waziri, H. (2017). *Impact of two wars on the educational system in Nigeria.* Clark University Clark Digital Commons International Development, Community and Environment (IDCE) Master's Papers5.

Oyesomi, K. O., Soola, E., Abioye, T., & Oyero, O. (2014). Perception of women on the role of indigenous communication in politics: A study of Ado-Odo Ota, Ogun State, Nigeria. *Vision 2020: Sustainable Growth, Economic Development, and Global Competitiveness - Proceedings of the 23rd International Business Information Management Association Conference, IBIMA 2014, 1*, 2622-2644.

Oyewobi, A. (2016). *NHRC Decries Neglect of 4000 IDPs in Taraba.* Retrieved from Premium Times: http://www.premiumtimesng.com/regional/nnorth-east/196920-nhrc-decries-neglect-of-4000-idps-in-taraba.html

Pham, J. P. (2012). Boko Haram's evolving threat. *Africa Security Brief*, 20. Retrieved from http://www.ndu.edu/press/lib/pdf/Africa-Security-Brief/ASB-20.pdf

Sahara Reporters. (2015). *How one school provides education for children in a Nigerian IDP camp.* Retrieved from http://saharareporters.com/2015/07/21/how-one-school-provides-education-children-nigerian-idp-camp

Sambo, A. S. (2017). Internal displaced persons and their information needs. *Library Philosophy and Practice, 1512.* Retrieved from http://digitalcommons.unl.edu/libphilprac/1512

Sanni, M. (2017). *Quality education for children in IDPs camps.* Retrieved from https://aljazirahnews.com/feature-quality-education-children-idps-camps/

Skujyte, D. (2011). *Rights of African children under the African Charter on the Rights and Welfare of the Child: The addition to the universal protection of a child.* University of Tilburg Master International and European Public Law (accent on Human Rights Law).

Sofoluwe, A. O. (2012). Human rights and quality education in Nigerian primary schools. *Academic Research International*, *2*(3), 459–468.

Soyinka-Airewele, P., & Yartey Ajayi, L. (2016). Reframing human security, borders and gendered violence in the Shadows of Chibok. *2016 International Conference of the Association of Third World Studies held in the Indiana University Southeast*, New Albany.

Tauson, M. (2017). Can technology substitute for the classroom? The ethical use of edtech in emergency and displaced settings. In *Proceedings of 14th International conference of education and development* (p. 39). Oxford, UK: University of Oxford.

Tong, A., Sainsbury, P., & Craig, J. (2007). Consolidated criteria for reporting qualitative research (COREQ): A 32-item checklist for interviews and focus groups. *International Journal for Quality in Health Care*, *19*(6), 349–357. doi:10.1093/intqhc/mzm042 PMID:17872937

UN (1998). *Guiding Principles on the United Nations Global Counter-Terrorism Strategy.* ADM 1.1, PRL 12.1, PR00/98/109.

UNESCO. (2008). Inclusive education: The way of the future. In *Proceedings of 48th International conference of education* (pp. 5-80). Geneva: International Conference Centre.

UNESCO. (2009). *UNESCO's 2009 Policy Guidelines on Inclusion*. Retrieved from http://www.unesco.org/new/en/media-services/single-view/news/unescos_new_policy_guidelines_on_inclusion_in_education/

UNESCO (2019). *Migration, displacement and education: building bridges, not walls.* UNESCO Global Education Monitoring Report.

United Nations Educational, Scientific and Cultural Organisation. (2011). *The hidden crisis: armed conflict and education.* EFA global monitoring report, 2011.

United Nations OCHA. (2004). *Guiding Principles on Internal Displacement.* Retrieved from http://www.unhcr.org/43ce1cff2.html

Universal Declaration of Human Rights (UDHR). (1948). Retrieved from https://www.un.org/en/udhrbook/pdf/udhr_booklet_en_web.pdf

Waldron, J. (1985). *Theories of rights.* Oxford, UK: Oxford University Press.

Zenn, J., Barkindo, A., & Heras, N. A. (2013). The ideological evolution of Boko Haram in Nigeria. *RUSI Journal, 158*(4), 46–53. doi:10.1080/03071847.2013.826506

Chapter 11
Transient Marriages, Child Rights Abuses, and Mediatic Gap:
A Theoretical Coverage of Crime Instigators in Nigeria

Jegede Ebenezer Ajibade
Department of Sociology, Covenant University, Nigeria

ABSTRACT

A few abusive occurrences in the Third World escape the lenses of the media, portending danger to our collective existence. One such social ill that defied the radar of news coverage is the growing transient consummation and abortion of conjugal relationship implicating male gender and instantiating abuses affecting the children from such relationships. Regrettably, the 'hit and run parenthood' posture attendant of this practice often populate the crime cells cross-culturally and raises the probability of social dislocation laden with colossal cost to societies. Consequently, this chapter attempts to descriptively investigate the depth of this sexual pervasion and the predicaments of children raised under such milieu. A passionate appeal is thus made to galvanize dissuasive participation in such practices and to generate more media attention in order to alleviate the excruciating socio-economic condition and discourage crime among the affected children.

DOI: 10.4018/978-1-7998-0329-4.ch011

BACKGROUND AND STATEMENT OF THE PROBLEM

The nature and conditions of children all over the world present myriad of setbacks in realizing their full potential as future adults. Mostly in their ages of 'human becoming', setbacks appear remarkable in their accessibility to functional education, qualitative health, self-protection and better condition of living. Comparatively, the lives of children are overwhelmingly more affected than those of adults due to their powerlessness and precariousness in confronting annihilable threats surrounding their existence. Due to the realization that we seem to live in violent and increasingly difficult times bearing its pernicious rage engulfing the world of children, pragmatic steps at arresting the tide then becomes necessary (Collins and Makowsky, 2005:262). Hitherto, deplorable attention has attended the deprivations affecting the children globally, only in the latter half of 20th century did the world community formally decide on a common accord that children should have rights and that violence of any kind against them constitute abuse and ultimately unacceptable infringement of those rights. This translated into a codified policy put in place to guide the handling and treatment of the minors, with the U.N.O. taking the lead. The United Nations Convention on the Rights of the Child sought to find means to protect children from abuse, to eliminate the root causes of abuse, to apprehend and heal the abuser and to rehabilitate and integrate abused children so that they can live normal lives. (Arnaldo, 2001: xvi). Drawing conclusions from the provisions enshrined in the international convention, children should have the right to a standard of living that is good enough to meet their physical and mental needs. Further supports were also put in place by regional blocks to drive the global concern on the inalienable rights of the children. In own region, the indigenous instrument "African Charter on the Rights and Welfare of the Child (1990), also represents a concerted effort to extricate children from all forms of maltreatment and this was formulated with the view of ushering them into a purposeful future and for the enhancement of better condition of living. Unfortunately, there are number of inhibitants that are making this unrealizable and setting children on a collision course with multiple abuses. With empirical cases of persistent abuses of children intercontinentally, it then behoves on governments across board to help families and guardians who cannot afford the basic requirements, to fill the gap by providing the most essential—with regard to food, clothing and housing (CRC, article 27). Outside the institutional mandates that are expected to be mitigated by governments, better living conditions for children is often a herculean task under the current milieu of economic condition across the globe and this is helping to fan abuses at varied levels. The core of inhibition threatening the existence of children which incidentally becomes the focus of this discourse resides in the private arena of the home, family patterns, parenting styles, and the consistently depreciating economic capacity of the caregivers. The problems emanating from the home front is made complex by other life threatening cues often engendered by the public institutions. At the core of the public lies the roles of schools, labour camps, community and the Criminal Justice System (CJS) in promoting secondary abuses of children. One should quickly notice that the structuration of families under which children are raised represents one of the sources of child abuse. Few number of children often got enmeshed in both overt and covert violence and these involves all forms of physical or mental violence, injury and abuse, neglect or negligent treatment, maltreatment or exploitation, including sexual abuse (UNICEF, 2016:1). The family is implicated in the promotion and persistence of these complications leading to myriad of abuses. The most potent of the family contributions to child abuse emanates from the quality of marital unions often contracted by parties across board in major societies of Africa. In a recessive environment of the Third world, there are diverse dimensions of marital relationships and parenting practices with correspondingly exposure children to risks of diverse magnitudes. Risk or vulnerability factors are fairly enduring characteristics of an individual's external and internal world that are likely to lead to maladaptive or negative functioning. It is that factor that increases the chance of an individual developing a psychopathological condition (Keenan, 2002:236). External factors of risk mitigating abuses include the family, social dynamics and the general environment of children mostly predisposing them to risks (p. 237). The epicentre of current discussion revolves around the family environment of most abused children and tinkering with the nature, dynamics and complexities affiliatory to sundry marital arrangements in Sub Saharan-Africa. The spate at which men contract women for affinal relationship and the unabated rates of disorganization of family units find representation in the global expression of postmodern shock identified by Dasgupta (2014). This singular destabilizing factor has generated visible annihilative risks concertedly requiring the attention of the intellectual community and other stakeholders. Expressions of public concern about deviant and inadequate parenting are frequently heard hence, an urgent need to understand the nature, their causes and their consequences for children's life course (Schaffer, 1996:227). The concern as portrayed hinges more or less on the dilapidated structures of modern family resulting from unabated separations of couples which often leave children to bowl under excruciating conditions. Consequently, this discourse being a relationship research attempts the descriptive of the growing trends and the prevalence of "hire and fire" model of marital relationship that are generative of mass abandonment of children to either of the spouse at the point of eventualities of separation. Apart from mediatic gap identified with the coverage of abuses emanating from transient marriages, it is also pathetic to inform that media research on the occurrences of single household are not often fully explored to investigate the situations of the children in such disorganized family arrangements. Studies of the implications of parental separation for children's well-being have consistently shown that children of divorced parents fare worse on different measures of well-being than children living in intact families (Barnadi and Radl, 2014:1654). Therefore, this paper also strives to serve as a wakeup call to the media organizations with the intent of re-directing attention to this subtle yet unidentified malignant devoursive of children's future. The centrality of the destructive potential of this malignant lies in the unabated marital dissolution and their after effects on the contractual parties with the children inclusive. In several cases of marital dissolution, women are always at the receiving ends while the custodial rule suffers a waver once the reckless observance of separation is set in motion. Absence of quality time devotable to tendering children by reason of family dislocation accounts majorly for the instigation of abuses in all its ramifications (Oti, 2012). The punitive measure of conjugal separation has often been borne in Africa by the women and it is quite unfortunate to know that women who mostly perform the roles of caregivers are often found to belonged to lower income bracket and oftentimes economically inactive (Musan, Kisovi and Otor, 2015: 146). In this context, there is prevalence of poverty risk and the carrying capacity of women often snaps at the point of saturation. Childhood separation from both biological parents or qualitative caregiver has the potential of destabilizing or altering the personality development of a child. Once there are existence of shaky relationship, acrimonies or unwholesome rivalries affecting the primary reference group, there is the high probability of experiencing either temporal or permanent disruption of life flow that will be suffered by the cohort. The shock of separation may also lead to health fatalism for both the mother and children since disorganization may likely engender negative wellbeing and health (Sbarra, 2015:2). Children are made precarious by virtue of the existence of natural ethics guarding custodial rules and the attendant responsibility of care givers. The ethics historically conferred on the parents and other caregivers vested authority and oversight function to decide on what to make out of children while in its manifest reinforces the helplessness of the children. Abuses are made handy by reason of deprivations; just as children end up earning low level of education often closely made deplorable by low school attendance rates (Kreidl Štípková and Hubatková, 2017), and basically furthered by complexities inherent in unhelpful exposure to different fatherly regimes coming and going in the process of consummating secondary transient relationship over the childhood lifetime of a cohort. Visible vacuum is often created in the life of a child as qualitative parenting is completely absent in few cases thus forcing the affected children to scavenge for substitutes. In recent times, children that are products of separated relationship are forced into meeting virtual strangers via social platform and thereby substituting inputs from such personalities for what they ought to have acquired from their biological parents. This is quite predatory in nature. Four dimensional forms of danger are contactable via the contamination often posed by virtual strangers on the Internet. These include danger revolving around the communication content (unethical, illegal and harmful) at the disposal of the deprived child; dangerous communication (cyber bullying, grooming and learning of illicit acts at meeting life challenges); electronically danger (stealing personal data and exposure to harmful software that may disrupt the life course of a child) and that which is inherent in media input consumption (cyber fraud and other virtual borne crimes) often made available to isolated children (Kocharyan, 2019). The propensity to evolve anti-social traits within this socio-climatic crisis lies in inadequate socialization or guidance and absence of support required to make children functional members of their societies. With the abortion of the early marital relationship, most women are left with nothing but non-controllable or unregulated come and go suitors carrying varied characters and preferring to be visiting partners and thus serving as mobile parentlike tutors rather than cohabiting tutors needed to sharpen the personality component of the children, hence the hub of crimogemic involvements.

THE CHALLENGES RELATING TO CHILD ABUSE

Child abuse is a constellation of multiple environmental risk factors. Risk contextual of child abuse is entrenched under the class of crimes against persons. Minors vulnerable crimes include homicide, rape or sexual abuse and assault or violence. Madjd-Sadjadi, (2013:151) disclosed that the scariest crime for most people including children are those against persons, so called violent crime. A UNICEF (2014) publication "Hidden in Plain Sight: A Statistical Analysis of Violence Against Children" reveals the magnitude of the risks confronting children globally. In a 2012 survey comprising of 190 countries, it was found that homicide took the lives of about 95,000 children and adolescents under the age of 20 and one billion children were said to have been subjected to physical punishment. Similarly, about 120 million girls under the age of 20 were estimated to have been subjected to forced sexual intercourse or other forced sexual acts during their life time (UNICEF, 2016). Globally, there are so many forensic medical assessment of child sexual abuse but there are limited research relating to assessment of grooming Internet abuse and other forms of child sexual abuse (Schrader-McMillan and Barlow, 2017:7). To further lay credence to the high prevalence rate of child abuse especially in Sub-Saharan Africa, Violence Against Children Surveys (VACS) conducted in Kenya, Tanzania, Swaziland, and Zimbabwe indicate that about one in three girls experienced sexual violence during their childhood. The prevalence of physical violence in childhood for the countries affected was puts at ranging between 53% and 76% with boys being more at the receiving ends than girls. The emotional violence during childhood in the surveyed countries was also between 24% and 38% respectively. The consequences of exposable violence directly affecting children vary along age of incidence of abuse, duration and severity of violence, nature of relationship co-existing between the victims and perpetrators; the availability of qualitative innate resilience in the risks takers and co-occurrence of other maltreatment or adverse exposure to health, drug, parental violence risks (UNICEF, 2016:2). However, the lifelong adverse effects of child abuse that are inherent in physical, mental and social health have been considerably documented in research (Daley et al, 2016: 29). The most germane effect to current discourse therefore involves the metamorphic potentials of maltreatment resulting in crime and other anti-social behaviours (Reavis, Looman, Franco & Rojas, 2013; Levenson and Socia, 2016 as cited in Daley et al, 2016:30). The family have also been recognized as most important factor in the life of a child. This is basically so for two reasons: one is the nature of the family structure which determines the personality acumen of the affected child and two is the family atmosphere affecting psycho-social interaction and the economic circumstances of the child (Papalia, Gross and Feldman, 2003:359). The correlates of anti-social behaviour are found to be quite endemic in the family atmosphere. The supportiveness of the home or otherwise, quality of treatment and the social security available, sufficiency of money resources and availability of basic necessities of life, and other things that goes on within the walls of the house with crisis between the spouses inclusive determines the situation of the child (Ruther and Quinton, 1987; Ruther, 1990; Ruther and Ruther, 1993 as cited in Keenan, 2002) have earlier identified six risk factors that are instigators of psychopathology or anti-social behaviour. The rallying point of the six so identified primarily lies in chronic family problems. The factors linkable to chronic family problem include, severe marital discord, maternal psychiatric illness, low economic status, overcrowding or large family size, parental criminality and the placement of a child out of the family home (p.257). In establishing the basis for child abuse in the six enumerated factors (Keenan, 2002: 257) educates that family discord breed ineffective parenting and maternal psychiatric illness triggers bizarre behaviour towards children coming as a result of depression and capable of spurring disorder in children. (It is worthy of note that research linked child abuse to risk factors such as parental substance abuse (Seay and Kohl, 2013), family violence (Nicklas and Mackenzie, 2012; Diderich et al, 2013) and community poverty and instability (Peterson et al, 2014) but these research findings fall short of investigating the uniqueness of family dysfunctionality located in transient marriages exposing children to multiple environmental risk factors. Studies have also found that childhood experience of physical violence is related to living in a violent, marital relationship (Cascadi, O'Leary, Lawrence and Schlee, 1995;). Longitudinal and retrospective studies as well as studies using a 'follow-back' strategy earlier reported relationship between violence and abusive child rearing practices alongside the specificity of parental abuses and later life violent criminality (Lewis, Mallouh and Webb, 1989; Luntz and Widom, 1994; McCord, 1996; Widom and White, 1997 as cited in Haapasalo, 2000). Transient marital relationship promotes high level risk to the children and it thus requires urgency in dealing with its prevalence. Ideally, there is the uniqueness of every child in term of socio-psychological composition, it is however important to know that as a child develops, he/she needs different types of stimulation and interaction to form a personality pattern which in turn becomes enduring ((Evans, Meyer and Ilfeld, 2000:11). Failure to learn to adjust to social circumstances and the incapability of conforming to collective expectation generate both risks to the affected child and general public. Risk instigator revolves around physical neglect or physical abuse both resulting in maltreatment. High risk problematic parenting with the likelihood of featuring power assertive, authoritarian and harsh childrearing practices and parental rejection and aggression has affinity with transient or disorganized homes which will promote myriad of abuses (Farrington, 1992; Patterson, Reid and Dishion, 1992; McCord, 1996; Haapasalo, 2000). Descriptively, the nature, severity chronicity and the axis of maltreatment of children implicate caretakers or parents, peers and intimate partners whose role is always at variance with their emotional and physical conditions and their probability of engagement in bizarre irrational behaviour ending in violent outburst, attitudinal problems with the law, stereotyping the child as either bad or evil, use of verbal or physical punishment for not meeting caregivers expectations, and quality of friendship on either side of both the child and the caregiver can be regarded as high. Children from transient relationship often belonged to disorganized blended family with low income that is far too short to sustain qualitative survival and grossly lacking in family support by reason of inaccessibility of the parent or caregiver (Kreidl, Štípková and Hubatková, 2017:174). Consequently, the correlation between the experientials of abuses and becoming prone to crime is quite high. Societies thus need to articulate the magnitude of occurrence with the view of arresting the tide. The main driver of conscientization for both government and the general public consist of the roles of the media in their varying degrees. Intensification of reporting the prevalence of abuses and the preoccupation with highlighting the consequences of abuse will further draw the attention of the stakeholders to the looming epidemics of crime across known cultures.

HISTORICITY AND AGENTIC-STRUCTURE POSTULATIONS OF CHILD ABUSE

Improvement to parenting and caregiving with the view of arresting child abuse rest solidly on cementing the gaps already created by the historical ideologies which commenced with John Locke's (1632-1704) notion of experiential child with tabula rasa and transitorily, the iniquitous child of the Puritans (17t and 18th century) known to be laden with sinful nature. Further complex thoughts produced in the virtuous child of Jean Jacques Rousseau (1712-78) proclaimed children as having inherent natural goodness and the competent child of David Elkind, (1987) portrayed modern child as having enhanced capabilities to learn academic skills regardless of background if not for the existence of abuses. In contrast, the postmodern child of Alasuutari and Karila, (2009), rested on the advocacy that children be rated as beings and possessing significant contribution to modern change rather than subject or collaborators in research and latter thought culminated into the thinking of the wired child of Slee, Cross, Campbell, Spear and Dooley (2010), which linked possession of capabilities by children towards the mass utilization of the cyber technologies as inalienable fact making children equal partners and abingers of qualitative socio-economic development in the modern world (Campbell and Spear, 2012). Irrespective of the historicity of development we explore, children deserve our respects and conferment of honour as equal beings. The role of parents or caregivers is quite also essential to the filling of the gaps created by most of the extant ideologies conferring both incapability and potentiality on the innate abilities of young people and the absence of which is capable of derailing the life course of childhood development. Young people has been touted as focus of our investment, hence the need to control their lives and manage their experiences with the intent of making them useful adults (Lee, 2003: 36). They are to be protected from the scourge of abuse and whenever such predatory symptom surfaces the amelioration of risks become quite important, hence the need to explore theoretical underpinnings of child abuse.

The theoretical basis of child abuse can be extrapolated from sociology of childhood. This branch classified the world of children under social structuralism with the defining character of children viewed as occupying unequal status both in power and the distribution of capital and their subjugation under the mandatory acquisition of normative knowledge needed to make them functional members of human society (Oswell, 2013:35). The importance of structuralism in understanding child abuse is made comprehensible from the work of Elliot (2014). In his observance of the roles of impersonal forces of politics, culture, family and the economy, he opined that these institutions exert pressure on the activities of individual agents thereby forcing them to make choices and decisions on how best to cope with their daily lives and in the process unintentionally producing social structures (p12)., Clarifying the advent of structure, Giddens considers structure as a duality with intense and consistent negotiation among the parties involved (Turner, 2013:712). The foundational structure implicated in abuses of children remains the family. In the context of child abuse having its prompting in family disorganization, Giddens posited that the predicament of the agency is implicated in the structure of the dislocated family and the structure is involved in exerting pressure on the agentic to adopt a particular type of lifestyle with the intent of appropriating a set benefit in the ensuing scenario. Just as the family structure is enabling to some set of children, it is also constraining in its impact on the developmental progression of significant others (Ritzer and Goodman, 2004:79). The world of children is a negotiated world, just as the parents or caregivers supply the lead, there is a complimentary followership by the cohorts. In this structural arrangement, there is a state of helplessness often promoting subserviency on one hand and the fear of non-existence of definable or collective support that is capable of arousing the potentiality of experimenting with anti-social behaviour ably serving as substitutes for societal requirements on the other hand. Children were also regarded as reckonable agents of change thus having the capacity to interpret, make meaning and materially manipulate their environment. The existence of these innate qualities portend the high probability for either using them for positive advancement or adapting them into negative uses by virtue of the placement of diverse children along the hierarchies of family structures. The family structure determines to a large extent the world view of children, their personality components and ultimately, successes in life. A well-structured family with maximum roles functionality tends to reproduce conformable children while disorganized family becomes an incendiary capable of ravaging and dislocating the equilibrium of any social setting. The relevance of agency now comes into play in role performance and abdication. Agency is what an actor actually does in a situation that has visible consequences and which in most reasonable cases operates outside the intended consequences (Giddens, 1984). The point of dislocation in agentic role performance occasioning child abuse lies in the variation affecting both the discursive and practical consciousness of the parents (vital agency) or caregivers and the children as identified by Giddens. Both consciousness within the structuralism of the family pungently directs the attention of reviewers to the likelihood of having both role realization and failure unfolding within the lifespan of permissible contact between the children and their caregivers. In essence, the discursive consciousness remarkably implicates the 'breadwinner' or sole caregiver but the practical consciousness, got to do more with the children that are exposable to abuses and their mothers in case of Sub-Saharan Africa. At the discursive plane, caregivers are often fixated but often rationalize the value of children and attempt to equate their role occupation as the ideal type within their various capacities yet inadvertently reneging in completing the life cycle of tendering children to maturity by reason of the transient nature of relationship leading to the suffocation of other members of the family of the love, care, warmth and resources needed for continuity or survival of the group. There are visible gaps inhibiting the finality of product development and standardization; which in the process reduces the competitiveness of children raise in organized homes and those coming from disorganized settings. The adjustment potential of the former appears more favourable or stress free while for the latter, adjustment often prove difficult and annihilating. The practical consciousness consists of the stock of knowledge that one implicitly uses to act in situations and to interpret the actions of others (Turner, 2013:713). In transient marriage relationships, two actors within the family network often utilize the practical input. The woman and her children often engage the faculty of qualitative reasoning towards making adjustment or coping with the ensuing challenges linkable with their 'breadwinner' separation. In the course of the two dwelling in unabated reflexivity, the assumed 'breadwinner' operate under the illusory of insulation against the vicissitude of life challenges infectible within the abandoned family unit. This form of fatherhood is considered in the current discourse as 'touch and go' or 'hit and run' model having partial or zero commitment to accountability in relation to the products of dislocated conjugal relationship. Pathetically, the 'touch and go' or 'hit and run' paternity or fatherhood seldom think of the consequences of their abandonment of children to their mothers and in the process relegating reflexivity on the consequences of making other vulnerable to predatory circumstances to the realm of unconsciousness. As a matter of fact, all acts of omission on the part of the 'breadwinner' is indexical and thereby forms the basis of interpreting and making decisions on the next line of action on the part of the victims. Oswell, (2013), discloses that there are many pressures to act in certain ways, which an actor under the gulag of deprivation or starvation does not perceive due to the dissatisfaction and pain attendant of shocks promoted by separation. Elliot (2014:146) corroborated that 'we seldom think of ourselves as catalyst using various reasoning skills to negotiate the social circumstance about us'. At the point of feeling disappointed, there is the tendency to permit emotional betrayal that is capable of leading to doing the opposite (Mena and Eyer, 2004:189). In most of the time, actors adopt natural attitude as distinct from social attitude of inclusiveness needed to cement our world and to make life bearable to others around us thereby making what we do, as well as why we do what we do a mystery. These mysteries are driven by the use we put our consciousness. The contextual interpretation of deprivation and the framework of what next to do mostly instantiated by practical consciousness, compulsively push the victims of 'breadwinner' separation into non-conventional practices. Worse still is the occupation of economic inactive positions by most African women which tends to lure them into becoming sex hawkers, 'call women' or accomplices in crime while for the children, the knowledgeability of fatherhood gaps pushes them into becoming incorrigible, vagabonds, playing truancy in school and invariably dropping out of school and thereby crescending into finding enlistment into criminal gangs. Although, the victims are pressured into embarking on anti-social conducts or behaviour but they can yet rationalize their nefarious activities as survival driven thus pointing to the fact that there is absence of correlation between the eventful acts and the underpinning motive according to Giddens. What propels action in transient marriage environment lies below consciousness and at best provides very general and diffused pressure to act. The man often acts to throws behind him what he perceives as moribund marital relationship and in-turn reaching forth towards new feminist frontiers to explore those pleasures that are derivable from novel discovery of sexual gratification while the victims (wife and children) which are product of broken homes are forced to act to evade extinction with excruciating pains.

VARIABILITY OF GENDER EXPOSURE TO MARITAL SEPARATION ABUSES

Research has found that children of women experiencing intimate partner's violence or who have suffered a certain degree of marital separation are more than twice as likely to experience neglect by their mothers (Daley et al, 2016: 30). Neglect often involves depriving a child of food, clothing, shelter, medical care, or other necessities of life. Neglect can also involve exposing a child to harmful substances or materials such as drugs, alcohol, or pornography, or to harmful practices such as violent behaviour (BSOA, 2015). There exists an affinal relationship between child abuse, neglect and substance abuse (Howard, 2000). Assessment about childhood symptom and family characteristics accounts substantially for reversion into drug use or supporting culture. Children whose parents abuse substances are almost three times more likely to be abused and four times more likely to be neglected than other children (CASA, 1999). Neglect has been classified as the most prevalent form of maltreatment associated with child abuse (Rosenzweig, 2017: iii). The drug culture is most prevalent among children from disorganized settings. The availability of drug deflects and ameliorates the pains often injected by marital separation. It becomes a substitute to filial support and provides artificial succour or joy to abuse threatened young people. The most connecting ill to the predicament of neglect associated with marital separation or conflict involve the growing trend in child exploitation and corruption. There is high probability of converting girl children into bargaining instruments between for instance a separated woman and her potential succourer's or benevolent males which thus increase the likelihood of moral pollution with its end result in prostitution, crime or other anti-social practices (WA, Health, 2015). There is the domesticity of class mutation in which the intergenerational conditions of the foster parent (Mostly women in Africa) is not remarkably different from what awaits the abuse child. Intergenerational mobility is often stifled and the trend of "lamb takes after its mother" begin to unfold in the life of an abandoned or neglected child. In most cases, there exists a scenario of reputational career for girls in which the mother occupation pursuit becomes transferred wholesomely as the child grows up. Research examination of gender dimension of child abuse reveals that the girl child is more likely to be the victim of sexual abuse, more predisposable to physical abuse, neglect and lacking care and guardianship due to the excessive mobility of the mothers in making efforts both licitly and illicitly to make ends meet for the products of marital separation or spousal abandonment (UNICEF, 2017:41). Complimentarily, boys have been discovered to possess genetic risk factors for problematic behaviours prior to engaging in anti-social related activities but the manifestation of which is often triggered by exposure to abuses emanating in part from their homes. In boys, three meta analyses have supported the association between neglect or maltreatment often occasioned by abuses and low activity alleles of the monoamines oxidase A (MAOA) gene, which appear to increase the risk of anti-social behaviour in boys especially with each successive exposure to episodic neglect or maltreatment (Raad and Apellbaum, 2015:12). Deficiency noticeable along this plane promote violent behaviour and ultimately resulting from abuses being experienced or hitherto suffered (Widom and Maxfield, 2001: Weder, Yang. Douglas-Palumberi, Massey, Krystal, Gelenter and Kaufman, 2009). For both gender, in its recent time, there is the incremental of nefarious activities with the enablement of Internet related technologies or ICT's which make the situation overtly precarious and defying control. Advances in ICT's facilitates cyber related immorality. Easy connectivity to the network of crime, prostitution and other secondary abuses are made handy to children that are produced by separated parents. ICT's promotes online risks such as sexual exploitation and abuse of children online (Hermandez et al, 2018:305) Sexual abuse and sexual exploitation is on the rise for girls and peer inducement to engage in crime is potentially high for boys. For both gender, concern has also grown with the incremental use of social media with its impact on the various aspects of young people's mental and physical health. With its potential negative effects, there are rising rates of physiological arousals, decreased attention, hyperactivity, aggression, anti-social and fearful behaviour, social isolation and excessive use of or technological addiction (Tartari, 2015: 322; Adcock, 2016:2). For products of most separated relationship, additional dose of depression and anxiety occasions attention deficits to the inculcation of group norms and socialization content. Poverty has been blamed for infectious vulnerability on line affecting the abused children.

MEDIA, CHILD ABUSE, AND CRIME ENVIRONMENT

The relationship between media input and the intensification of violence and crime has been established in research (Becker-Blease, Finkelhor and Turner, 2008: Kolhman et al, 2014). Although few research findings reported that the impact of media content cannot be considered a sufficient explanation for someone's criminal motivation (Gunter, 2008; Savage, 2008; Ferguson, 2014; Helfgott, 2015 cited in

Philips, 2017:), it has however been established that modern media is preoccupied with allurement to crime while judging from the exposure of minors and youths to violent content carefully selected to attract their attention (Ignjatovic and Ljubicic, 2017). The impact of the media is much felt in the alteration in the audience emotions, attitudes and behaviours (Philips, 2017). Of particular interest in this section is the relationship between separation emanating from transient marriages, child abuse and the development of anti-social behaviour as a result of children's exposure to media contents. Relationship is sought between child abuse, the experiential deprivation and the role of the media in the presentation of non-normative actions. Vast majority of children have access to multiple media in our today global environment and this singular advantage determines to a large extent, the choices at the disposal of such group on how best to put to use the media contents. Irrespective of the socio-biological condition of the children, it is most glaring that significant portion of them has access to the Internet via phones, iPods, video games which is both aiding their connectivity to social networking platforms such as Facebook twitters, Myspace and WhatsApp and in turn shape their worldview and the eventfulness of behavioural enactments carrying double-edged implication for interactors within the web of social relationship. In concrete terms, there appears to be opportunity to engage the mimickery of already portrayed violence from the media inputs by the affected group and there is a thin line between the inclination to stay put in the domain of acceptable behavioural mode or snapping into heinous behaviours. The pendulum of switching is closely knitted to the circumstantial situation constituting the pull factor from the family front and the media content indirectly serving as a push factor into the adoption of unacceptable behaviours by the victimized children. With increasing isolation and its attendant deprivation, the most illicit adaptation of media infrastructure is often recorded among children whose parents offer less physiological and emotional support. The response effect to the absence of survival comfort is mostly registrable in the development of aggressive personality which serves as a pre-condition to becoming suitable for criminal career. Warburton (2014) further corroborated that non-restriction to exposure to violent media often caused by parental neglect, deficient socialization and lack of censorship on children's activities increase the rate of crime participation among the vulnerable groups. Children under the gulag of child abusers are exposed to myriad of risk factors and this ultimately determines the life course of the already contaminated victims of abuses. The presence of risk factors as a precursor of the development of psychopathic personality traits was further support in the findings of Bushman and Anderson (2015). Once there is an existence of family dislocation, it produces secondary aggravators that predispose abuse victims to vagaries of life. Most children becoming the victims of transient relationship mutually reinforced by their parents often find life so difficult and in the process being entangled within the web of circle of confusion that makes a detour into crime and other anti-social conducts attractive. Abused children in this context are left with no other option than to emulate their pairs in bodily term while they elope with the media as a succourer in a virtual term. Virtualism here denotes schoolism for the deprived children (Helfgott, 2015). Asides the negativity induceable through the home front, young people's exposure to the media has not been devoided of maltreatments. Research for instance established that the internet has been shown to act as a new medium through which some commonly recognised forms of child maltreatment, sexual and emotional abuse, may be pursued (Feather, 1999; Stanley, 2014: 2). In a way, there is a double edged vulnerability encounterable by most abused children along the planes of human and technological inducible risks. Threats emanating from the home front becomes primary causative factor in crime participation while the externality of technological influence reinforces the habituality of becoming both incorrigible and deviant on the long run. Multiplicity of challenges are measurable along the flow of relational disorganization attendant of 'hire' n 'fire' model of marital contract that is voraciously engulfing the Nigeria's recessive environment and which invariably thwarted the developmental life course of most abused children as currently being experienced across the major boundaries of the nation.

EXPECTED MEDIA FOCUS AND CHILD RIGHTS IN THE GLOBAL ENVIRONMENT

From the beginning of modern history which holistically enunciated the contributions of media profession in the ordering of global relationship, experts in this field have often been found at the front burner of championing the rights of children. The important role of the media in the defence of children's rights involves protecting them from the risk of harm through the understanding of the vulnerabilities they are confronted with in the various domains of their relational environment (Livingstone and Bulger, 2014:1). So many giant strides have been recorded by the media in this regard but there are more rooms for improvement in the coverage of children's predicaments globally. There are lots of gaps in media coverage of their activities and endangerment when evaluated from one continent to another in terms of the effectiveness of championing a change. Despite knowing that children represent one of the group hardest hit by situations of violence and insecure environment, there is yet a lot of under reporting or media exclusion of those things that are of concern for their survival (IACHR, 2015: 31). This neglect is absolutely rife and being practice in most developing nations such as Nigeria. Notably, while playing the role of child defender most times, media coverage is more felt in the reportage of the plight of children in the war torn areas or at best, crisis ridden environments.

This by implication excludes the gamut of pressure imposable on children 's welfare and other broad arrays of issues confronting children most capable of annihilating or threatening their survival across major cultures globally. Most of the media coverage is limited to reportage laden with unwritten codes of ethics (UNICEF, 2005). There is also a disdainful treatment or public resentment to what is of major concern to the children (UNICEF, 2000). With this existence of gap in media coverage that is affecting the life chances of an average child, it then becomes important to reappraise the condition of children with the view of capturing occurrences that are affronting their survival. Global community therefore urgently requires the re-engineering of mediatic focus. Journalist and social media practitioners therefore need to show responsibility and sensitivity toward covering the vulnerabilities that children are made exposable to by unfriendly relationship such as endemic in marital fatalities. Consequently, the most germane to current discourse is investigative journalism that will enable risk prone children aired their plight to the public and thus necessitate the intervention of stakeholders to their rescue. Little has been recorded on the socio-material condition of children suffering by reason of family dislocations. More of journalistic roles is quite needed to salvage the situation and reduce the impact of family separation on the children particularly in Nigeria where the culture of silence exists in the handling and care of the product of marital separation. The mediatic intervention required in this context will take cognizance of the provisions enshrined in the Convention of the Rights of the Child. Hence, the media should see the children as an important subject of focus; just as their well-being is depended on the quality of media attention directed at them Children are known to be obsessed partner in progress alongside the media as they contribute a greater voice to media outputs (Calvert, 2008; McLanahan, Haskins, Paxson Rouse and Sawhill, 2008). Children in this regard are often referred to as invisible audience (Burton, 2014). Media has no choice but to accommodate and constructively engage all manner of threats confronting them in their diverse socio-economic environment. Another factor capable of wooing the media to the situation of the children is the fact that the media is in a best position to portray accurately the nuances of suffering and challenges affecting them and also, it is the only institution that best captures the voices and realities of children with adequate attention to the ethics and rights of the children. Those affected and requiring media attention in the context of this discourse are children commonly classified as vulnerable children. They are at risk of participating in crime due to their placement along the hierarchy of deteriorated families. (Penal Reform International, 2013:21). Children. under the excruitiating pain of marital separation often lose their sense of individuality and humanity which thus make them prone to crime related involvement. They are both active member in crime perpetration and crime victimization. This is equally depended on their placements in the hierarchy of conflict.

CONCLUSIONS AND RECOMMENDATIONS

The magnitude of vulnerabilities often projected toward young people are multi-dimensional along diverse spatial settings. Most unique to Sub-Saharan Africa in general and Nigeria in particular involves the unrestrainable practice of transient marriages promoting the exposure of significant number of children to untoward abuses and which invariably predisposes them to the acquisition of crime sub-culture and as a result, helplessly engaging in innumerable number of deviant events. Quite pathetic is the systemic mediatic under reporting or neglect in the coverage of the ensuing negative development. There is the culture of near viewing the event as normal when judged from the fact that the desired attention is yet to be elicited from the media class, and yet, the pain inflictable remained astronomical in its consequences for the victims of abuses. The overt occurrences of this omission is well represented in the sundry breaches of security which mostly affect lives and properties across Nigerian landscape. In response to this unfolding counter-culture therefore, an appeal is hereby put across to all well-meaning media practitioners to fill the gap created by the non-exposure of the growing trend of the dastard acts of hiring and firing women at will without sufficient or justifiable reasons and thereby causing the derailment of valuable destinies of tomorrow generations. Stakeholders are also expected to also rise up to the current challenges by sponsoring a re-amendment of the existing marriage dissolution bill that will reduce the spate of marital separation on one hand and peradventure if allowed to take place, such law must make it mandatory for the culturally recognized breadwinner of the family to continue the performance of his role to the products of the union even after the dissolution of the marriage. Although marriage dissolution bill and its attendant rights exist in a weak form and it seldom confers culpability on reckless men, it is quite important to the media community to commence the alarmist mode of reporting for the purpose of restoring the effective of the existing instrument. By this, a state of emergency should be declared to arrest the operational flexibility currently being enjoyed by men who mainly subscribed to the regime of transient marriages. It should be known to all and sundries that the absence of tangible legal framework that is capable of curbing the excesses of some men has resulted in today recklessness in perpetrating the procreation of so many children who suffer from the covertly intentions of the fathers not to pay the bills of their sustainability. The prevalent level of ignorance that is rife among women on the next line of action to take in case of this eventuality should be mitigated by mass orientation to be undertaking by NGO's with vested interest in women's affair. If pragmatic steps are taken, the scourge of young people involvement in crime would drastically reduce and Nigerian society will be a better place for all to live and be productive. Ideally, this advocacy hinges on one of the proverbs of the Yoruba people of Nigeria, which states "the state of peace of a tree will largely determine the quality of comfort that will be derived by a pitching bird." Once the practice of free for all kinds of misbehaviour and experimentation remained permissible and acquiesced as one of the ethos of marital culture, it then becomes real that Nigeria's future may grow bleak and become non-predictable, hence the need for all to stitch right on time.

REFERENCES

Adcock, A. (2016). Effect of social media on the mental health of young people. *Debate Pack*, Number CDP 2016-0196, 1 November, House of Common, Library.

Alasuutari, M., & Karila, K. (2009). Framing the picture of the child. *Children & Society*, *24*(2), 100–111. doi:10.1111/j.1099-0860.2008.00209.x

Arnaldo, C. A. (2001). Introduction. In *Child Abuse on the Internet: Ending the Silence*. New York: UNESCO.

Becker-Blease, K. A., Finkelhor, D., & Turner, H. (2008). Media Exposure Predicts Children's Reactions to Crime and Terrorism. *Journal of Trauma & Dissociation*, *9*(2), 225–248. doi:10.1080/15299730802048652 PMID:19042776

Bernardi, F., & Radl, J. (2014). *The long-term consequences of parental divorce for children's educational attainment*. Vol. 30. *Article*, *61*, 1653–1680.

Boys Scout of America (BSOA). (2015). *How to Protect your Children from Child Abuse: A Parent's Guide*. Retrieved from www.scouting.org

Burton, A. (Ed.). (2014). Protecting the Rights of Children: The Role of the Media, Lessons from Brazil, India and Kenya. Interview Europe.

Bushman, B. J., & Anderson, C. A. (2015). Understanding causality in the effects of media violence. *The American Behavioral Scientist*, *59*(14), 1807–1821. doi:10.1177/0002764215596554

Calvert, S. L. (2008). Children as Consumers: Advertising and Marketing. *The Future of Children*, *18*(1), 2005–2234. PMID:21338011

CASA. (1999). *National Center on Addiction and Substance Abuse at Columbia University*. CASA.

Cascardi, M., O'Leary, K. D., Lawrence, E. E., & Schlee, K. A. (1995). Characteristics of women physically abused by their spouses and who seek treatment regarding marital conflict. *Journal of Consulting and Clinical Psychology*, *63*(4), 616–623. doi:10.1037/0022-006X.63.4.616 PMID:7673539

Collins, R., & Makowsky, M. (2005). *The Discovery of Society* (7th ed.). New York: McGraw-Hill Companies Inc.

Daley, D., Bachmann, M., Bachmann, B. A., Pedigo, C., Thuy-Bui, M., & Coffman, J. (2016). Risk Terrain Modelling Predicts Child Maltreatment. *Child Abuse & Neglect*, *62*, 29–38. doi:10.1016/j.chiabu.2016.09.014 PMID:27780111

Dasgupta, S. (2014). Sociology and postmodern risks. In S. Dasgupta & P. Kivisto (Eds.), *Postmodernism in a Global Perspective*. New Delhi, India: SAGE Publications India Pvt Ltd. doi:10.4135/9789351507833.n7

Diderich, H., Fekkes, M., Verkerk, P., Pannbakker, F. D., Velderman, M. K., Sorenson, P. J., & Qudesluys-Murphy, A. M. (2013). A new protocol for screening adults presenting their own medical problems at the emergency department to identify children at high risk for treatment. *Child Abuse & Neglect*, *37*(12), 1122–1131. doi:10.1016/j.chiabu.2013.04.005 PMID:23768937

Elkind, D. (1987, May). The child yesterday, today and tomorrow. *Young Children*, 6–11.

Elliot, A. (2014). *Contemporary Social Theory: An Introduction* (2nd ed.). Abingdon, UK: Routledge.

Evans, J. L., Meyers, R. G. & Ilfeld, E. M. (2000). *Early Childhood Counts: A Programming Guide on Early Childhood Care for Development*. Washington, DC: IBRD.

Farrington, D. P. (1992). Explaining the beginning, progress and coding of anti-social behaviour from birth to adulthood. In J. McCord (Ed.), Advances in Criminological Theory: Vol. 3. *Facts, Frameworks and Forecasts* (pp. 253–286). New Brunswick, NJ: Transaction.

Feather, M. (1999). *Internet and child victimization*. Paper presented at the Children and Crime: Victims and Offenders Conference, convened by the Australian Institute of Criminology, Brisbane, Australia.

Ferguson, C. J. (2014). Does media violence predict societal violence? It depends on what you look at and when. *Journal of Communication*, *65*(1), E1–E22. doi:10.1111/jcom.12129

Giddens, A. (1984). *The Constitution of Society: Outline of the Theory of Structuration*. Oxford, UK: Polity Press.

Gunter, B. (2008). Media violence: Is there a case for causality? *The American Behavioral Scientist*, *51*(8), 1061–1122. doi:10.1177/0002764207312007

Haapasalo, J. (2000). Sons in prison and their mothers: Is there a relationship between childhood histories of physical abuse? In G. L. Fox & M. L. Benson (Eds.), *Contemporary Perspectives in Family Research: Families* (Vol. 2, pp. 73–90). Crime and Criminal Justice.

Health, W. A. (2015). *Guidelines for Protecting Children 2015. WA Health.* Government of Western Australia.

Helfgott, J. B. (2015). Criminal behaviour and the copycat effect: Literature review and theoretical framework for empirical investigation. *Aggression and Violent Behavior*, *22*(C), 46–64. doi:10.1016/j.avb.2015.02.002

Hermandez, S. C. L. S., Lacsina, A. C., Ylade, M. C., Adaba, J., Lam, H. Y., Estacio, L. R. Jr, & Lopez, A. L. (2018). Sexual Exploitation and Abuse of Children Online in the Philippines: A review of online news and Articles. *ACTA Medica Philppina*, *52*(4), 305–311.

Howard, J. (2000). *TIP 36: Substance Abuse Treatment for Persons with Child Abuse and Neglect Issues: Treatment Improvement Protocol (TIP) Series 36.* Academic Press.

Ignjatovic, D., & Ljubicic, M. (2017). Media and crime: The eternal criminological theme. In I. Stevanović & O. Pavićević (Eds.), *Judiciary & Media. Serbia: istraživanja.* Beograd: OEBS.

Inter-American Commission on Human Rights (IACHR) (2015). *Violence, Children and Organized Crime*. OEA/Ser.L/V/II, Doc. 40/15.

Jones, L. M., Finkelhor, D., & Beckwith, J. (2010). Protecting victims' identities in press coverage of child victimization. *Journalism*, *11*(3), 347–367. doi:10.1177/1464884909360925

Keenan, T. (2002). *An Introduction to Child Development.* London: SAGE Publication Ltd.

Kocharyan, A. (2019). *The Abuse of Social Media: Child Protection.* Retrieved from http://www.bearr.org/pdfs/BEARR_ArturKocharyan.pdf

Kohlman, S., Baig, A., Balice, G., DiRubbo, C., Placencia, L., Skale, K., ... Aquino, S. (2014). Contribution of Media to the Normalization and Perpetuation of Domestic Violence. *Austin Journal of Psychiatry and Behavioral Sciences*, *1*(4), 1–5.

Kreidl, M., Štípková, M., & Hubatková, B. (2017). Parental separation and children's education in a comparative perspective: Does the burden disappear when separation is more common? *Demographic Research*, *36*, 73–110.

Lee, N. (2003). *Childhood and Society: Growing up in an Age of Uncertainty*. Berkshire, UK: Open University Press.

Levenson, J. S., & Socia, K. M. (2016). Adverse childhood experiences and arrest pattern in a sample of sexual offenders. *Journal of Interpersonal Violence*, *31*(10), 1883–1911. doi:10.1177/0886260515570751 PMID:25711615

Lewis, D. O., Mallouh, C., & Webb, C. (1989). Child abuse, delinquency and violent criminality. In D. Cochetti & V. Carlson (Eds.), *Child Maltreatment, Theory and Research on the Causes and Consequences of Child Abuse and Neglect* (pp. 707–721). Cambridge, UK: Cambridge University Press. doi:10.1017/CBO9780511665707.023

Livingstone, S., & Bulger, M. E. (2014). A global research agenda for children's rights in the digital age. *Journal of Children and Media*, *8*(4), 317–335. doi:10.1080/17482798.2014.961496

Luntz, B. K., & Widom, C. S. (1994). Antisocial personality disorder in abused and neglected children grown up. *The American Journal of Psychiatry*, *151*(5), 670–674. doi:10.1176/ajp.151.5.670 PMID:8166307

Madjd-Sadjadi, Z. (2013). *The Economies of Crime*. New York: Business Expert Press, LLC.

McCloskey, L. A. (2011). The impact of intimate partner's violence on adolescents. In S. Graham-Bermann & A. A. Levendosky (Eds.), *How Intimate Partners Violence Affects Children: Developmental Research, Case Studies, and Evidence-Based Intervention* (pp. 225–246). Washington, DC: American Psychological Association. doi:10.1037/12322-011

McCord, J. (1996). Family and Crucible for Violence. Comment on Gorman-Smith, et al, 1996. *Journal of Family Psychology*, *10*(2), 147–152. doi:10.1037/0893-3200.10.2.147

McLanahan, S., Haskins, B., Paxson, C., Rouse, C., & Sawhill, I. (2008). Children and Electronic Media. *The Future of Children*, *18*(1).

Mena, J. G., & Eyer, D. W. (2004). *Infants, Toddlers, and Caregivers: A Curriculum of Respectful, Responsive Care and Innovation*. New York: McGraw-Hill Companies, Inc.

Musan, J. M., Kisovi, L. M., & Otor, S. C. J. (2015). Marital Instability and its Impact on Female-Headed Household Livelihoods in Machakos County, Kenya. *International Journal of Humanities and Social Science*, *5*(8), 145–153.

Nicklas, E., & Mackenzie, M. (2012). Internal partner violence and risk for child neglect during early childhood in a community sample of fragile families. *Journal of Family Violence, 28*(1), 17–29. doi:10.100710896-012-9491-8

Oswell, D. (2013). *The Agency of Children: From Family to Global Human Rights.* Cambridge, UK: Cambridge University Press.

Oti, O. A. (2012). *Parenting Child Sexual Abuse: A Parental Approach.* Faith Printers International.

Papalia, D. E., Gross, D., & Feldman, R. D. (2003). *Child Development: A Tropical Approach.* New York: McGraw-Hill Companies Inc.

Patterson, J. R., Reid, J. B., & Dishion, T. J. (1992). *Antisocial boys.* Eugene, OR: Castalia.

Penal Reform International. (2013). *Protecting children's rights in criminal justice systems A training manual and reference point for professionals and policymakers.* Retrieved from www.penalreform.org

Peterson, A. C., Joseph, K., & Feit, M. (2014). *New Directions in Child Abuse and Neglect Research.* Washington, DC: National Academies Press.

Philips, N. (2017). *Violence, Media Effects, and Criminology. In Oxford Research Encyclopaedia, Criminology and Criminal Justice.* Oxford, UK: Oxford University Press.

Raad, R., & Appelbaum, P. S. (2015). Impact of Behavioral Genetic Evidence on the Perceptions and Dispositions of Child Abuse Victims. *Public Health Genomics, 18*(1), 11–18. doi:10.1159/000364994 PMID:25060544

Reavis, J. A., Looman, J., Franco, K. A., & Rojas, B. (2013). Adverse childhood experiences and adult criminality: How long must we live before we possess our own lives. *The Permanente Journal, 17*(2), 44–48. doi:10.7812/TPP/12-072 PMID:23704843

Resenzweig, J. F. (2017). Understanding *Child Maltreatment.* Administration of Children, Youth and Families Children Bureau: US. Department of Health and Human Services.

Ritzer, R., & Goodman, D. J. (2004). *Modern Sociological Theory* (6th ed.). New York: McGraw-Hill Companies Inc.

Ruther, M. (1990). Psychosocial Resilience and protective mechanisms. In J. Rolf, A. S. Masten, & D. Cicchetti (Eds.), *Risk and Protective Factors in the Development of Psychopathology*. New York: Cambridge University Press. doi:10.1017/CBO9780511752872.013

Ruther, M., & Quinton, D. (1987). Parental mental illness as a risk factor for psychiatric disorder in childhood. In D. Magnusson & A. Ohman (Eds.), *Psychopathology: An Interaction Perspective*. Orlando, FL: Academic Press.

Ruther, M., & Ruther, M. (1993). *Developing Minds: Challenge and Continuity Across the Lifespan*. New York: Basic Books.

Savage, J. (2008). The role of exposure to media violence in the etiology of violent behavior: A criminologist weighs in. *The American Behavioral Scientist*, *51*(8), 1123–1136. doi:10.1177/0002764207312016

Sbarra, D. A. (2015). Divorce and Health: Current Trends and Future Directions. *Psychosomatic Medicine*, *77*(3), 227–236. doi:10.1097/PSY.0000000000000168 PMID:25829240

Schaffer, H. R. (1996). *Social Development*. Malden, MA: Blackwell Publishing.

Schrader-McMillan, A., & Barlow, J. (2017). *Improving the effectiveness of the child protection system: A review of literature*. Oxford, UK: Department of Social Policy and Intervention, University of Oxford.

Seay, K. D., & Kohl, P. L. (2013). Care giver substance abuse and children's exposure to violence in a nationally representative child welfare sample. *Journal of Social Work Practice in the Addictions*, *13*(1), 70–90. doi:10.1080/1533256X.2013.756335 PMID:23440502

Slee, P. T., Campbell, M., & Spears, B. (2012). *Child, Adolescent and Family Development*. Cambridge, UK: Cambridge University Press. doi:10.1017/CBO9781139196567

Slee, P. T., Cross, D., Campbell, M., Spears, B., & Dooley, J. (2010). *From research to policy and practices: Innovation and sustainability in cyberbullying prevention*. European Cooperation in Science & Technology and Department of Innovation, Industry, Science and Research Training School, Melbourne, Australia.

Stanley, J. R. (2014). Child Abuse and the Internet. *Issues (Chicago, Ill.)*, 1–20. Retrieved from https://www.researchgate.net/publication/242085433

Tartari, E. (2015). Benefits and Risks of Children and Adolescence Using Social Media. *European Scientific Journal*, *11*(, 13), 321–332.

Turner, J. H. (2013). *Theoretical Sociology: 1830 to the Present*. Thousand Oaks, CA: SAGE Publications, Inc.

UNICEF. (2000). *Children's Rights and the Media: A Resource for Journalists*. UNICEF.

UNICEF. (2005). *The Media and Children's Rights*. UNICEF.

UNICEF. (2014). *Hidden in Plain Sight: A Statistical Analysis of Violence Against Children*. UNICEF.

UNICEF. (2016). National Population Commission of Nigeria, UNICEF Nigeria and the U.S. Centers for Disease Control and Prevention, Violence Against Children in Nigeria: Findings from a National Survey 2014. Abuja, Nigeria: UNICEF.

UNICEF. (2017). *Situation Analysis of Children in Trinidad and Tobago*. UNICEF Office for Barbados and the Eastern Caribbean.

Warburton, W. (2014). Apples, oranges, and the burden of proof—Putting media violence findings into context. *European Psychologist*, *19*(1), 60–67. doi:10.1027/1016-9040/a000166

Weder, N., Yang, B. Z., Douglas-Palumberi, H., Massey, J., Krystal, J. H., Gelernter, J., & Kaufman, J. (2009). MAOA genotype, maltreatment, and aggressive behaviour: The changing impact of genotype at varying levels of trauma. *Biological Psychiatry*, *65*(5), 417–424. doi:10.1016/j.biopsych.2008.09.013 PMID:18996506

Widom, C. S., & White, H. R. (1997). Problem behaviour in abused and neglected children: Grown up, prevalence and co-occurrence of substance abuse, crime and violence. *Criminal Behaviour and Mental Health*, *7*(4), 287–300. doi:10.1002/cbm.191

Chapter 12
Child Swaddling or Back Wrapping During Street Trading:
Where Are the Media to Protect Child Rights?

Emmanuel O. Amoo
Demography and Social Statistics, Covenant University, Nigeria

Mofoluwake P. Ajayi
Sociology Department, Covenant University, Nigeria

Faith O. Olarewaju
https://orcid.org/0000-0002-5242-0889
Political Science and International Relations, Covenant University, Nigeria

Tomike Olawande
Sociology Department, Covenant University, Nigeria

Adebanke Olawole-Isaac
Demography and Social Statistics, Covenant University, Nigeria

ABSTRACT

The study is premised on social responsibility and social epidemiological theories and examined the exposure of back-wrapped babies to health risk during street trading. Data were collected using structured face-to-face interviews and snowballing techniques among 228 Street trading women (with children aged ≤ 11 months), in one local government area of Ogun State, Nigeria. Data analyses involved univariate and multivariate methods. The results show that 58.3% of women interviewed

DOI: 10.4018/978-1-7998-0329-4.ch012

wrapped their babies at their back while trading on the streets, ≥80% were not aware of any campaign against baby back-wrapping, 35% viewed baby back-wrapping as medicinal for the baby, and as traditional practice (59.2%). The multivariate analysis revealed that children wrapped while trading on the street are at higher risk of exposure to illness than those not back wrapped (OR=1.778, p=0.042). The authors suggested media campaign against back-wrapping baby while trading on the street to reduce exposure to diseases, mortalities and possibly achievement of sustainable development goal (SDG-3).

INTRODUCTION

The unemployment in developing countries without enabling infrastructural and institutional support releases more people into abject poverty with solace in petty trading with no official location but peddling on the streets (Amoo et al., 2018; Amoo, Ola-David, Olurinola, & Fadayomi, 2012, 2016; Bénit-Gbaffou, 2018; Mizen, 2018). However, with the rising level of street trading, the burden is titled towards women who are by traditional African setting characterized with low economic status (Amoo et al., 2018, 2012, 2016). Considering the nature of Nigerian population structure, the bulk of these women are young and mostly in their reproductive age and may probably be pregnant or nursing babies (Amoo et al., 2012, 2016). Apart from the fact that the nature of this job could pose a threat to the health of women, especially as mothers or potential mothers, the inherent consequences of wrapping baby at the back while trading on the road could be antithetical to the pursuit of Sustainable Development Goals, especially Goal 3.2, 3.6 and 3.9 (Amoo, 2018; Inter-Agency and Expert Group on SDG Indicators (IAEG-SDGs), 2016).

Specific few studies have identified certain childhood diseases such as asthma, atopy, bronchitis and chronic cough to be associated with air pollution (Bowatte et al., 2015; Landrigan, 2017; Mustapha, Blangiardo, Briggs, & Hansell, 2011; Peters et al., 2001; Schwartz, 2004). Amazingly, most of the media efforts on child safety, survival and rights often center on effect of children' exposure to media, and eventual psychosocial development, attitudes and behaviours (Buckley & Anderson, 2006; Mares & Kretz, 2015; Nieman, 2003), theories on child development also have omitted the issue of swaddling or back-wrapping (Buckley & Anderson, 2006). Many media campaigns only touched on sleeping hours and discouragement against bedsharing which in mothers' perspective aids child-mother bonding opportunity (Caraballo et al., 2016; Ndu, 2016). The popular back-to-sleep message that focused on safe sleep environment for children only centered on back or side sleeping position of infant and remained silent on back-wrapping (Caraballo et al., 2016; Ottolini et al., 1999). In Nigeria, the awareness of the medically recommended sleep position or the back-to-sleep message for infant has also been proven to be very low (Ndu, 2016; Okpere & Opara, 2014). The media silence or lack of popular campaign on child back-wrapping could be antithetical to the achievement of the current sustainable development goals related to child survival. Thus, the study examined the prevalence of street baby back-wrapping and swaddling, children risk to infections and role of new and mass media in mitigating street and baby back-wrapping and swaddling.

Specifically, two prominent goals of the Sustainable Development agenda are the reduction of the number of deaths, illnesses from air pollution (SDG-3.9) and child mortality, morbidity and maternal deaths (Inter-Agency and Expert Group on SDG Indicators (IAEG-SDGs), 2016). This also include reduction of injury that could accrue through accident on the road. These goals were planned to reduce the risks of vulnerability to morbidities, air pollution, injury through road accidents, and through non-communicable infections and eventual maternal and child mortalities (Abah & Ohimain, 2011; Agaba, Thacher, Angyo, & Agaba, 2003; Inter-Agency and Expert Group on SDG Indicators (IAEG-SDGs), 2016). However, the risk of health challenges and deaths that could ensue due to involvement of mothers on street activities as well as exposure to air pollution has not been conspicuously treated in literature, particularly in Nigeria and sub-Saharan Africa (SSA) in general (Abah & Ohimain, 2011; Agaba et al., 2003; Feigin et al., 2017; Landrigan, 2017). Worldwide, air-pollution-induced deaths range from cardiovascular deaths (19%), ischaemic heart disease (24%), stroke (21%) to lung cancer deaths (23%), and projected to reach 6-9 million annual deaths by 2060 (Landrigan, 2017). Higher proportions of these deaths would likely occur in developing countries (Feigin et al., 2017; Landrigan, 2017; Mustapha et al., 2011), especially in SSA, where infants and mothers are exposed to air pollution in the course of finding daily means of livelihood as mothers and fenders for the families.

BACKGROUND

Since the United Nation Convention on the Rights of the Child defines a child as any person under the age of 18 (Cohen & Naimark, 1991; UNICEF, 1989), a child could therefore be conjectured as a young human being below the age of puberty or below the legal age (≤ 17 year), and attracting different synonyms such as youngster, young girl, young boy, infant, toddler, school-boy, school-girl, adolescent, and teenager (Amoo et al., 2018; Wusu & Amoo, 2014). This category of population in most developing countries constitutes relatively half of the population considering the mean age that tends towards 17.0 years in countries like Nigeria, Ethiopia (<20), Congo (17.0), Uganda (16.0), Chad and Somalia (17.0 years) and Niger (15 years) (United Nations, Department of Economic and Social Affairs, Population Division,

2017). This invariably imply that almost half of sub-Saharan population are children (Amoo et al., 2018; United Nations, Department of Economic and Social Affairs, Population Division, 2017; Wusu & Amoo, 2014, 2016).

Global concern has been on the security and the protection of right of children. While there have been works on how to stop children from systematic abuse of their rights, and information on children living in hunger, homelessness and illiteracy, and suffer sexual, physical violence, forced labour, there are no data on the extent of their exposure to risk of disease (Angle, Baerthlein, Daftari, Rambaud, & Roshani, 2014a). One of the fundamental responsibility of parents is to keep children safe from harm and, the media campaigns and broadcast should be relatively solace in terms of child abuse. Specifically, while media campaigns or interventions have been proven to be effective in the areas of diarrheal disease, child immunization, the use of malarial-treated-net, nutrition, (e.g. breastfeeding practice), under-age work, child trafficking, prevention of mother-to-child HIV transmission, and other diseases, the import of media campaign on child back-wrapping seems obscured or perhaps unpopular in the literature (Angle, Baerthlein, Daftari, Rambaud, & Roshani, 2014b; Naugle & Hornik, 2014; Olufunlayo et al., 2019; Ottolini et al., 1999; Rollins et al., 2016)

There are several initiatives that have attempted to protect the right of children. These include but not limited to: the 1924 Geneva Declaration of the Rights of the Child, United Nations for Children's Fund (UNICEF), UN Convention on the Rights of the Child, Asia Summit on Child Rights and the Media, the UN Committee on the Rights of the Child, the First All African Summit, the Second World Summit on Television for Children, and the West African Regional Summit on Media for Children. Despite all these initiatives and programs, child abuse and its associate consequences are at alarming rate in most developing countries. However, the power of media has been identified to be of immense value in the matters related to the protection of children, especially in curbing child abuse and child undue exposure to adverse situation (Angle et al., 2014a; Mares & Kretz, 2015). However, this would be contingent upon the coverage of the media communication. Media communication would be effective if the supposedly target population have access or are aware of such campaign. Notwithstanding, avoidable illnesses, diseases, accidents and injuries are the leading causes of death among children (Angle et al., 2014a). The exposure of children to illnesses or infections is increasing the number of children at risk.

In all ramifications, the state of the child's health is a serious concern to both mothers, the family and the community as a whole. Although, many factors are attached to the health status of children, there is no gainsaying that it could be compounded if they are to be nursed or cared for not only in the open but along the streets considering the gamut of dirt log from vehicles, opened and unsanitized gutters and other pollutants along the streets. While there are innumerable literature on the health status of children or nursing mothers, there are some levels of reticent on the well-being of children wrapped at the back while the mothers pursue external chores especially selling on the road. This study therefore assessed the health status of children whose mothers pursue daily livelihood on the street.

Street trading is a sub sector of the micro and small businesses and pervades most towns and cities of developing world. Women are most visibly identified as operators and are noted to be exposed to low earnings, exploitation, limited access to finance and lack of social protection (Amoo et al., 2016; Bénit-Gbaffou, 2018; Mitullah, 2004; Muiruri, 2010; Okafor, Amoo, & Onugu, 2010; Olurinola, Fadayomi, Amoo, & Ola-David, 2014). Other studies produced mixed results, categorizing street traders as mostly found in poor geographical locations like blighted slums or settlements and areas often characterized by overcrowding (Amoo et al., 2016; Fagbohun, Oke, & Okesoto, 2010; Mitullah, 2004). They were noted to live generally in unplanned places with numerous social vices and places lacking essential infrastructures and social amenities such as shelter, roads, toilets, water and sewerage, and garbage collection. Today, street trading has taken over most street in the cities and towns and general observations have shown that they largely work in poor environmental conditions (Bromley, 2000; Fagbohun et al., 2010; Lund, 1999; Mitullah, 2004).

A prominent characteristic of informal sector and unemployment generally in developing countries is that the burden is tilted towards women due to vagaries of factors such as their low economic status, high fertility and inadequate or lack of external financial support and children most often bear the brunt (Amoo et al., 2016; Mitullah, 2004; Okafor et al., 2010; Olurinola et al., 2014). The peculiarities of street trading (like other informal businesses) allows free-entry, free-exit, small capital outlay, unstructured 'modus operandi' and accommodates wearing babies at their back while conducting street trading. The health consequences of these conditions could transcend their personal health but make their children more vulnerable.

Despite numerous initiatives across all continents to stop abuse of the rights of children, the level of violations against the rights of children are alarming in sub-Saharan African countries such as Nigeria, Kenya (to name but two) and most other economies such as India and Brazil (Angle et al., 2014a). In Kenya, India and Brazil alone, over 279 million children are faced with complex and serious risk factors in terms of their basic rights and wellbeing (Angle et al., 2014a). Today, Media concerns on protection of children against hunger, homelessness, illiteracy, sexual and physical abuse, and forced labour remain undeniable. However, in addition to these efforts, there is need for media to extend its efforts on protection of the rights of children to societal enlightenment on the adverse effects inherent in baby swaddling and back-wrapping.

The study is anchored on the theory of social responsibility that put media or other social organizations in the vanguard of promoting environment and socio-cultural aspects in relation to the economy of the place (Palmer, Oates, & Portney, 1995; Schiavo, 2013). In this regard, the media is socially obligated to act for the benefit of society at large (Namazova-Baranova et al., 2019; Schiavo, 2013; Oyesomi, Soola, Abioye & Oyero, 2014; Nelson, Kehinde, Oyero, Wiliams & Soola, 2013), which should include holistic children care and survival. The involvement of media campaign in this instance has conspicuously omitted campaign against child-wrapping at the back while trading on the streets (Caraballo et al., 2016; Ndu, 2016). The media is in better position to make known actions or behaviors that could cause harm, not only to the society or the environment, but also individuals (including children) in that society or environment (Namazova-Baranova et al., 2019; Schiavo, 2013). Another theory tangential to this study is the theory of social epidemiology that perceives social structure as a crucial determinant in the state of health (Honjo, 2004). The social epidemiology theory also assumes that the distribution of advantages and disadvantages in a society reflects the distribution of health and disease (Honjo, 2004; Neidell, 2004). Thus, this study considers the societal structure (street trading) and traders' traits (mothers in this case) and the state of the mother and health of their children. While few studies have expressed the advantages of appropriate infant wrapping and/or swaddling especially as good mother-care practice (Keall & Bond, 2011; Young, Gore, Gorman, & Watson, 2013), studies and media campaigns that have raised concerned about wrapping baby at the back while trading along the streets are very rare among the current literatures. Young, Gore, Gorman and Watson (2013) indicated that swaddling or wrapping of baby at the back has been in practices since the time immemorial with the perspective that it is meant to make the babies safe and secure (Young et al., 2013). The ignorant abuse of back-wrapping and swaddling baby at the back has not caught the media attention particularly in Nigeria. This study is concerned with how much risk is the child that is wrapped at the back while the mother is on street trading business. It is also meant to examine the depth of knowledge of street trading mothers on child exposure to air pollution.

DATA AND METHODS

Data were collected through structured face-to-face interviews intermediated with snowballing technique among 228 nursing mothers who trade on the streets with their children between ages 0 and 11 months. These techniques were adopted due to lack of sampling frame for street traders in the study location (Amoo et al., 2012, 2016). One Local Government Area (LGA) was randomly selected for the study among the 20 LGAs in the state (Ogun state) selected for the study. Two out of four

Central Business Districts (CBDs) identified in the location of study were selected. The state was chosen purposively due to proximity and cost. Data gathered were analysed using univariate and multivariate methods and the results were presented in tables. Also, only one model was formulated to ascertain the interconnections between exposure to back-wrapping during trading on the street and risk of the child to diseases/illness risk. The test was done using binary logistic regression with the aid of Stata 14. The mathematically expression of the model is denoted as follows:

$$logit\left\{\pi\left(x\right)\right\} = \beta_0 + \beta_{x1} + \beta_{x2} + \ldots + \beta_{xn} \quad (1)$$

Where, β_0, β_{xS} are the unknown parameters of the model estimated by likelihood techniques in the statistical software used (i.e. Stata 14).

RESULTS

Socio-Demographic Characteristics of Respondents

The target population were only mothers with baby below 12 months. The mean age of the respondents was 27 years. Respondents age classifications shows that majority were in the age group 25-34 years (69.7%), those in age group 15-24, 35-44 and 45 and above were 20.2% 5.7% and 4.4%, respectively. Marital status distribution indicated singes constituting 17.5%, married (73.2%) and others (9.2%). Less than 5% of the respondents have no formal education, those with secondary school and below are 70.1% (primary, 15.4% and secondary, 55.7%), implying that more than half of the mothers interviewed have had secondary education.

The result of the analysis revealed that 58.3% of the mothers identified were trading with their baby wrapped at their back as they trade along the street while the rest are also nursing mothers. Although, this might be relatively synonymous with Africa culture, the associated health risks are individual's or family's burden. The migration indicator shows that a large number of respondents (61.8%) were from Southwest zone of Nigeria, 13.2% were of Southeast origin, 15.8% from the Northern part of the country while only 9.2% indicated they were migrants from other geo-political zone of Nigeria such as Cross River, Edo, Kogi States, to mention but few (Table 1). Among those that have ever married, their partners' occupation distribution revealed that 5.9% were still schooling as at the time of the survey, 27.7% were skilled and unskilled artisans, 0.9% are civil servant while 24.5% and 11.2% were in trading and farming occupation categories.

Most of the street traders identified (relatively 48.2% of the respondents) are food traders/vendors selling food, water, drinks, confectioneries, and so on. Those who trade in clothing materials (e.g. shoes, bags) constitutes 19.3% while 32.5% sell accessories (household, car, phones, recharge cards, and so on). Majority of the street trading nursing mothers identified (88.2%) were roving or peddling traders while only 11.8% were sedentary holding small shops, kiosks, table tops and stalls by the road sides. Questions on the time and duration of trading on the streets were asked in order to have an overview of the extent to which mothers and their children are exposed to stress. The result of the analysis revealed that the daily duration of selling on the road was 2-7 hours and they only operated between morning and evening daily. The proportion that sell for relatively seven hours are 29.4%, 1.8% worked for 1-2 hours per day, 13.6% work for 3-4 hours and 55.3% work for 5-6 hours daily (see Table 1).

The study among others, investigated the reasons why the nursing mothers engaged in street trading considering their supposed role of nursing babies and the age of their children. More than one-third of the respondents (39.5%) claimed they resorted to trading on the street because they had no alternative means of livelihood, 18.4% engaged in the trade as a result of the spouse, partner, and parent decision. Only 16.2% prefer the trade as move to be self-employed. In addition, 26.4% of the total respondents engaged in the trade in order to get funding for other business or to fund their educational ambition. The distribution for this latter category is 11.8% (looking for money for other business) and 14.5% (school fees) as shown in Table 1. However, majority of the traders identified (65.4%) were own account workers, 25.4% were employees, 9.2% were unpaid family workers or volunteers. Other information gathered shows that 30.3% of the traders indicated that they had at certain time sustained injury or involved in accident in the course of trading on the street.

Health Status of Children

Among the crucial pursuits of this study was the assessment of the health status of children of street trading mothers and the mothers' awareness of the likely implications of exposure of infants to risky environment. Up to 35% of the respondent indicated that baby-wrapping is medicinal, 59.2% believed do so as a tradition and, only 5.7% believed it helps to secure the baby. The study also made enquiry about the precautionary measures the traders put in place to protect children from infections. The study revealed the proportion of respondents whose children' health conditions impact negatively on their work, not only in terms of cost, but due to the numbers of days they had to spend in hospital/clinic or stay at home attending to ill-health conditions of their children. The investigation also shows that 57.5% of the respondents indicated that their children often sick Out of this proportion,

40.4% confirmed they often lose up to two working days in a month as a result of their children ill-health, 28.1 percent sometimes unable to trade for 3-4 days/week while 26.3 percent have forfeited up to one-week work in the last 3 months to attend to the children ill-health condition.

The second category of respondents (42.5%) claimed that they rarely visit hospital/clinic or stay off the street because their children rarely or don't usually fall sick. The most common illness that affect the children of street traders is malaria as indicated by 46.1% of the respondents. The second common illness among the children of these women is diarrhea (43.0%) while high fever (known as *àisan ibà*) is identified to be frequent among 7.0% of the children. The proportion of women who indicated that typhoid (called locally as *ibà-ìponjú*) often affect their children is 2.6 percent, and those that their children have experienced gastro-intestinal diseases (locally called *àrùn inú*) is 1.3 percent. Relatively all the women (97.8%) indicated they could recognise the symptoms of children without medical personnel assistance. Asking the mothers, the first thing they would do if the child shows any sign of sickness, relatively half (50.4%) would administer the baby's drugs that they always kept within reach, 11.4 percent would pray or watch briefly before taking any major step. One-third (30.3%) would visit the chemist, and 7.9% would rather go to hospital. In the analysis of access of women street traders to health facilities for their children, majority indicated that there are health facilities within the selling central business district but expensive. However, 74.1 percent reported that the health facilities are not far but unaffordable, 19.7% claimed that health facilities are very far and also expensive. Visitation to health facility was rated on a scale of very often, often, not often and not all. Very few women (0.4 percent) visit hospital very often to treat children health condition, 86.8% often visit clinic, while 4.4 percent never visited the hospital because of their children.

The study shows that the manner in which children' foods are preserved was susceptible to infections. While 35.1 percent keep their children food in flask or cooler, more than half (59.2 percent) use cloth/nylon to wrap or cover the food while away (at a distance) selling to passerby or commuters. Tabulated responses from the traders show that 62.7 percent of them breastfeed their babies against 37.3 percent who do not practice breastfeeding.

Binary Logistic Regression Illustrating the Interrelationships Between Operation of Street Trading and Children Vulnerability to Illness

The binary logistic regression employed estimated the interrelationships between selected demographic characteristics of the respondents, street trading operation and the odds of children's exposure to sickness. The dependent variable is exposure to sickness. This was measured as a binary code (ever sick = 1 or never sick = 0). The result indicated that the longer the hours a nursing mother trades on the street, the more vulnerable the child is to illness. The specific statistics show that children of women that spend 3-4 hours, 5-6 hours and ≥ 7 hours daily are 1.057, 4.973 and 5.795 times more likely to be vulnerable to illness compared to those who trade briskly for ≤ 2 hours per day. The Beta coefficients reflect positive correlations at p-value (0.044 and 0.003, respectively). Although, the children of those that spent 3-4 hours are also more likely to be vulnerable to illness, the relationship is not statistically significant (r = 0.056, p-value > 0.05). The analysis revealed that there is a significant relationship between wrapping of baby at the back and the child's vulnerability to illness. The statistics shows that babies in this category are 1.778 times more likely to be vulnerable to illness compared to other babies not wrapped at the back while trading on the street.

The result revealed that children of women who are not peddling or roving around while selling wares on the street, i.e. sedentary) are less likely to be vulnerable to illness compared to children of mothers who are sedentary traders (odd ratio = 0.122, P-value = 0.031). The analysis indicated that higher the age of mother the more likely the child is to be exposed to illness. The specific statistics revealed that children of traders who are in age groups 25-34 and 35-44 years are respectively 1.466 and 1.064 times more likely to be exposed to sickness compared to the reference category (15-24 year). However, this is not statistically significant with the P-value > 0.05. There is a negative association between secondary education and children exposure to illness (Beta = -1.979) while children of women who had no formal or only primary education are more likely to be vulnerable to illness (odd ratio = 3.157 and 2.734 respectively) as shown in Table 3.

The study also evaluated the connection between the items of trade among the nursing mothers and exposure of their children to illness. The result revealed that children of mothers that sell edibles (such as food, water, drinks, confectioneries, and so on) are less likely to be vulnerable to illness (r =-0.81, odd ration = 0.445, p-value = 0.002). however, children of those that sell accessories (household, car and phone accessories) are more likely to be vulnerable to illness compared to the reference category (women that sell clothing and related wares). The statistics show that r = 0.022, odd ratio = 1.022, p-value >0.05). Overall, the model is statistically adjudged to be correct up to 93 percent as shown by the overall percentage of 92.7 percent. However, the model is averagely strong considering the Cox and Snell R-Square and Nagelkerke R-Square of 0.41 and 0.17 respectively (Table 3).

DISCUSSION

The study is located within the tripod or pillars of sustainable development agenda (economic, environmental and social) and could be crucial in achieving reduction in infant morbidity and mortality that pervade most developing countries. The study specifically investigated unnoticeable aspect of street trading activity, the trade that has become a formidable feature of urban environment in Nigeria, which is also common across other developing countries. While the trade itself is a significant trait of informal sector that portends positive development especially through the micro business sector, as it relates to job creation, creativity and its low capital base, the study revealed that the involvement of nursing mothers that trade with baby wrapped at their back should be considered a serious public concern considering the health risks involved for the children and mothers inclusive.

The research represents an extension of various studies that have confirmed the health benefits of baby wrapping at the back (Keall & Bond, 2011; Young et al., 2013). While this study is not disputing claims on the health benefits of wrapping practice, it specifically emphasised that the conditions under which the babies are wrapped at the back, especially the environment, are critical for maximization of such health benefits. Besides, improvement in infant and mother's health cannot be effectively analysed without considering inherent danger in roving and sedentary trading which exposes baby wrapped at back to outdoor pollution, and other combustion sources (Popoola, 2019; Prüss-Üstün & Corvalán, 2006; Prüss-Üstün & Neira, 2016). The study highlighted that roving with children wrapped at back is not absolutely benign in nature considering the level of air pollution that characterised most developing countries. This finding is in consonance with other studies that have raised similar concern and established the interconnection between infant exposure to outdoor pollution and acute illnesses, asthma, atopy, bronchitis and chronic cough (Abah & Ohimain, 2011; Bowatte et al., 2015; Landrigan, 2017; Mustapha et al., 2011; Peters et al., 2001; Schwartz, 2004).

The use of the theory of social responsibility relatively revealed omissions in media obligations towards promoting holistic child rights and healthcare. The study emphasised that media campaigns till date have not popularly included issues on back-wrapping of babies while trading on the streets (Namazova-Baranova et al., 2019; Palmer et al., 1995; Schiavo, 2013). Also, the use of social epidemiology theory perceives social structure as fundamental determinant of state of health of citizenry (Honjo, 2004; Neidell, 2004) and in this regard, mother and child's health. Generally, from the literature review, peddling on the streets or solace in petty trading are products of lack of enabling infrastructural and institutional support to address unemployment, and poverty particularly among women (Amoo et al., 2018, 2012, 2016; Mizen, 2018). Notwithstanding, the findings from this study could be relevant to curtailing children exposure to infant mortality and morbidities that have been serious obstacle to realisation of Sustainable Development Goals especially Goal 3.2, 3.6 and 3.9 (Amoo, 2018; Inter-Agency and Expert Group on SDG Indicators (IAEG-SDGs), 2016). These goals were planned to reduce the risks of vulnerability to morbidities, and eventual maternal and child mortalities (Inter-Agency and Expert Group on SDG Indicators (IAEG-SDGs), 2016).

The prevalence of this practice (prevalence of street baby back-wrapping and swaddling) as well as the near complete absence of media campaign or information on this practice is a great omission (Angle et al., 2014a; Mares & Kretz, 2015; Naugle & Hornik, 2014)and could require stakeholders' attention if the objective of SDGs (Goal 3.2, 3.6, 3.9) are to be achieved. Lack of popular media campaign to mitigating street back-wrapping and swaddling of baby could engender abuse of the practice of back-wrapping, and at the detriment of the baby health and wellbeing.

The significant relationship observed between the hours spent on the street with baby wrapped at back and child exposure to risk of illness could be integrated into the sustainable development initiative to achieve reduction in child morbidity and mortality in the location of study, Nigeria as a whole, and by extension other sub-Saharan Africa countries. While several studies have addressed infant mortality and morbidities (Popoola, 2019; Samuel & Amoo, 2014), the import of mothers engagement in odd jobs (street trading in this case), due to poverty, as well as, the inherent challenge for the accompanied babies could be regarded as important contribution of this study to the body of knowledge on this subject. The study signals that wrapping baby at the back for longer hours (>2 hours) while working under harsh weather condition could be inimical to child's health. The possible exposure to traffic-related pollution, noise pollution, heat or cold are dangerous factors when it comes to health and wellbeing issues.

Among other important findings is the educational profile of the women trading on the street. Specifically, that the majority of the street traders who are nursing mothers have some levels of basic education could be optimized for job provision. This is fundamental to women empowerment and, increased knowledge on child healthcare with possible improvement in child's health rather than morbidity and mortality. Education is critical in all issues relating to childcare and health. Mothers with higher education could be better informed on health matters and all other being equal, an educated women above primary school should be able to provide better level of cares to her children compared to the illiterates or those with lower level of education (United States Agency for International Development (USAID), 2012).

FUTURE RESEARCH DIRECTION

Among the major limitations of the study is lack of data for nursing mother who are trading on the street. There is no sampling frame for the street trader generally. Continuous research on the study could boost the level of data that could assist in mitigating the negative consequences of baby-wrapping while trading on the street. The role of new media especially the new digital media technologies could as well be properly investigated.

CONCLUSION AND RECOMMENDATIONS

The study highlighted that children wrapped at back is not absolutely benign in nature but the environment under which is being practiced is crucial for maximization of such benefits. The study highlighted that peddlers' children are more likely to be exposed to illnesses compared to the children of sedentary traders, and that consistent hustling/trading among the women of reproductive age could be hazardous to both baby and mothers' health. Where alternative jobs are difficult to get, the duration of roving on the street could be contained for possible less exposure to outdoor pollution. The authors suggest children care policy towards curtailment of children exposure to outdoor pollution, stress, and wrapping on the street for plausible reduction in infant mortality and morbidity to enhance the achievement of Sustainable Development Goals, especially Goal 3.2, 3.6 and 3.9. In addition, provision of mobile primary healthcare in Central Business Districts across the study location (and semi-urban or urban areas) could be vital for ease of access or to cater for the health needs of the street traders and their children. Also, sick-bays could also be provided within the CBDs to provide 'first aid' treatment to emergency health issues. It is also important that while media campaign about the danger inherent in street baby-back-wrapping and swindling could be necessary to create awareness among nursing mothers.

CONFLICT OF INTEREST

The authors declare that there is no conflict of interest regarding the paper.

ETHICS APPROVAL AND CONSENT TO PARTICIPATE

All research instruments were subjected to review by the ethical committees of Covenant University. Necessary permissions were secured from the proprietorship of the health facilities used for the main study and respondents were assured of confidentiality of their responses and anonymous reporting of the research findings. Notwithstanding that informed consent was obtained from every participant, prospective participants were encouraged to participate but were informed of their freedom to withdraw at any stage of the discussion.

FUNDING

This research received no specific grant from any funding agency in the public, commercial, or not-for-profit sectors.

ACKNOWLEDGMENT

The authors appreciate the Covenant University Centre for Research, Innovation and Development (CUCRID) for the funding of the survey and the publication of this article. We also recognise the responses from our anonymous respondents as their contributions to humanity.

REFERENCES

Abah, S. O., & Ohimain, E. I. (2011). Healthcare waste management in Nigeria: A case study. *Journal of Public Health and Epidemiology*, *3*(3), 99–110.

Agaba, P. A., Thacher, T. D., Angyo, I. A., & Agaba, E. I. (2003). Peak expiratory flow rates in healthy Nigerian children. *Journal of Tropical Pediatrics*, *49*(3), 157–159. doi:10.1093/tropej/49.3.157 PMID:12848205

Amoo, E. O., Igbinoba, A., Imhonopi, D., Banjo, O. O., Ajaero, C. K., Akinyemi, J. O., … Solanke, L. B. (2018). Trends, Determinants and Health Risks of Adolescent Fatherhood in Sub-Saharan Africa. *Ethiopian Journal of Health Sciences, 28*(4). Retrieved from https://www.ajol.info/index.php/ejhs/article/view/175550

Amoo, E. O., Ola-David, O., Olurinola, I. O., & Fadayomi, T. (2012). Street trading activities and maternal health in urban areas of Nigeria. *Global Journal of Human Social Sciences, 12*, 46–55.

Amoo, E. O., Ola-David, O., Olurinola, I. O., & Fadayomi, T. O. (2016). Female Youth in Street Trading: Implications for Sexual Harassment in HIV/AIDS Risky Environment. *Journal of South African Business Research, 2016*, 1–12. doi:10.5171/2016.975495

Amoo. (2018). Introduction to Special Edition on Covenant University's Perspectives on Nigeria Demography and Achievement of SDGs-2030. *African Population Studies, 32*(1). doi:10.11564/32-1-1170

Angle, S., Baerthlein, T., Daftari, N., Rambaud, B., & Roshani, N. (2014a). Protecting the Rights of Children: The Role of the Media–Lessons from Brazil, India and Kenya (Internews Europe). *Interviews Europe*. Retrieved from https://www.internews.org/sites/default/files/resources/InternewsEurope_ChildRightsMedia_Report_2014.pdf

Angle, S., Baerthlein, T., Daftari, N., Rambaud, B., & Roshani, N. (2014b). *Protecting the Rights of Children: The Role of the Media–Lessons from Brazil, India and Kenya*. Internews Europe.

Bénit-Gbaffou, C. (2018). Beyond the Policy-Implementation Gap: How the City of Johannesburg Manufactured the Ungovernability of Street Trading. *The Journal of Development Studies, 54*(12), 2149–2167. doi:10.1080/00220388.2018.1460468

Bowatte, G., Lodge, C., Lowe, A. J., Erbas, B., Perret, J., Abramson, M. J., ... Dharmage, S. C. (2015). The influence of childhood traffic-related air pollution exposure on asthma, allergy and sensitization: A systematic review and a meta-analysis of birth cohort studies. *Allergy, 70*(3), 245–256. doi:10.1111/all.12561 PMID:25495759

Bromley, R. (2000). Street vending and public policy: A global review. *The International Journal of Sociology and Social Policy, 20*(1/2), 1–28. doi:10.1108/01443330010789052

Buckley, K. E., & Anderson, C. A. (2006). A theoretical model of the effects and consequences of playing video games. *Playing Video Games: Motives, Responses, and Consequences*, 363–378.

Caraballo, M., Shimasaki, S., Johnston, K., Tung, G., Albright, K., & Halbower, A. C. (2016). Knowledge, Attitudes, and risk for sudden unexpected infant death in children of adolescent mothers: A qualitative study. *The Journal of Pediatrics, 174*, 78–83. doi:10.1016/j.jpeds.2016.03.031 PMID:27113377

Cohen, C. P., & Naimark, H. (1991). United Nations Convention on the Rights of the Child: Individual rights concepts and their significance for social scientists. *The American Psychologist, 46*(1), 60–65. doi:10.1037/0003-066X.46.1.60

Fagbohun, P., Oke, G., & Okesoto, J. (2010). Socio-Economic Characeristics of Street Trading in Sango-Otto, Ogun State: The implications on Urban Environment. *Editorial Board, 139*, 157.

Feigin, V. L., Abajobir, A. A., Abate, K. H., Abd-Allah, F., Abdulle, A. M., Abera, S. F., ... Aichour, I. (2017). Global, regional, and national burden of neurological disorders during 1990–2015: A systematic analysis for the Global Burden of Disease Study 2015. *Lancet Neurology, 16*(11), 877–897. doi:10.1016/S1474-4422(17)30299-5 PMID:28931491

Honjo, K. (2004). Social epidemiology: Definition, history, and research examples. *Environmental Health and Preventive Medicine, 9*(5), 193–199. doi:10.1007/BF02898100 PMID:21432303

Inter-Agency and Expert Group on SDG Indicators (IAEG-SDGs). (2016). *Final List of Proposed Sustainable Development Goal indicators. Report of the Inter-Agency and Expert Group on Sustainable Development Goal Indicators (E/CN.3/2016/2/Rev.1), Annex IV.* Retrieved from https://sustainabledevelopment.un.org/content/documents/11803Official-List-of-Proposed-SDG-Indicators.pdf

KeallJ. K.BondJ. A. (2011). *Baby wrap.* Retrieved from http://www.freepatentsonline.com/D644413.html

Landrigan, P. J. (2017). Air pollution and health. *The Lancet Public Health, 2*(1), e4–e5. doi:10.1016/S2468-2667(16)30023-8 PMID:29249479

Lund, B. (1999). 'Ask not what your community can do for you': Obligations, New Labour and welfare reform. *Critical Social Policy, 19*(4), 447–462. doi:10.1177/026101839901900402

Mares, M.-L., & Kretz, V. (2015). *Media effects on children* (2nd ed.). International Encyclopedia of the Social & Behavioral Sciences. doi:10.1016/B978-0-08-097086-8.95006-2

Mitullah, W. (2004). *A review of street trade in Africa.* Unpublished Manuscript. Cambridge, MA: WIEGO.

Mizen, P. (2018). Bringing the street back in: Considering strategy, contingency and relative good fortune in street children's access to paid work in Accra. *The Sociological Review, 66*(5), 1058–1073. doi:10.1177/0038026118771279

Muiruri, P. (2010). *Women street vendors in Nairobi, Kenya: A situational and policy analysis within a human rights framework*. African Books Collective.

Mustapha, B. A., Blangiardo, M., Briggs, D. J., & Hansell, A. L. (2011). Traffic air pollution and other risk factors for respiratory illness in schoolchildren in the niger-delta region of Nigeria. *Environmental Health Perspectives, 119*(10), 1478–1482. doi:10.1289/ehp.1003099 PMID:21719372

Namazova-Baranova, L., Carrasco-Sanz, A., Vural, M., Huss, G., Mestrovic, J., Barak, S., ... Pettoello-Mantovani, M. (2019). European Pediatricians: Speaking with One Voice to Advocate for Children and Their Health. *The Journal of Pediatrics, 211*, 227–228. doi:10.1016/j.jpeds.2019.05.071 PMID:31349917

Naugle, D. A., & Hornik, R. C. (2014). Systematic review of the effectiveness of mass media interventions for child survival in low-and middle-income countries. *Journal of Health Communication, 19*(sup1), 190–215. doi:10.1080/10810730.2014.918217

Ndu, I. K. (2016). Sudden infant death syndrome: An unrecognized killer in developing countries. *Pediatric Health. Medicine and Therapeutics, 7*, 1. PMID:29388586

Neidell, M. J. (2004). Air pollution, health, and socio-economic status: The effect of outdoor air quality on childhood asthma. *Journal of Health Economics, 23*(6), 1209–1236. doi:10.1016/j.jhealeco.2004.05.002 PMID:15556243

Nelson, O., Kehinde, O., Oyero, O., Wiliams, O. R., & Soola, E. O. (2013). Effective use of information sources for breast cancer care: Interplay of mass media and interpersonal channels. *Creating Global Competitive Economies: 2020 Vision Planning and Implementation - Proceedings of the 22nd International Business Information Management Association Conference, IBIMA 2013, 3*, 2231-2243.

Nieman, P. (2003). Canadian Paediatric Society Statement: Impact of media use on children and youth. *Paediatrics & Child Health, 8*(5), 301–306. doi:10.1093/pch/8.5.301 PMID:20020034

Okafor, C., Amoo, E. O., & Onugu, C. U. (2010). *Microfinance and-Gender Development Policy: Implications for Millennium Development Goals (MDGs)*. Academic Press.

Okpere, A., & Opara, P. (2014). Mothers' knowledge and practice of infant sleep position. *Nigerian Journal of Paediatrics, 41*(4), 312–315. doi:10.4314/njp.v41i4.4

Olufunlayo, T. F., Roberts, A. A., MacArthur, C., Thomas, N., Odeyemi, K. A., Price, M., & Jolly, K. (2019). Improving exclusive breastfeeding in low and middle-income countries: A systematic review. *Maternal and Child Nutrition*, *15*(3), e12788. doi:10.1111/mcn.12788 PMID:30665273

Olurinola, I. O., Fadayomi, T., Amoo, E. O., & Ola-David, O. (2014). Occupational Health and Safety among Street Traders in, Nigeria. *International Journal of Econornics and Finance*, *6*(4).

Ottolini, M. C., Davis, B. E., Patel, K., Sachs, H. C., Gershon, N. B., & Moon, R. Y. (1999). Prone infant sleeping despite the Back to Sleep campaign. *Archives of Pediatrics & Adolescent Medicine*, *153*(5), 512–517. doi:10.1001/archpedi.153.5.512 PMID:10323633

Oyesomi, K. O., Soola, E., Abioye, T., & Oyero, O. (2014). Perception of women on the role of indigenous communication in politics: A study of Ado-Odo Ota, Ogun State, Nigeria. *Vision 2020: Sustainable Growth, Economic Development, and Global Competitiveness - Proceedings of the 23rd International Business Information Management Association Conference, IBIMA 2014*, *1*, 2622-2644.

Palmer, K., Oates, W. E., & Portney, P. R. (1995). Tightening environmental standards: The benefit-cost or the no-cost paradigm? *The Journal of Economic Perspectives*, *9*(4), 119–132. doi:10.1257/jep.9.4.119

Peters, A., Fröhlich, M., Döring, A., Immervoll, T., Wichmann, H.-E., Hutchinson, W., ... Koenig, W. (2001). Particulate air pollution is associated with an acute phase response in men. Results from the Monica–Augsburg Study. *European Heart Journal*, *22*(14), 1198–1204. doi:10.1053/euhj.2000.2483 PMID:11440492

Popoola, O. T. (2019). An Empirical Analysis of Infant Mortality: Evidence from sub-Saharan Africa Countries. *Journal of Economics and Management Sciences*, *2*(1), 27–32. doi:10.30560/jems.v2n1p27

Prüss-Üstün, A., & Corvalán, C. (2006). *Preventing disease through healthy environments. Towards an Estimate of the Environmental Burden of Disease*. Geneva: World Health Organization.

Prüss-Üstün, A., & Neira, M. (2016). *Preventing disease through healthy environments: a global assessment of the burden of disease from environmental risks*. World Health Organization.

Rollins, N. C., Bhandari, N., Hajeebhoy, N., Horton, S., Lutter, C. K., Martines, J. C., ... Victora, C. G. (2016). Why invest, and what it will take to improve breastfeeding practices? *Lancet, 387*(10017), 491–504. doi:10.1016/S0140-6736(15)01044-2 PMID:26869576

Samuel, G. W., & Amoo, E. O. (2014). A statistical Analysis of child mortality: Evidence from Nigeria. *Journal of Demography and Social Statistics, 1*(1), 110–120.

Schiavo, R. (2013). *Health communication: From theory to practice* (Vol. 217). John Wiley & Sons.

Schwartz, J. (2004). Air pollution and children's health. *Pediatrics, 113*(Supplement 3), 1037–1043. Retrieved from https://pediatrics.aappublications.org/content/113/Supplement_3/1037 PMID:15060197

UNICEF. (1989). Convention on the Rights of the Child. *Cornell University ILR School DigitalCommons@ILR*, 17. Retrieved from http://digitalcommons.ilr.cornell.edu/child

United Nations, Department of Economic and Social Affairs, Population Division. (2017). *World Population Prospects: The 2017 Revision.* Retrieved from https://www.un.org/development/desa/publications/world-population-prospects-the-2017-revision.html

Wusu, O., & Amoo, E. O. (2014). 11 Sub-Saharan African Children and Adolescents. *Continuity and Change in Sub-Saharan African Demography*, 192.

Wusu, O., & Amoo, E. O. (2016). Fertility Behaviour and Wealth Situation in Nigeria: Evidence from 2013 Demographic and Health Survey. *Social Indicators Research, 128*(1), 1–14. doi:10.100711205-015-1016-4

Young, J., Gore, R., Gorman, B., & Watson, K. (2013). Wrapping and swaddling infants: Child health nurses' knowledge, attitudes and practice. *Neonatal, Paediatric, and Child Health Nursing, 16*(3), 2–11.

KEY TERMS AND DEFINITIONS

Baby: A very young child, especially one newly or recently born. In this context, a person aged (0-11 months).

Central Business Districts (CBDs): A central business district is the commercial and business center of a city. In larger cities, it is often synonymous with the city's financial district. Geographically, it often coincides with the city centre.

Child Protection: Child protection is the protection of children from violence, exploitation, abuse, and neglect.

Child Wrapping: Is the practice of covering baby with cloth. It is means to cover, envelop, or encase a child with cloths especially at the back of the mother.

Child's Rights: These are economic, social and cultural rights, such as the right to education, the right to a decent standard of living, the right to health, etc. Children's rights include individual rights: the right to live with his parents, the right to education, the right to benefit from a protection.

Disease: A disorder of structure or function in a human, animal, or plant, especially one that produces specific signs or symptoms or that affects a specific location and is not simply a direct result of physical injury. It is literally the absence of ease.

Illness: A disease or period of sickness affecting the body or mind. Illness is the persons experience with disease. It is that person's perception and interpretation of disease.

Media: The main means of mass communication (broadcasting, publishing, and the Internet) regarded collectively. Media are the communication outlets or tools used to store and deliver information or data. The term refers to components of the mass media communications industry, such as print media, publishing, the news media, photography, cinema, broadcasting, and advertising.

Street Trader: A street trader is someone who sells something in the street, either from a stall or van or with their goods laid out on the sidewalk.

Street Trading: The selling, or exposing for sale, of articles on certain streets. It means the selling or exposing or the offering for sale of any article (including a living thing) or the supplying or offering to supply any service in a street for gain or reward.

Sustainable Development: It is development that meets the needs and aspirations of the present without compromising the ability of future generations to meet their own needs. Thus, sustainable development is the organizing principle for sustaining finite resources necessary to provide for the needs of future generations of life on the planet.

Sustainable Development Goals (SDGs): The Sustainable Development Goals (SDGs), otherwise known as the Global Goals, are a universal call to action to end poverty, protect the planet and ensure that all people enjoy peace and prosperity.

Swaddling: Swaddling is an age-old practice of wrapping infants in blankets or similar cloths so that movement of the limbs is tightly restricted.

APPENDIX

Table 1. Demographic and trading profile of respondents

Selected Variables	(N=228)	%	Selected Variables	(N=228)	%
Gender			**Sales item/products**		
Female	228	100.0	Edibles (foo/drinks/confectioneries, etc)	110	48.2
Age Group			Clothing (shoes/watches/bags, etc)	44	19.3
15-24	46	20.2	Accessories (household/car/phone, etc)	74	32.5
25-34	159	69.7	**Employment status**		
35-44	13	5.7	Self employed	149	65.4
45-54	10	4.4	Employee	58	25.4
Marital status			Unpaid workers	21	9.2
Single	40	17.5	Nature of trade		
Married	167	73.2	Sedentary	27	11.8
Separated/others	21	9.2	Peddling/Roving	201	88.2
Educational level			**Average hour trading per day**		-
No schooling	11	4.8	1-2 hours	4	1.8
Primary Education	35	15.4	3-4 hours	31	13.6
Secondary Education	127	55.7	5-6 hours	126	55.3
Tertiary Education	55	24.1	7 hours & above	67	29.4
Place of origin			**Wrapped Baby at back**		
South East	30	13.2	Yes	133	58.3
South West	141	61.8	No	95	41.7
North	36	15.8	**Ever had Accident/injury while trading**		-
Others	21	9.2	Yes	69	30.3
Partner Occupation			No	159	69.7
Schooling	11	5.9	**Do you have other job(s)**		
Unskilled/unskilled artisan	52	27.7	Yes	47	20.6
Civil servant	58	30.9	No	181	79.4
Trading	46	24.5	**Why do you trade on the street?**		
Faming	21	11.2	No other job	90	39.5
			Partner/boss/parent's decision	42	18.4
Age of the child			Prefer self-employment	37	16.2
0-6 months	12	5.3	To get money for other business	27	11.8
7-11 months	216	94.7	To get school fees	33	14.5
Total	**228**	**100.0**	**Total**	**228**	**100.0**

Source: Field Survey, 2017

Table 2. Child's health condition and cares

Selected Variables	(N=228)	%	Selected Variables	(N=228)	%
Child' Health Status			**Lost Days/Month**		
Ever sick	131	57.5	Never	97	42.5
Never sick	97	42.5	1-2 Days/Month	61	26.8
Common Child illnesses			3-4 Days/Month	43	18.9
Malaria/Fever	105	46.1	5-6 Days/month	27	11.8
Typhoid	22	9.6	**Loss days due to child's illness**		
Diarrhea	98	43	1-2 Days/Month	61	46.6
Gastro-intestinal diseases	3	1.3	3-4 Days/Month	43	32.8
How close is health facility			5 Days and above	27	20.6
Very far and not trekable	14	6.1	**Ever heard Campaign against back-wrapping**		
Not far but not trekable	169	74.1	Yes	43	18.9
Not far and trekable	45	19.7	No	185	81.1
First step when child is sick			**Rate of visiting hospital**		
Pray/watch the situation	26	11.4	Often	52	22.8
Administer drugs	115	50.4	Not often	79	34.6
Visit the chemist	69	30.3	Not at all	97	42.5
Go to hospital	18	7.9	**Perspective on baby-wrapping**		
Practice Breastfeeding			It is medicinal	80	35.1
Yes	143	62.7	It is a tradition	135	59.2
No	85	37.3	Mother-to-child closeness	13	5.7
Frequency of Breastfeeding			**Place of Breastfeeding**		
Very often	30	13.2	Anywhere	101	44.3
Often	131	57.5	In the store	79	34.6
Not often	60	26.3	Under the Shade	48	21.1
Not at all	7	3.1			
Total	**228**	**100**	**Total**	**228**	**100**

Source: Field Survey 2017

Table 3. Binary logistic regression illustrating the interconnections between operation of street trading and child exposure to sickness

Selected Variables	B	S.E.	Wald	Sig.
Age of Mother				
15-24 years	RC			
25-34 years	0.382	1.814	0.044	0.833
35-44 years	0.062	2.005	0.001	0.975
Educational Attainment				
Tertiary Education	RC			
No schooling	1.15	0.815	1.99	0.158
Primary Education	1.006	0.944	1.135	0.287
Secondary Education	-1.979	1.94	1.04	0.308
Hours Spent Trading per Day				
1-2 Hours	RC			
3-4 Hours	0.056	0.165	0.114	0.736
5-6 hours	1.604	1.408	1.298	0.064
7 hours & above	1.757	1.248	1.982	0.003
Back-wrapping				
No baby at back	RC			
Wrapped baby at back	0.575	0.284	4.116	0.042
Sales item/products	RC			
Clothing (e.g. shoes, watches, bags) (RC)				
Edibles (e.g. food, water, drinks, confectioneries)	-0.81	0.263	9.487	0.002
Accessories (e.g. household, car, phone)	0.022	0.16	0.019	0.89
Nature of Trade				
Peddling	RC			
Sedentary	-2.107	0.979	4.636	0.031
Constant	-6.084	1.816	11.229	0.001

Overall Percentage = 97.4, Cox & Snell R-Square = 0.41, Nagelkerke R-Square = 0.17, -2Log Likelihood = 52.984 and RC = Reference Category

Source: Field Survey 2017

Chapter 13
Perception on Child Rights Protection and Media Performance Among Kuje Internally Displaced Persons' Camp, Abuja, Nigeria

Felix Chidozie Chidozie
Covenant University, Nigeria

Augustine Ejiroghene Oghuvbu
Covenant University, Nigeria

ABSTRACT

This essay examines media and child rights protection in Nigeria, using Kuje IDPs Camp in Abuja, FCT as a case study. It argues that the media has important and indispensable roles to play in enabling the promotion of the United Nations Convention on the Rights of the Child and Nigeria's Child Rights Act, 2003. The study adopted the qualitative method through interviews and focus group discussions conducted at the Kuje IDPs Camp. Findings suggest that the Nigerian government is not committed to implementing the prescription of the United Nations Convention on the Rights of the Child and the Child Rights Act, thus further jeopardizing the already fractured rights of the of children in IDPs camps in Nigeria. Similarly, the media is not paying attention to the plight of the displaced children. The prescriptions advanced in this study as well as the conclusions reached are relevant for policy makers at the national, regional, and international levels responsible for the rights of the children, especially the Nigerian child.

DOI: 10.4018/978-1-7998-0329-4.ch013

INTRODUCTION

Child Rights protection is a fundamental aspect of International Human Rights Law which serves to protect children and minors from political, economic or social repression by various national, regional and international actors. Hence, International Human Rights Law sets out the basic protections that all individuals are entitled to, including children and expressly recognizes the duty of states to respect, ensure and fulfill these rights. This has become necessary in view of the preponderance of state as an actor in international relations. To be sure, numerous cases of state violation of the rights of children have been clearly documented by scholars, policy makers, international and inter-regional agencies as well as the global media (Nordveit, 2010; Adesina, 2014; Gabel, 2014; Ogunniran, 2017). This systematic abuse of children's rights has manifested in forms of hunger, starvation, homelessness, illiteracy, sexual violence, physical abuse, forced labour, forced marriage, child trafficking, slavery, prostitution, forced recruitment into armed groups and other varied and complex risks (Internews Europe, 2014). Despite the national and international coalition efforts to arrest this ugly trend, shockingly, the high rise in child's rights violations continues. The reason often adduced for the general interest over the protection of the rights of children by multiple agencies and organizations at domestic and international levels, is simply the vulnerability of this segment of the population to the vagaries of international politics. Thus, scholarship on media protection of the rights of children has undoubtedly attracted volumes of literature over many decades (Davies, 2014; Morris and Davies, 2018; Livingstone, 2016; Oyero, 2010).

However, media coverage of the protection of the rights of Children is even more challenging in conflict situations because of the precarious and often violent nature of certain conflicts. Indeed, the United Nations High Commissioner for Refugees (UNHCR, 2012 p. 7) reports 'that almost half of all forcibly displaced persons globally are children – over 12 million girls and boys'. The report further stated 'that 46% refugees, 54% stateless persons, 47% Internally Displaced Persons (IDPs), and 56% refugees living in camps are children' (UNHCR, 2012 p. 7). For example, the Syrian civil war has claimed an estimated casualty of half a million since the war began in 2011 according to statistics released from Syrian Center for Policy Research (SCPR, 2018) with another 13 million displaced by the conflict (Connor, 2018). Precisely, it is estimated that there have been almost 207,000 civilian casualties since the beginning of the conflict, and about 25,000 of them were children (SCPR, 2018). Added to this is that the humanitarian crisis triggered by the war in Syria is similarly profound. According to the International Rescue Committee (2018), nearly 2 million children are out-of-school and another 3 million face dangers of malnutrition. In addition, Internews Europe (2014, p.7) reported that 'nearly 300 million children in India, Kenya and Brazil (over half of the children population) are living in conditions where their basic rights are violated. Not surprisingly, in the face of this carnage - indeed, staggering statistics - the politics within the Security Council of the United Nations and cascades of often conflicting interests by international actors have delayed intervention in Syria, and other conflict theaters, further escalating the violence in those countries.

In Nigeria, the situation is equally alarming. The plight of children caused by the recent rise in internal displacement, necessitated by the insurgencies of the Boko Haram and Hausa Fulani mayhem, including natural disasters leaves much to be desired (Isokpan and Durojaye, 2016). Following the havoc unleashed by Boko Haram insurgents since 2009, many children have been abducted, killed and even used as suicide bombers and human shields against the combating Nigerian Armed Forces. In some instances, entire villages have been left without clean water, electricity, health care, schools – or simply burned to the ground (Bappah, 2016; D'Amato, 2017; Olojo, 2017; Raineri and Martini, 2017). According to the United Nations International Children's Emergency Funds (UNICEF, 2018), among the 2.6 million people displaced, more than half of them are children, who have fled the brutal violence within Nigeria (northeast Borno state being the worst hit) and to Cameroon, Chad and Niger. To be sure, many more thousands are out-of-school and have since fled to settle in the IDPs camps established by the Nigerian government, and over 475,000 of them were likely to suffer severe acute malnutrition in 2018 (UNICEF, 2018). In short, UNICEF Nigeria (2017) put the total number of displaced children needing immediate relief materials at 1.3 million (cited in Punch, July 19, 2017: 10). According to the United Nations Child Agency (UNCA, 2017), an estimated 57 per cent of all schools are closed in Nigeria's Borno state, leaving a projected 3 million children in need of emergency education support. It is the combination of these humanitarian disasters that prompted the United Nations High Commissioner for Refugees (UNHCR) in Nigeria to declare the situation in northeast Nigeria a humanitarian crisis in 2017.

In retrospect, Nigeria adopted the Child Rights Act (CRA) in 2003 under the administration of President Olusegun Obasanjo (Toyo, 2006). The overall objective of the then Obasanjo administration was to domesticate the Convention on the Rights of the Child (CRC), a United Nations human rights treaty which sets out the civil, political, economic, social, health and cultural rights of children. UNICEF (2003) argued that the Child Rights Act (CRA) was created to serve as a legal documentation and protection of Children's rights and responsibilities in Nigeria. According to Nmeregini (2010), the CRA has three primary purposes: to incorporate the rights of the Convention on the Rights of the Child (CRC) and the African Charter on Human and Peoples' Rights into the national law, to provide the responsibilities of government agencies associated with the law and to integrate children-focused legislation into one comprehensive law. Kathryn (2009) further added that the CRC acts as a legislation against human trafficking since it forbids children from being separated from their parents against their will, except in situations where it is in the best interests of the child.

Indeed, while most literature parade relevant data on essential components of the CRC of the United Nations and the CRA of Nigeria, a few of them have clearly identified and defined the role(s) of the media - both at the global (where it concerns violations of the CRC) and national (where it concerns the violation of the CRA) levels – especially where it involves the children IDPs. Consequently, the protection of the rights of children may have suffered serious setback in Nigeria. This is a fundamental gap in the literature that this work intends to fill in view of the enormous powers and leverage of the media in reaching a wider audience, especially in this digital age.

It is against this background that this study raises the following questions: Are there any defined roles by the media – both electronic and print – in promoting the CRC? What are the identifiable responsibilities of the media in protecting the children's right under the CRA? Has the Nigerian government successfully incorporated the CRC into the CRA? What are the domestic challenges militating against the rights of the Nigerian child? The corresponding objective of the study is to answer the above research questions.

The essay is divided into six sections. Following the above introduction, the essay addresses the dominant conceptual and theoretical issues on children's rights. The third section reviews the existing literature on media and child rights protection in Nigeria. The fourth section presents the methodology of the study. The fifth segment is the data presentation and analysis while the last part of the essay is the conclusion and recommendations.

CONCEPTUAL AND THEORETICAL ISSUES ON CHILDREN'S RIGHTS

It has been alluded earlier that, children are one of the most vulnerable groups in any population in the world. This is because of their physical and emotional dependence on adults for protection, development and survival (Gabel, 2014). However, children in developing countries, unlike their counterparts in developed countries are exposed to greater vulnerability because of the higher incidence of poverty, induced by conflicts, failed government policies, low infrastructural development, absence of safety or social protection mechanisms, and social-cultural limitations (Gabel, 2014). Consequently, children in developing countries suffer serious health, physical, political, economic and social disadvantages compared to those in the developed societies. For instance, according to the Sustainable Development Goals Report

(2017, p. 3), 'in 2016, an estimated 155 million children under age 5 were stunted (low height for their age), 52 million were suffering from wasting (low weight for their height), and 41 million were overweight'. The report explicitly identified the most affected population of the children in the above category from the developing countries.

Similarly, Gabel (2014, p. 2) reported that 'about half of all the poor in developing countries (with incomes less than US $1:25 a day) are children and 40% of children in developing countries are poor'. If we add the direct and indirect impacts of the prevalence of adult poverty and inequalities to the conditions of children in the developing countries, the picture becomes grimmer. To illustrate, the SDGs Report (2017) estimated that,

767 million people lived below the extreme poverty line in 2013. Almost 10 percent of the employed population worldwide lives with their families on less than 1.90 US dollars per person per day in 2016. 9 percent of adult workers and their families lived in extreme poverty compared to 15 percent of youth workers. In 2016, only 22 percent of the unemployed worldwide received unemployment benefits, 28 percent of people with severe disabilities collected a disability pension, 35 percent of children were covered by social protection, 41 percent of women giving birth received maternity benefits, and 68 percent of people above retirement age collected a pension. Economic losses from natural hazards are now reaching an average 250 billion to 300 billion US dollars a year, with a disproportionate impact on small and vulnerable countries. (SDGs Report, 2017 p. 3)

It is in the bid to reverse these tragic statistics and provide the children with the necessary protection and safety nets that the United Nations Convention on the Rights of the Child (UNCRC or CRC for short) became operational in 1989 (Collins, 2014). The CRC is arguable the first international instrument to explicitly recognize children as social and active agents with delineated rights. It is described as 'the most ratified human rights treaty in the history of International Law' (Tobin, 2005 p. 86). It begins with a proviso that, like all human beings, children have rights; but acknowledges that certain rights are specific to children and must be reinterpreted in cases involving children (Gabel, 2014). The CRC has four cardinal principles which are: non-discrimination; the best interests of the child; the right to life, survival and development; and respect for the views of the child (Gabel, 2014 p. 3). It is instructive to mention that, even though 193 countries out of the 196 signatories to the Convention have ratified and integrated the basic elements of the CRC into their different national legislations and constitutional provisions, the exact application of certain instruments of the CRC in the countries concerned have been subject to a lot of controversy. For example, the correct application of highly volatile social-cultural issues such as female genital mutilation, child marriage and at times, child labour, has resulted in the blatant abuse of the CRC in certain countries. These abuses are often borne out of discontinuities, and at times, ambiguities between national legislative and international discourses in the field of child's rights.

According to Nordtveit (2010) the contradicting logics that govern the interpretation of childhood or definition of what constitutes 'children' in the national and international debates contributes to the abuse of children's rights. He stated that,

The international and national-legal discourses are classifying children and childhood according to several levels of dualism: dualism of age (defining a quantitative limit for when a child becomes an adult); dualism of activity (school attendance or child labour); dualism of employment (acceptable work or worst forms of child labour); and dualism of the response structure (depending on whether an abusive situation, based on international norms can be detected). These discourses are then defining in absolute terms, what is right and what is wrong: right age for schooling; wrong age for work. Child or youth employment, easily categorized as 'wrong', may also fall into the category of worst forms of child labour, and automatically, abuse is detected. In most such cases of abuse, 'removal' (from work) and 'reinsertion' (into school, most often in the child's community of origin) are prescribed. (Nordveit, 2010 p. 700)

Correspondingly, the United Nations Convention on the Rights of the Child (UNCRC, 1989) and the African Charter on the Rights and Welfare of the Child (ACRWC, 1990) are two instruments on child protection, both of which define a child in dual labels. According to these texts, a child is 'every human being below the age of 18 years', although the United Nations Convention provides an exception related to national jurisdiction (cited in Nordveit, 2010 p. 702). Accordingly, the UNCRC and ACRWC have placed the international narrative above the national norms, religions and culture. Specifically, the African Charter on the Rights and Welfare of the Child (ACRWC, 1990 p. 2) stated that, 'any custom, tradition, cultural or religious practice that is inconsistent with the rights, duties and obligations contained in the present Charter shall to the extent of such inconsistency be discouraged' (cited in Nordveit, 2010 p, 702).

It is this same tension between international legal obligations of states and the constitutionalization of children's rights that necessarily creates dilemmas of policy and practice (Smith, 1991). Nothing epitomizes this friction more profoundly than the allegations of cultural imperialism by some developing states over the principles and subjects (this time, children) of International Human Rights Law. According to Pupavac (1998):

An examination of the provisions of the Convention reveals that the universal standards of the Convention are based on a Western concept of childhood and Western social policies which emphasize the role of individual causations and professional interventions and de-emphasize the influence of the wider, social, economic, political and cultural circumstances. (cited in Tobin, 2005 p. 91)

In short, the unintended consequences of this 'conflict of laws' led Smith (1991, p. 469) to conclude 'that the legislation intended to protect and promote children's interests can only be implemented selectively, and in ways contrary to its own spirit'. Since, till date, compliance with international human rights obligations varies across national jurisdictions, the impasse between the two bodies of law may not readily be resolved in the nearest future. We can only seek a balance in order not to completely jeopardize the rights of children. Such balance can only be reached when state actors recognize that 'the significance of child rights highlights the influence of international human rights in the national context' (Collins, 2013 p. 608). Thus, currently, there is much international impetus to incorporate child rights into national constitutions as evidenced by developing countries in Africa such as Ethiopia, Rwanda, South Africa, Burkina Faso, Togo and Nigeria (Collins, 2013).

MEDIA AND CHILD RIGHTS PROTECTION IN NIGERIA

Child rights protection in Nigeria is a familiar theme in contemporary literature. Scholars have attempted to present the predicaments of the Nigerian child despite all the international, regional and national legal provisions available to protect the latter (Amdi, 1990; Toyo, 2006; Adesina, 2014; Enakhimion, 2014; Obiechina, 2014; Chinwuba, 2015; Tajudeen, 2015; (Nelson, Kehinde, Oyero, Wiliams & Soola, 2013; Oyesomi, Soola, Abioye & Oyero, 2014). Apart from the UNCRC and the ACRWC instituted in 1989 and 1990 respectively, Section 34 of the 1999 Constitution of the Federal Republic of Nigeria eloquently provides for the protection of the rights of the Nigerian child to dignity of his/her person. This section 'prohibits all forms of torture, inhuman or degrading treatment, and slavery, forced or compulsory labour' (cited in Awosola and Omoera, 2008 p. 126).

Likewise, the passage of the Child Rights Bill by the National Assembly in 2003, and later promulgated as the Child Rights Act (aimed at principally enacting into law in Nigeria the principles enshrined in the Convention on the Rights of the Child and the AU Charter on the Rights and Welfare of the Child), as well as its subsequent passage into law by some states' Houses of Assembly in Nigeria, supposedly created much anticipation and respite for the Nigerian child (Anho and Christopher, 2016). However, it will be safe to infer that despite the legal provisions available through the country's 1999 Constitution and the Child Rights Bill, the Nigerian child has been subjected to harrowing experiences resulting in emotional and physical trauma, leaving them overwhelmed and shattered in some instances.

In an interesting study by Awosola and Omoera (2008), the role of the media (in their case television) in raising awareness on the challenges of the Nigerian child was persuasively presented. They portrayed the media in Nigeria as 'undoubtedly persuasive instruments in man's struggle for self-liberation and development' (p. 126); regretting rather, that the advocacy and massive campaigns by the Nigeria media to draw attention to the plights of the Nigerian child and galvanize support for the latter, have been aggressively rebuffed by the Nigeria public. Their findings suggest that factors such as rising cost of living, grinding poverty, prohibitive cost of schooling, indiscriminate child bearing and other competing demands 'may have blurred the residents' consciousness about child rights' (p. 130). Awosola and Omoera's study succeeded in reporting the indispensable role of the media in alerting the general public about the abuses suffered by the Nigerian child; but their study did not identify the role of the media in integrating the two dominant legal instruments – CRC and CRA in achieving this objective. This is the gap that this study fills.

Similarly, Ige and Fawole (2011) studied the prevalence of Child Sexual Abuse (CSA) in a selected community in southwest Nigeria, which they portrayed as a human rights issue. They argued that the myths and cultural beliefs surrounding certain diseases such as HIV/AIDS may have contributed to the rise in the epidemic. They further posited that parental negligence due to other pressing economic factors usually left the children unsupervised, thus, increasing the frequency of CSA. They admitted to high rate of awareness of CSA among the parents pooled in their sample, an awareness attributed to the assertive crusade and mounting media coverage of CSA in Nigeria. They summarized the consequences of CSA among the Nigerian children to include both physical (genital trauma, pregnancy, and sexually transmitted diseases) and psychological (suicide attempts, post-traumatic stress disorder, PTSD and emotional and behavioural difficulties). Again, this study presented the role of the media in creating awareness about the rise in the incidences of CSA in Nigeria, but did not contextualize the roles of the media in harmonizing the CRC and CRA. Another study by Ogunniran (2017) discussed similar narrative with the above study but basically focused on the role of the media in protecting the Nigerian child from pornography, trafficking and prostitution.

Again, Anho and Christopher (2016) presented a compelling case for the media coverage of children's rights in Nigeria using data generated from two prominent national dailies (The Vanguard and The Punch) as case studies. They argued that there were serious cases of under reportage of the children's rights by the two national dailies covering a two-year period, 2011-2013. They maintained that the 'mass media, in line with its information dissemination and agenda setting roles', had tremendous opportunity 'to contribute immensely in raising awareness, influencing attitude, and promoting debates on the need to promote and protect the rights of the child' (p. 1); but unfortunately, had failed to do so. They concluded that ironically, the two national dailies had failed to fulfill the major roles of the mass media in shaping public opinion and influencing public policy, especially on the issues surrounding children's rights in Nigeria. Again, the above study did not address how the media can synergize the CRC and CRA with a view to providing adequate latitude in the protection of child rights in Nigeria. This explains the significance of this study. We turn our attention to the methodology and later to the data presentation and discussion of findings.

METHODOLOGY OF THE STUDY

The study adopted a qualitative method of enquiry. Data was generated from interviews conducted at the Kuje IDPs Camp in Abuja. The respondents for the oral interview were six, comprising camp officials and government agencies that are responsible for the needs of IDPs, especially children. The interview sessions were recorded with the aid of tape recorder and were listened to several times by the researchers in order to identify recurring themes. Focus group discussions (FGD) were conducted on three occasions as well in the camp with selected categories of children respondents within the age brackets of 14- 17 resident in the camp. Since, most of the children involved in the FGD could neither speak nor understand English Language; the researchers involved a Hausa Language interpreter who played a mediatory role in the conversations. Thus, purposive sampling technique was used to select the study sample. Secondary sources of data such as journal articles, periodicals, newspapers publications, research projects and internet sources from national and international organizations and agencies engaged in protection of children's rights were used to augment the primary sources of data.

DATA PRESENTATION AND DISCUSSION OF FINDINGS

The authors tested the research questions through interviews and focus group discussions conducted at the Kuje IDPs Camp in Abuja, FCT. Below are the results of the findings.

Research Question 1: Are There Any Defined Role by the Media—Both Electronic and Print—in Promoting the Convention on the Rights of the Child (Crc)?

A notable official of the Communication Unit of the National Commission for Refugees, Migrants and Internally Displaced Persons (NCRMIDP), maintained that even the Convention itself, probably Article 17, recognizes the importance and roles of the media and print in the lives of children. Though in Nigeria, there may not be defined roles stipulated by the Act, but however, the country, being a signatory to the Treaty and having ratified it, it means that the provision regarding the media and print is legally applicable here.

The above official's view is in order here, since in concrete terms, the UNCRC's Article 17 recognizes the child's need for information. It discloses that,

States Parties recognize the important function performed by the mass media and shall ensure that the child has access to information and material from a diversity of national and international sources, especially those aimed at the promotion of his or her social, spiritual and moral well-being and physical and mental health (1989, p. 5 cited in Nordveit, 2010 p. 702).

The Vice-President, Kuje IDPs Camp, held the view that the media are always expected to cover and promote issues that concern women and children, and this is what they should actually do. However, he argued that in their camp, the media do not come around to cover and report activities in the camp, not even the government agencies visit them. The only agencies that make efforts are the Non-Governmental Organizations (NGOs) which sometimes visit. For him, the media covers and reports only IDP Camps that are accessible which they often listen to on the radio from their own camp.

Research Question 2: What Are the Identifiable Responsibilities of the Media in Protecting the Children's Rights Under Child Rights Act (CRA)?

A notable official of the Communication Unit of the National Commission for Refugees, Migrants and Internally Displaced Persons (NCRMIDP), reported that, following his earlier response, the media is charged with the responsibility of covering and reporting any act that contravenes the Convention at international level. In Nigeria, the Act does not prevent the media from covering or reporting behaviours or actions that contravenes the Child Rights Act. In most cases, some contraventions come to the notice of government through the media, be it electronic or print. He asserted that, "the Act did not specify or list the responsibilities of the media, but at the same time did not prohibit the media from covering or reporting activities of such".

The Vice-President, Kuje IDPs Camp posited that, the basic duty expected from the media is the coverage and reportage of activities concerning children. By this primary responsibility, the media is promoting and protecting the children's rights. He lamented that the media do not cover camps, and the children in camps suffer as a result. He continued that, the rights of the children are denied by the government itself even when the Act is to ensure the protection of the rights of all the children, including those in the IDP camps.

Research Question 3: Has the Nigerian Government Successfully Incorporated the Convention on the Rights of the Child Into the Child Rights Act?

An official of the Communication Unit of the National Commission for Refugees, Migrants and Internally Displaced Persons argued that, in theory, the Nigeria government has integrated the Convention on the Rights of the Child into the Child Rights Act. But in practice, there are entrenched socio-cultural norms and religious impediments, and that is why its implementation may be successful in one part of the country and otherwise in another part of the country. For instance, he mentioned that, there are some clauses in the Convention on the Rights of the Child that do not totally agree with the Islamic teachings and beliefs in the country. Accordingly, the approach of affected regions to the identified stipulations may be hostile. This is one of the reasons why Nigeria is seen as a big and heterogeneous country and this will continue to hinder the domestication of some important provisions of the CRC.

The above view corresponds with Ayesha Iman's (a leading feminist and Muslim scholar in Nigeria) submission. According to her:

Nigeria is in fact a state party to several international human rights covenants. However, although such agreements may give rise to obligations under international law, unless they have been specifically incorporated into domestic law, they give no basis for claims in national courts. The interplay between domestic Nigerian multiple and parallel legal systems of secular, Muslim and customary laws is also problematic as they give differential rights on different issues, and jurisdiction can be contentious (cited in Toyo, 2006 p. 1300)

The Vice-President, Kuje IDPs Camp maintained that, in Nigeria most of the policy pronouncements end in paper work. The major problem, according to him lies in implementation. For him, this is evident as both government and media hardly visit them in their camps, even when IDPs' Camps should be part of the area of priority in implementing such Act. He further stressed that, it is obvious that there are many communities and villages that do not have the presence of government or media, yet these communities and villages have children whose rights are supposed to be protected and promoted by this Act.

Research Question 4: What Are the Domestic Challenges Militating Against the Rights of the Nigerian Child?

An official of the Communication Unit of the National Commission for Refugees, Migrants and Internally Displaced Persons reported that, illiteracy is one of the challenges limiting the rights of the Nigerian child. This factor, according to him has a double tragedy in that, it originates from both the child and the parents or guardians. Consequently, most of the children are not aware that they even have some legal rights. The parents on the other hand do not know if there is anything called Child Rights Act, let alone Convention on the Rights of the Child.

Another challenge is deep-rooted cultural and religious beliefs. According to this official, Africans have peculiar ways of raising a child which in most cases are not in tune with the legal provisions in the document. He further explained that, the religious injunctions have already stipulated conditions on how to raise children in some instances, which also, in most cases are not in conformity with the requirements in the legal document. And in this part of the world, he emphasized, Nigerians are a very religious people. Religion, he submitted, permeates the entire fabric of the country's politics, economic, legal, cultural, and even educational structures as demonstrated by the Sharia laws

The Vice-President, Kuje IDPs Camp, on his part, recounted that the orientation and ideology of the political class in Nigeria is a big threat not only to child's rights but to all Nigerians. He reported that, the politicians in the country are not concerned about such issues as child rights, but rather how to grab and retain power. According to him, this was evident in the last contentiously concluded general elections where the protection of the rights of the children was not part of their campaign manifesto. Again, he maintained that, some cultural practices in some parts of the country are not friendly with the child's rights. And in most cases, he argued that, the cultures are sacred and must be observed and revered. This, in his opinion, is where the media should step-in and mount sensitization and awareness campaigns, concentrating in the most affected regions and areas.

The researchers conducted FGD involving seven children within the age brackets of 14- 17 cutting across different gender in the Kuje IDPs Camp to ascertain their views on the questions under investigation. This is in line with the UNCRC and

ACRWC's definitions of children as 'every human being below the age of 18 years' (UNCRC, 1989 p. 9 cited in Nordtveit, 2010 p. 702).

On the question whether there are any defined role(s) by the media, both electronic and print in promoting the Convention on Rights of Child: the individual respondents deliberated on the question and arrived at a common view that the handling of child rights by media is very poor. For instance in their camp they claimed that they have only seen the media personnel twice. They reiterated that the media personnel only come when there is a government official who pays them a visit.

When asked what they thought were the identifiable responsibilities of the media in protecting the children's rights under the Child Rights Act: the group members both individually and collectively submitted that the media was supposed to come and witness what the children are passing through in the camps so that members of the public will be aware that their rights are not being protected.

When we posed the question on whether the Nigerian government had successfully incorporated the Convention on the Rights of the Child into the Child Rights Act, having properly explained to them what that meant: the group members were of the view that the government has not fully integrated the Convention on the Rights of the Child into the Child Rights Act. According to them, this is evident in what the children in different IDPs Camps are passing through. They submitted that the basic needs of the children such as their rights to feeding; shelter and security are still serious challenges despite how long they had stayed in the camp.

On the question of what the domestic challenges militating against the rights of the Nigerian child was: the group respondents distilled all their responses into four main challenges after intensive deliberations: Corruption; Poor Educational System; Lack of a Sense of Priority and Nigeria's Brand of Politics.

CONCLUSION AND RECOMMENDATIONS

This study has contributed to the volume of literature on the role of the media in protecting children's rights in Nigeria. Its point of departure borders on the urgency for successful implementation of the existing provisions of the CRC as an integral part of the International Human Rights Law with the CRA, and their implications on the rights of the Nigerian child. The study was set at Kuje IDPs Camp in Abuja, FCT where relevant questions were raised through interviews and focus group discussions to ascertain the level of incorporation of the CRC into the CRA in Nigeria. The paper consistently advanced the view that the role of the Nigeria media in effectively holding accountable the government and other agencies responsible for protecting the rights of the children, especially the IDPs category, can never be overemphasized. In so doing, the Nigeria media can be in the vanguard of driving the complete coordination of all relevant international and domestic legal obligations for the protection of the children in Nigeria. In view of the above, the study makes the following recommendations:

The role of the media in this era of 'new wars' resulting in 'new threats' to global peace should involve new approaches and dynamic coverage to protect the vulnerable group, of which children are the worst hit. The 'new wars' such as insurgency, terrorism, genocide, intra-state conflicts and fratricidal wars resulting in 'new threats' to global peace such as IDPs, Refugees, Migration, diseases, poverty, starvation, and environmental disasters require new forms of reportage by the media in a rapidly changing international system. Similarly, there is an urgent need for effective coordination of the agendas and operations of all international, regional, inter-regional and national agencies/organizations responsible for the protection of the rights of children, especially during conflicts. One of the reasons for the failures of these multiple agencies in ensuring the protection of children is often the conflicting and unnecessary duplication of responsibilities and functions. By drawing attention of the public to these issues, the agencies concerned will be forced to play complementary rather than conflicting roles.

With specific reference to Nigeria, the media must relentlessly put the plight of the Nigerian children littered in the numberless IDPs Camps in the country on the front burner of public consciousness. This can be achieved through inundating the visual and airwaves with powerful educational programmes, images, documentaries, videos, interviews and the likes with a view to consistently directing the attention of both the public and relevant agencies to the challenges of children in the camps. As a corollary, since many children lose the opportunity to continue their education while in the IDPs Camps, the media can raise public awareness about the need to reintegrate these categories of children into their host communities and provide education for them.

This can be more effective when Non-governmental organizations interested in the problems of displaced children are involved. In addition, social protection programmes must be initiated and implemented to better the conditions of the children in the camps. This is important since 'there is a growing evidence from a range of developing countries that social protection programmes…can effectively increase the nutritional, health, and educational status of children; reduce their risk of abuse and exploitation; ensure their rights; and offer long-term development benefits' (Gabel, 2014 p. 2). The media, must in addition, compel and demand accountability from the Nigerian government and her various agencies, and challenge powerful related international groups and organizations to the issues concerning the abuse and violations of children's rights in Nigeria.

It is important to mention that, this study has not in any way provided complete information on the media and child rights protection in Nigeria. Further studies in this area are recommended because of the obvious limitations encountered in this study. The study is limited in the sense that, it only gathered data from one IDPs Camp in Nigeria among several others. Thus, the views presented here may not be fully representative of the roles of the media in protecting child's rights in Nigeria. More so, the data for this study was generated during the just concluded national elections in Nigeria. Consequently, the general atmosphere of uncertainty and political tension in the country pervaded the IDPs Camp covered in this study, as some of the IDPs had either fled the camp or compromised by politicians who visited the camp. Hence, other studies that could engage a more comprehensive and robust research methods, covering more of the IDPs camps in Nigeria would be necessary. Despite these identifiable limitations, this study is significant in its objective by distinguishing the role of the media in addressing the gaps in effective harmonization of the CRC and CRA in Nigeria, with specific reference to the IDPs. By so doing, it has contributed to the literature on conflict, peace and communications studies.

REFERENCES

Adesina, O. S. (2014). Modern day slavery: Poverty and child trafficking in Nigeria. *African Identities*, *12*(2), 165–179. doi:10.1080/14725843.2014.881278

Amdi, V. (1990). The cause of child abuse and neglect and their effects on the development of children in Samaru Zaria, Nigeria. *Early Child Development and Care*, *58*(1), 31–43. doi:10.1080/0300443900580105

Anho, E. J., & Christopher, C. (2016). Mass Media Coverage of Children's Rights in Nigeria. *Multidisciplinary Journal of Research Development*, *25*(1), 1–9.

Awosola, R. K., & Omoera, O. S. (2008). Child Rights and the Media: The Nigerian Experience. *Study Home Communication Science*, *2*(2), 125–131. doi:10.1080/09737189.2008.11885263

Bappah, H. Y. (2016). Nigeria's military failure against the Boko Haram insurgency. *African Security Review*, *25*(2), 146–158. doi:10.1080/10246029.2016.1151799

Chinwuba, N. N. (2015). Human Identity: Child Rights and the Legal Framework for Marriage in Nigeria. *Marriage & Family Review*, *51*(4), 305–336. doi:10.1080/01494929.2014.938286

Collins, T. M. (2013). International Child Rights in National Constitutions: Good Sense or Nonsense for Ireland? *Irish Political Studies*, *28*(4), 591–619. doi:10.1080/07907184.2013.838951

Collins, T. M. (2014). The relationship between children's rights and business. *International Journal of Human Rights, 18*(6), 582–633. doi:10.1080/13642987.2014.944805

Connor, P. (2018). *Most displaced Syrians are in the Middle East, and about a million are in Europe*. Retrieved from www.reliefweb.int/report

D'Amato, S. (2017). Terrorists Going Transnational: Rethinking the Role of States in the Case of AQIM and Boko Haram. *Critical Studies on Terrorism, 11*(1), 151–172. doi:10.1080/17539153.2017.1347238

Davies, L. (2014). Working positively with the media to protect children. *Journal of Social Welfare and Family Law, 36*(1), 47–58. doi:10.1080/09649069.2014.886877

Enakhimion, E. (2014). *Child Protection System Strengthening, Mapping and Assessment in Edo State, Nigeria*. Edo State Ministry of Women Affairs and Social Development.

Gabel, S. G. (2014). Social protection and children's rights in developing countries. *Journal of International and Comparative Social Policy, 30*(3), 199–216. doi:10.1080/21699763.2014.921233

Ige, O. K., & Fawole, O. I. (2011). Preventing Child Sexual Abuse: Parents' Perceptions and Practices in Urban Nigeria. *Journal of Child Sexual Abuse, 20*(6), 695–707. doi:10.1080/10538712.2011.627584 PMID:22126111

Internews Europe. (2014). *Protecting the Rights of Children: The Role of the Media*. Author.

Isokpan, A. J., & Durojaye, E. (2016). Impact of the Boko Haram Insurgency on the Child's Right to Education in Nigeria. *Potchefstroom Electronic Law Journal*, 19.

Kathryn, C. D. (2009). *Human Trafficking*. Infobase Publishing.

Livingstone, S. (2016). Reframing media effects in terms of children's rights in the digital age. *Journal of Children and Media, 10*(1), 1, 4–12. doi:10.1080/17482798.2015.1123164

Morris, B., & Davies, M. M. (2018). Can children's privacy rights be adequately protected through press regulation? What press regulation can learn from the courts. *Journal of Medicine and Law, 10*(1), 92–113. doi:10.1080/17577632.2018.1467597

Nelson, O., Kehinde, O., Oyero, O., Wiliams, O. R., & Soola, E. O. (2013). Effective use of information sources for breast cancer care: Interplay of mass media and interpersonal channels. *Creating Global Competitive Economies: 2020 Vision Planning and Implementation - Proceedings of the 22nd International Business Information Management Association Conference, IBIMA 2013, 3*, 2231-2243.

Nmeregini, A. S. (2010). *Do African Children Have Rights?: A Comparative and Legal Analysis of the United Nations Convention on the Rights of the Child*. Universal-Publishers.

Nordtveit, B. H. (2010). Discourses of education, protection, and child labor: Case studies of Benin, Namibia and Swaziland. *Discourse (Abingdon), 31*(5), 699–712. doi:10.1080/01596306.2010.516954

Obiechina, G. O. (2014). Violation of Child's Rights in Nigeria: Implications for Child Health. *Social Science and Humanities, 5*(1), 151–159.

Ogunniran, I. (2017). Forward Looking or Backward Stepping: Evaluating Child Protection from Sexual Exploitation in Nigeria. *Journal of Human Trafficking, 3*(3), 167–181. doi:10.1080/23322705.2016.1146519

Olojo, A. E. (2017). Resistance through Islamic clerics against Boko Haram in northern Nigeria. *African Security Review, 26*(3), 308–324. doi:10.1080/10246029.2017.1294092

Oyero, O. (2010). Child rights and media democratization: An agenda for realization of the MDGs in Nigeria. *International Journal of Communication*, (11): 202–215.

Oyesomi, K. O., Soola, E., Abioye, T., & Oyero, O. (2014). Perception of women on the role of indigenous communication in politics: A study of Ado-Odo Ota, Ogun State, Nigeria. *Vision 2020: Sustainable Growth, Economic Development, and Global Competitiveness - Proceedings of the 23rd International Business Information Management Association Conference, IBIMA 2014, 1*, 2622-2644.

Raineri, L., & Martini, A. (2017). ISIS and AL-Qaeda as Strategies and Political Imaginaries in Africa: A Comparison between Boko Haram and Al-Qaeda in the Islamic Maghreb. *Civil Wars, 19*(4), 425–447. doi:10.1080/13698249.2017.1413226

Smith, R. (1991). Child Care: Welfare, protection or rights? *Journal of Social Welfare and Family Law, 13*(6), 469–481. doi:10.1080/09649069108413575

Tajudeen, O. I. (2015). Legal Framework for the Protection of Child Rights in Nigeria. *AGORA International Journal of Juridical Sciences, 1*(3), 46–52.

Tobin, J. (2005). Increasingly Seen and Heard: The Constitutional Recognition of Children's Rights. *South African Journal on Human Rights*, *21*(1), 86–126. doi:10.1080/19962126.2005.11865129

Toyo, N. (2006). Revisiting Equality as a Right: The Minimum Age of Marriage Clause in the Nigerian Child Rights Act, 2003. *Third World Quarterly*, *27*(7), 1299–1312. doi:10.1080/01436590600933677

UNHCR. (2012). *A Framework for the Protection of the Children*. Retrieved from www.globalcitizen.org www.statista.com www.unicefusa.org www.un.org

Chapter 14
Dilemma of Child Actors and the Nigerian Video Film Industry

Uduakobong Sunday
Lagos State University, Nigeria

Rotimi Williams Olatunji
Lagos State University, Nigeria

ABSTRACT

Demands on the actors include ability to interpret the writer's scripts, memorise the lines, and be at rehearsals anywhere, anytime, and anyhow; obvious dilemma is associated with the involvement of child actors. A child has the right to survival and development, education, leisure, amongst others, which are to be undertaken under the guidance, supervision, and care of parents. If a child actor has a dutiful parent or guardian, effectiveness may be attained in creating a balance between acting and other areas of needs; without a conscientious parent, where the child actor is overwhelmed by the acting environment, his education may suffer even as he can commit himself to the lifestyle of the make-believe world of acting. Drawing from two child actresses in Nigeria, this chapter exemplifies the dilemma of child actors and the challenge it poses to such child rights. It offers suggestions on how the effect of the dilemma could be resolved.

DOI: 10.4018/978-1-7998-0329-4.ch014

INTRODUCTION

There seems to be a consensus on the power of video film in this contemporary age (Adenugba, 2007, Alawode & Sunday, 2013, Giwa, 2014) & Ekwuazi, 1991); where the primary essence of the video film, like all other forms of media, is to provide enlightenment, education and information to the audience, while also entertaining them. These are done through employing characters in screen plays to represent real life persona in order to effectively convey required messages and situations convincingly. The characters would necessarily constitute all kinds of individuals who are representatives of the real world and societies which the situations and story lines subsist. These would include children, youths and all categories of older people as represented in every human society. While all categories of people are connected to video films as actors and actresses, the involvement of children in acting careers, particularly in very major roles which requires serious rehearsals and participation evokes streams of questions, considering their age and expected development levels with associated expectations. The implications can be overwhelming, if they are not effectively harnessed. One of the questions that can readily occur is the possibility of balancing the rights of the child actor with the demands of the acting as a professional.

Acting places high demand on the characters to be nothing but real in their portrayals. A child of school age is expected to concentrate on his or her education in order to learn as effectively as expected; as well as have lots of play and rest schedules to enhance proper development and growth. The child's involvement in acting places exceedingly great demand on him/her as he/she has to grapple with studying of scripts, research into roles, characters and situations as well as auditions and rehearsals. The film industry, being a make-believe world is associated with show business and fantasy, which can expose the child actor to situations that may have untoward implications on the child's growth and development as well as eventual lifestyle, if he or she is not properly guided. On the other hand, a child actor, who is well guided to function in such manner that is viewed as acceptable within the norms and values of the society may be deemed as a positive model, even as such can undoubtedly be known as a celebrity. While the acting profession enables the actor (of whatever age) to serve the society as one that interprets roles for effective communication, a disconnect between being a message carrier as a child actor and his/her rights, will make a mess of whatever message is being passed across by film producers in correcting the errors of the society. Definetly, it would be most unlikely for any film with good storylines which reveals happenings in the society to be produced without involvement of children. The video films cannot possibly be sustained without the involvement of children as performers because there would always be scenes of families, schools, and the like where children should be represented otherwise the storylines would not be realistic. This is why it is necessary to resolve the dilemma of child actors and its implication on the Rights of the Child as stipulated in the Child Right Acts of 2003.

This chapter which is primarily based on desk research discusses the dilemma of child actors and actresses in the light of some items in the Child Right Act of 2003. Towards ensuring effective understanding of the subject, the concept of children would be explained, followed by identification of Child Rights Acts of 2003. The chapter shall also establish the role of film as a communication medium before giving insight into the Nigerian film industry. Reflection of the person of an actor as well as the actor as a child would be clarified, before identifying relevant theory that guides the subject matter. This would lead to discussion on dilemma of child actors in Nigeria and probable suggestions to tackle the identified challenges.

UNDERSTANDING CHILDREN

Article 1 of United Nations Convention on the Rights of the child (UNCRC, UNICEF, 2011), defines a child as "a person under the age of 18 unless the laws of a particular country sets the legal age for adulthood younger" (UNICEF, 2007). Garba (2015, p. 12) citing Bellingham (2007), defines "a child is defined as a person, known as a minor from birth to legal age of maturity, for whom a parent and/or caretaker, foster parent, public or private home institution or agency is legally responsible." Olatunji and Akhagba (2013) classify children in biological, legal and economic terms. In biological term, children are persons age 12 years and below… or a preteen. Legally, a child refers to a minor, otherwise known as a person younger than the age of majority… and legally must always be under the care of a responsible adult (Olatunji & Akhagba 2013, p. 28).

This leads to economic categorisation that considers children as persons highly dependent on responsible elders for economic needs, along with physical protection and emotional support.

Kumuyi (2010) gives the stages of childhood development to include the following: infancy – 0 -2 years; early childhood (preschool years) (3 -8years); and late childhood (9 – 12years). These are the formative ages of life that are critical to what a person becomes later in life. The early childhood is considered as very important and distinct in childhood development. Associated noticeable characteristics are as follows: cognition, self-regulation, moral development, physical growth, personality development and gender socialization and emotional development.

In Piaget's (1969) theory of cognitive development, Olatunji and Akhagba identify four stages of cognitive development as Sensori-motor period (birth to 18-24 months); Preoperational period (2 -7 years); the Operational period (7-11years); and the Formal Operational Period (over 11years). They assert that the child's cognitive development is based on four kinds of operations being: assimilation, accommodation, conservation and reversibility. The first two being closely related, Piaget asserts that the child develops units of knowledge about the world called 'schemata'. As the child takes in new information about the environment, the information gets assimilated into his or her consciousness which would change the thinking and behaviour to reflect those new perceptions. In assimilation, the individual adapts the environment to his or her own purpose, although it may be limited by the ability to consolidate the new experiences with previous experience. Accommodation is the reverse of assimilation and occurs when the person modifies existing thought structures to enable him or her incorporate new experiences. Progressively, through all these stages, children develop a range of faculties relevant to distinguishing diverse kinds of media content and can recall and become aware of the media messages. They can understand persuasive intent of advertising; like and become sceptical of advertising; and can be defensive of media content, messages and position that they are persuaded about. Children of these ages who are involved in acting as professionals definitely need effective guidance and counselling in order to live a balanced life.

RIGHTS OF THE NIGERIAN CHILD

The Nigerian Child's Right Act 2003, categorically states that the child's best interest shall remain paramount in all consideration; and that a "child is to be given protection and care necessary for his well-being" (Part I, Child's Right Act 2003). Super User (NAIJALEGALTALK, 9 Nov 2016) states that the fundamental human right in Nigeria provided in Chapter 4 of the 1999 Constitution is one of the reasons that necessitated the passage of the Child Rights Act in 2003 by the National Assembly. The *Rights and Responsibilities* listed under Part II of the Child's Right Act 2003 include:

Rights of a Child

1. Application of Chapter IV of 1999 Constitution, etc.
2. Right to survival and development.
3. Right to name.
4. Freedom of association and peaceful assembly.
5. Freedom of thought, conscience and religion.
6. Right to private and family life.
7. Right to freedom of movement.
8. Right to freedom from discrimination.
9. Right to dignity of the child.

10. Right to leisure, recreation and cultural activities.
11. Right to health and health services.
12. Right to parental care, protection and maintenance.
13. Right of a child to free, compulsory and universal primary education, etc.
14. Right of a child in need of special protection measure.
15. Right of the unborn child to protection against harm, etc.
16. Contractual rights of a child.
17. Responsibilities of a child and parent.
18. Parent, etc. to provide guidance with respect to child's responsibilities.

The above listed *Rights and Responsibilities of a Child* are in addition to the two earlier mentioned in Part I under *"Best Interest of a Child to be of Paramount Consideration in all Actions"*. It is important to note that Part II provides the content of children's Rights and all the stipulations are subject to the guidance, supervision and care of the parents. Implicit therein is the fact that the child should ensure that he or she undertakes expected responsibilities while exercising his/her rights even as the parents must ensure that they provide care, guidance and supervision. These facts are very pertinent to any child under the age of 18 or under the custody of any parent or guardian who may be involved in acting for production of movie films. The nature of operations associated with film production further makes parental guidance and supervision undeniably necessary, yet the fact that child actors would often be exceedingly exposed to scenarios, settings, associations and actions without the physical presence of their parents could make it very difficult for their parents to exercise effective care and supervision on sight. What can thus sustain effectiveness in such situations would be consistent parental guidance and counselling which may also depend on the child to apply. The responsibility of the child to the exercise of the respective rights towards his or her well-being and the good of the society remains as necessity. Hence, this will identify some of the child actors in the Nigerian film industry to assess their effectiveness in acting in comparison with the exercise of identified r*ights and responsibilities of the child.*

FILM AS COMMUNICATION MEDIUM

Adenugba (2007) posits that film is a prolific source of entertainment which has worldwide acclamation, associated with its aesthetic appeal. It has been recognised as a popular genre because it does not only mirror and tell stories of societies which it represents; it also depicts the lifestyle, attitudes, environments and activities of audiences. This gives expression of the mirroring and influencing role of the film.

Citing Ekwuazi (1991, p.7), Idegu (2014) explains that compared to all other forms of entertainment media, the screen has only one language, which is the language of images. That is why in film, thought and image exists, yet the image is primary. In the screen, thought is extracted from the image, while image is extracted from the thought in literature. Films therefore tries to achieve making the audience to hear, see and feel. The total experience of audio – visual medium is based primarily on the image, and the ability to match vision to sound. Nnaemeka (2017) avers that films are powerful tools that use visual effects to communicate. They cover a wider audience even as they have extraordinary influence on the children which consequently causes them to imbibe the culture of the society and/or the thematic microcosm showcased in the films. The implication is that it affects the orientation that they have of their own culture or preconception before watching the films. On their part, Nkete and Ikiroma – Owiye (2014) state that the film industry in Nigeria has been receiving increasing public patronage which has given rise to significant growth and expansion in the industry. Their reason is largely because of the importance of film as a medium for socialization, in promoting national integration and advancement of civilization.

THE NIGERIAN VIDEO FILMS

Nigerian video films are products of the Nigerian film industry whose history has been researched and documented in several publications by scholars and professionals in media and related spheres. Professionals involved in the production of the video films include scriptwriters, producers, directors and actors and actresses, without whom the films would not come alive. Scriptwriters Guild of Nigeria, Actors Guild of Nigeria, Directors Guild of Nigeria, and Producers Guild of Nigeria are some of the professional groups involved in film production. The overall body that regulates the film industry in Nigeria is National Films and Videos Censors Board (NFVCB), a body that specifies how films should be packaged and produced for the benefit of the film audience. NFVCB determines rating and classification for the video films. Film makers are also expected to adhere to guidelines provided by the Nigerian Broadcasting Code (NBC, 2016) on issues relating to broadcasting and as applicable to children as well as The Nigerian Code of Advertising Practice generated by Advertising Practitioners Council of Nigeria (APCON).

Nigerian video films have promoted certain identities and images about the country's reputation (Akaso, 2009). Citing cases of video films which have shot up the socio-economic profile of the nation (especially during the era of notorious military coups and political instability), he infers that such films had portrayed Nigerians as innovative, creative and balanced in spite of the social upheaval in the country. It also negated the bad image which had been generated in the Western press about the nation. According to Akaso, Nigerian video films have helped to change the perspective of Nigeria and indeed Africa in the eye of the rest of the world. Through portrayals in Nigerian video films which have demonstrated that Africans are just like other human beings in other nations of the world; who could be honest, corrupt, bad, good, greedy, selfish, nice or wicked regardless of their nationalities and locations, people outside the continent have also consequently come to understand that Africans do not live on trees nor walk about naked (Alawode & Sunday (2013).

Nnaemeka (2017) surmises that the spate of kidnapping, armed robbery, bunkering, credit card scam, internet fraud, ritual killing, occultism, secret cults, incessant quest to travel abroad, Ponzi schemes (get –rich –quick syndrome) are undoubtedly indices of exposure to the movie films. The implication is that excessive and unrestricted exposure to video films often makes film audience to want to practice what they see in the films. Just as the viewer could be induced to learn what he views from the film medium, the child actor can indeed not be exempted from the influence of the medium as he or she may adopt the make-believe life, identified with him or her as a career as reality. The Biblical counsel – "Train up a child in the way he should go: when he is old, he will not depart from it" (Proverbs 22:6KJV) need not be taken lightly as far as issues concerning the child actor and child audience are concerned. Following the above and in relation to exercise of the *rights and responsibility of a child*, it is obvious that the responsibility of child development is primarily vested on parents or legal guardians as well as educators and coaches. In contemporary times and diverse settings, careers and disciplines, training of children spans beyond the jurisdiction of the parents and guardian. While trainings may also be obtained variously through exposure to diverse kinds of media which include video films and postings in social media, they can also be obtained through associations at job settings and otherwise. This is also where the child actor can also be positively or negatively influenced.

Reflection on The Actor, as a Professional

The author of collegegrad (n.d) asserts that the actor is one who expresses ideas and portrays characters in theatre, film, television and other performing art media. He interprets the writer's script to entertain or inform an audience. Actors work in various settings like production studios, theatres, theme parks and sometimes on location. Their work engagement can range from one day to a few months.

The actor is expected to read scripts and meet with agents and other professionals before accepting a role. He should necessarily undertake auditions in front of directors, producers and casting directors. He or she needs to research the character traits and circumstances of given role in order to portray the character more authentically to the audience. He needs to memorize the lines and rehearse same as well as perform on stage or in front of the camera with other actors. Actors must of necessity discuss their roles with the director, producer or other actors in order to enhance the overall performance of the film. His or her acting must be according to the director's cue.

Actors may sometimes perform in unpleasant conditions such as outdoors in bad weather, under hot stage lights or while wearing uncomfortable costume or make –up. Work hours for actors are often extreme and irregular; it can be early in the morning, evening, weekend or during the holiday. Film actors would usually travel to work on location.

Actors should be able to interpret their characters' feelings and motives so as to portray their characters in the most compelling way. Television actors could be asked to appear on camera with little notice to memorize even as the scripts can frequently be revised or even be written moments before filming.

Actors may audition many roles before getting a job. They must be able to accept rejection and keep going. They are expected to always be in good physical health condition in order to endure the heat from stage to studio lights and the weight of heavy costume or make – up. They may work over long hours, including acting in more than one performance in a day; and they must do so without getting overly stressed or exhausted.

They must read their scripts and be able to interpret how the writer had developed their characters. Actors, especially those who act on stage must say their lines clearly, projecting their voices and pronouncing words so that the audience would understand them. They must be physically coordinated to perform predetermined, sometimes complex movements with other actors. Such may include – dancing or stage fighting in order to complete a scene.

It can take many years of practice to develop the skills required to be a successful actor. Acting training does not totally finish; actors need to regularly work to improve their acting skills throughout their careers. Many actors continuously undertake their trainings through workshops, rehearsals or being mentored by drama coach. As an actor's reputation soars, he or she may have opportunity to work on bigger projects or more prestigious venues.

On his part, Omeh (n.d) revealing more attributes of the actor asserts that apart from the take –home earnings made by actors, the real money that comes to the acting profession accrue from product endorsements and contracts that top organisations get to sign actors up when the actor would have become popular. He asserts that acting career is associated with huge glamour and seemingly enjoyment which are identified with the entertainment industry all over the world. There are usually opportunities to attend the finest events in the country, travel to exciting places and get to meet great people in the society, amongst other kinds of excitement, which other people watch on the television. Many celebrities from the film industry are readily given political appointments in their States of origin and at national level, due to the popularity which they attain through their acting career. The basic qualification of an actor is being talented. Omeh surmises that money and fame is associated with acting, which is indeed pretending to be what a person is not and assuming different characters at different times and circumstances.

THE CHILD ACTOR

Attributes for an actor who is a child is not so much different from an adult actor. The major difference is that the child actor is a minor; and he is identified as 'child actor'. A 'child actor' or 'child actress' is thus a minor who acts or performs on stage, motion picture and/or television; whereas an adult who started acting as a child is also qualified as 'former child actor'(Educalingo, n.d). While actors at all levels and ages are caught up with diverse kinds of challenges, without doubt, the challenges of the child actor would be different from those of individuals that are already matured in age and are acting. This is why consideration is given to the child actor in this chapter, to identify their ability to cope with the acting profession while also adapting to all other expectations associated to being a child.

The actor as a child is seen in different light as are suggested by the contributions of different people who associate with them. The impacts and implications on them can be double –sided; positively and negatively. Writing as a coach who works with lots of kids and teens, who also started as a child actor, Hartt (2015), views that acting is good for a child if he or she has a good parent. It allows helps the parent to support his or her child's dream. She suggests that just like Boy's Scout, music, baseball, academics, acting is just another activity that children have doing. It builds confidence. It can be a way to get the child to overcome his or her shyness, to gain confidence.

It gives the child something that makes him feel special. Since everybody needs something that can make them feel special, kids and teens that are busy with something they love doing would be less inclined to hang out looking for something to do with their friends who can get them into trouble. It builds strong work ethics when the child actor is working on a film, they work long hard hours. It teaches them social skills as actors because children in acting profession work with different people of all ages and have huge variety of life experiences. It makes weird to mean something good. Children who love the arts are looked at as plain weird, "but acting is a world that celebrates weirdness and being different" (Hartt, 2015). It encourages the synergy of community. Theatre especially teaches the child actors the strength of working with others to create something together.

Pireyn (movie.stachexchangecom, n.d) reveals that children in acting careers are exposed to violent situations through the characters they are featured. Such could range from crude language to extreme horror that may include torture or gore situations. The author rhetorically enquiring if the directors would usually avoid exposing the children in acting career to such types of experiences goes further to also add if there are laws that require them to do so? He quickly launches into the need for the parents of children in acting profession to be made aware of what roles their children would be acting before the children are allowed to venture into such acting. His explanation brings to focus the need to recognise the disposition of the child actor: where the child is not comfortable with what he or she is exposed to do–such as rape or murder, the director under the law cannot allow the use of that particular child for such a role or scene.

The author submits that it is about safety too. If a child in acting career feels protected from any real hazard, then he or she can indeed be allowed to be involved in whatever role and settings that his or her character suggests. The child also needs to know that the scene is not real therefore psychological and mental considerations should not be disregarded when involving children in the acting profession. Where blood and stabbing, threatening with blades and knifes apply, depending on the age of the child, even as the child needs to know safe and proper handling of the knife, sharp knives should not be used. Consideration needs to be given to how the child can cope with the scene.

Issues relating to child acting and their well-being are multifaceted which cannot be exhausted in one chapter. However, while the child actor is the one undertaking the role of acting, as implied in the content of the *Rights and Responsibilities of the child* in the Child Rights Act 2003, the parents are also undeniably involved as they necessarily need to provide adequate care, guidance, counselling and supervision. Without that, the child actor's performances would be anything but good, even as such a child can never live a normal life. Considering this, Risinger (2017) notes that acting is business and does not wait for school concerts, trips, accidental black eyes and does not care much about the life of the child nor his or her family concern; if a child who is involved in acting is not ready to fit into whatever role the individual may have been assigned, another person can easily fill it up.

The child actor has automatically become an income earner at a very tender age. By this, he or she would begin to think like everyone else who is doing business. She further adds, there are all kinds of parents with children in acting profession who variously survive through the earnings of their children. This is a real dilemma and a typical case of role reversal. Whereas, the parent of a child is supposed to work hard to provide for the well being of their children, the children in this case become the workers to sustain their families.

While the child actor needs to succumb to all expectations due to his or her acting role, Risinger identifies that the child could be missing school too often and can be taken out of classes too many times. She nevertheless underscores the fact the teachers may not be very happy with the tendency or frequency of setting up independent study situations to enable the child adapt and adjust with the vicissitude associated with the acting business as negative impact on the child's educational development.

THEORETICAL PERSPECTIVES

The connection between the child who is an actor or actress in relation to exercising his rights and responsibilities can also be underpinned within the framework of Social Learning Theory. Social learning theory, which was propounded by Albert Bandura in 1977, reveals that behaviour is learnt from the environment through the process of observational learning. Through observing people, children begin to model learnt behaviours. This implies that children begin to pattern their lives after observed behaviour (McLeod, 2016) having been exposed to certain kinds of environment or characters. Considering that children watch different characters whom they admire in films and television, acting aggressive, sexual pervert, occult, corrupt, honest, dishonest, irresponsible and just any identifiable role or character, there is a tendency for them to learn all such roles especially from those whom they admire or model after. They would therefore be imitating both acceptable and unacceptable models. Children learn from models –actors/actresses whom they see, hear and read about. Since the models could be rewarded or disciplined (punished) for actions in films, media scholars have come to believe that the audience - children (and adults alike) get to change their behaviours based on the observations of the models. This is why Kofi Annan's (n.d) and Robert Fulghum's (n.d) quote become relevant. According to them:

To look into some aspects of the future, we do not need projections by supercomputers. Much of the next millennium can be seen in how we care for our children today. Tomorrow's world may be influenced by science and technology, but more than anything, it is already taking shape in the bodies and minds of our children. Kofi Annan (AZ Quotes n.d)

Do not worry that children never listen to you; worry that they are watching you Robert Fulghum (AZ Quotes n.d)

The above quotes reveal that children are consciously or unconsciously drawn to learn and imitate models. The child actor is more susceptible to being impacted by the environment of acting than the audience that could be influence externally. This is because the child who is acting is directly involved in observational learning even as he or she operates in participatory capacity, being one of the contributors to producing the films. The child actor must of necessity be available at rehearsals with other actors, observing all the processes. The child actors therefore stands exposed to both vices and virtues associated with their work environment. Learning from the acting environment as well as cultivation of corresponding lifestyles can become undeniably obvious as they can consciously or unconsciously adopt new values or vices that are different from their parental upbringing. Conscious efforts to have the child actors to understand their place as individuals who serve in an industry that mirrors the society not as those to fall prey of negative portrayals needs to be effectively entrenched. That way, the child actor can through his or her acting career take advantage of valuable opportunities offered through acting to learn and become a lot smarter and enterprising than his or her peer who is not privileged to have opportunity in acting.

DILEMMA OF CHILD ACTORS IN NIGERIA

Two fast rising child actors in Nigeria are adopted in this chapter to explain the dilemma faced by children in acting profession. They are Emmuanuella Samuel, a seven-year old comedienne of Mark Angel Comedy who started acting at the age of five; and Regina Daniels, a nineteen year old undergraduate of Igbenindion University who started acting in Nollywood at the age of seven. Both actresses are classified as ‘sensation’.

Emmanuella, born on 22nd July 2010, who ‘is naturally funny’, according to her family friend, manager and patron, Mark Angel ‘is already a celebrity minor’. Earlier this year (2019), she got adopted to act in a Hollywood movie by Walt Disney. It is a noble achievement for a Nigerian child of her age. During an interview with Mark Angel and Emmanuella (Omatayo, September 8, 2019), some of the issues that are pertinent to this chapter were raised and adequately addressed through the responses offered by the duo. In response, Mark Angel revealed that he has been ‘pushing up Emmanuella brand’; even though it started as a family business between him and Emmanuella, ‘it is no longer family business’ (www.youtube, March 2017). He intimated further said that he decided to use her as the main face of Mark Angel Comedy when he noticed that she was getting attention and the fact that there was a huge vacuum in the comedy industry because children did not have content to consume. Using Emmanuella therefore became a strategic move to reach the children. He explained that he always allowed her a lot of freedom to behave like the child she is; although they carefully tell her that she is a superstar. Her payment and remuneration are currently defined, even as that is handled by her manager, her parents are also involved. At every location, it is ensured that there is a teacher to aid her studies, so she does not fall short of expectation in her education.

According to Naij.com News (March 8, 2018 & February 2018), Regina Daniels, born on October 16, 2000 and currently described as a superstar who has captured the hearts of many in the Nigerian film industry within a short time, also has her mother, Rita Daniels, as an actress who recently was appointed as the Chairperson of the Delta State Actors Guild. Regina's first role provided her a clear vision that she was natural in acting. Her dedication to work distinguished her amongst the other young actors and helped her to achieve fantastic results at a very tender age. That first movie brought her popularity. She first started with an acting fee of ten thousand naira (N10, 000) and has grown to be receiving up to five hundred thousand naira (N500, 000) per movie appearance.

In 2017, Regina Daniels got admission into the Igbinedion University to study Mass Communication. Report has that she goes to school in SUV Lexus, yet she did not attend lectures throughout the first few months in school and was sanctioned by the university (Naijgists.com, November 9, 2017). Below are some comments from contributions from social media platform Naijgists.com News regarding the actions and attitude of this superstar child actor to her pursuit of university education:

She will pay her way to graduation, which is common among celebrities. (Salem Godi, November 9, 2017)

If this girl can crown her beauty with academics, the sky will be her limit. Beauty alone cannot get her up there if not the sugar daddies or play boys with sugar coated tongues will mess her up. Her parents better advise her well. (Uzoma, November 9, 2017)

Don't the tertiary institutions provide orientation session to new students with dos and don'ts expected of them by the school? ... The girl should try and comply because gaining admission is only the first step to positive success and to an end in itself. (Big Aunty Koks, November 10, 2-17)

Flaunting her riches on campus does it make good vibes? A young girl below 18 is already driving a big car on campus. A fresher indeed who needed to build GP (grade point) in school; big girl you have bad advisers. There is time for everything. Stop all vain glory and concentrate on your academics first. Fetch knowledge first before making any endeavours on life. (Obi Eugene Chukwuemeka, November 11, 2018)

Baby Girl, suspend all your celebrity and fame for now and humble down like a commoner in the name of succeeding in your academic career. Remember fame will prove it! Make the best use of your youthly time today and we'll forever be proud of you. (Oala Emma, November 12, 2017)

Following the excerpts from the articles cited above, which give reflection of Regina Daniels lifestyle outside the screen, it is clear that the circumstance with child actors in Nigeria can be understandably challenging. The individual can tend to consciously or unconsciously replicate and/or translate his or her character on the screen to real life situation. The glamorous life associated with the screen show can consciously and unconsciously be carried into the real world. Where the child actor has become exceedingly wealthy and sophisticated, it may be difficult for such an individual to lower his or her standard in a situation that may require little or no sophistication. It can thus be difficult for the child actor to give effective balance to his or her life outside the screen, while pursuing such other engagement as in an academic setting. The author of Medicalbag, April 22, 2014 asserts that while the fame and fortune that go along with being a celebrity may seem glamorous, it can be extremely tasking for the child who suddenly has to work full time hours on the business and to deal with pressure of maintaining an image in front of millions of fans. The effects can also be detrimental to health, particularly of a child who has been in the public view.

Suggestions from interview with Emmanuella's patron, Mark Angel (March 2017) reveal that in order for the little girl to be functionally in her acting career as well as give balance to her educational pursuits, she has to be subjected to make up classes. On the part of Regina Daniel, the information revealed by the audience (above) suggests her inability to be able to balance her celebrity status with her education. Indeed, it shows that she had already grown far above her level as a university student and cannot adjust to operate simply as other students of her age. This has further made it difficult for her to cope as a student hence she is said not to have been attending lectures. Flaunting riches and driving big cars on campus by an undergraduate whose age is within the range of 18 and 21 years should not be encouraged by the any right-thinking parent no matter how rich they are. An individual who is a student, particularly of undergraduate status, should subject him/herself to discipline that would enable him/her to concentrate on attainment of the benefit offered by university education. Flaunting wealth would not only serve as a distraction to the student who engage in such an exhibition, it can also serve as an allurement to other students on campus, who may be distraction and seek for both positive and negative means to identify with the sophisticated child actor on campus. Certain other persons in different capacities within the university environment can also be tempted to associate with him or her towards having the benefit of eating out of the rich student's wealth. Regina Daniels therefore failed to "fetch knowledge" (Obi Eugene Chukwuemeka, Naijgists.com, November 11, 2018) through university education either before or alongside the university education. Although she may be very wealthy and comfortable as a university student and at a very young age, if she subjects herself to learning, she would enjoy the best of both her acting career and university education, which should impact greatly to ensure sustenance of her fame, relevance and wealth.

The author of Medicalbag (April 22, 2014) also notes breakdown syndrome associated with child star to the fact that fame comes along with attention, which they suddenly lose as they grow. Child stars live in fantasy world where everything revolves around them, but as they reach puberty, the chances that it would remain in the business become slim. They are loved because they are young and cute, but as they grow, that becomes changed and they lose the adorable charm that had once captivated the world; they get quickly replaced and forgotten. As fame gets withdrawn from child stars so quickly, they may lack ability to handle the loss of attention so they fill the vacuum with drugs and alcohol. This is why effective guidance from counsellors and parental guidance are necessity to sustain a child actor (actress) as an enviable model to people who look up to them. Referring to the comment of a psychologist, who is also an Associate Professor of Clinical Education at the University of South California, the author of Medicalbag (April 22, 2014) asserts thus "if the parents are able to keep every other aspect of the child's life controlled and normal and there are continued boundaries and rules, those are kids can do well." He further added thus: "If you don't have a really stable parental unit that is setting limits ahead of time, then the roles get flipped easily and the child becomes the parent" (Medicalbag, April 22, 2014).

The above has been effectively demonstrated in this life of Regina Daniels as she is already married at the age of nineteen (19). Whether she is continuing with her education or not, and to what extent that may be cannot be effectively explained. This is because most newspaper reports suggest that she is busy spending her time on very exotic lifestyle with her husband without much mention made of her education (*Vanguard* online, June 5, 2019, *Premium Times*, August 2, 2019)

The influence of Mark Angel, having been a family friend to the much celebrated comedienne, little Emmanuella, and now relating with as her patron and guardian can be acknowledged as a progressive and profitable association. At her very tender age, she is already making impact, travelling and acting all over the world. Omatayo (September 8, 2019) writes about her having "broken another ground internationally" in a new Australian movie titled *Survive or Die*. The movie is said to have been filmed in 2016 and released in 2018. It was co-directed by Daniel Okoduwa and Mike Kang and also co-written by them. Although Mark Angel is not mentioned as an actor in the movie, the report reveals that she made her trip to Australia with Mark Angel.

That came after Emmanuella made a debut in Hollywood earlier. Akwei (February 19, 2018) reports that "she has performed at comedy events in West Africa and East Africa while her YouTube skits and page have gained more than a million views and subscribers respectively". Referring to news from *The Guardian* (n.d), Akwei adds that "she is the first African to have one million subscribers on her YouTube comedy channel." He further adds that her breakthrough into Hollywood was welcomed by a Nigeria former Senate President, Bukola Saraki who had described her as an inspiration, and had invited her to the Senate to discuss the development of the potential of young talents in the creative industry.

Just as Social learning theory has alluded to the effects of film content on its audience (and indeed – the children), research findings on the effects and implications of film content are not scarce. Most of the reactions to Regina Daniels conduct within the university environment have given support to the fallout of influence of the glamour associated with film acting and lack (or inadequacy) of effective parental control and counselling, which further suggests the need not to be silent, to be cautious and to operate within regulations as well as to involve parental guidance and control.

In an interview with Ademola Olonilua of *The Punch* Newspaper, it was reported in naijaloaded.com (August 13, 2016), that little Emmanuella demystifies the fact of being a celebrity. She reveals that she still lives a normal life, plays with her mates in her neighbour and wears the kinds of clothes other children around her wear as well as things children of her age do. She repeatedly asserts in her responses that she is still a kid. She explains that coping with fame through acting does not affect her schooling so much because she starts shooting during the holidays for the next season before school resumes. It is only when there are emergencies that she can be permitted to shoot during school session and such shootings are usually done on Fridays.

She expresses delight that her uncle (Mark Angel) is not treating her like an adult, but as a child that she is because if that had been the case, things can go wrong because she cannot become an adult overnight. By the nature of her life as an actress, she is not usually at home most weekends because there are often several events that she should attend; when she is at home she lives a normal life.

She clarifies that she does not go to anywhere without an adult, particularly her uncle; she only attends events that are child-friendly. She would not attend any events that children are not supposed to attend neither would she "go to places that they do bad things". Her uncle usually ensures that organisers of events that she needs to perform at night would call her on stage early to ensure that she would return home early to sleep. She recalls an occasion when they had gone for an event and she slept off. By that singular act, there was no show because she didn't wake. She sleeps a lot during the day, particularly when there is an event because like she says, she is still a child and needs to rest at night.

Emmanuella explains that when they first started, her parents were not comfortable with the idea of her acting, but her uncle has several meetings with them and explained everything to them. He also assured them that her acting would not affect her schooling and that she would live like every child. Responding to attribution by some people who say that she does not behave like a star, she declares that they did not start the projects which she undertakes with her Uncle Mark angel for her to become a star, rather it was intended to satisfy the need to have a voice.

Little Emmanuella's responses provide adequate solution to resolving some of the dilemma surrounding the child who is involved in the limelight of acting as a business as well as the conflict that the profession can place of the exercise of his or her rights and responsibilities. While the child could have attained the status whose life is predominantly occupied with acting and entertainment, it is important to recognise that the child actor is a child in the first instance and still have a future that cannot be predicted ahead. Such an individual should be encouraged and guided to live a life in the manner that fits his or her age, while still protecting his or her status as a celebrity. That way, he or she can without fail adequately fit into any situation that is required of him or her at any particular time without feeling unfitted.

CONCLUSION AND RECOMMENDATIONS

Whilst the child actor generates income as remuneration from their vocation, the nature of films they act can also build or destroy their lives even as they would define the kinds of association they keep. The necessity to ensure that the child actor lives a normal and balance life deserving for the person of his or her age should be ascertained. By implication, the child needs to be in school at the time; he or she needs to play as expected as well as observe adequate rest and sleep during the day and at night. Acting should not rob the child of his or her rights in order that such an individual would grow and develop well.

The child actors can be saved from the corrupt and wild lifestyle identified with the film industry by strictly adhering to set standards of the society, which abhor immorality, corruption and indecency. There should be stipulations to attach a child actor to a supervisor even as it should insist that the parents provide parental guidance. A child actor should understand that life is transient and without a solid educational and moral foundation, the euphoria associated with stardom at an early age may not last forever. Such a person would thus ensure that he/she conducts himself/herself as a child and in conformity with acceptable norms of the environment and situation he/she is identified with.

Much of positive parental guidance is critical towards addressing associated challenges in the sphere of child actors and the film industry. Child acting should be to the advantage of the actor or actress who would have identified his/her career path early enough and strive to harness same for future sustainable gain. Accordingly, the benefits should not be turned to destruction. Such opportunities, if well-harnessed should cause the child actor to serve as a model and remain a positive influence to his/her peers and future generation. Parents/guardians, counsellors and educators are thus encouraged to allow their children and wards to venture into acting under informed guidance for mutual benefit of child actors and the society at large.

REFERENCES

Actor, Jobs, Career, Salary and Education. (n.d.). Retrieved from http://www.collegegrad.com

Actress Regina Daniels Shares First Official Photos with billionaire husband. (2019, Aug. 2). *Premium Times*.

Adenugba, O. O. (2007). *Motion Picture and the Nigerian image*. Retrieved from filminnaija.blogspot.com

Akaso, H. (2009). *Is Nollywood giving Nigeria a bad name?* Retrieved from http://www.ModernGhana.com

Akwei, I. (2018). *7-year –old Nigerian comedy star Emmanuella to debut in Hollywood*. Retrieved from www.face2faceafrica.com

Alawode, S. O., & Sunday, U. (2013). Home Video as Nigerian Image Maker. *European Scientific Journal*, *9*(11).

Bandura, A. (1977). *Social Learning Theory*. Englewood Cliffs, NJ: Prentice Hall.

Bellingham, J. (2007). *Academic's dictionary of education*. Academic Publishers.

Child Actor. (n.d.). Retrieved from www. Educalingo.com

Child Employment. (n.d.). Retrieved from http://www.gov.uk/employment

Child Labor Laws in Texas. (2018). Texas Film Commission/Texas Workforce Commission.

Ekwuazi, H. (1991). The Communicative import of film in National Development. In S. Unoh (Ed.), Topical Issues in Communication Arts. Uyo: Modern Business Press.

Garba, V. (2015). *Influence of Home Television Viewing on Academic Achievement of Children in Upper Basic Education in Kaduna State* (Master's thesis). University of Nigeria, Department of Vocational Education.

Giwa, E. T. (2014). *Nollywood: A Case Study of Rising Nigerian Film Industry - Content & Production* (Master's thesis). South Illinois University, Department of Mass Communication and Media Arts.

Hartt, C. (2015). *14 ways Acting is beneficial for kids and teens.* Retrieved from www.backstage.com

"I started acting after I gave Uncle Mark Angel an apple" – Kid Comedian Emmanuella grants her first interview. (2016). *Kemi Filani News*. Retrieved from www. Femikilani.ng

Idegu, E. U. (2014). Which change, which change? Glamourising social misfits in selected Nigerian home movies. *International Journal of English and Literature, 5*(8), 174-181.

Interview with Hilarious Emmanuella, the Comedian and Mark Angel. (2017). Retrieved from www.youtube.com

Kumuyi, A. (2010). *Christian women mirror.* Lagos: Life Press.

Mcleod, S. A. (2016, February 3). Bandura – Social learning Theory. *Simply Psychology*. Retrieved from http://www.simplypsychology.org/bandura.html

Nbete, A. D. & Ikiroma, O. (2014). Film and Cultural Imperialism in Nigeria: A Critical Developmental Perspective. *The Crab: The Journal of Theatre & Media Arts, 9*, 123-138.

Nnaemeka, F. O. (2017). COOU Undergraduates perspective portrayals in Nollywood movies. *COOU Journal of Multidisciplinary Studies, 1*(1).

"No matter the fame, I'm still a kid" – Emmuanuella. (2016). Retrieved from www. naijaloaded.com.ng

Olatunji, R. W., & Akhagba, O. (2013). Children and advertising literacy: A Study of Selected Schools in Lagos, Nigeria. *Global Advanced Research Journal of Social Science, 2*(6), 134–142.

Omatayo, J. (2019). *Popular star kid Emmanuella plays role in Australia movie Survive and Die*. Retrieved from http://www.Legit.com

Omeh, D. (n.d.). *How to become a Nigerian Nollywood actress or actor*. Retrieved from www.wealthresult.com

Pireyn, L. (n.d.). *To what extent are child actors exposed to the violent aspects of the movie they perform?* Retrieved from http://www.movie.stachexchange.com

Regina Daniels breaks silence after marriage to Ned Nwoko. (2019). Retrieved from www.vanguardngr.com

Regina Daniels' Network and Life story. (2018). Retrieved from http://www.Naij.com

Regina Daniels reportedly sanctioned by Igbinedion university for not attending lectures in a month. (2017). Retrieved from http://www.Naijagists.com

Risinger, H. (2017). *10 Things to know about raising a child actor.* Retrieved from www.huffpost.com

The Convention on the Rights of the Child. Guiding principles requirements for all rights. (n.d.). UNICEF.

The life of a Child Star: Why Some go crazy and others don't. (2014). Retrieved from www.medibag.com/paeditrics/the-life-of-a-child-star-why-some-go-crazy-and- others-don't/article/472544/

The Nigerian Child Rights Act 2003.

Top 20 facts about young Nollywood Actress Regina Daniels. (2017). *Hot Vibes Media.* Retrieved from smedia.com.ng/2017/06/top-20-facts-about-young-nollywood-actress-regina-daniels-.html?m=1/

Top facts from Regina Daniels Personal Life. (2018). Retrieved from http://www.Naij.com

UNICEF. (2011). *Nigeria – Fact Sheet: Child Right Legislation in Nigeria.* UNICEF.

User, S. (2016). *Child Rights in Nigeria.* Retrieved from www.naijalegaltalkng.com

KEY TERMS AND DEFINITIONS

Audience: Consumer or beneficiary of media content who views or listens to media contribution.

Child: A boy or girl whose age is not up to eighteen years.

Film: An audio-visual recorded medium of communication which consists of moving pictures, to provide entertainment, information, and/or education to its audience.

Model: Emulate, copying to be like another person or an individual whom another person copies or aspire to be like.

Nollywood: Identity of Nigerian (video) film industry.

Superstar: An actor or performer who has exceptionally exceeded his or her peers in the media industry in performance.

Talent: Actor/actress, performer, or star (who is involved in the film production).

Compilation of References

"I started acting after I gave Uncle Mark Angel an apple" – Kid Comedian Emmanuella grants her first interview. (2016). *Kemi Filani News*. Retrieved from www. Femikilani.ng

"No matter the fame, I'm still a kid" – Emmuanuella. (2016). Retrieved from www.naijaloaded.com.ng

Abah, S. O., & Ohimain, E. I. (2011). Healthcare waste management in Nigeria: A case study. *Journal of Public Health and Epidemiology*, *3*(3), 99–110.

Abdulrasheed, O., Onuselogu, A., & Obioma, U. G. (2015). Effect of insurgency on Universal Basic Education in Borno State of Nigeria. *American Journal of Educational Research*, *3*(4), 490–494.

Abideen, Z., & Salaria, M. (2009, December 4). *Effects of television advertising on children: with special reference to Paskitani Urban Children*. Available at https://mpra.ub.uni muenchen.de/22321

Abioye, T., Oyesomi, K., Ajiboye, E., Omidiora, S. & Oyero, O. (2017). *Impacts of the media on African socio-economic development*. Academic Press. doi:10.4018/978-1-5225-1859-4

Aboyi, A. E. (2014). Mass literacy and the attainment of sustainable democracy in African: The Nigeria Senario. *The 2014 WEI International Academic Conference Proceedings*.

Actor, Jobs, Career, Salary and Education. (n.d.). Retrieved from http://www.collegegrad.com

Actress Regina Daniels Shares First Official Photos with billionaire husband. (2019, Aug. 2). *Premium Times*.

Adamu-Issah, M., Elden, L., Forson, M., & Schrofer, T. (2007). *Achieving universal primary education in Ghana by 2015: A reality or a dream?* New York: UNICEF.

Adcock, A. (2016). Effect of social media on the mental health of young people. *Debate Pack*, Number CDP 2016-0196, 1 November, House of Common, Library.

Adedokun, N. (2013). Has Nigeria really made any progress? *The Punch*. Retrieved February 24, 2014 from http://www.punchng.com/opinion/has-nigeria-reallymade-any-progress/

Ademokun, F. (2002, Nov. 14). Children and the Lawmakers. *The Guardian*.

Adeniran, R., Hassan, S., Ajaga, M., & Kayode, J. (2015). *Representation of children in Nigeria News Media on ResearchGate.net*. Retrieved from https://www.researchgate.net/publication/316794864_Representation_of_children_in_Nigerian_News_Media

Adeniran, R., Suleiman, H., Ajaga, M., & Kayode, J. (2015). Representation of Children in the Nigerian News Media. *The Nigerian Journal of Communication*, *12*(1), 160–183. Retrieved from https://www.researchgate.net/.../316794864_Representation_of_children_in_Nigerian_N

Adenugba, O. O. (2007). *Motion Picture and the Nigerian image*. Retrieved from filminnaija.blogspot.com

Adepegba, A. (2019, May 3). 43% of Nigerian Children engaged in Child Labour-ILO. *The Punch*. Retrieved from https://punchng.com/43-of-nigerian-children-engaged-in-child-labour-ilo/

Adesina, O. S. (2014). Modern day slavery: Poverty and child trafficking in Nigeria. *African Identities*, *12*(2), 165–179. doi:10.1080/14725843.2014.881278

Adler, P. S. (2006). Technological Determinism. In S. Clegg & J. R. Bailey (Eds.), *The International Encyclopedia of Organization Studies*. Thousand Oaks, CA: Sage Publishing.

Advocacy Institute. (2001). *What is 'advocacy'?* Retrieved on October 2, 2008 from http://www.advocacy.org/definition.htm

Afolayan, A. (1984). The Six-Year Primary Project in Nigeria. In A. Bamgbose (Ed.), Mother Tongue Education. The West African Experience, (pp. 113-134). London: Hodder and Stoughton.

African Child Policy Forum. (2015). *Implementing child rights in Tanzania: What is working well, what is not? Background paper to the African report on child well being*. Addis Ababa, Ethiopia: ACPF.

African Develeopment Bank. (2018). African. *Economic Outlook, 2018*. Retrieved from https://www.afdb.org/fileadmin/uploads/afdb/Documents/Publications/African_Economic_Outlook_2018_-_EN.pdf

African Union Commission. (2015) Concept note on the DAC 2015. Addis Ababa, Ethiopia: The African Committee of Experts on the Rights and Welfare of the Child (ACERWC).

Agaba, P. A., Thacher, T. D., Angyo, I. A., & Agaba, E. I. (2003). Peak expiratory flow rates in healthy Nigerian children. *Journal of Tropical Pediatrics*, *49*(3), 157–159. doi:10.1093/tropej/49.3.157 PMID:12848205

Agba, G., Otuchikere, C., & Odemwingie, E. (2013). *Nigeria: Boko Haram attack on Yobe school, "You'll burn in hell, Jonathan tells sect."* Retrieved from http://allafrica.com/stories/201307080649.html

Agbiboa, E. (2013). No retreat, no surrender: Understanding the religious terrorism of Boko Haram in Nigeria. *African Study Monographs*, *34*(2), 65–84.

Agbo, C. M. (2017). The health and educational consequences of child labour in Nigeria. *Health Science Journal, 11*(1). Retrieved from http://www.hsj.gr/medicine/the-health-and-educational-consequences-of-child-labour-in-nigeria.php?aid=18408

Ahiuma-Young, V. (2012). Stakeholders re-strategize to combat human trafficking and child labour. *The Vanguard Newspaper*. Retrieved from https:// vanguardngr.com/Stakeholders-re-strategize-to-combat-human-trafficking-and-child-labour

Ajaegbu, O. O., Alao, S. E., & Oloyede, D. B. (2018). Press Coverage of Child Labour Issues in Nigeria (2010-2014). *International Review of Social Sciences*, *6*(12), 618–632. www.irss.academyirmbr.com

Ajayi, A. (2015). *Boko Haram: Nigerian Human Rights Commission laments number of out-of-school children.* Retrieved from http://www.premiumtimesng.com/regional/nnorth-east/194074-boko-haram-nigeria-human rights-commission-laments-number-of-out-of-school-children. html

Ajayi, L. A., Fayomi, O. O., Abasilim, U. D., & Adepoju, O. (2015). Girl-Child Education and Nigeria's National Development: A Study of selected Private and Public Secondary Schools in Ado-Odo Ota Local Government Area, Ogun State. *8th International Conference of Education, Research and Innovation (ICERI2015) held in Seville, Spain, 16th-18th November, 2015. Conference Proceedings*, 4819-4831.

Ajayi, I. A. (2007). Achieving Universal Basic Education (UBE) in Nigeria: Strategies for improved funding and cost-Effectiveness. *Social Sciences*, *2*, 342–345.

Ajayi, L. A., & Soyinka-Airewele, P. (2018). Key Triggers of domestic violence in Ghana: A victim centered analysis. *African Population Studies*, *32*(1), 4097–4108.

Akaso, H. (2009). *Is Nollywood giving Nigeria a bad name?* Retrieved from http://www.ModernGhana.com

Akinbote, O., Osuji, U., & Salawu, I. (2006). *Origin and development of early childhood and education.* Lagos: National Open University of Nigeria.

Akinbote, O., Osuji, U., & Salawu, I. (2014). *Origin and development of early childhood (Course Module).* Lagos: National Open University of Nigeria.

Akinnaso, F. (1993). Policy and Experiment in Mother Tongue Literacy in Nigeria. *International Review of Education / Internationale Zeitschrift Für Erziehungswissenschaft / Revue Internationale De L'Education, 39*(4), 255-285. Retrieved from http://www.jstor.org/stable/3445126

Akinrotimi, A. A., & Olowe, P. K. (2016). Challenges in implementation of early childhood education in nigeria : The way forward. *Journal of Education and Practice*, *7*(7), 33–38.

Akwei, I. (2018). *7-year–old Nigerian comedy star Emmanuella to debut in Hollywood.* Retrieved from www.face2faceafrica.com

Al Odhayani, A., & Ratnapalan, S. (2011). Teaching communication skills. *Canadian Family Physician Medecin de Famille Canadien, 57*(10), 1216–1218. Retrieved from http://www.ncbi.nlm.nih.gov/pubmed/21626902%0Ahttp://www.pubmedcentral.nih.gov/articlerender.fcgi?artid=PMC3076489 PMID:21998240

Alakwe, K., & Ogbu, S. (2018). Communication and the Shaping of Human Personality; Deconstructing the Nature/Nurture Debate in Light of the Menace of Street Children in Nigeria. *Advanced Journal of Social Science*, 23-33.

Alakwe, K., & Ogbu, S. U. (2017). *Media and Society: Deconstructing the Role of the Media in Fostering Social Cohesion in Contemporary Nigerian Society*. Research on Humanities and Social Sciences.

Alasuutari, M., & Karila, K. (2009). Framing the picture of the child. *Children & Society, 24*(2), 100–111. doi:10.1111/j.1099-0860.2008.00209.x

Alawode, S. O., & Sunday, U. (2013). Home Video as Nigerian Image Maker. *European Scientific Journal, 9*(11).

Alder, C., & Polk, K. (2001). *Child victims of homicide*. Cambridge.

Allwell, O. N., & Ogbu, S. U. (2018). Mediatization of Life: Exploring the influence of the mobile and other media in Nigeria. *Observatorio (OBS*)*, 72-84.

Al-Shail, E., Hassan, A., Aldowaish, A., & Kattan, H. (2012). *The cultural reinforcers of child abuse*. Retrieved from http://cdnintechopen.compdfs-wm/37763.pdf.

Altheide, D. (2002). *Creating fear: News and the construction of crisis*. New York: Aldine de Gruyter.

Altheide, D. L., & Schneider, C. J. (2013). *Qualitative media analysis* (2nd ed.). Thousand Oaks, CA: SAGE Publications. doi:10.4135/9781452270043

Aluko, O. (2018). *Agency to train 60 education planners for IDP camps*. Retrieved from https://punchng.com/agency-to-train-60-education-planners-for-idp-camps/

Amadioha, S. (2018). Challenges of early childhood education in Nigeria: implication for assessment of early childhood curriculum implementation in Port Harcourt, Rivers State. *Australian Journal of Arts and Scientific Research, 22*, 125–129.

Amalu, C. (2010, June 29). Nigerian child and the Child Rights Act. *The Vanguard*. Retrieved from http://www.vanguardngr.com/2010/06/nigerian-child-and-the-child-rights-act/

Amante, L. (2016). Childhood, digital culture and parental mediation. In The Digital Literacy and Multimodal Practices of Young Children: Engaging with Emergent Research (pp. 205-212). Braga: Centro de Investigação em Educação (CIEd).

Amdi, V. (1990). The cause of child abuse and neglect and their effects on the development of children in Samaru Zaria, Nigeria. *Early Child Development and Care*, *58*(1), 31–43. doi:10.1080/0300443900580105

Amineh, R. J., & Davatgari, H. A. (2015). Review of Constructivism and Social Constructivism. *Journal of Social Sciences. Literature and Languages*, *1*(1), 9–16.

Amolloh, O. P., Lilian, G. K., & Shaji, M. G. (2017). *Adopting Digital Technology in Teaching and Learning Environment in Early Childhood Education Classes in Nairobi County*. Asian Education Studies.

Amoo, E. O., Igbinoba, A., Imhonopi, D., Banjo, O. O., Ajaero, C. K., Akinyemi, J. O., … Solanke, L. B. (2018). Trends, Determinants and Health Risks of Adolescent Fatherhood in Sub-Saharan Africa. *Ethiopian Journal of Health Sciences, 28*(4). Retrieved from https://www.ajol.info/index.php/ejhs/article/view/175550

Amoo, E. O., Ola-David, O., Olurinola, I. O., & Fadayomi, T. (2012). Street trading activities and maternal health in urban areas of Nigeria. *Global Journal of Human Social Sciences, 12*, 46–55.

Amoo. (2018). Introduction to Special Edition on Covenant University's Perspectives on Nigeria Demography and Achievement of SDGs-2030. *African Population Studies, 32*(1). doi:10.11564/32-1-1170

Amoo, E. O., Ola-David, O., Olurinola, I. O., & Fadayomi, T. O. (2016). Female Youth in Street Trading: Implications for Sexual Harassment in HIV/AIDS Risky Environment. *Journal of South African Business Research, 2016*, 1–12. doi:10.5171/2016.975495

Amoo, E. O., Omideyi, A., Fadayomi, T., Ajayi, M., Oni, G., & Idowu, A. (2017). Male reproductive health challenges: Appraisal of wives coping strategies. *Reproductive Health, 14*(1), 90. doi:10.118612978-017-0341-2 PMID:28754166

Anderson, C. A. (2003). An update on the effects of violent video games. *Journal of Adolescence*, *27*(3), 113–122. PMID:15013264

Angle, S., Baerthlein, T., Daftari, N., Rambaud, B., & Roshani, N. (2014a). Protecting the Rights of Children: The Role of the Media–Lessons from Brazil, India and Kenya (Internews Europe). *Interviews Europe*. Retrieved from https://www.internews.org/sites/default/files/resources/InternewsEurope_ChildRightsMedia_Report_2014.pdf

Angle, S., Baerthlein, T., Daftari, N., Rambaud, B., & Roshani, N. (2014b). *Protecting the Rights of Children: The Role of the Media–Lessons from Brazil, India and Kenya*. Internews Europe.

Anho, E. J., & Christopher, C. (2016). Mass Media Coverage of Children's Rights in Nigeria. *Multidisciplinary Journal of Research Development*, *25*(1), 1–9.

Anju, M. (2011). Solutions to end child marriage: what the evidence shows. International Center for Research on Women, 11.

Ansell, N. (2005). *Children, youth and development*. London: Routledge.

Ardèvol-Abreu, A. (2015). Framing theory in communication research in Spain. Origins, development and current situation. *Revista Latina de Comunicación Social*, *70*, 423-450.

Arnaldo, C. A. (2001). Introduction. In *Child Abuse on the Internet: Ending the Silence*. New York: UNESCO.

Arnett, J. J. (2007). *Encyclopedia ofchildren, adolescents, and the media*. Thousand Oaks, CA: Sage Publications. doi:10.4135/9781412952606

Arthur, J. B. (2012). *Framing child neglect: A content analysis of national and regional U.S. newspaper coverage* (Unpublished Master's Thesis). A Capstone Project Presented to the Faculty of the School of Communication.

Asare-Donkoh, F. (2017). Children in the media: How much space do they get in Ghanaian newspapers? *Journal of Children and Media*, *11*(4), 417–435. doi:10.1080/17482798.2017.1348370

Attoh, N. R. (2016, August 8). *The Child's Rights and Responsibility Law just passed in Enugu state*. Retrieved from https://www.educationalresourceproviders.com/child-abuse-and-the-childs-rights-and-responsibility-law-just-passed-into-law-in-enugu-state/

Atuma, U. (2018). Day stakeholders converged in Osun against human trafficking, child labour. *The Sun Newspaper*. Retrieved from https://sunnewsonline.com/Day-stakeholders-converged-in-Osun-against-human-trafficking-childlabour

Awosola, R. K., & Omoera, O. S. (2008). Child Rights and the Media: The Nigerian Experience. *Communication Science*, *2*(2), 1255-131. Retrieved from http://www.krepublishers.com/02-Journals/S-HCS/HCS-02-0-000-08-Web/HCS-02-2-087-08-Abst-Text/HCS-02-2-125-08-047-Awosola-R-K/HCS-02-2-125-08-047-Awosola-R-K-Tt.pdf

Awosola, R. K., & Omoera, O. S. (2008). Child Rights and the Media: The Nigerian Experience. *Studies on Home and Community Science*, *2*(2), 125-131. Retrieved from www.krepublishers.com/...Awosola.../HCS-02-2-125-08-047-Awosola-R-K-Tt.pdf

Awosola, K., & Omoera, O. (2008). Child Rights and the Media: The Nigerian Experience. *Study Home Communication Science*, *2*(2), 125–131. doi:10.1080/09737189.2008.11885263

Bakken, L., Brown, N., & Downing, B. (2017). Early childhood education: The long term benefits. *Journal of Research in Childhood Education*, *31*(2), 255–269. doi:10.1080/02568543.2016.1273285

Bandura, A. (1977). *Social Learning Theory*. Englewood Cliffs, NJ: Prentice Hall.

Bappah, H. Y. (2016). Nigeria's military failure against the Boko Haram insurgency. *African Security Review*, *25*(2), 146–158. doi:10.1080/10246029.2016.1151799

Baran, S. J., & Davis, D. K. (2003). *Mass communication theory: Foundations, ferment and future*. Belmont: Thomas-Wardworth.

Baran, S. J., & Davis, D. K. (2003). *Mass Communication Theory: Foundations, Ferment, and Feature*. Belmont: Thomson-Wardsworth.

Barber, K. (2009). Orality, the media and new popular cultures in Africa. In K. Njogu & J. Middleton (Eds.), *Media and Identity in Africa* (pp. 3–18). Edinburgh, UK: Edinburgh University Press/International African Institute. doi:10.3366/edinburgh/9780748635221.003.0001

Batson, D., Lishner, D., Cook, J., & Sawyer, S. (2005). Similarity and nurturance: Two possible sources of empathy for strangers. *Basic and Applied Social Psychology*, *27*(1), 15–25. doi:10.120715324834basp2701_2

Becker-Blease, K. A., Finkelhor, D., & Turner, H. (2008). Media Exposure Predicts Children's Reactions to Crime and Terrorism. *Journal of Trauma & Dissociation*, *9*(2), 225–248. doi:10.1080/15299730802048652 PMID:19042776

Beers, H., Invernizzi, A., & Milne, B. (2006). *Beyond Article 12: Essential Readings in Children's Participation*. Black on White Publications.

Bellingham, J. (2007). *Academic's dictionary of education*. Academic Publishers.

Bénit-Gbaffou, C. (2018). Beyond the Policy-Implementation Gap: How the City of Johannesburg Manufactured the Ungovernability of Street Trading. *The Journal of Development Studies*, *54*(12), 2149–2167. doi:10.1080/00220388.2018.1460468

Bento, M., Lencastre, J. A., & Pereira, Í. (2016). The use of mobile devices in the development of reading comprehension skills. In The Digital Literacy and Multimodal Practices of Young Children: Engaging with Emergent Research (pp. 24-35). Braga: Centro de Investigação em Educação (CIEd).

Bernardi, F., & Radl, J. (2014). *The long-term consequences of parental divorce for children's educational attainment*. Vol. 30. *Article*, *61*, 1653–1680.

Berry, D. (2013). *Ethics and Media Culture: Practices and Representations*. Oxford, UK: Focal Press. doi:10.4324/9780080573809

Bhati, A., & Eikenberry, A. (2016). Faces of the needy: The portrayal of destitute children in the fundraising campaigns of NGOs in India. *International Journal of Nonprofit and Voluntary Sector MarketingInt*, *21*(1), 31–42. doi:10.1002/nvsm.1542

Bioulac, S., Arfi, L., & Bouvard, M. P. (2008). Attention deficitlhyperactivity disorder and video games: A comparative study of hyperactive and control children. *European Psychiatry*, *23*(2), 134–141. doi:10.1016/j.eurpsy.2007.11.002 PMID:18206354

Bissell, K. (2000b). Culture and Gender as Factors in Photojournalism Gatekeeping. *Visual Communication Quarterly*, *7*(2), 9–12. doi:10.1080/15551390009363429

Bissell, K. L. (2000a). A return to "Mr. Gates": Photography and objectivity. *Newspaper Research Journal*, *21*(3), 81–93. doi:10.1177/073953290002100307

Blackwell, C., Lauricella, A., Carway, A., & Wartella, E. (2014). Children and the internet: Developmental implications of websites preferences among 8 to 12 years children. *Journal of Broadcasting & Electronic Media*, *58*(1), 1–20. doi:10.1080/08838151.2013.875022

Bossen, H. (1985). Zone V: Photojournalism, ethics, and the electronic *age. Studies in Visual Communication*, *11*(2), 22–32. doi:10.1111/j.2326-8492.1985.tb00031.x

Bowatte, G., Lodge, C., Lowe, A. J., Erbas, B., Perret, J., Abramson, M. J., ... Dharmage, S. C. (2015). The influence of childhood traffic-related air pollution exposure on asthma, allergy and sensitization: A systematic review and a meta-analysis of birth cohort studies. *Allergy*, *70*(3), 245–256. doi:10.1111/all.12561 PMID:25495759

Boys Scout of America (BSOA). (2015). *How to Protect your Children from Child Abuse: A Parent's Guide*. Retrieved from www.scouting.org

Brito, R., & Dias, P. (2016). 'The tablet is my BFF': Practices and perceptions of Portuguese children under 8 years old and their families. In The Digital Literacy and Multimodal Practices of Young Children: Engaging with Emergent Research (pp. 35-43). Braga: Centro de Investigação em Educação (CIEd).

Bromley, R. (2000). Street vending and public policy: A global review. *The International Journal of Sociology and Social Policy*, *20*(1/2), 1–28. doi:10.1108/01443330010789052

Brooks, P. (2008). Narrative in and of the law. In J. Phelan & P. J. Rabinowitz (Eds.), *In a companion to narrative theory*. Malden, MA: Blackwell Publishing Ltd.

Buckley, K. E., & Anderson, C. A. (2006). A theoretical model of the effects and consequences of playing video games. *Playing Video Games: Motives, Responses, and Consequences*, 363–378.

Burton, A. (Ed.). (2014). Protecting the Rights of Children: The Role of the Media, Lessons from Brazil, India and Kenya. Interview Europe.

Bushman, B. J., & Anderson, C. A. (2015). Understanding causality in the effects of media violence. *The American Behavioral Scientist*, *59*(14), 1807–1821. doi:10.1177/0002764215596554

Bushman, B., & Cantor, J. (2003). Media ratings for violence and sex. Implications for policymakers and parents. *The American Psychologist*, *58*(20), 130–141. doi:10.1037/0003-066X.58.2.130 PMID:12747015

Business Insider. (2018, February 14). *Lifestyle 50% of Nigerian children engage in child labour – NBS- Pulse Nigeria*. Retrieved from https://www.pulse.ng/bi/lifestyle-50-of-nigerian-children-engage-in-child-labour-nbs/bnqqk33

Calvert, S. L. (2008). Children as Consumers: Advertising and Marketing. *The Future of Children*, *18*(1), 2005–2234. PMID:21338011

Cantor, J., & Omdahl, B. (1999). Children's acceptance of safety guidelines after exposure to televised drama depicting accidents. *Western Journal of Communication*, *63*(1), 1–15. doi:10.1080/10570319909374628

Caple, H., & Bednarek, M. (2016). Rethinking News Values: What a Discursive Approach Can Tell Us about the Construction of News Discourse and News Photography. *Journalism, 17*(4), 435–455. doi:10.1177/1464884914568078

Caraballo, M., Shimasaki, S., Johnston, K., Tung, G., Albright, K., & Halbower, A. C. (2016). Knowledge, Attitudes, and risk for sudden unexpected infant death in children of adolescent mothers: A qualitative study. *The Journal of Pediatrics, 174*, 78–83. doi:10.1016/j.jpeds.2016.03.031 PMID:27113377

Carlsson, U. (Ed.). (2006). Regulation, awareness, empowerment: Young people and harmful media content in the digital age. The UNESCO International Clearing House on Children, Youth and Media, 239-251.

Carter, M. J. (2013). The hermeneutics of frames and framing: An examination of the media's construction of reality. *SAGE Open*, 1–12.

CASA. (1999). *National Center on Addiction and Substance Abuse at Columbia University*. CASA.

Cascardi, M., O'Leary, K. D., Lawrence, E. E., & Schlee, K. A. (1995). Characteristics of women physically abused by their spouses and who seek treatment regarding marital conflict. *Journal of Consulting and Clinical Psychology, 63*(4), 616–623. doi:10.1037/0022-006X.63.4.616 PMID:7673539

Center for Literacy Studies. (2017). Communication process. In *Learning guide Communication process theory* (2nd ed.; pp. 79–86). Christchurch, New Zealand: Careerforce. Retrieved from www.cls.utk.edu/pdf/ls/Week1_Lesson7.pdf

Chaffee, S. H., & Metzer, M. J. (2001). The End of Mass Communication. *Mass Communication & Society, 4*(4), 365–379. doi:10.1207/S15327825MCS0404_3

Cheit, R. E., Shavit, Y., & Reiss-Davis, Z. (2010). Magazine coverage of child sexual abuse (1992 -2004). *Journal of Child Sexual Abuse, 19*(1), 99–117. doi:10.1080/10538710903485575 PMID:20390781

Child Actor. (n.d.). Retrieved from www. Educalingo.com

Child Employment. (n.d.). Retrieved from http://www.gov.uk/employment

Child Labor Laws in Texas. (2018). Texas Film Commission/Texas Workforce Commission.

Child Rights Act. (2003). *Understanding the Child Rights Act 2003 (UNICEF)*. Ministry of Social Welfare Rehabilitation.

Child Rights International Network (CRIN). (2009). *MEDIA: Representations of Children in News Media: Revisiting the Oslo Challenge*. Retrieved February 24, 2014 from http://crin.org/en/library/publications/mediarepresentations-children-news-media- revisiting-oslochallenge

Child Rights International Network (CRIN). (2018). *Civil Rights: Freedom Of Expression And Children's Rights*. Retrieved from https://archive.crin.org/en/library/publications/civil-rights-freedom-expression-and-childrens-rights

Children Act (2001). Retrieved from www.kenyalaw.org

Chinwuba, N. N. (2015). Human Identity: Child Rights and the Legal Framework for Marriage in Nigeria. *Marriage & Family Review*, *51*(4), 305–336. doi:10.1080/01494929.2014.938286

Christians, C. G., Glassier, T. L., McQuail, D., Nordenstreng, K., & White, R. A. (2009). *Normative Theories of the media: Journalism in democratic societies*. Urbana, IL: University of Illinois Press.

Chumbow, B. S. (1990). The place of the mother tongue in the national policy on education. In E. N. Emenanjo (Ed.), *Multilingualism, minority languages and language policy in Nigeria* (pp. 61–72). Agbor, Nigeria: Central Books Limited and Linguistic Association of Nigeria.

Clements, D. H., & Nastasi, B. K. (2012). *Electronic media and early childhood education*. doi:10.1080/00094056.2014.952218

Cohen, B. C. (1963). *The press and foreign policy*. Princeton, NJ: Princeton University Press.

Cohen, C. P., & Naimark, H. (1991). United Nations Convention on the Rights of the Child: Individual rights concepts and their significance for social scientists. *The American Psychologist*, *46*(1), 60–65. doi:10.1037/0003-066X.46.1.60

Collins, R. (1985). *Four sociological traditions: Revised and expanded edition of the three sociological traditions*. New York, NY: Oxford University Press.

Collins, R., & Makowsky, M. (2005). *The Discovery of Society* (7th ed.). New York: McGraw-Hill Companies Inc.

Collins, T. M. (2013). International Child Rights in National Constitutions: Good Sense or Nonsense for Ireland? *Irish Political Studies*, *28*(4), 591–619. doi:10.1080/07907184.2013.838951

Collins, T. M. (2014). The relationship between children's rights and business. *International Journal of Human Rights*, *18*(6), 582–633. doi:10.1080/13642987.2014.944805

Colvert, A. (2016). Teachers supporting transmedia play with classes of young children in the UK: Exploring new literacies through Alternate Reality Game design. In The Digital Literacy and Multimodal Practices of Young Children: Engaging with Emergent Research (pp. 51-60). Braga: Centro de Investigação em Educação (CIEd).

Connor, P. (2018). *Most displaced Syrians are in the Middle East, and about a million are in Europe*. Retrieved from www.reliefweb.int/report

Constitution of the Federal Republic of Nigeria. (1999). *Cap 23 LFN 2004*. Lagos: Simon Printers.

Convention on the Rights of the Child. (1989). *Adopted and opened for signature, ratification and accession by General Assembly resolution 44/25 of 20 November 1989 entry into force 2 September 1990, in accordance with article 49*. Retrieved from https://www.ohchr.org/documents/professionalinterest/crc.pdf

Corry, S. (2017). *Celebrating the day of the African child*. Retrieved from https://www.trustedclothes.com/blog/2017/06/19/celebrating-the-day-of-the-african-child/

Cotroneo, A. (2017). Specificities and challenges of responding to internal displacement in urban settings. *International Review of the Red Cross*, *99*(1), 283–318. doi:10.1017/S1816383118000164

Creswell, J. W. (2015). Research design: A qualitative, quantitative, and mixed method approaches. Thousand Oaks, CA: Saga.

Creswell, J. W. (2012). *Educational Research: Planning, Conducting, and Evaluating Quantitative and Qualitative Research* (4th ed.). Boston, MA: Pearson Education, Inc.

Crewe, E. (2010). Protecting children in different contexts: Exploring the value of rights and research. *Journal of Children's Services*, *5*(1), 43–55. doi:10.5042/jcs.2010.0116

Cunningham, S. B. (1999). Getting It Right: Aristotle's "Golden Mean" as Theory Deterioration University of Windsor. *Journal of Mass Media Ethics*, *14*(1), 5–15. doi:10.1207/S15327728JM140101

D'Amato, S. (2017). Terrorists Going Transnational: Rethinking the Role of States in the Case of AQIM and Boko Haram. *Critical Studies on Terrorism*, *11*(1), 151–172. doi:10.1080/17539153.2017.1347238

Daily Post. (2018, July 28). Retrieved from http://dailypost.ng/2018/01/01/sacked-22000-teachers-kaduna-el-rufai-finally-speaks/

Daily Sun. (2017). *Nigeria's internet users rise to 91.6*. Retrieved from https://www.ncc.gov.ng/thecommunicator/index.php?option=com_content&view=article&id=1572:nigeria-s-internet-users-rise-to-91-6m&catid=32&Itemid=179

Daley, D., Bachmann, M., Bachmann, B. A., Pedigo, C., Thuy-Bui, M., & Coffman, J. (2016). Risk Terrain Modelling Predicts Child Maltreatment. *Child Abuse & Neglect*, *62*, 29–38. doi:10.1016/j.chiabu.2016.09.014 PMID:27780111

Dasgupta, S. (2014). Sociology and postmodern risks. In S. Dasgupta & P. Kivisto (Eds.), *Postmodernism in a Global Perspective*. New Delhi, India: SAGE Publications India Pvt Ltd. doi:10.4135/9789351507833.n7

Davie, G. (n.d.). *Framing Theory. Mass Communication Theory. Mass Communication Theory: From Theory to Practical Application*. Retrieved from https://masscommtheory.com/theory-overviews/framing-theory/

Davies, L. (2014). Working positively with the media to protect children. *Journal of Social Welfare and Family Law*, *36*(1), 47–58. doi:10.1080/09649069.2014.886877

De Silva, S. (n.d.). *Role of Education in the Prevention of Violent Extremism.* Retrieved from http://documents.worldbank.org/curated/en/448221510079762554/120997-WP-revised-PUBLIC-Role-of-Education-in-Prevention-of-Violence-Extremism-Final.pdf

de Vreese, C. H. (2005). News framing: Theory and typology. *Information Design Journal and Document Design, 13*(1), 51–62. doi:10.1075/idjdd.13.1.06vre

Diderich, H., Fekkes, M., Verkerk, P., Pannbakker, F. D., Velderman, M. K., Sorenson, P. J., & Qudesluys-Murphy, A. M. (2013). A new protocol for screening adults presenting their own medical problems at the emergency department to identify children at high risk for treatment. *Child Abuse & Neglect, 37*(12), 1122–1131. doi:10.1016/j.chiabu.2013.04.005 PMID:23768937

Director of Security Services, Babcock University. (2019). Speech delivered at the 2019 Annual Colloquium, Babcock University, Ilisan-Remo, Ogun State, Nigeria.

Donnelly, E., Mausi, S., & Dele-Adedeji, I. (2016). *Boko Haram impacts on education in Northeast Nigeria.* London: Chatham House.

Duruji, M., Azuh, D., Oviasogie, F. O., & Ajayi, O. (2014). Education and Gendered Roles In Post-Adjustment Igbo Society. *International Conference on Education and New Learning Technologies EDULEARN14 Proceedings*, 5054-5061.

East African Commission. (2016). *EAC child policy.* Arusha, Tanzania: EAC secretariat.

Eastwood, A., & Imbiri, H. (2017). Local language as a means to inclusive education in Indonesia: A remote area pilot project for kindergarten and primary children. In *Proceedings of 14th International conference of education and development* (p. 124). Oxford, UK: University of Oxford, United Kingdom.

Eco, U. (1976). *A Theory of Semiotics.* Bloomington, IN: Indiana University Press. doi:10.1007/978-1-349-15849-2

Edgar, P., & Edgar, D. (2008). *Television, Digital Media and Children's Learning.* Discussion Paper. Victorian Curriculum and Assessment Authority.

Education Crisis Response Program. (n.d.). *Nigeria.* Retrieved from https://www.creativeassociatesinternational.com/past-projects/nigeria-education-crisis-response-program/)

Education for All Global Monitoring Report. (2011). *Armed conflict and education (part 2).* Retrieved from http://www.ungei.org/paris2011/docs/gmr2011-part2-intro.pdf

Egbas, J. (2018). *13.2 million Nigerian children now out of school, highest in the world, UNICEF says.* Retrieved from https://www.pulse.ng/news/local/132-million-nigerian-children-now-out-of-school-highest-in-the-world-unicef-says/ge754pc

Ekwuazi, H. (1991). The Communicative import of film in National Development. In S. Unoh (Ed.), Topical Issues in Communication Arts. Uyo: Modern Business Press.

Elkind, D. (1987, May). The child yesterday, today and tomorrow. *Young Children*, 6–11.

Elliot, A. (2014). *Contemporary Social Theory: An Introduction* (2nd ed.). Abingdon, UK: Routledge.

Elliott, D. (2017). Systematic moral analysis. *Ethics Unwrapped.* Accessed June 28, 2017 from http://ethicsunwrapped.utexas.edu/video/systematic-moral-analysis

Elo, S., & Kyngas, H. (2008). The qualitative content analysis process. *Journal of Advanced Nursing, 62*(1), 107–115. doi:10.1111/j.1365-2648.2007.04569.x PMID:18352969

Enakhimion, E. (2014). *Child Protection System Strengthening, Mapping and Assessment in Edo State, Nigeria.* Edo State Ministry of Women Affairs and Social Development.

Entman, R. M. (1993). Framing: Toward Clarification of a Fractured Paradigm. *Journal of Communication, 43*(4), 51–58. doi:10.1111/j.1460-2466.1993.tb01304.x

Europe, I. (2014). *Protecting the Rights of Children: The Role of the Media. Lessons from Brazil, India and Kenya.* Retrieved from https://internews.org/sites/default/files/resources/InternewsEurope_ChildRightsMedia_Report_2014.pdf

Evans, J. L., Meyers, R. G. & IIfeld, E. M. (2000). *Early Childhood Counts: A Programming Guide on Early Childhood Care for Development.* Washington, DC: IBRD.

Evans, R. (2012). *Understanding Young People's Rights to decide.* Retrieved from http://www.ippf.org

Facer, K. (2012). After the moral panic? Reframing the debate about child safety online. *Discourse (Abingdon), 33*(3), 397–413. doi:10.1080/01596306.2012.681899

Fafunwa, A. B., Macauley, J. I., & Sokoya, J. A. F. (1989). *Education in Mother Tongue: The Ife Primary Education Research Project (1970-1978).* Ibadan: University Press.

Fagbohun, P., Oke, G., & Okesoto, J. (2010). Socio-Economic Characeristics of Street Trading in Sango-Otto, Ogun State: The implications on Urban Environment. *Editorial Board, 139*, 157.

Farrington, D. P. (1992). Explaining the beginning, progress and coding of anti-social behaviour from birth to adulthood. In J. McCord (Ed.), Advances in Criminological Theory: Vol. 3. *Facts, Frameworks and Forecasts* (pp. 253–286). New Brunswick, NJ: Transaction.

Fatokun, K. V. (2007). Child abuse and the educational attainment of secondary school students in science subjects. *Journal of Research in National Development, 5*(2), 1596–8308.

Fayoyin, A. (2011). Promoting children's rights through the new media: The Nigerian Experience. *Journal of Communication, 2*(2), 57–65. doi:10.1080/0976691X.2011.11884782

Feather, M. (1999). *Internet and child victimization.* Paper presented at the Children and Crime: Victims and Offenders Conference, convened by the Australian Institute of Criminology, Brisbane, Australia.

Federal Government of Nigeria. (2004). *National policy on education* (4th ed.). Lagos: Nigeria NERCD.

Feeny, T., & Boyden, J. (2003). *Children and poverty: Shaping a response to poverty: A conceptual overview and implications for responding to children living in poverty, Children and Poverty Series Part III*. Christian Children's Fund.

Feigin, V. L., Abajobir, A. A., Abate, K. H., Abd-Allah, F., Abdulle, A. M., Abera, S. F., ... Aichour, I. (2017). Global, regional, and national burden of neurological disorders during 1990–2015: A systematic analysis for the Global Burden of Disease Study 2015. *Lancet Neurology*, *16*(11), 877–897. doi:10.1016/S1474-4422(17)30299-5 PMID:28931491

Ferguson, C. J. (2014). Does media violence predict societal violence? It depends on what you look at and when. *Journal of Communication*, *65*(1), E1–E22. doi:10.1111/jcom.12129

Ferguson, H. B., Bovaird, S., & Mueller, M. P. (2007). The impact of poverty on educational outcomes for children. *Paediatrics & Child Health*, *12*(8), 701–706. doi:10.1093/pch/12.8.701 PMID:19030450

Flavell, J. H., Miller, P. H., & Miller, S. A. (2002). *Cognitive development*. Englewood Cliffs, NJ: Prentice Hall.

Folarin, B. (2005). *Theories of Mass Communication: An Introductory Text*. Stirling: Horden.

Foley, M., Hayes, N., & O'Neill, B. (2012). Journalism Education and Children's Rights: New Approaches to Media Development in CEE/CIS Countries. *Irish Studies in International Affairs*, *23*, 47-58. Retrieved from http://www.jstor.org/stable/23489213

Folorunsho, A.H., Imam-Tamim, M.K., & Abdulraheem, T.A. (2014). Children's right to education in Nigeria: Challenges and solutions. *Journal or Public Law and Constitutional Practice*, *6*, 104-117.

Foster, E., & Bochner, A. P. (2008) Social constructionist perspectives in communication research. Handbook of constructionist research, 85-106.

FrameWorks Institute (2011). *Framing Early Childhood Development in a Global context: An Analysis of Children's Issues in International News Media*. A FrameWorks Research Report.

Franzosi, R. (2007). *Introduction*. Retrieved from http://www.unive.it/media/allegato/Scuola-Dottorale/2011/allegato/Content_Analysis_-_Introduction.pdf

Friedman, L., & Friedman, H. (2008). The New Media Technologies: Overview and Research Framework. *Electronic Journal*, 1-30.

Frierson, M. (2018). *Film and Video Editing Theory Film*. Abingdon, UK: Focal Press. doi:10.4324/9781315475011

Gabel, S. G. (2014). Social protection and children's rights in developing countries. *Journal of International and Comparative Social Policy*, *30*(3), 199–216. doi:10.1080/21699763.2014.921233

Garba, V. (2015). *Influence of Home Television Viewing on Academic Achievement of Children in Upper Basic Education in Kaduna State* (Master's thesis). University of Nigeria, Department of Vocational Education.

Gee, J. P. (2011). *Introduction to discourse analysis* (3rd ed.). New York, NY: Routledge.

Geraci, P. C. (1984). *Photojournalism: New Images in Visual Communication*. Dubuque, IA: Kendall/Hunt Publishing Company.

Gernsheim, H. (1969). *The history of photography*. New York: McGraw-Hill.

Giddens, A. (1984). *The Constitution of Society: Outline of the Theory of Structuration*. Oxford, UK: Polity Press.

Giwa, E. T. (2014). *Nollywood: A Case Study of Rising Nigerian Film Industry - Content & Production* (Master's thesis). South Illinois University, Department of Mass Communication and Media Arts.

Goddard, C., & Saunders, B. (2001). Child abuse and the media. *Child Abuse Prevention, 14*(2).

Goddard, C., & Saunders, B. J. (2000). The gender neglect and textual abuse of children in the print media. *Child Abuse, 9*(1), 37–48. doi:10.1002/(SICI)1099-0852(200001/02)9:1<37::AID-CAR586>3.0.CO;2-2

Goldsmith, C., & Lotyam, M. L. (2017). Using real-time, disaggregate, national education data to drive inclusive school enrolment and attendance in fragile and conflict-affected settings. In *Proceedings of 14th International conference of education and development*. (p. 26). Oxford, UK: University of Oxford.

Gordon, F., McAlister, S., & Scraton, P. (2015). *Behind the headlines: Media representation of children and young people in Northern Ireland. Summary of research Findings*. Belfast, UK: Queen's University.

Goretti, L. K. (2009). Reflections on the media in Africa: strangers in a mirror? In K. Njogu & J. Middleton (Eds.), *Media and Identity in Africa* (pp. 49–61). Edinburgh, UK: Edinburgh University Press/International African Institute.

Grange, A. (2013). *Basic Critical Theory for Photographers*. Abingdon, UK: Focal Press.

Greene, E., Wilder, A., Levine, M., & Nemeth, K. N. (n.d.). *Technology and digital media in the early years : big ideas, best practices and future directions*. Academic Press.

Green, L. (2002). *Technoculture: From Alphabet to Cybersex*. Sydney: Allen & Unwin.

Gunter, B. (2008). Media violence: Is there a case for causality? *The American Behavioral Scientist, 51*(8), 1061–1122. doi:10.1177/0002764207312007

Guru, B. P. M. C., Nabi, A., & Raslana, R. (2013). Role of Television in Child Development. The International Institute for Science, Technology and Education (IISTE). *New Media and Mass Communication, 18*, 38-44. Retrieved from https://www.iiste.org/Journals/index.php/NMMC/article/view/8412/8512

Gynnild, A., Nilsson, M., Simonsen, A. H., & Weselius, H. (2017). Introduction: Photojournalism and editorial processes: Global similarities, local differences. *Nordicom Review, 38*(Special Issue 2), 1-5.

Haapasalo, J. (2000). Sons in prison and their mothers: Is there a relationship between childhood histories of physical abuse? In G. L. Fox & M. L. Benson (Eds.), *Contemporary Perspectives in Family Research: Families* (Vol. 2, pp. 73–90). Crime and Criminal Justice.

Hachten, W. (1993). *The growth of media in the third world: African failures, Asian successes.* Ames, IA: Iowa State University Press.

Harper, C., Jones, N., & McKay, A. (2009, Sep.). *Including Children in Policy Responses to economic Crises: Lessons from the Past and Policies for a Sustainable Future.* ODI and UNICEF Synthesis Conference Paper.

Hartley, C. (1981). *The reactions of photojournalists and the public to hypothetical ethical dilemmas confronting press photographers* (Unpublished master's thesis). University of Texas, Austin, TX.

Hartt, C. (2015). *14 ways Acting is beneficial for kids and teens.* Retrieved from www.backstage.com

Hastings, E. C., Karas, T. L., Winsler, A., Way, E., Madigan, A., & Tyler, S. (2009). Young children's video/computer game use: Relations with school performance and behavior. *Issues in Mental Health Nursing, 30*(10), 638–649. doi:10.1080/01612840903050414 PMID:19742374

Hauer, T. (2017). Technological determinism and new media. *International Journal of English, Literature and Social Science.*

Hayne, H., Herbert, J., & Simcock, G. (2003). Imitation from Television by 24- and 30-Month-Olds. *Developmental Science, 6*(3), 254–261. doi:10.1111/1467-7687.00281

Health, W. A. (2015). *Guidelines for Protecting Children 2015. WA Health.* Government of Western Australia.

Heim, J., Brandtzaeg, P. B., Karre, B. H., Endestad, T., & Torgersen, L. (2007). Children's usage of media technologies and psychosocial factors. *New Media & Society, 9*(3), 425–454. doi:10.1177/1461444807076971

Helfgott, J. B. (2015). Criminal behaviour and the copycat effect: Literature review and theoretical framework for empirical investigation. *Aggression and Violent Behavior, 22*(C), 46–64. doi:10.1016/j.avb.2015.02.002

Herman, D. (2008). Histories of narrative theory (I): A genealogy of early developments. In J. Phelan & P. J. Rabinowitz (Eds.), *In a companion to narrative theory.* Malden, MA: Blackwell Publishing Ltd.

Hermandez, S. C. L. S., Lacsina, A. C., Ylade, M. C., Adaba, J., Lam, H. Y., Estacio, L. R. Jr, & Lopez, A. L. (2018). Sexual Exploitation and Abuse of Children Online in the Philippines: A review of online news and Articles. *ACTA Medica Philppina, 52*(4), 305–311.

Hestres, L.E. (2017, April). Tools beyond control: Social media and the work of advocacy organizations. *Social Media + Society,* 1-11.

Hjarvard, S. (2008). The mediatization of society: A study of media as agents of social and cultural change. *Nordicom Review*, 105–134.

Hofferth, S. L. (2010). Home media and children's achievement and behavior. *Child Development*, *81*(5), 1598–1619. doi:10.1111/j.1467-8624.2010.01494.x PMID:20840243

Honjo, K. (2004). Social epidemiology: Definition, history, and research examples. *Environmental Health and Preventive Medicine*, *9*(5), 193–199. doi:10.1007/BF02898100 PMID:21432303

Hooker, J. (2018). *Taking ethics seriously: Why ethics is an essential tool for the modern workplace.* London: Productivity Press. doi:10.4324/9781315097961

Howard, J. (2000). *TIP 36: Substance Abuse Treatment for Persons with Child Abuse and Neglect Issues: Treatment Improvement Protocol (TIP) Series 36.* Academic Press.

HRW. (2016). *They set the classrooms on fire: Attacks on education in Northeast Nigeria.* Retrieved from https://www.hrw.org/report/2016/04/11/they-set-classrooms-fire/attacks-education-northeast-nigeria#

Huston, A. C., & Ripke, M. N. (2006). *Middle childhood: Contexts of development.* New York: Cambridge University Press. doi:10.1017/CBO9780511499760

Ibhaze, F. O. (2016). *Issues and challenges of implementation of early childhood education in Nigeria.* Academic Press.

Idegu, E. U. (2014). Which change, which change? Glamourising social misfits in selected Nigerian home movies. *International Journal of English and Literature*, *5*(8), 174-181.

Ige, O. K., & Fawole, O. I. (2011). Preventing Child Sexual Abuse: Parents' Perceptions and Practices in Urban Nigeria. *Journal of Child Sexual Abuse*, *20*(6), 695–707. doi:10.1080/10538712.2011.627584 PMID:22126111

Ignjatovic, D., & Ljubicic, M. (2017). Media and crime: The eternal criminological theme. In I. Stevanović & O. Pavićević (Eds.), *Judiciary & Media. Serbia: istraživanja*. Beograd: OEBS.

Imo, N. A. (2015). Working with emotionality and sexually abused children: The therapeutic value of effective communication. *International Journal of Research in Arts and Social Sciences*, *8*(1), 151–161.

Inter-Agency and Expert Group on SDG Indicators (IAEG-SDGs). (2016). *Final List of Proposed Sustainable Development Goal indicators. Report of the Inter-Agency and Expert Group on Sustainable Development Goal Indicators (E/CN.3/2016/2/Rev.1), Annex IV.* Retrieved from https://sustainabledevelopment.un.org/content/documents/11803Official-List-of-Proposed-SDG-Indicators.pdf

Inter-American Commission on Human Rights (IACHR) (2015). *Violence, Children and Organized Crime*. OEA/Ser.L/V/II, Doc. 40/15.

International Labour Organisation. (2010). *Mainstreaming child labour issues in key development policies and programmes in Sri Lanka. Report of a Preliminary Review*. Colombo, Sri Lanka: ILO.

Internews Europe. (2014). *Protecting the Rights of Children: The Role of the Media*. Author.

Internews. (2014) *Protecting the rights Of children: the role of the media Lessons from Brazil, India and Kenya.* Internews Europe.

Interview with Hilarious Emmanuella, the Comedian and Mark Angel. (2017). Retrieved from www.youtube.com

Interviews Europe, . (2014). *Protecting the rights of children: the role of the media lessons from Brazil.* India Internews Europe. Available at https://www.internews.org/sites/default/files/resources/InternewsEurope_ChildRightsMedia_Report_2014.pdf

ION and NEMA Displacement Tracking Matrix. (2018). *Nigeria. Round 23 Report - June 2018*. Retrieved from https://reliefweb.int/sites/reliefweb.int/files/resources/Nigeria%20-%20Displacement%20Report%2023%20%28June%202018%29.pdf

Isokpan, A. J. (2016). *The Boko Haram insurgency and the child's right to education in Nigeria.* A Thesis submitted in partial fulfilment of the requirements for the degree of masters of Law (Llm (Ii)) In International and Human Rights Law.

Isokpan, A. J., & Durojaye, E. (2016). Impact of the Boko Haram Insurgency on the Child's Right to Education in Nigeria. *Potchefstroom Electronic Law Journal*, 19.

Isua, N. (2009). An examination of the child rights protection and corporal punishment in Nigeria: The Legislative and institutional framework of environmental protection in the oil. Academic Press.

Itat, U. D. (1999). *A Critical Analysis of the United Nations Convention on the Rights of the Child and the Constitution of the Federal Republic of Nigeria.* A paper presented at a seminar organised by Law Reform Commission, Akwa Ibom State, Nigeria.

Iyanda, R. O., & Nwogwugwu, N. (2016). Globalization and Rising Human Trafficking in Nigeria. *Kuwait Chapter of Arabian Journal of Business and Management Review*, *5*(6), 17–31. doi:10.12816/0019031

Iyengar, S. (1991). *Is anyone responsible? How television frames political issues*. Chicago: University of Chicago Press. doi:10.7208/chicago/9780226388533.001.0001

Jackson, C., Brown, J. D., & Pardun, C. J. (2008). A TV in the bedroom: implications for viewing habits and risk behaviors during early adolescence. *Journal of Broadcasting and Public Media*, 349-367.

Jacomy, S., & Stevens, A. (2004). *Rights of the child in Nigeria: Report on the implementation of the convention on the rights of the child by Nigeria*. Geneva: OMCT and Cleen Foundation.

Jandt, F. E. (2007). *Introduction to intercultural communication: Identities in global community* (5th ed.). Thousand Oaks, CA: SAGE Publications.

Jolicoeur, D. (2011). *Understanding poverty and conflict.* Retrieved from https://www.mercycorps.org/research-resources/understanding-poverty-and-conflict

Jolin, E. M., & Weller, R. A. (2011). Television viewing and its impact on childhood behaviors. *Current Psychiatry Reports, 13*(2), 122–128. doi:10.100711920-011-0175-5 PMID:21267680

Jones, L. M., Finkelhor, D., & Beckwith, J. (2010). Protecting victims' identities in press coverage of child victimization. *Journalism, 11*(3), 347–367. doi:10.1177/1464884909360925

Jones, L. M., Finkelhor, D., & Halter, S. (2006). Child maltreatment trends in the 1990s: Why does neglect differ from sexual and physical abuse? *Medline, 11*(2), 107–120. PMID:16595845

Jørgensen, M., & Phillips, L. (2002). *Discourse analysis as theory and method.* London: Sage. doi:10.4135/9781849208871

Joshua, S. & Olanrewaju, F. O. (2016). The impacts of terrorism on education: The North Eastern Nigeria's experience. *Journal of International Politics and development, 14*(1), 59-74.

Kadiri & Muhammed. (2011). Mass media as correlates of children's behavioural problems in Kwara State, Nigeria. *Journal of Media and Communication Studies, 3*(5), 198–202. Retrieved from http://www.academicjournals.org/app/webroot/article/article1380115207_Kadiri%20and%20Muhammed.pdf

Kadiri, K. K., & Muhammed, A. Y. (2011). Mass media as correlation of children's behavioural problems in Kwara state, Nigeria. *Journal of Media and Communication, 3*(5), 198–202.

Kadiri, K. K., Muhammed, Y. A., Raji, A., & Sulaiman, A. L. (2015). Constraints And Challenges Of The Media In The Development Of Nigeria. *Journal of Sustainable Development in Africa, 17*(1), 44–60.

Kahiu, C. W. (2015). *An investigation into the extent of child labor issues content in the Kenyan media: A case study of the Daily Nation and the Standard newspapers (Unpublished master's thesis).* University of Nairobi. Retrieved from https://journalism.uonbi.ac.ke/sites/default/files/chss/journalism/journalism/Caroline

Kathryn, C. D. (2009). *Human Trafficking.* Infobase Publishing.

KeallJ. K.BondJ. A. (2011). *Baby wrap.* Retrieved from http://www.freepatentsonline.com/D644413.html

Keenan, T. (2002). *An Introduction to Child Development.* London: SAGE Publication Ltd.

Kilimwiko, L. (2009). *Media power and political in Tanzania: Critical analysis of media trends and practice.* Dar es Salaam: Friedrich Ebert Stiftung.

Kilkelly, U. (2006). Operationalizing children's rights: lessons from research. *Journal of Children's Services, 1*(4), 35-46. doi:10.1108/17466660200600030

Kimuyu, H. (2019, January 14). Form girl kicked out of school for being Rastafarian. *Nairobi News*. Retrieved from https://nairobinews.nation.co.ke/new

King'ori, M. E., & Bitrus-Ojiambo, U. A. (2016). Newspaper framing of gender-based (domestic) violence of women-on-men from Nyeri County. *African Multidisciplinary Journal of Research*, *1*(1), 4–25.

Kirkorian, H. L., Wartella, E. A., & Anderson, D. R. (2008). Media and Young Children's Learning. In Children and Electronic Media (pp. 39-63). Princeton, NJ: Princeton-Brookings.

Kjartansdóttir, S. H. (2016). Creative and playful learning with Biophilia in preschool, after-school classes and primary schools in Iceland. In The Digital Literacy and Multimodal Practices of Young Children: Engaging with Emergent Research (pp. 90-103). Braga: Centro de Investigação em Educação (CIEd).

Kocharyan, A. (2019). *The Abuse of Social Media: Child Protection*. Retrieved from http://www.bearr.org/pdfs/BEARR_ArturKocharyan.pdf

Kohlman, S., Baig, A., Balice, G., DiRubbo, C., Placencia, L., Skale, K., ... Aquino, S. (2014). Contribution of Media to the Normalization and Perpetuation of Domestic Violence. *Austin Journal of Psychiatry and Behavioral Sciences*, *1*(4), 1–5.

Kolucki, B., & Lemish, D. (2011). *Communicating with children*. UNICEF Factsheet. Retrieved from http://www.unicef.org.ng/cwc/

Kramer, M. H. (2004). *Where law and morality meet*. Oxford, UK: Oxford University Press.

Kramer, M. H. (2010). Refining the interest theory of rights. *The American Journal of Jurisprudence*, *55*(1), 31–39. doi:10.1093/ajj/55.1.31

Kreidl, M., Štípková, M., & Hubatková, B. (2017). Parental separation and children's education in a comparative perspective: Does the burden disappear when separation is more common? *Demographic Research*, *36*, 73–110.

Kruger, R. A. (2002). *Designing and conducting focus group Interviews - EIU*. Retrieved from http://www.eiu.edu/ihec/Krueger-FocusGroupInterviews.pdf

Kumuyi, A. (2010). *Christian women mirror*. Lagos: Life Press.

Kunkel, Suding, & Biely. (2002). *Coverage in context: How thoroughly the news media report five key children"'s issues*. Retrieved August 18, 2013, from http://www.mediawise.org.ukldisplay

Landrigan, P. J. (2017). Air pollution and health. *The Lancet Public Health*, *2*(1), e4–e5. doi:10.1016/S2468-2667(16)30023-8 PMID:29249479

Lansdown, G. (2005). The evolving capacities of the child. Firenze.

Lasica, J. D. (2003). *We media: How audiences are shaping the future of news and information. The Media Centre*. New York: The American Press Institute.

Lee, D. (n.d.). *Developing Effective Communications*. Retrieved from https://extension2.missouri.edu/cm109

Lee, N. (2003). *Childhood and Society: Growing up in an Age of Uncertainty*. Berkshire, UK: Open University Press.

Lemish, D. (2007). *Children and television: A global perspective*. Hoboken, NJ: Blackwell Publishing.

Lenshie, N. E., & Yenda, H. B. (2016). Boko haram insurgency, internally displaced persons and humanitarian response in Northeast Nigeria. *The International Journal of Humanities & Social Studies*, *4*(8), 141–150.

Lester, M. (2018). *Visual ethics*. Oxford, UK: Focal Press. doi:10.4324/9781315455136

Lester, P. (1991). *Photojournalism: An ethical approach*. Lawrence Erlbaum Associates, Incorporated.

Levenson, J. S., & Socia, K. M. (2016). Adverse childhood experiences and arrest pattern in a sample of sexual offenders. *Journal of Interpersonal Violence*, *31*(10), 1883–1911. doi:10.1177/0886260515570751 PMID:25711615

Lewis, D. O., Mallouh, C., & Webb, C. (1989). Child abuse, delinquency and violent criminality. In D. Cochetti & V. Carlson (Eds.), *Child Maltreatment, Theory and Research on the Causes and Consequences of Child Abuse and Neglect* (pp. 707–721). Cambridge, UK: Cambridge University Press. doi:10.1017/CBO9780511665707.023

Listverse. (2009, July 6). *Top 10 terrible issues facing children worldwide*. Retrieved from http://listverse.com/2009/07/06/ top-10-terrible-issues-facing-children-worldwide/

Littlejohn, S. W., & Foss, K. A. (2009). *Encyclopedia of communication theory*. London: SAGE Publications Inc. doi:10.4135/9781412959384

Livingstone, S. (2009). *Children and the internet*. Cambridge, UK: Polity Press.

Livingstone, S. (2016). Reframing media effects in terms of children's rights in the digital age. *Journal of Children and Media*, *10*(1), 1, 4–12. doi:10.1080/17482798.2015.1123164

Livingstone, S., & Bulger, M. E. (2014). A global research agenda for children's rights in the digital age. *Journal of Children and Media*, *8*(4), 317–335. doi:10.1080/17482798.2014.961496

Longe, O.B., & Longe, F.A. (2005). The Nigerian web content: Combating pornography using content filters. *Journal of Information Technology Impact, 15*(2), 59-64.

Longe, O. B., Chiemeke, S. C., Onifade, O. F., Balogun, F. M., Longer, F. A., & Otti, V. U. (2007). Exposure of children and teenagers to internet pornography in South Western Nigeria: Concerns, trends and implications. *Journal of Information Technology Impact*, *7*(4), 195–212.

Lonne, B., & Parton, N. (2014). Portrayals of child abuse scandals in the media in Australia and England: Impacts on practice, policy, and systems. *Child Abuse & Neglect*, *38*(5), 822–836. doi:10.1016/j.chiabu.2014.04.020 PMID:24942126

Lull, J. (2000). *Media, communication, culture: A global approach* (2nd ed.). New York, NY: Columbia University Press.

Lund, B. (1999). 'Ask not what your community can do for you': Obligations, New Labour and welfare reform. *Critical Social Policy*, *19*(4), 447–462. doi:10.1177/026101839901900402

Luntz, B. K., & Widom, C. S. (1994). Antisocial personality disorder in abused and neglected children grown up. *The American Journal of Psychiatry*, *151*(5), 670–674. doi:10.1176/ajp.151.5.670 PMID:8166307

Madjd-Sadjadi, Z. (2013). *The Economies of Crime*. New York: Business Expert Press, LLC.

Mahkonen, S. (n.d.). *Children's rights and the media*. Malaysia: AIBD. Retrieved on August 6, 2008 from http://download.aibd.org.my/books/Childrens_Rights_and_the_Media.pdf

Maley, B. (2000). *The elite gatekeepers-How the media capture public policy*. Policy. Winter.

Manderson, L., & Liamputting, P. (2002). *Youth and sexuality in contemporary Asia societies in coming age in South East Asia*. Richmond: Curzon Press.

Manovich, L. (2002). New Media from Borges to HTML. In *The New Media Reader* (pp. 1–29). Cambridge, MA: The MIT Press.

Manyasa, E. (2017, June 16). *Challenges the African child faces in our time*. Retrieved from https://www.standardmedia.co.ke/article/2001243683/challenges-the-african-child-faces-in-our-time

Mares, M.-L., & Kretz, V. (2015). *Media effects on children* (2nd ed.). International Encyclopedia of the Social & Behavioral Sciences. doi:10.1016/B978-0-08-097086-8.95006-2

Mastin, T., Choi, J., Barboza, G. E., & Post, L. (2007). Newspapers' Framing of Elder Abuse: It's Not a Family Affair. *Journalism & Mass Communication Quarterly*, *84*(4), 777–794. doi:10.1177/107769900708400408

Mburu, S. (2004). *Shocking rise in rape cases unveiled. In The Daily Nation Newspapers*. Nairobi: Nation Media Group.

McCloskey, L. A. (2011). The impact of intimate partner's violence on adolescents. In S. Graham-Bermann & A. A. Levendosky (Eds.), *How Intimate Partners Violence Affects Children: Developmental Research, Case Studies, and Evidence-Based Intervention* (pp. 225–246). Washington, DC: American Psychological Association. doi:10.1037/12322-011

McCombs, M., & Shaw, D. (1972). The agenda-setting function of mass media. *Public Opinion Quarterly*, *36*(2), 176–185. doi:10.1086/267990

McCord, J. (1996). Family and Crucible for Violence. Comment on Gorman-Smith, et al, 1996. *Journal of Family Psychology*, *10*(2), 147–152. doi:10.1037/0893-3200.10.2.147

McCoy, D. C., Peet, E. D., Ezzati, M., Danaei, G., Black, M. M., Sudfeld, C. R., ... Fink, G. (2016). Early childhood developmental status in low-and middle-income countries: National, regional, and global prevalence estimates using predictive modeling. *PLoS Medicine*, *13*(6), e1002034. doi:10.1371/journal.pmed.1002034 PMID:27270467

McLanahan, S., Haskins, B., Paxson, C., Rouse, C., & Sawhill, I. (2008). Children and Electronic Media. *The Future of Children*, *18*(1).

Mcleod, S. A. (2016, February 3). Bandura – Social learning Theory. *Simply Psychology*. Retrieved from http://www.simplypsychology.org/bandura.html

McLeod, S. A. (2018, June 6). *Jean Piaget's theory of cognitive development.* Retrieved from www.simplypsychology.org: https://www.simplypsychology.org/piaget.htm

McLuhan, M. (1962). *The Gutenberg Galaxy: The making of typographic man.* London: Routledge.

McLuhan, M. (1964). *Understanding Media: The Extensions of Man.* MIT Press.

McManus, J., & Dorfman, L. (2002). *How U. S. newspapers portray child care. Issue 11.* Berkeley, CA: Berkeley Media Studies Group.

McNamara. (n. d.). *Silent victims and pretty props: The representation of young people in Irish national.* Retrieved from newspapers.www.nordicom.gu.se/cl/publ/electronic/PaulMcIreland1.pdf

McQuail, D. (2005). McQuail's mass communication theory (5th ed.). New Delhi: Vistaar Publications.

McQuail, D. (1989). *Mass communication theory: An introduction.* London: SAGE publications.

McQuail, D. (2005). *McQuail's Mass Communication Theory* (5th ed.). Sage Publications Inc.

McQuail, D. (2005). *McQuail's mass communication theory: An introduction.* London: SAGE publications.

McQuail, D. (2007). *Mass communication theory.* London: Sage Publication Limited.

McQuail, D. (2010). *McQuail's mass communication theory.* London: Sage Publications.

Media Council Act (ACT). (2013). *Laws of Kenya. Media Council Act No. 46 of 2013.* National Council for Law Reporting with the Authority of the Attorney-General. Available at www.kenyalaw.org

Media Council of Tanzania. (2016). *Code of ethics for media professionals.* Dar es Salaam: Media Council of Tanzania.

Media Institute of Southern Africa. (2013). *Promoting ethical reporting on children's issues in the SADC region.* Retrieved February 24, 2013 from http://misa.org/component/k2/item/2354-promotingethical-reporting-on-childrens-issues-in-the-sadcregion?Itemid=101#topofthepage

Mediawise. (2010). *The Media and Children's Rights.* Retrieved from http://www.mediawise.org.uk/wp-content/uploads/2011/04/The-Media-and-Children-Rights-2005.pdf

Mena, J. G., & Eyer, D. W. (2004). *Infants, Toddlers, and Caregivers: A Curriculum of Respectful, Responsive Care and Innovation.* New York: McGraw-Hill Companies, Inc.

Methodist Church in Kenya vs. Mohamed Fugicha & 3 others. (2016). *Petition 16 of 2016.* Nairobi: Supreme Court of Kenya. Retrieved from http://kenyalaw.org/caselaw/cases/view/170043/

Meyer, J. H. F. (1991). Study orchestration: The manifestation, interpretation and consequences of contextualised approaches to studying. *Higher Education, 22*(3), 297–316. doi:10.1007/BF00132293

Meyer, J. H. F. (2000). The modelling of 'dissonant' study orchestration in higher education. *European Journal of Psychology of Education, 15*(1), 5–18. doi:10.1007/BF03173163

Mitullah, W. (2004). *A review of street trade in Africa.* Unpublished Manuscript. Cambridge, MA: WIEGO.

Mizen, P. (2018). Bringing the street back in: Considering strategy, contingency and relative good fortune in street children's access to paid work in Accra. *The Sociological Review, 66*(5), 1058–1073. doi:10.1177/0038026118771279

Momanyi, L., Norby, R., & Strand, S. (2006). The need for integration of technology in K-12 school settings in Kenya, Africa. Association for the Advancement of Computing in Education Journal, 154-177.

Momoh, S. O., Aigbomian, D., & Longe, B. O. (2008). Students' perception of the prevalence, forms and causes of child abuse in Edo state, Nigeria. *Investigaciones-REOP, 19*(1), 5–11.

Moody, Z. (2015). The United Nations Declaration on the Rights of the Child (1959): Genesis, transformation and dissemination of a treaty (re)constituting a transnational cause. *Prospects, 45*(1), 15–29. doi:10.100711125-015-9343-4

Morris, B., & Davies, M. M. (2018). Can children's privacy rights be adequately protected through press regulation? What press regulation can learn from the courts. *Journal of Medicine and Law, 10*(1), 92–113. doi:10.1080/17577632.2018.1467597

Morrison, J. W. (2001). Early Care and Education in Ghana. *Childhood Education*, 77–85.

Mosby's Medical Dictionary. (2009). *Child* (8th ed.). Elsevier. Retrieved May 29, 20 II http://medical dictionary.thefreedictionmy.com/Childrens

Mtahabwa, L. (2009). Early Child Development and Care in Tanzania: Challenges for the Future. *Early Child Development and Care, 179*(1), 55–67. doi:10.1080/03004430600923436

Muigai, R. (2019, March 27). Debate as court proposes sex consent age to be lowered to 16 years. *Citizen Digital.* Retrieved from https://citizentv.co.ke/news

Muiruri, P. (2010). *Women street vendors in Nairobi, Kenya: A situational and policy analysis within a human rights framework.* African Books Collective.

Musa, M. M., Abubakar, I. B., & Danladi, N. Y. (2017). Early childhood education : Development, challenges and prospects in Nigeria. *International Journal of Education and Evaluation*, *3*(10), 47–58.

Musan, J. M., Kisovi, L. M., & Otor, S. C. J. (2015). Marital Instability and its Impact on Female-Headed Household Livelihoods in Machakos County, Kenya. *International Journal of Humanities and Social Science*, *5*(8), 145–153.

Mushoriwa, T., & Muzembe, H. (2011). Attitudes of Primary school teachers towards Early Childhood Development in Zimbabwean primary schools. *International Journal of Educational Studies*, 117-128.

Mustapha, B. A., Blangiardo, M., Briggs, D. J., & Hansell, A. L. (2011). Traffic air pollution and other risk factors for respiratory illness in schoolchildren in the niger-delta region of Nigeria. *Environmental Health Perspectives*, *119*(10), 1478–1482. doi:10.1289/ehp.1003099 PMID:21719372

Muste, D. (2016). The Role of Communication Skills in Teaching Process. *The European Proceedings of Social and Behavioural Sciences.*, *430-434*, 430–434. doi:10.15405/epsbs.2016.12.52

Mutembei, P. (2012, May 6). Children's parliament launched. *Standard Digital*. Retrieved from https://www.standardmedia.co.ke

Muthoni, K. (2019, March 26). Why court proposed lowering sex consent to 16 years. *Standard Digital*. Retrieved from https://www.standardmedia.co.ke

Mwamwenda, T. S. (2014). Early Childhood Education in Africa. *Mediterranean Journal of Social Sciences*. doi:10.5901/mjss.2014.v5n20p1403

Nakpodia, E. D. (2011). Early childhood education : Its policy formulation and implementation in Nigerian educational system. *African Journal of Political Science and International Relations*, *5*(3), 159–163.

Namazova-Baranova, L., Carrasco-Sanz, A., Vural, M., Huss, G., Mestrovic, J., Barak, S., ... Pettoello-Mantovani, M. (2019). European Pediatricians: Speaking with One Voice to Advocate for Children and Their Health. *The Journal of Pediatrics*, *211*, 227–228. doi:10.1016/j.jpeds.2019.05.071 PMID:31349917

NAN. (2016). *910 students destroyed, 952, 029 pupils displaced by insurgency in North east.* Retrieved from https://guardian.ng/news/910-schools-destroyed-952029-pupils-displaced-by-insurgency-in-north-east/

Nation Team. (2019, March 29). Lowering the age of sexual consent talk divides Kenyans. *Daily Nation*. Retrieved from https://mobile.nation.co.ke/news/

National Bureau of Statistics. (2015). *Nigerian Formal Education Sector: Summary Report 2010-2012*. Author.

National Children Authority (Uganda). (2018). Day of the African Child. *Souvenir Magazine*.

Naugle, D. A., & Hornik, R. C. (2014). Systematic review of the effectiveness of mass media interventions for child survival in low-and middle-income countries. *Journal of Health Communication, 19*(sup1), 190–215. doi:10.1080/10810730.2014.918217

Nbete, A. D. & Ikiroma, O. (2014). Film and Cultural Imperialism in Nigeria: A Critical Developmental Perspective. *The Crab: The Journal of Theatre & Media Arts*, *9*, 123-138.

Ndu, I. K. (2016). Sudden infant death syndrome: An unrecognized killer in developing countries. *Pediatric Health. Medicine and Therapeutics*, *7*, 1. PMID:29388586

Neidell, M. J. (2004). Air pollution, health, and socio-economic status: The effect of outdoor air quality on childhood asthma. *Journal of Health Economics*, *23*(6), 1209–1236. doi:10.1016/j.jhealeco.2004.05.002 PMID:15556243

Nelson, O., Kehinde, O., Oyero, O., Wiliams, O. R., & Soola, E. O. (2013). Effective use of information sources for breast cancer care: Interplay of mass media and interpersonal channels. *Creating Global Competitive Economies: 2020 Vision Planning and Implementation - Proceedings of the 22nd International Business Information Management Association Conference, IBIMA 2013, 3*, 2231-2243.

Newton, J. H. (1991). *In front of the camera: Ethical issues of subject response in photography* (Unpublished doctoral dissertation). University of Texas, Austin, TX.

Nicklas, E., & Mackenzie, M. (2012). Internal partner violence and risk for child neglect during early childhood in a community sample of fragile families. *Journal of Family Violence*, *28*(1), 17–29. doi:10.100710896-012-9491-8

Nieman, P. (2003). Canadian Paediatric Society Statement: Impact of media use on children and youth. *Paediatrics & Child Health*, *8*(5), 301–306. doi:10.1093/pch/8.5.301 PMID:20020034

Nigeria, P. R. (2018). *Labour Ministry champions renewed fight against child labour in Nigeria*. Retrieved from www.prnigeria.com

Nikander, P. (2008). Working with Transcripts and Translated Data. *Qualitative Research in Psychology*, *5*(3), 225–231. doi:10.1080/14780880802314346

Nikolopoulou, K. (2014). ICT Integration in Preschool Classes: Examples of Practices in Greece. *Creative Education*, 402-410.

Nkememena, A. C. (2009). *Press coverage of child trafficking in Nigeria: a content analysis of* Daily Sun *and* Vanguard *newspapers* (Master's thesis). University of Nigeria, Nsukka.

Nmeregini, A. S. (2010). *Do African Children Have Rights?: A Comparative and Legal Analysis of the United Nations Convention on the Rights of the Child.* Universal-Publishers.

Nnaemeka, F. O. (2017). COOU Undergraduates perspective portrayals in Nollywood movies. *COOU Journal of Multidisciplinary Studies, 1*(1).

Nnam, M., & Njemanze, V. (2016). Culture as a determinant of child abuse in Nigeria: A sociological standpoint. *International Journal of Arts. Management and Humanities*, *1*(3), 1–22.

Nordtveit, B. H. (2010). Discourses of education, protection, and child labor: Case studies of Benin, Namibia and Swaziland. *Discourse (Abingdon)*, *31*(5), 699–712. doi:10.1080/01596306.2010.516954

Nottingham, E. (1978). *From both sides of the lens: Street photojournalism and personal space* (Unpublished doctoral dissertation). Indiana University, Bloomington, IN.

Nwankwo, E. H., & Okwemba, A. (2002). *How the Kenyan media covers the children's rights issues: A content analysis.* A paper presented to International Federation of Journalists (IFJ), Nairobi, Kenya. Retrieved on October 22, 2008 from www.ifj.org/assets/docs/089/021/36f1759-cbfee15.pdf

Nwankwo, V. C. (2011). *The Role of The Media in Promoting Human Rights: An analysis of the BBC documentary, 'chocolate: the bitter truth'*. An Unpublished MA Dissertation. Retrieved from http://munin.uit.no/bitstream/handle/10037/3500/thesis.pdf?sequence=1

Nwodu, L. C., & Ezeoke, C. B. (2013). An Evaluation of Press Coverage of Children's and Women's Rights in Nigeria. *Higher Education of Social Science*, *4*(2), 41–51.

Nwosu, I. E., & Nwodu, L. C. (2007). An Empirical analysis of the factors influencing child labour abuses and control in Nigeria. Towards the application of ACADA model. *The Nigerian Journal of Development Studies*, *6*(1), 23–45.

Obiechina, G. O. (2014). Violation of Child's Rights in Nigeria: Implications for Child Health. *Social Science and Humanities*, *5*(1), 151–159.

Obiweluozor, N. (2015). Early Childhood Education in Nigeria, Policy Implementation: Critique and a Way Forward. *African Journal of Teacher Education*, *4*(1), 1–9. doi:10.21083/ajote.v4i1.2930

Obozuwa, D. E. (2010). *Nigeria @ 50 ... Protecting the future of this Nigerian child – The future leaders of this Nation: A look again at the Child Rights Act.* Retrieved from http://www.wali-uwais.com/?page_id=784

Ogila, J. (2019, January 14). Kibera girl seeks justice after being rejected by school over dreadlocks. *Standard Digital.* Retrieved from https://www.standardmedia.co.ke/article/2001309413/k

Ogunniran, I. (2017). Forward Looking or Backward Stepping: Evaluating Child Protection from Sexual Exploitation in Nigeria. *Journal of Human Trafficking*, *3*(3), 167–181. doi:10.1080/23322705.2016.1146519

Ohunene, O. C., & Ozoji, B. (2014). Science education and sustainable development in Nigeria. *American Journal of Educational Research*, *2*(8), 595–599. doi:10.12691/education-2-8-6

Okafor, C., Amoo, E. O., & Onugu, C. U. (2010). *Microfinance and-Gender Development Policy: Implications for Millennium Development Goals (MDGs).* Academic Press.

Okewole, J. O., Iluezi-Ogbedu, V. A., & Osinowo, O. A. (2015). An evaluation of the implementation of early childhood education curriculum in Osun State. *Journal of Education and Practice*, *6*(4), 48–54. Retrieved from http://www.iiste.org/Journals/index.php/JEP/article/viewFile/19793/20357

Okewole, J. O., Veronica, I.-O. A., & Osinowo, O. A. (2015). An evaluation of the implementation of early childhood education curriculum in osun state. *Journal of Education and Practice*, *6*(4), 48–55.

Okpere, A., & Opara, P. (2014). Mothers' knowledge and practice of infant sleep position. *Nigerian Journal of Paediatrics*, *41*(4), 312–315. doi:10.4314/njp.v41i4.4

Okunola, M. I. (2002). *A handbook for Nigeria Social Workers*. Daybis Limited.

Olagoke, A. (2017). *Sustainable Development Goals In Nigeria: What Role(S) For Nigeria's Indigenous Languages?* Retrieved from https://www.idpublications.org/wp-content/uploads/2017/06/full-paper-sustainable-development-goals-in-nigeria.pdf

Olaiya, T. T. (2018). *Nigeria: Sparing a thought for harsh realities of refugees, IDPs*. Retrieved from https://allafrica.com/stories/201806210093.html

Olanrewaju, F. O. (2018). *Boko Haram insurgency and the crisis of internal displacement of women in Nigeria (2009-2017)* (Thesis). Covenant University, Ota, Nigeria.

Olanrewaju, F. O., Omotoso, F., & Alabi, J. O. (2018a). Datasets on the challenges of forced displacement and coping strategies among displaced women in selected Internally Displaced persons' (IDP) Camps in Nigeria. *Data in Brief*, *20*, 152–158. doi:10.1016/j.dib.2018.07.042 PMID:30112431

Olanrewaju, F. O., Omotoso, F., & Alabi, J. O. (2018b). Boko Haram insurgency and the crisis of internally displaced women in Nigeria: A situational analysis. *African Population Studies*, *32*(1), 3622–3633.

Olatunji, R. W., & Akhagba, O. (2013). Children and advertising literacy: A Study of Selected Schools in Lagos, Nigeria. *Global Advanced Research Journal of Social Science*, *2*(6), 134–142.

Olojo, A. E. (2017). Resistance through Islamic clerics against Boko Haram in northern Nigeria. *African Security Review*, *26*(3), 308–324. doi:10.1080/10246029.2017.1294092

Olowu, D. (2002). Protecting children's rights in Africa: A critique of the African charter on the Rights andWelfare of the Child. *International Journal of Children's Rights*, *10*(2), 127–136. doi:10.1163/157181802401005403

Olson, C. K., Kutner, L. A., Baer, L., Beresin, E. V., Warner, D. E., & Nicholi, A. M. II. (2009). Mrated video games and aggressive or problenl behavior among young adolescents. *Applied Developmental Science*, *13*(4), 188–198. doi:10.1080/10888690903288748

Olube, F. K. (2015). The influence of mass communication on social change: a study of press reports on child labour and women trafficking. *New Media and Mass Communication*, *36*, 31- 40. Retrieved from https://www.iiste.org/Journals/index.php/NMMC/article/viewFile/21765/21793

Olufunlayo, T. F., Roberts, A. A., MacArthur, C., Thomas, N., Odeyemi, K. A., Price, M., & Jolly, K. (2019). Improving exclusive breastfeeding in low and middle-income countries: A systematic review. *Maternal and Child Nutrition, 15*(3), e12788. doi:10.1111/mcn.12788 PMID:30665273

Olugbode, M. (2017). *Boko Haram: 57 percent of schools in Borno closed, says UNICEF.* Retrieved from https://www.thisdaylive.com/index.php/2017/09/30/boko-haram-57-percent-of-schools-in-borno-closed-says-unicef/

Olurinola, I. O., Fadayomi, T., Amoo, E. O., & Ola-David, O. (2014). Occupational Health and Safety among Street Traders in, Nigeria. *International Journal of Econornics and Finance, 6*(4).

Olusegun, O., & Idowu, A. (2016). Child abuse in Nigeria: Dimension, reasons for its persistence and probable. *Child and Family Law Journal, 4*(1), 1–23.

Omatayo, J. (2019). *Popular star kid Emmanuella plays role in Australia movie Survive and Die.* Retrieved from http://www.Legit.com

Omeh, D. (n.d.). *How to become a Nigerian Nollywood actress or actor.* Retrieved from www.wealthresult.com

Omodara, O. D., & Adu, E. (2014). Relevance of Educational Media and Multimedia Technology for Effective Service Delivery in Teaching and Learning Processes. *Journal of Research & Method in Education*, 48-51.

Omojola, O., Amodu, L., Okorie, N., Imhonopi, D., Yartey, D., & Adesina, E. (2018). Assessing the One-Lecture-One-Test Learning Model in Undergraduate Journalism Program Using Cohort Design. *The Journal of Social Sciences Research, 4*(12), 591–597.

Omojola, O., Odiboh, O., & Amodu, L. (2018). Opinions as Colors: A Visual Analysis Technique for Modest Focus Group Transcripts. *Qualitative Report, 23*(8), 2019–2035. Retrieved from https://nsuworks.nova.edu/tqr/vol23/iss8/16

Omotosho, Y., Oyero, O., & Salawu, A. (2015). Children's Programmes on Nigerian Television Stations: a Case of Media Negle. *E-Bangi: Journal of Social Sciences and Humanities, 10*(1), 135–153. Retrieved from http://www.ukm.my/e-bangi/papers//2015/135-153 Olusola CHILDREN'S programme on TV.pdf

Onumah, D. (2004). Media literacy and the Nigerian child. *The Guardian,* 65.

Onuoha, F. C. (2014). Why do youth join Boko Haram? Special Report. United States Institute of Peace. Special Report 348, June 2014.

Onwuegbuzie, A. J., & Leech, N. L. (2004). *Enhancing the interpretation of significant findings: The role of mixed methods research.* Paper presented at the annual meeting of the Eastern Educational Research Association, Clearwater, FL.

Onyemelukwe-Waziri, H. (2017). *Impact of two wars on the educational system in Nigeria.* Clark University Clark Digital Commons International Development, Community and Environment (IDCE) Master's Papers5.

Organization of African Unity (OAU). (n.d.). *African Charter on the Rights and Welfare of the Child.* Addis Ababa: OAU.

Ortiz-Ospina, E., & Roser, M. (2019). *Child Labor.* Retrieved from: 'https://ourworldindata.org/child-labor'

Ortum, L. L. (2011). *An investigation into the extent of children content in Kenyan media: A case study of the Nation and Standard newspaper (Unpublished master's thesis).* University of Nairobi. Retrieved http://erepository.uonbi.ac.ke/bitstream/handle/11295/60127/Ortum

Oswell, D. (2013). *The Agency of Children: From Family to Global Human Rights.* Cambridge, UK: Cambridge University Press.

Oti, O. A. (2012). *Parenting Child Sexual Abuse: A Parental Approach.* Faith Printers International.

Ottolini, M. C., Davis, B. E., Patel, K., Sachs, H. C., Gershon, N. B., & Moon, R. Y. (1999). Prone infant sleeping despite the Back to Sleep campaign. *Archives of Pediatrics & Adolescent Medicine, 153*(5), 512–517. doi:10.1001/archpedi.153.5.512 PMID:10323633

Overseas Development Institute. (2009). *Raising the game: mainstreaming children's rights.* Briefing paper, 56.

Ow-Yeong, W. (2014). Our Failure of Empathy': Kevin Carter, Susan Sontag, and the Problems of Photography. *Think Pieces: A Journal of the Joint Faculty Institute of Graduate Studies, 1*(1), 9-17.

Oxford Advanced Learner's Dictionary . (2015). (9th ed.). Oxford University Press.

Oyama, O.-A., & Ogbu, S. U. (2017). Television and Content Censorship: The Impact of Violent Content on the Developmental Stages in the Personality of the Nigerian Child. *Advanced Journal of Social Science*, 30-39.

Oyero, O. (2010). Child rights and media democratization: An agenda for realization of the MDGs in Nigeria. *International Journal of Communication, 11*, 202-215.

Oyero, O. (2010). Children: as 'invisible' and voiceless as ever in the Nigerian news media. *Estudos em Communicacado, 7*(2), 25-41. Retrieved from www.ec.ubi.pt/ec/07/vol2/oyero.pdf

Oyero, O. (2010). Media Ownership and the Coverage of Child's Rights in the Nigerian Newspapers. *Nigerian Journal of Communication, 8*(1).

Oyero, O. (2011a). Presenting Children's Right Issues in Nigerian and Ghanaian Newspapers. Multidisciplinary Journal of the University of Fort Hare, 17.

Oyero, O. S. (2009). *A comparative study of child rights coverage in selected Nigerian and Ghanaian newspapers (1999-2003)* (Unpublished doctoral thesis). Covenant University, Ota, Nigeria.

Oyero, O. S. (2011). How children are reported in Nigerian newspapers: Implications for the right of the child. *International Journal of Social and Management Sciences, 4*(1), 37-56.

Oyero, O. (2010). Child rights and media democratization: An agenda for realization of the MDGs in Nigeria. *International Journal of Communication*, (11): 202–215.

Oyero, O. (2011). How children are reported in Nigerian Newspapers: Implications for the realization of the rights of the child. *International Journal of Social and Management Sciences*, *4*(1), 37–56.

Oyero, O. S. (2003). Indigenous Language Radio for Development Purposes. In E. O. Soola (Ed.), *Communicating for Development Purposes* (pp. 185–195). Ibadan: Krafts Books.

Oyero, O., & Salawu, A. (2018). Building media capacity for children sustainability in Africa: Educational and partnership imperatives. *SAGE Open*, *8*(1), 1–10. doi:10.1177/2158244018763930

Oyesomi, K. O., Soola, E., Abioye, T., & Oyero, O. (2014). Perception of women on the role of indigenous communication in politics: A study of Ado-Odo Ota, Ogun State, Nigeria. *Vision 2020: Sustainable Growth, Economic Development, and Global Competitiveness - Proceedings of the 23rd International Business Information Management Association Conference, IBIMA 2014, 1*, 2622-2644.

Oyewobi, A. (2016). *NHRC Decries Neglect of 4000 IDPs in Taraba*. Retrieved from Premium Times: http://www.premiumtimesng.com/regional/nnorth-east/196920-nhrc-decries-neglect-of-4000-idps-in-taraba.html

Palmer, K., Oates, W. E., & Portney, P. R. (1995). Tightening environmental standards: The benefit-cost or the no-cost paradigm? *The Journal of Economic Perspectives*, *9*(4), 119–132. doi:10.1257/jep.9.4.119

Panos Eastern Africa. (2013). *The role of media in child protection: Challenges and opportunities in Uganda*. Kampala: Panos Eastern Africa.

Papalia, D. E., Gross, D., & Feldman, R. D. (2003). *Child Development: A Tropical Approach*. New York: McGraw-Hill Companies Inc.

Parajuli, B. (2004, March 23). Child rights and media role. *The People's Review: A Political and Business Weekly*. Retrieved from http: //www.peoplesreview.com.np /2004/10/14102004 /c10.html

Parliament of Kenya. (2018). *Senate debates*. Retrieved from http://www.parliament.go.ke/sites/default/files/2018-11/Thursday%2C%2029th%20November%2C%202018.pdf

Patterson, J. R., Reid, J. B., & Dishion, T. J. (1992). *Antisocial boys*. Eugene, OR: Castalia.

Patterson, P., & Wilkins, L. (2008). *Media ethics issues and cases*. New York: McGraw-Hill.

Pearsall, S. (2013). *A photojournalist's field guide: In the trenches with combat photographer*. San Francisco: Peachpit Press.

Penal Reform International. (2013). *Protecting children's rights in criminal justice systems A training manual and reference point for professionals and policymakers*. Retrieved from www.penalreform.org

Perebinossoff, P. (2012). *Real-world media ethics*. Oxford, UK: Focal Press. doi:10.4324/9780080557106

Peters, A., Fröhlich, M., Döring, A., Immervoll, T., Wichmann, H.-E., Hutchinson, W., ... Koenig, W. (2001). Particulate air pollution is associated with an acute phase response in men. Results from the Monica–Augsburg Study. *European Heart Journal*, *22*(14), 1198–1204. doi:10.1053/euhj.2000.2483 PMID:11440492

Peterson, A. C., Joseph, K., & Feit, M. (2014). *New Directions in Child Abuse and Neglect Research*. Washington, DC: National Academies Press.

Peterson, A., & Spratt, M. (2005). Choosing Graphic Visuals: How Picture Editors Incorporate Emotion and Personal Experience into Decision Making. *Visual Communication Quarterly*, *12*(1-2), 4–19. doi:10.1080/15551393.2005.9687439

Pham, J. P. (2012). Boko Haram's evolving threat. *Africa Security Brief,* 20. Retrieved from http://www.ndu.edu/press/lib/pdf/Africa-Security-Brief/ASB-20.pdf

Philips, N. (2017). *Violence, Media Effects, and Criminology. In Oxford Research Encyclopaedia, Criminology and Criminal Justice*. Oxford, UK: Oxford University Press.

Piaget, J. (1936). *Origins of intelligence in the child*. London: Routledge & Kegan Paul.

Piaget, J. (1945). *Play, dreams and imitation in childhood*. London: Heinemann.

Piaget, J. (1957). *Construction of reality in the child*. London: Routledge & Kegan Paul.

Pickering, T. (2016). *Print media and child welfare: A discourse analysis* (Master's Thesis). The University of Manitoba.

Pireyn, L. (n.d.). *To what extent are child actors exposed to the violent aspects of the movie they perform?* Retrieved from http://www.movie.stachexchange.com

Plaisance, P. L. (2014). Privacy. In *Media ethics: Key principles for responsible practice* (2nd ed., pp. 175–199). Los Angeles, CA: SAGE Publications. doi:10.4135/9781544308517.n10

Pohio, L. (2009). *The implementation and integration of information and communication technologies in early childhood education: Teachers' perspectives* (Unpublished thesis). UNITEC Institute of Technology, Waitakere.

Popoola, O. T. (2019). An Empirical Analysis of Infant Mortality: Evidence from sub-Saharan Africa Countries. *Journal of Economics and Management Sciences*, *2*(1), 27–32. doi:10.30560/jems.v2n1p27

Prensky, M. (2006). *Don't bother me mom, I'm learning*. St. Paul, MN: Paragon House.

Priest, S. H. (2010). *Doing media research: An introduction* (2nd ed.). Sage Publications.

Prüss-Üstün, A., & Corvalán, C. (2006). *Preventing disease through healthy environments. Towards an Estimate of the Environmental Burden of Disease*. Geneva: World Health Organization.

Prüss-Üstün, A., & Neira, M. (2016). *Preventing disease through healthy environments: a global assessment of the burden of disease from environmental risks*. World Health Organization.

Raad, R., & Appelbaum, P. S. (2015). Impact of Behavioral Genetic Evidence on the Perceptions and Dispositions of Child Abuse Victims. *Public Health Genomics*, *18*(1), 11–18. doi:10.1159/000364994 PMID:25060544

Raineri, L., & Martini, A. (2017). ISIS and AL-Qaeda as Strategies and Political Imaginaries in Africa: A Comparison between Boko Haram and Al-Qaeda in the Islamic Maghreb. *Civil Wars*, *19*(4), 425–447. doi:10.1080/13698249.2017.1413226

Rawls, J. (1999). *A theory of justice* (2nd ed.). Cambridge, MA: Harvard University Press.

Ray, M., & Jat, K. R. (2010). Effect of electronic media on children. *Indian Pediatrics*, *47*(7), 561–568. doi:10.100713312-010-0128-9 PMID:20683108

Reavis, J. A., Looman, J., Franco, K. A., & Rojas, B. (2013). Adverse childhood experiences and adult criminality: How long must we live before we possess our own lives. *The Permanente Journal*, *17*(2), 44–48. doi:10.7812/TPP/12-072 PMID:23704843

Reddy, K. J. (2002). Socio-Political Turmoil and the Role of Media. *Journal of Communication Studies*, *1*(3), 12–17.

Regina Daniels breaks silence after marriage to Ned Nwoko. (2019). Retrieved from www.vanguardngr.com

Regina Daniels reportedly sanctioned by Igbinedion university for not attending lectures in a month. (2017). Retrieved from http://www.Naijagists.com

Regina Daniels' Network and Life story. (2018). Retrieved from http://www.Naij.com

Resenzweig, J. F. (2017). Understanding *Child Maltreatment*. Administration of Children, Youth and Families Children Bureau: US. Department of Health and Human Services.

Risinger, H. (2017). *10 Things to know about raising a child actor*. Retrieved from www.huffpost.com

Ritzer, G. (2004). *The McDonaldization of society (Revised New Century Edition.)*. Thousand Oaks, CA: Pine Forge Press/Sage Publications.

Ritzer, R., & Goodman, D. J. (2004). *Modern Sociological Theory* (6th ed.). New York: McGraw-Hill Companies Inc.

Roberts-Holmes, G. (2013). Playful and creative ICT pedagogical framing: A nursery school case study. *Early Child Development and Care*, 1–14.

Rollins, N. C., Bhandari, N., Hajeebhoy, N., Horton, S., Lutter, C. K., Martines, J. C., ... Victora, C. G. (2016). Why invest, and what it will take to improve breastfeeding practices? *Lancet*, *387*(10017), 491–504. doi:10.1016/S0140-6736(15)01044-2 PMID:26869576

Ross, W. D. (1930). *The right and the good.* Oxford, UK: Clarendon Press.

Ruggiero, T. E. (2000). Uses and gratifications theory in the 21st century. *Mass Communication & Society*, *3*(1), 3–37. doi:10.1207/S15327825MCS0301_02

Ruther, M. (1990). Psychosocial Resilience and protective mechanisms. In J. Rolf, A. S. Masten, & D. Cicchetti (Eds.), *Risk and Protective Factors in the Development of Psychopathology*. New York: Cambridge University Press. doi:10.1017/CBO9780511752872.013

Ruther, M., & Quinton, D. (1987). Parental mental illness as a risk factor for psychiatric disorder in childhood. In D. Magnusson & A. Ohman (Eds.), *Psychopathology: An Interaction Perspective*. Orlando, FL: Academic Press.

Ruther, M., & Ruther, M. (1993). *Developing Minds: Challenge and Continuity Across the Lifespan*. New York: Basic Books.

Sadeeq, A. A. (2016). *Appraisal Of The Legal Framework For Protecting Rights Of The Child And The Role Of Unicef In Promoting Rights Of The Child In Nigeria* (Unpublished dissertation). Ahmadu Bello University, Zaria. Retrieved from http://kubanni.abu.edu.ng/jspui/bitstream/pdf / http://kubanni.abu.edu.ng/jspui/bitstream/123456789/9087/1/APPRAISAL%20OF%20THE%20%20LEGAL%20FRAMEWORK%20FOR%20%20PROTECTING%20RIGHTS%20OF%20THE%20CHILD%20AND%20THE%20ROLE%20OF%20UNICEF%20IN%20PROMOTING%20%20RIGHTS%20OF%20THE%20CHILD%20IN%20NIGERIA.pdf

Sahara Reporters. (2015). *How one school provides education for children in a Nigerian IDP camp.* Retrieved from http://saharareporters.com/2015/07/21/how-one-school-provides-education-children-nigerian-idp-camp

Saint-Jacques, M. C., Villeneuve, P., Turcotte, D., Drapeau, S., & Ivers, H. (2012). The role of media in reporting child abuse. *Journal of Social Service Research*, *38*(2), 292–304. doi:10.1080/01488376.2011.627232

Salami, I. A. (2016). Nigerian early childhood education policies and practices for sustainability. *European Journal of Research and Reflection in Educational Sciences*, *4*(5), 71–85.

Sambe, J. A. (2005). *Introduction to mass communication practice in Nigeria*. Ibadan: Spectrum Books Limited.

Sambo, A. S. (2017). Internal displaced persons and their information needs. *Library Philosophy and Practice, 1512*. Retrieved from http://digitalcommons.unl.edu/libphilprac/1512

Samuel, G. W., & Amoo, E. O. (2014). A statistical Analysis of child mortality: Evidence from Nigeria. *Journal of Demography and Social Statistics*, *1*(1), 110–120.

Sanni, M. (2017). *Quality education for children in IDPs camps.* Retrieved from https://aljazirahnews.com/feature-quality-education-children-idps-camps/

Sarı, B., Başal, H. A., Takacs, Z. K., & Bus, A. G. (2016). Using Electronic Storybooks to Foster Word-learning in Turkish Children. In The Digital Literacy and Multimodal Practices of Young Children: Engaging with Emergent Research (pp. 116-173). Braga: Centro de Investigação em Educação (CIEd).

Saunders, M., Lewis, P., & Thornhill, A. (2009). *Research methods for business students* (5th ed.). Harlow: Pearson Education Harlow.

Savage, J. (2008). The role of exposure to media violence in the etiology of violent behavior: A criminologist weighs in. *The American Behavioral Scientist*, *51*(8), 1123–1136. doi:10.1177/0002764207312016

Save the Children. (2014). *A lesson from Kenyan children*. Retrieved from https://kenya.savethechildren.net/news/lesson-kenyan-children

Save the Children. (2014). Universal Periodic Review: Successful examples of child rights advocacy. *Child Rights Governance Global Initiative*. Save the Children.

Sbarra, D. A. (2015). Divorce and Health: Current Trends and Future Directions. *Psychosomatic Medicine*, *77*(3), 227–236. doi:10.1097/PSY.0000000000000168 PMID:25829240

Schaffer, H. R. (1996). *Social Development*. Malden, MA: Blackwell Publishing.

Scheufele, D. A., & Tewksbury, D. H. (2007). Framing, agenda setting, and priming: The evolution of three media effects models. *Journal of Communication*, *57*(1), 9–20.

Schiavo, R. (2013). *Health communication: From theory to practice* (Vol. 217). John Wiley & Sons.

Schrader-McMillan, A., & Barlow, J. (2017). *Improving the effectiveness of the child protection system: A review of literature*. Oxford, UK: Department of Social Policy and Intervention, University of Oxford.

Schwartz, J. (2004). Air pollution and children's health. *Pediatrics*, *113*(Supplement 3), 1037–1043. Retrieved from https://pediatrics.aappublications.org/content/113/Supplement_3/1037 PMID:15060197

Schwartzman, K. C. (1998). Globalization and Democracy. *Annual Review of Sociology*, *24*(1), 159–181. doi:10.1146/annurev.soc.24.1.159

Seay, K. D., & Kohl, P. L. (2013). Care giver substance abuse and children's exposure to violence in a nationally representative child welfare sample. *Journal of Social Work Practice in the Addictions*, *13*(1), 70–90. doi:10.1080/1533256X.2013.756335 PMID:23440502

Secretariat, C. (2017). *Youth Mainstreaming in Development Planning: Transforming Young Lives*. Loughborough, UK: Commonwealth.

Serag, E. M. (2015). *The Coverage of Children's Issues in Egyptian Newspapers* (Unpublished MA Thesis). American University in Cairo, Egypt.

Servaes, J., & Lie, R. (2008). Media Globalization through Localization. In J. Servaes (Ed.), *Communication for Development and Social Change* (pp. 58–68). Thousand Oaks, CA: Sage Publications. doi:10.4135/9788132108474.n4

Severin, W. J., & Tankard, J. W. (1979). *Communication Theories: Origins, Methods and Uses*. Toronto, Canada: Copp Clark Ltd.

Sharanappa, A. (2018). *Mass media and social problem*. Raleigh, NC: Laxmi Book Publication.

Shen, C., & Williams, D. (2011). Unpacking time online-connecting internet and massively multiplayer online game use with psychosocial well-being. *Communication Research, 38*(1), 123–149. doi:10.1177/0093650210377196

Siddegowda, Y. S., & Srinivasa, D. (2015). Intervention Of Media In Child Rights Protection. *International Research Journal Of Commerce, Arts And Science, 6*(12), 64-73. Retrieved From http://www.casirj.com

Skujyte, D. (2011). *Rights of African children under the African Charter on the Rights and Welfare of the Child: The addition to the universal protection of a child.* University of Tilburg Master International and European Public Law (accent on Human Rights Law).

Slee, P. T., Cross, D., Campbell, M., Spears, B., & Dooley, J. (2010). *From research to policy and practices: Innovation and sustainability in cyberbullying prevention*. European Cooperation in Science & Technology and Department of Innovation, Industry, Science and Research Training School, Melbourne, Australia.

Slee, P. T., Campbell, M., & Spears, B. (2012). *Child, Adolescent and Family Development*. Cambridge, UK: Cambridge University Press. doi:10.1017/CBO9781139196567

Sloth-Nielsen, J., & Mezmur, B. (2014). A dutiful child: The implications of Article number 31 of the African Children's Charter. *Journal of African Law*.

Smith, R. (1991). Child Care: Welfare, protection or rights? *Journal of Social Welfare and Family Law, 13*(6), 469–481. doi:10.1080/09649069108413575

Sofoluwe, A. O. (2012). Human rights and quality education in Nigerian primary schools. *Academic Research International, 2*(3), 459–468.

Sontag, S. (2003). *Regarding the pain of others*. New York, N.Y.: Picador. doi:10.3917/dio.201.0127

Sooter, T. (2013). Early Childhood education in Nigeria: Issues and Problems. *Journal of Education and Social Research., 3*(5), 173–179.

Soyinka-Airewele, P., & Yartey Ajayi, L. (2016). Reframing human security, borders and gendered violence in the Shadows of Chibok. *2016 International Conference of the Association of Third World Studies held in the Indiana University Southeast*, New Albany.

Staksrud, E., & Milosevic, T. (2017). Adolescents and children in global media landscape: From risks to rights. *Annals of the International Communication Association*, *41*(3-4), 235–241. doi:10.1080/23808985.2017.1387503

Stanley, J. R. (2014). Child Abuse and the Internet. *Issues (Chicago, Ill.)*, 1–20. Retrieved from https://www.researchgate.net/publication/242085433

Steinberg, C. S. (1972). *The Communicative Arts: An Introduction to Mass Media*. New York: Hasting House Publishers.

Stubbs, M. (1985). Discourse Analysis: The Sociolinguistic Analysis of Natural language. *Language*, *61*(2).

Subrahmanyam, K., & Lin, G. (2007). Adolescents on the Net: Internet use and well-being. *Adolescence*, *42*, 659–677. PMID:18229503

Sutherland, G., McCormack, A., Pirkis, J., Eastal, P., Holland, K., & Vaughan, C. (2015). *Landscapes: Media representations of violence against women and their children: State of knowledge paper. Landscapes, No. 15*. ANROWS.

Sylva, K. (1994). School influences on children's development. *Child Psychology & Psychiatry & Allied Disciplines*, *35*(1), 135–170. doi:10.1111/j.1469-7610.1994.tb01135.x PMID:8163626

Tajudeen, O. I. (2015). Legal Framework for the Protection of Child Rights in Nigeria. *AGORA International Journal of Juridical Sciences*, *1*(3), 46–52.

Tartari, E. (2015). Benefits and Risks of Children and Adolescence Using Social Media. *European Scientific Journal*, *11*(, 13), 321–332.

Tauson, M. (2017). Can technology substitute for the classroom? The ethical use of edtech in emergency and displaced settings. In *Proceedings of 14th International conference of education and development* (p. 39). Oxford, UK: University of Oxford.

Terr, L. (2010). Childhood trauma: An outline and overview. *The American Journal of Psychiatry*, *148*(12), 10–20. PMID:1824611

ThankGod-Amadi, S. (2012, May 27). *Domesticating Child Rights Law …The Rivers Example*. Retrieved from http://www.thetidenewsonline.com/2012/05/27/domesticating-child-rights-law-%E2%80%A6the-rivers-example/

The Convention on the Rights of the Child. Guiding principles requirements for all rights. (n.d.). UNICEF.

The Good Planet Foundation. (2013). *Accelerating progress to 2015. Nigeria.* A report series to the UN Special Envoy for Global Education. Working Paper. Retrieved from http://educationenvoy.org/wp-content/uploads/2013/07/Nigeria-Unse-Final.pdf

The humanities in media and communication research. (2002). In *Handbook of media and communication research: Qualitative and quantitative methodologies*. London, UK: Routledge.

The Kenyan Constitution. (2010). Retrieved www.kenyalaw.org

The life of a Child Star: Why Some go crazy and others don't. (2014). Retrieved from www.medibag.com/paeditrics/the-life-of-a-child-star-why-some-go-crazy-and- others-don't/article/472544/

The MediaWise Trust. (2003). *The Oslo challenge*. Retrieved May 8, 2007 from http://www.mediawise.org.uk/display_page.php?id=130

The Nigerian Child Rights Act 2003.

The state of convergence in media and communication research. (2002). InJensen, K. B. (Ed.), *Handbook of media and communication research: Qualitative and quantitative methodologies*. London, UK: Routledge.

Thompson, K., & Anita Sharma, A. (1998, September). Secularization, Moral Regulation and the Mass Media. *The British Journal of Sociology*, *49*(3), 434–455. doi:10.2307/591392

Tobin, J. (2005). Increasingly Seen and Heard: The Constitutional Recognition of Children's Rights. *South African Journal on Human Rights*, *21*(1), 86–126. doi:10.1080/19962126.2005.11865129

Tong, A., Sainsbury, P., & Craig, J. (2007). Consolidated criteria for reporting qualitative research (COREQ): A 32-item checklist for interviews and focus groups. *International Journal for Quality in Health Care*, *19*(6), 349–357. doi:10.1093/intqhc/mzm042 PMID:17872937

Top 20 facts about young Nollywood Actress Regina Daniels. (2017). *Hot Vibes Media*. Retrieved from smedia.com.ng/2017/06/top-20-facts-about-young-nollywood-actress-regina-daniels-.html?m=1/

Top facts from Regina Daniels Personal Life. (2018). Retrieved from http://www.Naij.com

Toyo, N. (2006). Revisiting Equality as a Right: The Minimum Age of Marriage Clause in the Nigerian Child Rights Act, 2003. *Third World Quarterly*, *27*(7), 1299–1312. doi:10.1080/01436590600933677

Tuchman, G. (2002). The production of news. In K. B. Jensen (Ed.), *Handbook of media and communication research: Qualitative and quantitative methodologies*. London, UK: Routledge.

Turner, J. H. (2013). *Theoretical Sociology: 1830 to the Present*. Thousand Oaks, CA: SAGE Publications, Inc.

Ugal, D., & Undyaundeye, F. (2012). *Child labour in Nigeria: causes and consequences for national development*. Retrieved from https://www.researchgate.net/publication/228217064_Child_Labour_in_Nigeria_Causes_and_Consequences_for_National_Development

Ugangu, W. (2012). *Normative media theory and the rethinking of the role of the Kenyan media in a changing social economic context* (PhD thesis). University of South Africa.

UN (1998). *Guiding Principles on the United Nations Global Counter-Terrorism Strategy*. ADM 1.1, PRL 12.1, PR00/98/109.

UNESCO (2019). *Migration, displacement and education: building bridges, not walls.* UNESCO Global Education Monitoring Report.

UNESCO. (2008). Inclusive education: The way of the future. In *Proceedings of 48th International conference of education* (pp. 5-80). Geneva: International Conference Centre.

UNESCO. (2009). *UNESCO's 2009 Policy Guidelines on Inclusion.* Retrieved from http://www.unesco.org/new/en/media-services/single-view/news/unescos_new_policy_guidelines_on_inclusion_in_education/

UNHCR. (2012). *A Framework for the Protection of the Children.* Retrieved from www.globalcitizen.org www.statista.com www.unicefusa.org www.un.org

UNICEF fact sheet on child labour in Nigeria. (2006). Retrieved from https://www.unicef.org/wcaro/english/WCARO_Nigeria_Factsheets_ChildLabour.pd

UNICEF, Joint United Nations Programme on HIV/AIDS, World Health Organization, & United Nations Population Fund. (2010). *Children and AIDS: Fifth stocktaking report.* Retrieved from https://www.unicef.org/publications/files/Children_and_AIDS-Fifth_Stocktaking_Report2010_EN.pdf

UNICEF. (1989). Convention on the Rights of the Child. *Cornell University ILR School DigitalCommons@ILR*, 17. Retrieved from http://digitalcommons.ilr.cornell.edu/child

UNICEF. (1996, March 9). *FACT SHEET: A summary of the rights under the Convention on the Rights of the Child.* Retrieved from UNICEF for Every Child: www.unicef.org/crc

UNICEF. (2000). *Children's Rights and the Media: A Resource for Journalists.* UNICEF.

UNICEF. (2002). *A World Fit for Children.* New York: UNICEF.

UNICEF. (2005). *The Media and Children's Rights.* UNICEF.

UNICEF. (2009). *Childhood under Threat.* Retrieved from http://www.unicef.org/sowc05/english/sowc05.pdf

UNICEF. (2011). *Nigeria – Fact Sheet: Child Right Legislation in Nigeria.* UNICEF.

UNICEF. (2011). *Social Protection Diagnostic and Forward Agenda for UNICEF.* Retrieved from http://bit.ly/social-protection-nigeria

UNICEF. (2012). *State of the World's Children 2012: Children in an urban world.* Retrieved from https://www.unicef.org/sowc2012/pdfs/SOWC-2012-Main-Report_EN_21Dec2011.pdf

UNICEF. (2013). *Towards an AIDS-free generation—Children and AIDS: Sixth Stocktaking Report, 2013.* Retrieved from https://data.unicef.org/wp content/uploads/2015/12/str6_full_report_29-11-2013_78.pdf

UNICEF. (2014). *Hidden in Plain Sight: A Statistical Analysis of Violence Against Children.* UNICEF.

UNICEF. (2014). *Idea Box: Engaging stakeholders on children's rights (First ed.). A tool for companies*. Retrieved from www.unicef.org/cs

UNICEF. (2016). National Population Commission of Nigeria, UNICEF Nigeria and the U.S. Centers for Disease Control and Prevention, Violence Against Children in Nigeria: Findings from a National Survey 2014. Abuja, Nigeria: UNICEF.

UNICEF. (2016). *State of the World's Children 2016: A fair chance for every child*. Retrieved from https://www.unicef.org/publications/files/UNICEF_SOWC_2016.pdf

UNICEF. (2017). *Annual Report 2017 Nigeria*. Retrieved from https://www.unicef.org/about/annualreport/files/Nigeria_2017_COAR.pdf

UNICEF. (2017). *Reporting on children: An ethical guideline for journalists*. United Nations.

UNICEF. (2017). *Situation Analysis of Children in Trinidad and Tobago*. UNICEF Office for Barbados and the Eastern Caribbean.

Unite for Sight. (n.d.). *The role of social media in early childhood education: the sesame workshop*. doi:10.1598/RT.58.1.9

United Nations Children Fund (UNICEF). (2016). *The State of the World's Children*. UNICEF.

United Nations Children's Fund (UNICEF). (2007). *Children's rights and journalism practice: a rights - based perspective*. Dublin Institute of Technology.

United Nations Convention on the Rights of the Child (UNCRC). (1989). *Adopted by the General Assembly of the United Nations on 20th November*. Geneva: United Nations Publication.

United Nations Educational, Scientific and Cultural Organisation. (2011). *The hidden crisis: armed conflict and education*. EFA global monitoring report, 2011.

United Nations OCHA. (2004). *Guiding Principles on Internal Displacement*. Retrieved from http://www.unhcr.org/43ce1cff2.html

United Nations, Department of Economic and Social Affairs, Population Division. (2017). *World Population Prospects: The 2017 Revision*. Retrieved from https://www.un.org/development/desa/publications/world-population-prospects-the-2017-revision.html

United Nations. (1989). *Convention on the Rights of the Child (A/RES/44/25)*. New York: General Assembly.

United Nations. (2000). *Assembly adopts two protocols on rights of child: Children in armed conflict; Sale of children, Child prostitution, Child pornography*. Accessed October 9, 2019 from https://www.un.org/press/en/2000/20000525.ga9711.doc.html

Universal Declaration of Human Rights (UDHR). (1948). Retrieved from https://www.un.org/en/udhrbook/pdf/udhr_booklet_en_web.pdf

User, S. (2016). *Child Rights in Nigeria*. Retrieved from www.naijalegaltalkng.com

Uwaleke, I., & Eghagha, B. (2009, June 9). *Child's Rights Act: The Cure For Trafficking*. Retrieved from http://www.nigerianbestforum.com/generaltopics/childs-rights-act-the-cure-for-trafficking/

Uzochukwu, C. E., Morah, N. D., & Okafor, E. G. (2015). Coverage of Child Rights and Protection Issues: Analysis of Selected Broadcast Media in Nigeria. *The Nigerian Journal of Communication, 12*(1), 272–297. Retrieved from http://tnjc.org.ng/wp-content/uploads/October2015/Coverage-of-Child-Rights-and-Protection-Issues.pdf

Valkenburg, P. M., Schouten, D., & Peter, J. (2007). Preadolescents' and adolescents' online communication and their closeness to friends. *Developmental Psychology, 43*(2), 267–277. doi:10.1037/0012-1649.43.2.267 PMID:17352538

Vandenhole, W., Hammonds, R., & Vlieghe, K. (Eds.). (2008). Children's rights in a globalized world: From Principles to Practice (comprehensive report). International Interdisciplinary Course.

Vasterman, K., & Ruigrok, C. (2013). Pandemic Alarm in the Dutch Media: Media coverage of the 2009 Influenza A (H1N1) Pandemic and the Role of the Expert sources. *European Journal of Communication, 28*(4), 436–453. doi:10.1177/0267323113486235

Vermunt, J. D., & Verloop, N. (2000). Dissonance in students' regulation of learning processes. *European Journal of Psychology of Education, 15*(1), 75–89. doi:10.1007/BF03173168

Vlad, D. (2017) Perspectives on media representation of children. *Social Sciences and Education Research Review, 4*(1), 114-124.

Vlad, D. (2017). Perspectives on media representation of children. *Social Sciences and Education Research Review., 1*(4), 114–124.

Vossen, H., Poitrowski, J., & Valkenburg, P. (2014). *Media Use and Effects in Childhood. In Handbook of Lifespan Communication Chapter*. Peter Lang Publishers.

Vos, T. P. (2018). *Journalism*. Boston: Walter de Gruyter Inc. doi:10.1515/9781501500084

Waldron, J. (1985). *Theories of rights*. Oxford, UK: Oxford University Press.

Wambui vs. Republic. (2019). *Criminal Appeal 102 of 2016*. Nairobi: Court of Appeal. Retrieved from http://kenyalaw.org/caselaw/cases/view/170043/

Wanguba, F. M. (2011). *Subservience of children's rights in media coverage in Kenya* (Unpublished master's thesis). University of Nairobi. Retrieved from http://erepository.uonbi.ac.ke/handle/11295/4471

Wang, Y., & Lobstein, T. (2006). Worldwide trends in childhood overweight and obesity. *International Journal of Pediatric Obesity; IJPO, 1*(1), 11–25. doi:10.1080/17477160600586747 PMID:17902211

Warburton, W. (2014). Apples, oranges, and the burden of proof—Putting media violence findings into context. *European Psychologist, 19*(1), 60–67. doi:10.1027/1016-9040/a000166

Warren, C. (2006). *The nexus between independent journalists' unions, press freedom and poverty eradication: A Strategic Policy Discussion Between Donors and UNESCO* (Unpublished master's thesis). International Federation of Journalists.

Warrier, S., & Ebbeck, M. (2014). Children's rights: Television programmes aired in Singapore. *Early Child Development and Care, 184*(1), 138–148. doi:10.1080/03004430.2013.773991

Watch, H. R. (2018). *World Report 2018.* Washington, DC: HRW.

Waters, J. K. (2011). *The everything guide to social media.* Adams Media.

Weatherred, J. L. (2015). Child sexual abuse and the media: A literature review. *Journal of Child Sexual Abuse, 24*(1), 16–34. doi:10.1080/10538712.2015.976302 PMID:25635896

Weder, N., Yang, B. Z., Douglas-Palumberi, H., Massey, J., Krystal, J. H., Gelernter, J., & Kaufman, J. (2009). MAOA genotype, maltreatment, and aggressive behaviour: The changing impact of genotype at varying levels of trauma. *Biological Psychiatry, 65*(5), 417–424. doi:10.1016/j.biopsych.2008.09.013 PMID:18996506

White, P. (2008). *Representations of children in a monopoly print medium* (Unpublished Doctoral dissertation). University of Western Australia, Perth, Australia.

Whitehead, P. C., Chiodo, D. G., Leschied, A. W., & Dermot, H. (2004). Referrals and admissions to the children's aid society: A test of four hypotheses. *Child and Youth Care Forum, 33*(6), 425–440. doi:10.100710566-004-5265-7

Widom, C. S., & White, H. R. (1997). Problem behaviour in abused and neglected children: Grown up, prevalence and co-occurrence of substance abuse, crime and violence. *Criminal Behaviour and Mental Health, 7*(4), 287–300. doi:10.1002/cbm.191

Wilkins, L., & Clifford, G. C. (2009). *The handbook of media ethics.* New York: Routledge.

Woodruff, K. (1997). *Children's health in the news. Issue 4.* Berkeley, CA: Berkeley Media Studies Group.

Woodruff, K., & Dorfman, L. (2001). *Newspaper coverage of child nutrition policies.* Berkeley Media Studies Group.

Wright, J. C., Huston, A. C., Murphy, K. C., St. Peters, M. F., Piñon, M. F., Scantlin, R. M., & Kotler, J.P. (2001). The relations of early television viewing to school readiness and vocabulary of children from low-income families: The early window project. *Child Development, 72*, 1347–1366. doi: 0009-3920/2001/7205-0005

Wusu, O., & Amoo, E. O. (2014). 11 Sub-Saharan African Children and Adolescents. *Continuity and Change in Sub-Saharan African Demography*, 192.

Wusu, O., & Amoo, E. O. (2016). Fertility Behaviour and Wealth Situation in Nigeria: Evidence from 2013 Demographic and Health Survey. *Social Indicators Research, 128*(1), 1–14. doi:10.100711205-015-1016-4

Wyness, M. (2006). *Childhood and society: An introduction to the sociology of childhood.* Hampshire: Palgrave, Macmillan.

Young, J., Gore, R., Gorman, B., & Watson, K. (2013). Wrapping and swaddling infants: Child health nurses' knowledge, attitudes and practice. *Neonatal, Paediatric, and Child Health Nursing*, *16*(3), 2–11.

Zakeri, A., Zainab, B., & Yakubu, I. (2016). Examining children learned violent behaviour through mass media content: A study of Obasanjo model school, Jos, Nigeria. *Global Journal o Arts. Humanities and Social Sciences*, *4*(11), 12–21.

Zaleza, P. T. (2009). The media in social development in contemporary Africa. In K. Njogu & J. Middleton (Eds.), *Media and Identity in Africa* (pp. 19–35). Edinburgh, UK: Edinburgh University Press/International African Institute. doi:10.3366/edinburgh/9780748635221.003.0002

Zenn, J., Barkindo, A., & Heras, N. A. (2013). The ideological evolution of Boko Haram in Nigeria. *RUSI Journal*, *158*(4), 46–53. doi:10.1080/03071847.2013.826506

Zguri, P. (2014). *Ethical issues in photojournalism* (Unpublished Doctoral Thesis). University of Tirana.

About the Contributors

Olusola Oyero is a researcher and an associate professor in the Department of Mass Communication, Covenant University, Ota, Ogun state, Nigeria. He has written several articles in international and national journal. He is currently the postgraduate chair for the department of Mass Communication, Covenant University.

* * *

Oluwafolafunmi Afolabi is an Assistant Lecturer and PhD candidate in the Department of Mass Communication, Covenant University, Ota, Nigeria.

Abdulhameed Agboola is currently a senior lecturer in the Department of Information and Media Technology, School of Information and Communication Technology, Federal University of Technology, Minna. He obtained his bachelor and master degrees in Mass Communication from the International Islamic University, Malaysia (IIUM) in 1998 and 2002 respectively. Also, he obtained his first Phd in Instructional Technology in 2006 at IIUM but my second Phd in Media Studies at the University of Malaya. His area of research interests focuses on Mass Communication, Media Studies, Instructional Technology, Media Technology, etc. Also, he is interested in health information communication and related areas.

Oguchi Ajaegbu is a lecturer in the department of mass communication, Babcock University, Ilisan-Remo, Ogun State, Nigeria. She holds a B.A and M.Sc. degrees in mass communication from Babcock University. Her research interests include development communication, international communication and studies on gender in relation to the media. She has co-authored books, published chapters in books and scholarly publications in revered journals both local and international.

Lady Adaina Ajayi holds a Ph.D in International Relations and is a faculty in the Department of Political Science and International Relations at Covenant University, Nigeria. Recently, she became an African-German Network of Excellence in Science

(AGNES) Junior Research Fellow. She was an active participant of the Classrooms Beyond Borders (CBB) Program which was an International Communications and Negotiations Simulation amongst Covenant University (Nigeria), Ithaca College (USA), UNISA (South Africa) and An Najah University (West Bank) in 2011. She has been a two-time visiting scholar at Ithaca College, New York. She is affiliated to reputable academic and professional associations including the International Political Science Association (IPSA), African Studies and Research Forum (ASRF; where she is currently the Chair, Standing Committee on Projects), Association of Global South Studies (AGSS) and the Lagos Studies Association (LSA). She has published scientific articles in locally and internationally peer-reviewed journals. Having investigated the effectiveness of homegrown (VAWA) versus transplanted (CEDAW) human rights regimes on gendered violence in diverse socio-political/cultural landscapes, she continues to engage in advocating and advancing the quest for an effective regime of human rights while exploring the pervasive influence of culture and patriarchy on the global struggle to protect women's rights.

Mofoluke Akoja is a lecturer in the department of Mass Communication, Babcock University, Nigeria.

Lanre Amodu is a communication scholar with research interest in technological advancement and communication.

Emmanuel Amoo is a PhD holder in Demography and Social Statistics and Senior Lecturer at Covenant University. His research areas are on men's reproductive health, gender health education/promotion, adolescent and sexology (sexual relationships), family demography and population studies. He has authors and co-authored several articles in reputable journals including book chapters in university-level textbooks.

Ukaiko A. Bitrus-Ojiambo holds an MA in Communication from the University of South Alabama and a BA in Psychology from USIU-A. She teaches human communication courses with research interests in media analysis. She is a member of AFELT, a regional faculty development network.

Felix Chidozie is a Lecturer in the Department of Political Science and International Relations, Covenant University, Ota, Nigeria. He had his B.Sc. in Political Science (2000); M.Sc. Political Science (2003), M.A. in Peace and Conflict Studies (2007), where his research work focused on the Politics of Humanitarian Intervention in the Horn of Africa. He has his PhD in International Relations, focusing on Comparative Foreign Policy (2014) where he examined Nigeria-South Africa Relations. His PhD Thesis won the CODESRIA Grant for Thesis Writing (2013).

He is widely published in the areas of Foreign Policy, African Development Issues, Global Governance Issues and Regional Conflict Issues. His articles are published in reputable national and international outlets, some of which are indexed in ISI and SCOPUS. He is an International Visitor Leadership Programme (IVLP) Fellow, USA (2009), Council for the Development of Social Science Research in Africa (CODESRIA) Fellow and a Visiting Doctoral Fellow to the University of Pretoria, South Africa (2013). His current area of research is in Comparative Development Models of Emerging Market Economies.

Oluwatimilehin Deinde-Adedeji is a faculty and a graduate student (currently pursuing a Master's degree in Public Administration) in the Department of Political Science and International Relations, Covenant University, Nigeria. His research centers on E-governance, Public-Private Partnership, Sustainable Development, Open Government and Public Administration.

Kaanaeli Kaale is a Mass Communication Lecturer at St. Augustine University of Tanzania, who teaches Mass Communication and Media Studies. She is an Editorial Director for International Research Journal (IRJ) of International Association of Research Scholars. She is keen to use her knowledge and skills to enhance effective journalism in Tanzania. She is a founding chairperson of the Tanzania Media and Youth Development Association and Active member of Tanzania Media Women Association. Dr. Kaale has 15 years working experience as an editor and senior feature writer in leading private and government media companies. Her writing focuses on human rights issues aimed at promoting women and youth development, and rights for children, elders and people with disabilities. She is interested in using her knowledge and experience in media to make a positive contribution towards effectively using journalism to promote stronger democracies. She believes that promoting democracy and making leaders accountable are the best ways of fighting poverty and promoting gender equity and human rights.

Muthoni E. King'ori has a PhD in Communication with a specialisation in Media Studies. She teaches media/film courses at Daystar University, Kenya. Prior to joining the academia, Muthoni worked as a journalist for a number of Kenyan media organisations. Her research interests are in media ethics, film, media framing/ representations of various issues in society.

Ejiroghene Loromeke is a Doctoral Student and Lecturer in the Department of Political Science and International Relations Covenant University, Ota, Ogun State, Nigeria. His research focus is on Conflict and Conflict Resolution. He has published a couple of papers in his area of research.

Mashaka Boniface Mgeta is a veteran journalist who has worked with major newspapers in Tanzania for almost 20 years. He has a certificate in Journalism awarded by the Tanzania School of Journalism (1997), a Diploma in Journalism awarded by the Time School of Journalism (2008), a Bachelor of Arts in Sociology awarded by the Open University of Tanzania (2013) and a Master of Arts in Mass Communication degree from St Augustine University of Tanzania (2018). Mgeta has participated in several national, regional and international journalism events. In March 2018, he attended the 17th World Conference on Tobacco or Health, held in Cape Town, South Africa from 7-9 March 2018 where he presented a paper titled, "Investigative Journalism Perspective on Tobacco Control in Tanzania." Mgeta also is Chairperson of the Association of Tanzania Health Journalists (THJ) and a member of the AMREF Media Health Network (AMHN) and Tanzania Editors' Forum (TEF). He is interested with politics, human rights and environmental conservation.

Joseph Njuguna is lecturer and Ag Dean of the School of Journalism and Communication at the University of Rwanda. His current research interests are in media convergence, media education and policy, textual analysis and development communication. Joseph is a Phd in Mass Communication candidate at the Jomo Kenyatta University of Agriculture and Technology (JKUAT), Kenya. He has wide experience in media training, consultancy and policy development in the East African region (Rwanda, Uganda, Kenya and South Sudan).

Silk Ugwu Ogbu is a public affairs and communication strategist. His early education was at the University of Calabar, where he received a B.sc in Political Science. He later proceeded to Enugu State University of Science and Technology, from where he earned both M.sc and Ph.D. in Political Science (International Relations). He also holds an M.sc degree and another Ph.D. in Marketing (Public Relations) from the University of Nigeria. He is currently in pursuit of a third Ph.D. in Public Administration. His research interests are in the areas of conflict resolution, rhetorical communication, negotiation, political communication, leadership strategies, development communication, brand management, and stakeholder relationship Management. He is a public relation and customer service consultant, a political analyst and a public communication strategist. He has extensive experience from many years of private sector practice and has contributed immensely through training, conferences, and publications to the pursuit of excellence both in the academia and the industry. He teaches currently at and also heads the Communication & Media Enterprise Department of the School of Media and Communication, Pan Atlantic University, Lagos.

Taiwo Ogunwemimo is a data analyst per excellence and is currently on his PhD, specializing in Business Information Management in Babcock University.

Stellamaris Ngozi Okpara teaches media and communication ethics, media and society, and human communication theory and practice; she has a background in media and communication and educational psychology. She studied at the University of Nigeria, Nsukka and the Pan- Atlantic University. Her research and consultancy are in the areas of media and communication ethics, media and society and human communication. She is also interested in the discourse on the impact of digital literacy on human communication, particularly verbal and nonverbal communication as means of deception in the era of social media and how this affects effective human communication. Her publications in the above areas have appeared in reputable local and international peer-reviewed journals. Dr. Okpara is a member of many professional associations such as Advertising Practitioners Council of Nigeria (APCON) and the International Association for Media and Communication Research (IAMCR).

Adekunle Olanrewaju is a Doctoral Student and Lecturer in the Department of Political Science and International Relations Covenant University, Ota, Ogun State, Nigeria. His research focus is on Democracy, Good Governance and Development. He has published a couple of papers in his area of research.

Faith Osasumwen Olanrewaju holds a PhD in International Relations. She is a lecturer in the Department of Political Science and International Relations Covenant University, Ota, Ogun State, Nigeria. She started teaching and research work in the university system in 2009. Her research focus is on Gender Issues, Displacement and Conflict. She has participated in some conferences within Nigeria and some of her works have been presented at local and international conferences. She has published articles in reputable local and international journals.

Rotimi Williams Olatunji is Professor, Public Relations and Advertising and Dean, School of Communication, Lagos State University, Lagos, Nigeria. He is a highly resourceful and self-motivated scholar. His major areas of research are in Advertising, Economy and Society; Media and Cultural Studies; Political Communication; Entertainment Education; Health Communication; Consumer Studies; Public Relations; Media & Communication Research Methods. He has over 18years of teaching, research and community services at the university level. Professor Olatunji is an author of Advertising, economy and societies in Africa: The Nigerian Perspective (2010); co-author of Soft Sell Magazines in Nigeria (2014); edited Dimension of Advertising Theory and Practice in Africa (2014); and Co-edited along with Professor Lai Oso and Owen –Ibie, N. (2014) Journalism and Media in

Nigeria: Context, Issues and Practice. Ontario (Canada: Canada University Press). He has over 70 research publications in peer reviewed books and learned journals, including Public Relations Review, Journal of Promotions Management, and International Journal of Integrated Marketing Communications. Professor Olatunji is Fellow of American Academy of Marketing Science; Senior Member, African Federation of Public Relations Association; Member, Nigerian Institute of Public Relations (MNIPR); Associate Registered Practitioner in Advertising (arpa); Member, African Council of Communication Education (ACCE): and Vice President, South –West Zone, Association of Communication Scholars and Professionals of Nigeria (ACSPN). Some of the most recent works of Professor include "Advertising Cultures and Global Influences in Sub-Saharan Africa- Nigerian, South African and Kenyan Models" ((2017, pp 127-143). In Brennan, L. Crawford, R., and Parkar, L. (Eds.). Global advertising practice in a borderless world. London & New York: Rutledge Tarlor & Francis Group (ISBN 978-1-138-91830-6 (hbk); and "Trends in advertising and cultures in Nigeria", Communication Cultures in Africa, A Journal of Academics and Practitioners, Vol. 1, No. 1, (2018, pp. 54-76). Professor Olatunji is Fellow, American Academy of Marketing Science; Senior Member, African Federation of Public Relations Association; member, Nigerian Institute of Public Relations (MNIPR); member, International Management Development Association (IMDA), Hummelstown, P.A, (U.S.A. Based); Member, International Academy of Business Disciplines (IABD), Beltsville, M.D. (USA); Associate registered practitioner in advertising (arpa); Member, African Council for Communication Education (ACCE); Vice-President, South-West Zone, Association of Communication Scholars and Professionals of Nigeria (ACSPN); Member, Nigerian Institute for Training and Development, (NITAD), and Secretary General, Zionists International Club, Ota, Nigeria, among others.

Adebanke Olawole-Isaac is a Lecturer and Researcher in Demography and Social Statistics of Covenant University, Nigeria. She received her PhD from Covenant University Nigeria. Adebanke has successfully executed funded research projects with grants from reputable research institutions with her research team members and has co-authored a number of publications in respected international journals. Her research interests includes sexual and reproductive health, non-communicable diseases, demographic research, gender issues and Migration.

Uduakobong Sunday is a Ph.D student with Lagos State University, Lagos. She hold a B.sc in Political Science from University of Calabar; Master in Business Administration from Obafemi Awolowo University, Ile -Ife, PGD and MSc in Communication Studies, both from Lagos State University. She has worked in the banking industry handling Risk Assets projects as well as a Project Manager handling UNDP and British Council/DFID projects with a consulting firm. Udua-kobong also holds a Certificate in Script Writing from PEFTTI Institute, Lagos. Her research interests are in Film Studies, Marketing, Public Relations, Advertising (Integrated Marketing Communication), Communication for Development, Political Communication and Health Communication. She is a member of African Council for Communication Education (ACCE).

Index

www.ingramcontent.com/pod-product-compliance
Lightning Source LLC
LaVergne TN
LVHW080014210926
848481LV00011B/3018
9781799803300